Living Ethics

Living Ethics

Developing Values in Mass Communication

Michael J. Bugeja
Ohio University

Allyn and Bacon

Boston • London • Toronto • Sydney • Tokyo • Singapore

Editor in Chief, Humanities: Joseph Opiela
Editorial Assistant: Susannah Davidson
Marketing Manager: Karon Bowers
Production Administrator: Annette Joseph
Production Coordinator: Susan Freese
Editorial-Production Service: TKM Productions
Composition Buyer: Linda Cox
Manufacturing Buyer: Aloka Rathnam
Cover Administrator: Suzanne Harbison

Library of Congress Cataloging-in-Publication Data

Bugeja, Michael J.
    Living ethics : developing values in mass communication / Michael
J. Bugeja
        p.   cm.
    Includes bibliographical references and index.
    ISBN 0-205-17323-3
    1. Mass media—Moral and ethical aspects.   I. Title.
P94.B84   1995   95-11987
302.23—dc20   CIP

Printed in the United States of America

10   9   8   7   6   5   4   3   2   1   00   99   98   97   96   95

Photo Credits: p. 32: Jared Lazarus; pp. 41 and 140: Pepsi-Cola Company; p. 96:
© John Kaplan; p. 110: © Terry E. Eiler; pp. 231, 232, and 233: Brogan and Partners;
p. 258: Ellen Lorentzson; p. 287: © Therese Frare; pp. 298 and 308: Diane-Sears
Bugeja.

Contents

Preface

Generally speaking, a journalist is anyone who works for a media outlet and delivers information or images to an audience (or helps others do so). Studies have shown that journalism majors may enroll in a specific sequence—advertising, say—only to graduate and secure a job in another field—such as public relations or magazine publishing. Many take jobs outside the mainstream media. Statistics vary from school to school and from region to region and are influenced by the economy and job market. As many as half the graduates in any given sequence, however, find work outside their areas of specialization.

A recent nationwide study by Lee B. Becker published in *Journalism Educator* reports that upon graduation about 20 percent of journalism majors found jobs outside their sequence or departmental specialty. A large percentage were still unemployed. Overall, six months after graduation, only 25 percent of graduates had found work in the area in which they majored.[1]

Even these students, though, had to know the tenets of other sequences because we live in an era of mass communication and multimedia. For instance, photojournalists not only must know how to shoot and process pictures these days, but they also must know how to write, edit, and process words along with computer visuals. Newspaper and television employees must know computer software programs to access art, images, information, and graphics traditionally associated with magazine journalism. In turn, magazine writers and editors must know all of these skills, in addition to the facts and lifestyle characteristics of their readers, targeting an audience much the way advertisers do. Increasingly, there is a blurring of lines between advertising and public relations agencies, as managers of both deal with newspapers, magazines, radio and TV stations, syndicates, and mass media conglomerates. Corporate public relations attracts specialists whose duties range from newswriting, editing, broadcasting, photography, desktop publishing, magazine production, and product/service promotion.

That is why this book is targeted at the journalist instead of at the sequence. You may be enrolled in a journalism school or a mass communication department, specializing in news-editorial, broadcasting, advertising, public relations, or photo- or magazine journalism. The specialty does not matter; the audience does.

If you target an audience or help other people do so, you are a journalist. Simply put, the cartoonist who draws for the opinion page is as much a journalist as the publisher who provides the opinion. Reporters, editors, and photographers are journalists, too, as are advertising representatives and promotions managers who help outlets underwrite the news. The term applies to radio or television reporters, along with the various producers, video editors, salespeople, and general managers of those outlets. It includes magazine journalists, editors, publishers, and free-lance writers. It extends to account executives, copywriters, media buyers, planners, managers, partners, and creative teams of advertising agencies. When the term *journalist* is used in this book, it encompasses public relations managers and practitioners in agencies, industries, and government.

Living Ethics is an inclusive book because media ethics are not defined by diploma, job title, or sequence but by professional values. Journalists are tempted to make unethical choices because of pressure from *outside* forces such as competition or profit margin. Values dictate choices and are determined by *inner* forces such as honesty and fairness. These forces influence your actions and ethics and so apply to all sequences. Thus, while people working in various types of media jobs may encounter different sets of situations or circumstances, these people also will tend to exhibit predictable moral behaviors.

Think about a newspaper or broadcast reporter who plagiarizes a story. He or she might have a motive similar to that of a marketer who steals a rival's research or a photojournalist who stages a documentary picture. Now think about a public relations manager who misleads the media at the client's request. He or she may have a motive similar to that of a magazine editor who reviews and recommends inferior products—at an advertiser's request. To ascertain motive, you must analyze the pressure exerted from the outside force and determine what, if any, moral value—or inner force— is lacking or counteracting the urge to behave unethically.

Usually, we do not approach ethics this way in the classroom. Aspiring journalists are too busy learning to cover or target the outside world and sometimes get caught up in circumstances. We think we might find ourselves in those circumstances one day—on a beat, a shoot, or an account— and want to know the ethics surrounding a particular event or incident. So we filter out information about other sequences without realizing that ethical lessons involved are quite similar.

Here is a typical scenario: You are a photojournalism major, say, reading about a reporter who plagiarizes a story because the competition has a scoop. You are not interested in plagiarism because the chances of your stealing a cutline are rather remote. What you would rather read is a case study about a photojournalist who stages pictures, intent on selling dramatic ones to photo syndicates such as Black Star, where competition is always keen. Or maybe you are an advertising, public relations, or magazine major. What, if anything, do these newsroom situations have to do with your chosen profession? The future advertiser wants to hear about the marketer stealing numbers in a rival's report to identify a need for a new product line. The public relations major wants to know why that manager sent the media on a false trail, perhaps because the client was worried about a liability suit. And the magazine major wants to hear all about the editor who reviewed inferior products favorably just to maintain an advertising base.

On the surface, these situations have little in common. That is because we have been approaching them from the wrong direction. *Ethics emanate from within.* If you approach ethics from the outside, emphasizing sequence, you can get lost in the situations and circumstances and miss the ethical lesson.

It is easy to lose interest when we think a topic or lesson does not apply to us. At first blush, some of these case studies may not seem to apply to your life or life goals. But if you approach ethics from the inside, emphasizing motives and values, you not only may discover answers to difficult issues but you may also end up discovering *yourself.*

Now let's approach these case studies from the *right* direction and determine how they are related. Certainly the reporter, marketer, and photojournalist have one thing in common: They feared the competition (outside force) and lacked a value (inner force) to counter that fear. The public relations manager and magazine editor were worried about profit margin (outside force) and feared the loss of a client and an advertiser more than the loss of their credibility (inner force). They, too, lacked a value to counter their concerns.

If these journalists had strong value systems, they would not have succumbed to the fear of competition or failure. The ethical journalist who embraces honesty as a value would never steal a rival's story or marketing report or stage a photo. The ethical journalist who embraces fairness as a value would never mislead the media or audience to keep a client or advertiser.

Good values are that important. They liberate journalists from sleepless nights and complicated lives. The more you become familiar with ethical issues in print, broadcast, advertising, photojournalism, and public relations, the more you will see how circumstances may vary but solutions usually do not. It is all a matter of counteracting outside forces with inner ones to remain whole as a journalist.

One way to document this is to keep an ethics journal as you read *Living Ethics*. Simply open up a notebook or computer file at the end of the day and record what you learned about your goals and the values you will need to achieve them. You have devoted much of your college career learning methods to cover or target the outside world. It is time to map the inner one before you enter the profession. Use your journal in tandem with this book. When you read an interesting passage in the text or encounter a difficult case study or problem, jot down your thoughts in your journal and relate them to your developing values. This process will help you execute assignments at the end of each chapter.

The structure of the book and the Values Exercises (at the end of each chapter) are meant to help you build, test, and improve your professional values. We all have them, by the way. Some of us have more developed value systems than others, but that is all right. Each chapter here contains enough information, examples, and anecdotes to engage every one of us in serious thought and discussion. At the end of each chapter is a "readings" section with interviews and articles from journalists who live their ethics, providing another level of instruction and more issues for discussion. By the time we reach the last chapter on values, our destination, we should arrive as a group.

That is why the chapter on values is the last and not the first in *Living Ethics*. We need to cover the basics to build an ethical foundation. So in the opening chapters, we will analyze influence (why we believe the things we believe), responsibility (accepting consequences), and truth (facts to satire). We will discuss these and other concepts in plain language and see how they apply to professional journalists. Then, in Part II, your value system will be tested in chapters on lies (from white ones to propaganda), manipulation (hoaxes, large and small), temptation (conflicts and crises), and bias (racial and ethnic stereotypes). Again, exercises at the end of each chapter will help you become more aware of hidden or overt weaknesses or prejudice. Finally, Part III of this book focuses on issues of fairness (balancing viewpoints and strengthening values) and power (tapping your own strengths and practicing restraint), reminding you of the influence you will wield and the lives you will touch as a journalist.

We will have come full circle. *Living Ethics* begins with the influences on you and ends with your influences on others, preparing you for the final all-important chapter on values. Here, you will learn about personal and professional values of journalists and the institutions for which they work. You will also learn how to codify your own values and create a document for your clipbook or portfolio. So there is a practical payoff at the end of our journey.

Ethics should be one of the most practical courses in your journalism curriculum. Don't be daunted by philosophical-sounding concepts such as truth or temptation. As the respected educator and writer Christina Hoff

Sommers states, "Once the student becomes engaged with the problem of what kind of person to be, and how to *become* that kind of person, the problems of ethics become concrete and practical and, for many a student, moral development is thereafter looked on as a natural and even inescapable undertaking."[2]

By the time you finish this book, you will have more confidence in your abilities and a better chance to secure the job of your choice. In today's fast-paced competitive world, you can assume that your rivals for entry-level jobs will have hefty clipbooks or portfolios. But they may not possess the qualities that will help them keep and enjoy their jobs: strong professional values.

Media companies take values seriously. For instance, at Ketchum, the prestigious communications agency, new employees are required to read the company's code of ethics and sign a document agreeing to honor it. There is a reason for this: Ethical employees make good decisions during crises or deadlines; unethical ones take shortcuts that can cause embarrassment, paperwork, or legal problems. At most companies, sound judgment is cause for a promotion, whereas a lapse is a firing offense. Thus, developing a value system is in your best long-term interests. But that should not be the sole motivation. A value system builds confidence, bestows character, and fulfills potential.

Unfortunately, many media companies lack employee training programs. Typically, you will be given a code of ethics, a corporate mission statement, and a company handbook. For instance, the Freedom Forum found that 70 percent of newspaper hires were given such a handbook and told to "sink or swim."[3] The lesson here is that now is the time to learn about ethics and to establish, test, and enhance your values. You are mistaken if you think that ethical issues are easy to resolve or that you can put off learning about them while you are at college.

Because of deadlines and other obligations, journalists have precious little time to devote to ethics. Investigative reporter Gail Taylor of the *Dominion Post* in Morgantown, West Virginia, says that "the subject of ethics only seems to come up as an afterthought on the job. Maybe during a slow news day some reporters might spark a discussion by setting up a 'what if' scenario. More often," Taylor adds, "it is our readers who bring up ethics questions."

At that stage, the issue may be too late and you will be responsible for your actions. That is the opinion of C. Howard Buford, founder and president of a New York City ad agency called Prime Access. Buford states, "It's important to have a pre-thought-out or internalized system of values, basically because of the deadlines and pressure involved in day-to-day business. Unless you think about ethics ahead of time, when faced with pressure, you're just going to do whatever is most expedient."

And that can get you fired.

The sad truth is that many journalism programs do not offer an ethics course. Professors are supposed to add an ethical element or dimension to each class, from newswriting to advertising copywriting. That is hardly enough, according to Linda Percefull, who worked as a reporter for several years at the *Tulsa World* and now is director of public relations at Littlefield in Tulsa—a marketing, advertising, public relations firm (a good example, incidentally, about how journalists cross lines to other sequences). Percefull says, "I have to admit when I was a student at Oklahoma State University I was a little naive about ethics. I figured I would be presented with situations and like a neon light I would recognize 'the ethical questions ahead.' I figured such dilemmas were black and white, presenting a clear choice: good vs. evil. . . . But I've found that ethical dilemmas rarely present themselves so boldly. Instead, ethics come into question in more subtle ways."

That is why values are so important. They help make the subtle more obvious so that you can make the correct choices on the job.

Professionals understand this, of course. Most view ethics in the practical way you might expect, as a tool to help them make good judgment calls—deciding whether to run a controversial story or picture, say, or accept a questionable account. They also know that value systems are efficient and help them manage stress, eliminating the need to waste time rehashing or worrying about their actions. At professional conferences and workshops, sessions on ethics often are the best attended. Although similar statistics are not available for other sequences, the Freedom Forum newspaper study cited earlier showed that 86 percent of journalists said they had a high or moderate interest in ethics, whereas only about 40 percent showed any interest in skills-related topics such as headline writing and court and police reporting.[4]

Perhaps skills are overemphasized in journalism programs and more significance should be placed on the inner journalist. At any rate, we will do so in *Living Ethics*. As the Freedom Forum study indicates, ethics is by far the most popular subject for working professionals—because it is the most important.

Acknowledgments

This book could not have been written without the help of dozens of professional journalists from newspapers, broadcast outlets, advertising and public relations agencies, magazines, professional associations, and universities. Contributors range from Dan Rather of CBS News, Tom Brokaw of NBC News, and Helen Thomas of United Press International to Jared Lazarus, photojournalism student at the University of Florida and several of my former students at Ohio University and Oklahoma State University.

Acknowledging each contributor here would fill several pages. For the most part, you won't recognize their names as much as their places of employment: Scripps-Howard Company, CBS, NBC, CNN, National Public Radio, Pepsi, Ruder-Finn, Ketchum, Oglivy Adams & Rinehart, Hill & Knowlton, *Writer's Digest, News Photographer,* the *Washington Post,* and the *New York Times.* What you should know, however, is that almost every contributor took time from busy schedules to address ethical issues in this book. Almost all did so without asking for anything in return—no permission fees, no tributes, no special treatments. One photojournalist asked that I contribute to an AIDS charity, which says something about her own strong value system and why so many have admired her work.

Contributors were selected because their work or work ethic impressed or influenced me. I know some of these journalists on a personal basis. A few are former students. But most contributors were strangers whom I came to know while researching this book. For instance, one day I spotted a news item about Jared Lazarus, the photojournalist mentioned earlier, while browsing through alumni publications in my school's library. The headline in the *Communigator,* a publication of the University of Florida, stated, "Intern puts photos on hold, helps save drowning child." I tracked down Lazarus and interviewed him, as I did others, telephoning or faxing at all hours. And still, these journalists put their reporting or duties aside and contributed because they care so deeply about ethics, sharing their anecdotes, case studies, and values.

It would be remiss of me to overlook those colleagues, family members, and friends who encouraged me to compose this book. First and foremost, I thank Joseph Opiela and Stephen Hull, editors at Allyn and Bacon, for their enthusiasm about this project. I appreciate the efforts, contributions, and support of Terry Eiler, Chuck Scott, Guido Stempel, Eddith Dashiell, Walter Friedenberg, Hugh Culbertson, Virginia Mansfield Richardson, Michael Sweeney, Bob Stewart, Nancy and Hub Burton, Cassandra Reese, and Tom Hodson, who teach with me in the College of Communication. Special thanks go to Ben Blackstock, director of the Oklahoma Press Association; Harry Heath, regents service professor at Oklahoma State University; Susan Porter, editor of *Scripps-Howard News;* and John Consoli, managing editor of *Editor & Publisher,* who helped me locate several journalists included in the text. Also, I wish to thank the following reviewers of the manuscript for their comments and suggestions: Benjamin J. Burns, Wayne State University; James Highland, West Kansas University; James Hoyt, University of Wisconsin; Harry Marsh, Kansas State University; Joe W. Milner, Arizona State University; Jon Roosenraad, University of Florida; Jeffery A. Smith, University of Iowa; and Carl Sessions Stepp, University of Maryland.

Finally, I thank my wife, Diane Sears-Bugeja, former coordinator of photojournalism at Oklahoma State University, who helped illustrate the text, and my children Erin and Shane, who tolerated my long hours away from home while I was researching and writing *Living Ethics*.

M. J. B.

ENDNOTES

1. Lee Becker, "Finding work was more difficult for graduates in 1990," *Journalism Educator,* Summer 1992, pp. 65–73.

2. Christina Hoff Sommers, "Teaching the virtues," *Chicago Tribune Magazine* reprint, 12 September 1993, p. 16.

3. Brian J. Buchanan, *No Train, No Gain: Continuing Training for Newspaper Journalists in the 1990s* (Arlington, VA: The Freedom Forum, 1993), p. 5.

4. Buchanan, pp. 10–11.

About the Author

Michael J. Bugeja has been a journalist and journalism professor for more than 20 years. He earned a bachelor's degree at Saint Peter's College, studying under Pulitzer Prize–winning reporter Anthony F. Shannon, and began his career as editor for a weekly newspaper in New Jersey. He earned a master's degree in mass communications at South Dakota State University and then joined United Press International, covering the legislature out of Pierre, South Dakota. He rose to the rank of correspondent in Omaha, Nebraska, and later to state editor for North and South Dakota.

In 1979, Bugeja left UPI to advise the student newspaper at Oklahoma State University, where he earned a doctorate in English and an assistant professorship in journalism. The student body at OSU chose him for an AMOCO Foundation Outstanding Teacher Award. In 1986, he joined the faculty of the E. W. Scripps School of Journalism at Ohio University, where he teaches ethics and magazine writing. The student body named him University Professor in 1987 for his work in ethics, and *Writer's Digest* named him contributing editor in 1991 for his work in publishing.

Bugeja has published more than 500 articles, essays, and short creative works in *Journalism Quarterly, Journalism Educator, Editor & Publisher, Quill, Harper's, Georgia Review,* and *New England Review,* among others. He is author of 12 books, including an investigative analysis of higher education, *Academic Socialism* (Orchises Press, 1994). He and his wife, Diane, a photographer, live in Athens, Ohio, with their children, Erin and Shane.

Living Ethics

Part I

Building Your Ethical Base

In this section you will identify basic influences affecting your perception and values. Only then can you understand the concepts of right and wrong and learn to accept responsibility for your actions. Then you will analyze various types of "truths"—facts to archetypes—and base your own beliefs on universal principles. Each chapter contains advice from, interviews with, and articles by working professionals from all sequences, which will sharpen your awareness and lay the foundation for a solid value system.

1

Influence

Basic Terms

The term *values* was defined in the Preface as an inner force (such as honesty or fairness) that helps people counter pressure from outside forces (such as competition or profit margin). Outside forces are neither moral nor immoral; they simply exist as a natural part of the world or the workplace. It is how we respond to those outside forces that counts. For example, there is nothing unethical about competition or profit—especially in journalism; competition challenges us to perform at our peak and profit can give us a reason to invest time and energy in our work. The focus here is on the *pressure* that outside forces exert on our lives. Competition requires us to try harder to succeed, and profit entails an element of risk. That is why moral shortcuts such as cheating or lying seem so attractive in the short term. They can fulfill our ambitions quicker, helping us arrive at a destination (meeting a deadline, say) or attain a goal (stealing an account, for example) while others struggle to play by the rules or obey the laws. Although we might experience an immediate sense of relief by taking ethical shortcuts, they also exert another type of pressure.

Shortcuts compromise values. They make us less honest or fair than we really are or want to be—this is precisely why living an immoral life is so complicated and self-defeating. First, we start hiding aspects of our true selves, and soon we start hiding evidence of our actions. If we persist, our values metamorphose from fairness to bias or from honesty to deceit, allowing outside forces to dominate or control our lives (as you will see in upcoming chapters). In the long run, as you might imagine, a journalist who takes ethical shortcuts encounters more pressure and expends more energy at greater risk than his or her ethical counterpart. The problem is, you might not be able to imagine this *without a value system*.

This is a circular argument with which all ethics teachers and students must grapple. The tendency is to avoid this very basic concern and discuss or study media coverage of social issues such as euthanasia or capital punishment that often have little impact on our lives. Typically, when addressing such issues in textbooks or classrooms, we divide up sides—pro and con—and argue according to our beliefs instead of investigating the values *behind* such beliefs. Even when the media issue engages us, as debates on abortion or gun control often do, usually we do not change our stance.

This is why philosophers such as Michael Levin question whether ethics can be taught at all. In an article condensed from the *New York Times* and reprinted in *Reader's Digest*, Levin states: "Moral behavior is the product of training, not reflection. As Aristotle stressed thousands of years ago, you get a good adult by habituating a good child to doing the right thing."[1] In sum, Levin believes that people learn ethics at home, not in the classroom, because by then it might be too late.

This is a powerful argument. In an ideal world, stable parents would discipline and rear their children morally so that they would lead ethical lives. In an ideal world, no other adult would mistreat those children or violate their trust so that they could embrace parental values. In an ideal world, these children would grow to adulthood without experiencing personal tragedies such as disease, accidents, poverty, unemployment, natural disasters, or violence. If so, we could rest assured that these individuals would apply those parental values and contribute to America's moral fiber. And indeed, millions have been that fortunate. But millions also have not. What about this latter group? Are they doomed to lead unethical lives?

The whole issue of values is provocative if we believe that parents are the sole moral providers. Other relatives may contribute as well, along with educators, clergy, friends, acquaintances, neighbors, coworkers, coaches, journalists—anyone with whom we have contact. Thus, Levin's article can easily be misinterpreted, the same way many voters in 1992 misinterpreted then Vice President Dan Quayle when he spoke about the importance of family values in a speech in San Francisco to the Commonwealth Club.

The issue of family values was deemed safe at the time. A *New York Times*/CBS poll indicated that only 1 percent of the voters considered this a crucial concern.[2] The controversy flared when Quayle, acting on advice from a speechwriter, questioned the morals of a fictive celebrity broadcaster—Murphy Brown—played by actor Candice Bergen in a CBS show by the same name. Scriptwriters for the show had prepared a plot over several segments so that Murphy Brown, a single, professional woman, would have a baby. Babies attract viewers and increase ratings, scriptwriters know, as documented by such TV shows as *I Love Lucy, The Flintstones,* and *Bewitched!* (to name a few). But this particular baby would soon attract a different kind of attention.

Back in San Francisco, Quayle spoke about such issues as social responsibility and personal integrity. He noted that children need discipline and love and bemoaned the breakdown of the American family. Then he added: "It doesn't help matters when prime-time TV has Murphy Brown—a character who supposedly epitomizes today's intelligent, highly paid professional woman—mocking the importance of fathers by bearing a child alone and calling it just another 'lifestyle choice.'"[3]

Quayle's speech became one of the most quoted in the 1992 campaign. For more than a year, the issue consumed Americans. Lance Morrow, writing for *Time,* was one of the first journalists to acknowledge how mass media influences social debate. In an article titled "But Seriously, Folks," Morrow asserted:

> This is national theater: surreal, spontaneous, mixing off-hours pop culture with high political meanings, public behavior with private conscience, making history up with tabloids and television personalities like Oprah Winfrey. The trivial gets aggrandized, the biggest themes cheapened. America degenerates into a TV comedy—and yet Americans end up thinking in new ways about some larger matters. The little television screen, the bright and flat and often moronic medium of these spectacles, works in strange disproportions of cause and effect.[4]

Three weeks later, Candice Bergen was on the cover of *Time,* wearing a political button that proclaimed "Murphy Brown for President." Pundits were debating how a conservative like Quayle could be a pro-life advocate and then put down single mothers—exactly the type of so-called theoretical debate that goes on in most ethics classes, by the way. Riding the publicity, the producers of *Murphy Brown* scheduled a one-hour premiere episode in which the fictive broadcaster rebutted Quayle's speech. The show attracted 44 million viewers. The advertising trade magazine *ADWEEK* noted that Quayle had helped make an ordinary show the most expensive slot on television. Public affairs spokespersons for Saturn and Reebok International issued releases stating that they supported their sponsorship of *Murphy Brown.* Representatives of the long-distance telephone company Sprint, for which Bergen was a spokesperson, seemingly had no ethical problem with a fictive TV character taking on the vice president of the United States.

Within a few months, the term *Murphy Brown* no longer applied to a situation comedy on CBS but to a social situation. In a column in *Money,* titled "What's a 'Murphy Brown' Like Me Supposed to Do?," writer Marlys Harris gave investment advice for single mothers.[5] About a year after the controversy over family values began, *Newsweek* published an article titled "Daughters of Murphy Brown," noting the "most rapid rise in single motherhood is among educated, professional women."[6] In a word, *Murphy Brown* had become a term in the lexicon of pop culture.

There are several ethical lessons to note at this point:

- The media influenced public debate, stirring a topic in which Americans had little (1 percent) interest into a premiere television show that attracted roughly one-fifth of the entire population.
- Journalism sequences became involved in aspects of such debates, from the Quayle speechwriter who suggested the idea to the *Murphy Brown* sponsors and spokespersons who rebutted it, from the newspapers and networks that covered the debate to the talk shows and magazines that popularized it.
- *Murphy Brown* became a term with a distinct definition, illustrating the flexibility and power of the English language.
- Ethical debate concerned the definition of *family* but not *values*, providing participants with enough distance to judge someone else rather than themselves.

Indeed, Quayle's comment seemed to imply that only traditional male/female, two-parent families were capable of transferring values to children. Opponents were right to press him on this point. They seemed to be asking the vice president: What about children of single, divorced, deceased, or gay/lesbian parents? What about children who are reared in extended families of other cultures in which grandparents, say, have a particularly influential role? What about social conditions like unemployment that contribute to the breakup of marriages? Do these children lack families or values or both?

To this day, the topic of values is powerful and controversial, influenced by a fictive TV show *about* a TV show. The problem is that people are still defining the wrong word in a two-word phrase: *family* values. By discussing *family* instead of *values*, we can voice our passionate, wise, or angry opinions and judge others without looking inward at ourselves. Moreover, despite massive coverage, Quayle and Brown (or Bergen—a former photojournalist, by the way) didn't change their opinions on this topic when the debate ended with the election of President Bill Clinton and Vice President Al Gore.

No doubt each player in this argument had something to gain or lose during the controversy, from voters to ratings. But we also sensed that each side was also committed to its agenda. Instead of noting common ground—

respect for the influence of families on values—and building paths to each other, each side challenged the other and defined the qualifier of the two-word phrase instead of the noun: *values.*

Definitions are as important as influences. If we do not set the parameters for ethical debate, we will argue what we already believe with closed minds. That is why some philosophers dislike ethics classes. How does an educator teach closed minds? Values give people a foothold on common ground. Even in the heated discussions of abortion debates, the two sides share the value of compassion—one for the mother and the other for the child. The journalist who knows how to keep an open mind to understand this basic principle will report to or target an audience with greater insight. Thus, the first step in building a value system is to define terms and identify tools that define ourselves. The goal is not to program your moral agendas, but to make you aware of the influences that have programmed them for you already. As the nineteenth-century philosopher Schoppenhauer maintained, we all have free will; the issue is, Who has determined that will?

Before you will be able to build a value system, you have to answer that basic question.

Basic Influences

So far, we have defined *values* and discussed their importance in mass communication. But little has been said about the concepts of right and wrong, upon which the definition of *ethics* is based. According to the *Random House Dictionary of the English Language, ethics* deals with "values relating to human conduct, with respect to the rightness or wrongness of certain actions . . . and the motives and ends of such actions." These concepts were developed in almost all ancient civilizations, beginning with Babylonian laws and Hebrew Ten Commandments and including Indian writings of the Vedas and Chinese virtues of the Tao. Western culture is heavily influenced by ancient Greece, which gave us the word *ethics,* derived from *ethos* ("customs"). It was the great thinker Socrates who said, "The unexamined life is not worth living."

The unexamined professional life is not worth much either. The concepts of right and wrong help us examine our lives at the workplace as surely as they do our lives at home. With regard to journalism, employees must be aware that an action or deed *is* right or wrong in the first place. Then they must make a conscious decision to do the right or wrong thing. Finally, they need to ascertain what influence, if any, caused them to make that choice.

You have probably heard the phrase "Ignorance is no excuse when it comes to breaking the law." For instance, if a person mistakenly thinks that posters of a local band on display at a record store are free samples and takes one out of that store, he or she can be prosecuted for shoplifting. But ignorance *is* an excuse when it comes to ethics. If that same person is an intern at a radio station and borrows a poster from there, intending to study local musicians, this is not a serious breach of ethics—until someone informs the intern that this is against company policy. Then, if the intern takes home the poster and lies about doing so, he or she is making a conscious decision and a serious ethical breach. Ultimately, the intern may have been influenced to make that choice because of a family motto: "Stealing is okay as long as you don't get caught!"

For now, ignorance of right and wrong is immaterial at this juncture. You may or may not know the ethics of every issue presented in this book. For instance, if you are a magazine major used to working with illustrators of a publication, you may not realize that altering documentary photographs is considered a serious ethical breach in photojournalism. The photojournalist might not realize that lack of quotations to indicate previously published material in an article can be deemed plagiarism in magazine journalism, even if the material contains a proper attribution. And so on through the various sequences. The goal of this book is to expose you to, discuss the rights and wrongs of, and analyze the values associated with such issues (among other things). Once you become familiar with these issues, you no longer can claim ignorance.

Then the more interesting aspect of ethics begins. When you know the specific rights and wrongs of a certain issue, and then act according to your conscience, you are making a voluntary choice for which you will be held accountable. "It's not oversimplifying the matter to claim that ethics is doing something or deciding not to do something for a payoff or other consideration," says Ben Blackstock, director of the Oklahoma Press Association. Blackstock represents dozens of Oklahoma newspapers and so must know journalism ethics to address the many right/wrong inquiries his office fields regularly from reporters and editors. He also lobbies for their newspapers at the state capital in Oklahoma City and must rely on his character and reputation when dealing with legislators. "Ethics is doing right instead of wrong," Blackstock remarks. "It's no use saying that you don't have any ethics because you haven't examined world philosophy enough. When you don't have any, that becomes your decision: *not to have any*."

When a person chooses to do wrong, Blackstock notes, he or she should feel "a stab of conscience"—a phrase that has become cliché because it is so true. If a person does not feel that stab, Blackstock maintains, this says something about the erosion of values. To stress this point, Blackstock tells a Native American story:

> An elder spoke about conscience. He said, "A conscience is a sharp stone someplace inside that has very sharp points and edges. When a person does something wrong it turns and hurts. But if the person keeps doing it long enough it will turn back and forth until it's smooth. Then it doesn't hurt any more."

Blackstock adds: "May your stone stay sharp. May it continue to hurt."

Although we may make conscious ethical choices, other factors often influence these decisions. Determining the various influences is complex and consumes much of this chapter and parts of others. For now, four basic influences on values will be considered: familial, experiential, generational, and cultural.

Familial

Family values have already been discussed in this chapter. However, families also pass along to children mottoes that play a big role in influencing actions. Margaret A. Taylor, past president of the Oklahoma Press Association, and Jim Mayo, publisher of the *Sequoyah (Oklahoma) Times,* are both members of that state's Journalism Hall of Fame. When asked to cite the key to their success as journalists, each recites familial mottoes.

Taylor says her life as a child and her marriage to a weekly newspaper publisher formed the basis of her ethics as a journalist.

> As a child of the South, I had parents who worked hard to give my brother and me an education, and I was taught to do the correct thing. There was no question as to telling the truth and treating everyone equally. Those words—"Treat everyone equally"—were the same standards we practiced in newspaper publishing and in everyday life. And my daddy's words—"Always be good"—say it all. You can't be good in journalism without being *fair* to everyone.

Mayo remarks that two mottoes

> have seen me through some tight spots that required close decisions in journalism: "Pick your enemies as carefully as you pick your friends." (Good advice from my granddad.) "Don't try to fight wars on two fronts at once." (Good advice from my dad—or maybe Dwight Eisenhower.)

Familial mottoes vary, however. Some are basically true or prudent, such as Taylor's and Mayo's, and some are basically false, especially ones that stereotype race or religious preference. Some fall in between—part true, part false—but are adopted by children and cause problems in adulthood. Such was the case with Barbara Neikirk, community development manager for Sprint/United Telephone.

> I was reared with the belief that anyone older than me knows more than me. "Respect your elders" was a frequently repeated rule in my family whose south- ern roots charged its offspring to address anyone over the age of 30 as "Sir" and "Ma'am." Initially in my communications career, I suffered some hard lessons as a result of this inbred conception, usually involving decisions based upon false trust.

As Neikirk correctly notes, a motto such as "Respect your elders" depends on the morality of the elder in question. On the other hand, Neikirk empha- sizes, the whole issue of age is problematic ethically in certain media posi- tions. She acknowledges that her very common family motto "automatically bestows knowledge" to older employees, which is confusing enough, but then there is a contradiction: "At some point," Neikirk states, "aging simply is not deemed fashionable in the workplace—especially in highly visible positions, such as public relations and other media jobs." The best method to overcome influences regarding such mottoes is to work hard, believe in yourself, and keep an open mind, Neikirk adds. The concept of hard work means focusing on job responsibilities and executing them ethically. Believ- ing in one's self means having the confidence to meet challenges on the job. Finally, keeping an open mind is key to resolving such challenges.

Experiential

Experience is such a strong influence on values that it is addressed in every chapter in this book, especially in Chapter 3 and later in this chapter. What you encounter in your life influences how you perceive the world and that, as you shall learn, colors your values. The most effective way to begin, then, is to assess what experience, if any, prompted you to pursue a career as a journalist.

Gail Taylor, who spoke about newsroom ethics in the Introduction, is an investigative reporter for the *Morgantown (West Virginia) Dominion Post.* She specialized in magazine journalism and interned at *Advertising Age* in Chicago, so she could have pursued a job in three media-related disciplines. However, she chose newspaper journalism because of a combination of parental influence and personal experience.

> Whenever I think of how the subject of ethics applies to my job as a newspaper reporter, I think of this statement: "Without truth, there is no integrity."

Although I am paraphrasing that quote, I wish that I had said the words first because they sum up my personal philosophy—a philosophy shaped by my parents. I was born in the late 1960s to parents who, along with thousands of other Americans from all faiths and ethnic backgrounds, fought for civil rights. I was two years old when my parents and I lived in Washington, D.C. My dad tells me that he took me to the rooftop of the apartment building where we lived so I could see the city afire. People were rioting because Dr. Martin Luther King had been murdered.

Shortly after that, we moved to Illinois. My dad thought the Midwest would be a better place to bring up a toddler. Then came the escalating Vietnam protests. I don't remember anything about these events, but I grew up hearing stories.

My parents never discouraged me from asking questions. More importantly, if I asked them questions they could not answer, they would say so—and then try to refer me to someone who *could* answer them.

Since we lived, for the most part, in college towns, that meant we usually had a coterie of scholars with whom we could discuss current events. All were avid readers of newspapers, news magazines, and books.

Early on, I got the sense that if smart people read newspapers, then newspapers must be written by equally smart people. It wasn't until much later in my life, really not until I became a journalist, that I realized that people don't read newspapers to become smart so much as to become informed. And that often, they take what journalists write with a grain of salt.

It is interesting to analyze the combination of influences that led Taylor to a career in investigative journalism. The one experience with her father on the apartment rooftop watching the nation's capital aflame in the aftermath of the King murder probably was etched in her unconscious, although we will never know. But the interaction with scholars who visited the family was a function of experience, as was all the reading of newspapers, magazines, and books that went on in her household. It is not surprising that Gail Taylor believed a newspaper career was related somehow to her intellect. If you read her testimonial closely, however, you can see that even her powerful experiences with regard to print journalism did not hold up entirely when she began working for the *Dominion Post*. Readers purchase newspapers for information, not for self-improvement; moreover, Taylor realized, they don't often believe the information that they consume in the newspaper.

Like Barbara Neikirk earlier, Gail Taylor had to adjust her beliefs to the reality of the workplace. Rather than succumb to the skepticism of readers and lowering her standards, Taylor emphasizes accurate reporting. "If even one person perceives a story I have written to be inaccurate, then I am less than pleased with my effort." Taylor believes that hard work and high standards are important values and aspects of her credibility as a journalist.

Generational

Each generation comes with its own set of experiences dictated by such influences as history, economy, weather patterns, technology, and war (to name a few). These situations and events combine to create generational filters through which people born in a specific era tend to view the world. For instance, only a few years separated the Roaring Twenties era—known for its prosperity and capriciousness—from the Great Depression era—known for its hardships and determination. Similarly, your own generation has its unique set of experiences in store for you.

U.S. society is experiencing rapid change. In a report distributed by computer via the Information Highway, the Johnson Foundation challenged educators to prepare for these changes and influences:

> The United States is becoming more diverse: by the year 2020, about one-third of Americans will be members of minority groups. . . . New information and technologies are accelerating change: with a half life of less than five years, they are reshaping the way the world lives, works, and plays. Our society is aging: in 1933, 17 Americans were employed for every Social Security recipient; by 2020, the ratio will have dropped from 17-to-1 to 3-to-1. In 1950, the Ford Motor Company employed 62 active workers for every retiree; by 1993, the ratio dropped to 1.2-to-1. . . .
>
> A generation ago, Americans were confident that the core values which had served our nation well in the past could guide it into the future. These values were expressed in homey statements such as: "Honesty is the best policy"; "Serve your country"; "Be a good neighbor." Today we worry that the core values may be shifting and that the sentiments expressed are different: "Don't get involved"; "I gave at the office"; "It's cheating only if you get caught.". . .
>
> A generation ago, computers took up entire rooms; punch cards for data processing were the cutting edge of technology; operators stood by to help with transatlantic calls; many families watched the clock each afternoon until local television stations began their evening broadcasts. Today, microprocessors, miniaturization, and fiber optics have made information from the four corners of the world instantaneously available to anyone with a computer, transforming the way we manage our institutions, the way we entertain ourselves, the way we do our business."[7]

The report went on to note that citizens who were reared in other generations thought that American society would continue to prosper. All that has changed, the report noted. "Americans may be aware of all this, but we are prisoners of our past." The framers of the report—some of America's most influential business and education leaders—said the solution to keep pace with changes and meet challenges is, in large part, to develop a strong value system.

Cultural

This is the catchall category that includes predominant beliefs within segments of society such as entertainment, sports, education, arts and sciences, and races, regions, and religions. Influences and examples from these segments are too lengthy to cite now and are covered in other chapters (particularly Chapters 5 and 7). However, to introduce you to the complexities of such influences, perhaps there is no better example than an American cartoonist employed by an Asian newspaper to discuss society in that country from a cross-cultural perspective.

Such is the case of Mike Woolson, free-lance writer and satirist, who has to deal with cultural influences each week in preparing a comic strip—"West Meets East"—for the *China Post,* Taiwan's leading English-language daily. The strip is about Woolson as an expatriate American experiencing how to live in Taipei.

"In my strip I'm trying to offer to a primarily Asian audience my own perspective on living and existing in Asia," Woolson says. "I worry a lot less about stereotyping Americans than I do about stereotyping Chinese. But I really ride the rail because I write for other expatriates within an Asian community. Because I don't speak Chinese I'm really very limited understanding the culture."

Woolson ran into a cross-cultural problem when he did a strip about English slogans seen on T-shirts and jackets in Taiwan.

> One person was wearing a shirt that had a picture of a bear with [the slogan] "Imposing Bear Is The Best Friend." So I made the bear into a character in the strip. Then I got an anonymous letter, probably from an American, saying it was culturally insensitive. . . . At the same time the Chinese may be thinking I am making fun of their inability to handle English which is a serious thing because I don't speak Chinese.
>
> One of the dangers ethically is how you render people of another nationality in a comic strip. There's a very unfortunate history of racial caricature in American cartooning. I avoid things like buck teeth, thick glasses [World War II stereotypes] and try to look at the people around me just as people. Nonetheless, what I see is seen through a filter. You are that filter.

While Woolson doesn't believe he can eliminate or adjust for *all* of his Western perspectives, he does believe he has a duty to identify and adjust for cultural influences. To ease matters, he often makes himself a stereotype. "I can abuse myself more than I can abuse anyone else without fear of offending," he says. "So I draw myself in a loud Hawaiian shirt and do a lot of cartoons about my own ineptitude in dealing with Taiwan."

Mike Woolson, American cartoonist for the China Post *in Taipei, ran into cultural problems with the character of "Imposing Bear" in the top panel. The bottom panel shows how he would rather offend himself than Asians, easing cultural misinterpretations.*

The Impact of Social Mores

As already noted, a person perceives the world through familial, experiential, generational, and cultural filters. If you could assess these influences for every person in the United States and somehow tally and condense them, you would end up with another important element: mores (pronounced mor'-ez from the Latin, meaning "conventions"). *Mores,* or *social mores* as they often are called, are beliefs—specific rights and wrongs—that a society or group accepts without question *at a certain point in time.*

Beliefs change over time. In the 1950s, for example, cigarette smoking was considered sophisticated and a symbol of progress. An L&M cigarette ad in the late 1950s stated: "Live modern! Smoke modern!" In the 1990s, smoking is considered dumb and a symbol of bad health habits, replete with the Surgeon General's warnings. But even this belief is a social more, subject to time. Maybe some future society will consider smoking brave—a symbolic affront to Big Brother government—or cowardly—a cop-out to avoid some type of community service.

Identifying social mores can be complicated because of time considerations. As historians know, people can assess the mores of the past only by understanding the influences of a specific era. It is more difficult to assess developing mores as events transpire in your own era. For instance, in the 1950s, a typical car slogan, such as "Only Ford gives you these modern features," symbolizes that era's emphasis on progress. But you may see no social influence regarding this 1990s Volvo slogan emphasizing safety concerns: "Where would you rather sit? Behind the front end or in it?" However, as in the earlier tobacco example, the social more seems to imply that we can circumvent health problems (or death) by being smart consumers. Think about that statement for a moment. Feeling uncomfortable? You might be thinking "Well, you *can* control these types of health problems" without realizing the relationship of genetics (determining who is more prone to develop certain ailments) and psychographics (determining who is more prone to have certain car accidents). You can bet that insurance companies know all about these statistics, explaining why applicants must provide information from medical and traffic records. Nonetheless, we don't have to debate the truth about tobacco or Volvos; for the purposes of this chapter, it is sufficient to note that the process of evaluating current mores also indicates the pressure that society can place on your values and perception. Even more difficult to discern are *future* mores because the events that will shape and define them have yet to happen and may only be predicted with imprecision. The lesson here is elusive: What society believes is right and moral today may be deemed wrong and immoral tomorrow (apart from moral absolutes, which will be discussed in Chapter 3). Finally, what society believes is right and moral or wrong and immoral today may still be so tomorrow—for a completely opposite reason.

For instance, in the 1940s, in a certain southern state, laws prohibited Blacks from attending White universities. People of color had their own segregated colleges, and this was considered equality: "separate but equal." In 1949, a young Black woman in this state was allowed to hear lectures at a White institution because a professor circumvented the law by positioning her outside an open window. (During this era, school officials helped two Blacks at another White institution circumvent the law by allowing them to attend class in metal enclosures so that the students, technically, were not "inside" the building.) In our time these would be atrocious examples of wrong and immoral behavior and, again, as you shall learn in Chapter 3, they may be deemed immoral in *any* era. Certainly, in this state in the 1940s, there were White and Black activists who recognized the racist symbolism of open windows and metal enclosures. But stop a minute and think about whether the particular professors who circumvented the law would be invited to tea that afternoon by racist citizens in these college towns. Although you might condemn the methods of these educators, think about their goals: accommodating people of color who wanted to attend White institutions. The educators believed they were acting in a right and moral fashion. Now think about social movements in your time concerning African Americans who, because of the continuing specter of racism, believe the best and most liberating educational experiences for people of color can be had only at predominantly Black institutions. As you can see, the issue of right and wrong becomes increasingly murky.

To test social mores about another controversial subject—gender— Renee Neeley, a broadcasting major at Ohio University, spent an afternoon impersonating an expectant mother. "I took my summer jumper, which is very baggy, and put that on over a pair of shorts I had stuffed with padding to make me look pregnant," she recalls. "My rules were simple: I wasn't allowed to reveal the fact that I wasn't pregnant to people I knew unless they asked. I knew this might start some rumors about me, but that was okay because I knew I would have my figure back the next day." Then she strolled down the main street in her college town. "I normally cross the street without regard to approaching cars because pedestrians have the right of way. Drivers don't usually recognize this fact and beep and yell profanities at me if I hold them up." On this day, however, a driver beeped, stopped and "started to yell, but then saw my stomach, and said, 'Oh, I'm sorry.'" As Neeley continued to walk, people were mostly indifferent. "An older man smiled and tipped his hat," she says.

But Neeley encountered different reactions on campus. Some students who knew her but hadn't seen her in a while seemed shocked. In the newsroom where she worked, classmates openly stared but avoided asking her if she was pregnant. One complimented her dress. Neeley began patting her stomach until her coworkers openly began wondering about "my new weight gain." Neeley confronted them, wondering why "they just didn't ask me about it, and they said they didn't want to be rude. I thought it was rude that they stared at me and didn't ask." Finally, she concluded that the experience showed that "people might be nicer to young pregnant women because they think you're married and expect you to have children, but when you're unwed and in school people are shocked or embarrassed." Neeley identified a social more.

The Impact of Language

Language encompasses ideas. Because it does, it also encompasses social mores. Advertisers know that slogans include key words—"The *Real* Thing" or "The *King* of Beers"—geared to give the product a certain identity that attracts consumers. However, words change along with mores. Since the 1950s, trendy synonyms for the operative word *real* in the Coca-Cola slogan have ranged from *true-blue* to *bitchin'*. If you plugged *true-blue* into the Coke slogan, as in "Coke, the true-blue thing," the slogan would depict a colorful beverage rather than a genuine one. If you plugged *bitchin'* into the slogan, it would depict a "hip" drink rather than one for all age groups. In the 1990s, words such as *true-blue* and *bitchin'* were rapidly losing their allure, consigned to the fad junkheap of words such as *swell* and *groovy*. Likewise, the word *king* in "The King of Beers" once may have connoted *tops,* as in the old childhood game King of the Hill. But now this particular Budweiser slogan may no longer appeal to younger consumers who might consider the word *king* too aggressive or arrogant, associating the product with their parents' generation.

Advertisers spend billions of dollars each year researching new products and their slogans, according to Cassandra Reese, former manager of consolidated brand purchases for Kraft USA. "One time at Kraft USA a slogan used over 40 years—'Good Food, Good Food Ideas'—was challenged by the new marketing managers." The phrase "good food" rang "apple pie and Mom," remarked Reese, "and that was not what the younger generation was responding to. Conversely, if Mom used the product, the slogan implied it must not be for *my* generation, a younger consumer might think." Reese says that advertisers test words and align slogans with products using scientific research, consumer panels, taste-test kitchens, focus groups, and telephone surveys. "Sometimes research will lead marketers to a word if a product is really 'whiter' or 'fluffier.' Then you can say, 'Our brand is *whiter*' or 'Our brand is *fluffier*.' You would give those words to your copywriters and then they would have to test those words in a slogan."

Words, especially proper nouns, also can affect us personally and influence us, coloring how we view the world. These are called *trigger words* because they trigger a reaction inside us and, consequently, cause us to lose perspective. Here is a short list of common trigger words:

1.	Jesus	6.	UFO
2.	Satan	7.	Kennedy
3.	Communist	8.	*Roe* v. *Wade*
4.	Nazi	9.	Elvis
5.	Ku Klux Klan	10.	CIA

You have heard these potent words thousands of times via mass media and probably have an opinion or a feeling about several of them. These opinions and feelings are associated with social mores and/or basic influences. Depending on your awareness, these words can trigger certain reactions—arguing instead of listening, for instance—or cloud perception—such as believing someone is a friend or an enemy based on his or her use of one of these words.

If you cover news, your reaction to certain trigger words can cause you problems with or impress your employer. John Lenger, the former Sunday editor of the *Post-Star* in Glens Falls, New York, recalls an incident with a reporter that did both.

"Police had told her [the reporter] that teenagers were conducting Satanic rituals that included animal sacrifices," Lenger says. "She had an interview with a police informant who said he had witnessed a sacrifice, and an interview with the anti-Satanist leader of a Christian group. The reporter told me she was ready to go with a three-part series." Lenger asked her to balance the story by talking to Satanists, but the reporter refused. "She was morally opposed to giving such people any outlet for their message," Lenger remarks. "I was her boss, so I won. The reporter interviewed the high priest of the largest organized Satanic church in the country. That interview made her story. And that story won her awards and made her a star."

"Playing devil's advocate was not just the ethical thing to do," Lenger adds. "It was also the smart thing to do" because it provided information to the community.

In that case, the reporter was responding to a trigger word—*Satan*—that somehow was associated with her basic influences. She adjusted for that influence and wrote an informative article. But what about social mores? Can they influence groups of people in the same way? Is it possible to overcome them, given peer pressure to conform?

In 1986, during the presidency of Ronald Reagan, many young people were attracted to conservatism. The president's name evoked favorable opinions and trustworthy feelings in students. In part, Reagan deserved this for instilling hope in millions of citizens for a better America. But these positive feelings also were influencing the perception of aspiring journalists. For instance, in an ethics class at Ohio University, students refused to consider whether our government would use a kind of propaganda called *disinformation,* which would entail officials supplying misleading data to mass media as part of foreign policy. This was a breaking story and mass media issue at the time, so it was appropriate to bring it up in class in an objective manner. Nonetheless, students seemed uncomfortable with the subject, which was unusual, inasmuch as students were relatively open minded when discussing controversial subjects such as racism or equal rights. In sum, they were being influenced by trigger words. To test that, students were given a doctored wire service story on disinformation that substituted Soviet and European proper nouns for American ones:

> MOSCOW (AP)—Soviet officials acknowledge the Kremlin plotted to deceive Afghan leader Sayid Mohammad Najibullah into thinking he faced a new round of Russian bombing and a possible coup. General Secretary Mikhail Gorbachev insisted yesterday there was "not any plan of ours" to deceive the people and the press.
>
> The aim of the secret plan was to convince Najibullah that a Soviet raid, such as the 1980 attack by MIG fighters against rebels in the Khyber Pass, was being planned against him, said unidentified sources.
>
> Meanwhile, the Politburo conducted an immediate inquiry into whether the KGB had violated Gorbachev prohibitions against planting phony stories with international news agencies and reached a conclusion that no regulations were broken either in letter or spirit.
>
> The German news magazine *Der Spiegel* reported yesterday that an elaborate Kremlin campaign included "a disinformation program with the basic goal of making Najibullah think there is a high degree of internal opposition against him within Afghanistan, that his key trusted aides are disloyal, that the Soviet Union is about to move against him militarily."

Stop here for a moment and isolate specific trigger words substituted from a wire story that appeared in an area newspaper under the headline "Officials detail plot to deceive Gadhafi," a Libyan leader against whom a U.S. airstrike was launched earlier that spring:

AP Report	*Class Example*
Administration	Soviet
White House	Kremlin
Libyan leader Moammar Gadhafi	Afghan leader Sayid Mohammad Najibullah
President Ronald Reagan	General Secretary Mikhail Gorbachev
Tripoli and Benghazi	Khyber Pass
U.S. bombers	MIG fighters
Senate Intelligence Committee	Politburo
CIA	KGB
U.S. news agencies	International news agencies
Washington Post	*Der Spiegel*

No student analyzing the doctored story realized that the proper nouns did not make sense. For instance, "Afghan leader" is never defined and the Soviet Union had more than 100,000 troops in the country at the time, so the notion of a military strike was obviously erroneous. When students were asked whether they believed that the Gorbachev government was capable of such deception, almost everyone answered yes. This was what they had expected from the old Soviet Union. Then they were asked whether the Reagan administration would plan a plot like this against Libyan leader Moammar Gadhafi. Roughly two-thirds of the students thought this unlikely or impossible. The class was showed the original Associated Press (AP) report and learned about the power of proper nouns on perception.

One year later, the class exercise was useless. By then, the Iran-Contra scandal had broken, a complex international story involving the trade of arms for hostages and tainting the credibility of the Reagan administration. When the same experiment was done with another class, the results reversed themselves, with more than two-thirds of the class believing that the United States would use disinformation to plot against Gadhafi.

The first exercise proved how proper nouns can trigger reactions within us. The second exercise proved how quickly those same words can fall from favor or change meaning.

Perception and Objectivity

Perception, or how one interprets the outside world, is perhaps the most important element in any journalism job. Perception is also key in developing *objectivity*, which is to view things, people, and events as they actually exist without filtering them through basic influences or accepting or rejecting them without question because of social mores. Objectivity, by the way, applies to all journalism sequences—not just print, broadcast news, and photojournalism. True, reporters and photographers try to perceive the outside world as it exists to cover it accurately. But advertisers and public relations practitioners also must target audiences with a keen, objective eye to determine the need or effectiveness of a product or campaign. They also must evaluate dispassionately such aspects of an account as slogan or copywriting, product or statistical research, market distribution, or crisis management. Thus, to report to or target an audience effectively, *all* journalists have to identify and adjust for basic influences and social mores. Only then will perception improve and with it, objectivity.

Many successful journalists relate objectivity to their value systems. Helen Thomas, who has covered seven presidents during her tenure with United Press International, bluntly states, "I wasn't hired for my opinions. It's a point of honor." Thomas has enjoyed an exciting career as a White House correspondent because she has been able to clear her mind of influences and report objectively on world-changing events as they happen in the nation's capital or on *Air Force One.* Anyone who knows or has worked with her understands that she is a woman of strong opinions and equally strong values (honor chief among them, as will be discussed in the next chapter). In sum, her principles counteract her opinions when she is on the presidential beat.

Too often, print and broadcast journalists believe objectivity means getting two sides of the story and giving them equal play. If so, they contend, a story is "balanced." That formula may work in legislative or election coverage—interviewing supporters and opponents of a bill in Congress or candidates of all parties in a campaign—but it falls short on other, more common types of assignments. In essence, a journalist must clear his or her mind of influences and mores and try to perceive a situation as it exists, highlighting the most important aspects of a story in the lead, broadcast summary, or cutline. Otherwise, objectivity is a tone of voice—words that sound dispassionate but miss the mark, the newspeg, the truth.

To determine how elusive objectivity can be, analyze the illustration entitled The Fine Line of Objectivity. You will learn two sides of an unfortunate story that happened in the 1980s in California. The dateline "Los Angeles" has been used, although that is not necessarily the city in which the incident occurred. An adolescent girl and defendant in an incest case refused to testify against her father, was charged with obstructing justice, and was threatened with jail by a prosecuting attorney. This example pertains to news coverage, but advertising and public relations majors will want to test their objectivity by analyzing it closely.

The Fine Line of Objectivity indicates just how subtle influence and objectivity can be. Many journalists believe that people cannot be truly

THE FINE LINE OF OBJECTIVITY

Below are three *X*s representing three objective-sounding leads, which are provided beneath the graph. At both ends of the graph is a "truth"—*Side A* on the left and *Side B* on the right. Read each lead and decide which truth should be emphasized: Side A, both, or Side B.

Side A: *Incest victim who fears her father will kill her.*

Side B: *Prosecutor who believes in the letter of the law.*

X1	*X2*	*X3*

X1:
LOS ANGELES—An 11-year-old incest victim, charged with obstructing justice, has told authorities she would rather go to jail than testify against her father because he has threatened to kill her.

X2:
LOS ANGELES—Prosecutors have threatened to jail an 11-year-old girl who has refused to testify against her father in an incest case, charging her with obstruction of justice.

X3:
LOS ANGELES—An 11-year-old girl who refused to testify against her father was charged with obstruction of justice, setting a precedent that may result in more sexual abuse convictions, prosecutors said.

All of the preceding leads sound objective but focus on different truths. The first lead, *X1*, uses the phrase "incest victim" and focuses on the girl's fear, explaining why she would rather go to jail than confront her father. The second lead, *X2*, notes that the prosecutor has charged an 11-year-old girl in an incest "case" with obstruction of justice but doesn't focus on the girl's fear or the prosecutor's reasoning. The third lead, *X3*, notes the reason that the prosecutor has jailed the girl and doesn't mention "incest," substituting "sexual abuse." Where would you draw *your* X on the line?

objective because human beings are subjective and often misperceive or misinterpret what they see because of basic influences and social mores. But these same journalists also believe that it is a person's responsibility to acknowledge and adjust for as many influences and mores as one can identify. Although we may be incapable of true objectivity, we must strive to achieve it as journalists.

Perception, as was noted, is your most important asset in any media job. It is also key in the development of values. The Introduction of this book said that ethics is simply a matter of balancing outside pressures with inner principles. To do that, you must view the world as objectively as possible to ascertain those pressures and then, as you shall learn in upcoming chapters, develop appropriate values.

ENDNOTES

1. Michael Levin, "Ethics courses: Useless," *New York Times,* 25 November 1989, Sec. A, p. 23.

2. Barbara Lippert, "Dream Sequence: Dan Quayle's family values fail to motivate apathetic voters," *ADWEEK Eastern Edition,* 21 September 1992, p. 41.

3. Lance Morrow, "But seriously, folks," *Time,* 1 June 1992, p. 29.

4. Morrow, p. 29.

5. Marlys Harris, "What's a 'Murphy Brown' like me supposed to do?" *Money,* November 1992, p. 191.

6. Michele Ingrassia, "Daughters of Murphy Brown," *Newsweek,* 2 August 1993, p. 58.

7. *An American Imperative: Higher Expectations for Higher Education,* multiple authors (Racine, WI: The Johnson Foundation, 1993), pp. 8–9.

L I V I N G   E T H I C S

Read the following interviews and articles and record your reactions in your ethics journal and/or discuss them with peers or mentors.

❊ **EDITOR'S NOTE**: *Eli Flournoy began working for Cable News Network (CNN) in 1990 on an internship through Indiana University. Since then, he has worked on* Headline News *as a writer and associate producer and now is a producer on the International Desk. In the following essay, Flournoy responds to the question, What would you tell readers of this text if you were a guest speaker today in their classroom?*

The Ethical Journalist

Eli Flournoy, Producer, *CNN International Newsource*

Ethics, or how to behave ethically, is something I think about every day at CNN. I work at CNN's International Desk handling relations with overseas affiliates, so I am especially sensitive to how CNN presents news about other countries. Criticism about underreporting and misreporting on the Third World is of particular interest to me.

Ethics in news means deciding what stories are newsworthy, making sure that they get reported and, most importantly, making sure the reporting is fair and accurate. Of course every case is different and it's a huge world so there is a tremendous amount of gray area.

If I were speaking to your class, I would give you an idea of the spectrum of situations you confront everyday here.

In the summer of 1990 one international wire service reported that a faction of the military in Zambia had revolted and sent the government into exile. The *New York Times* picked up the story as did CNN and probably other news services. Twenty-four hours later the story was corrected, and it became clear the government was not in exile and no military coup had taken place. Months later a Zambian television official explained to me what happened: a renegade soldier entered the state radio facility, forced the announcer off at gunpoint, and broadcasted his own message. The military had taken over and the government was in exile, he claimed. The wire service reporter in a neighboring country monitoring state radio reports in the region heard the report and filed it. Essentially, the story held uncorrected for 24 hours. Now imagine the financial and political implications internationally of a country appearing to be in anarchy.

On the other hand, sometimes a real story possibly should not be reported at all. In 1992 government soldiers rioted in Zaire because their pay was decreased and currency devalued again, causing Belgium and France to send in troops and evacuate expatriates. I was a writer at *Headline News* assigned to write a 25-second update on the story. After struggling with it a while I asked for more time to give some context to the story. Time wasn't available so I ultimately recommended to the producer that he drop the story because what I could do in that amount of time would be so misleading it would be better not to tell it at all. I was thinking the average viewer may not know anything about Zaire or even where it's located. It's very unlikely he or she would know that this was just one incident in a pattern of corruption. Or that several devaluations had already occurred and soldiers' pay had been withheld many times before. So what would the viewer get out of the update? "Black people riot in Zaire with little reason.The entire country is in chaos. White people are in danger in that country. Another case of an African country self-destructing despite the diligent help of First World governments and development/relief organizations." This may not have been giving the audience enough credit but after having majored in African Studies in college, I felt the assessment was accurate. Anyway, the story ran.

In a domestic story, CNN carried nearly gavel-to-gavel coverage of the William Kennedy Smith rape trial in Florida in 1991. First of all I thought the media's insistence on calling him William "Kennedy" Smith was unethical because he never used the "Kennedy" in his name. Even his college roommate did not know he was a Kennedy. So I refused to use the "Kennedy" in my copy. Some of my copy editors left it out, some added it. During the trial he testified that he had intercourse with the plaintiff twice, ejaculating once; I noticed that one of pieces juxtaposed the sound bite of him saying "I ejaculated" next to the reporter's description of the wrong incident, essentially making it seem as if he was caught in a lie. I was not involved in the show airing at the time but I still felt responsible to point this out to the supervising producer to check. He did and it turned out to be an unintentional error. The piece was killed. It would have been easier for him to let it slide and not make the reporter redo the story, but that was an ethical decision.

Another example in CNN writing which comes up frequently is what to call those who support or oppose the right to have an abortion. Reporters in many of our stories were calling them "anti-abortion activists" and "abortion-rights supporters." Despite my own personal feelings on abortion I felt this was presenting a negative slant against those who oppose abortions. *Anti* is a negative word versus *rights,* which is essentially a positive word. The word *activists* tends to carry a negative connotation versus *supporters,* which is generally positive. I brought this up to the senior editor and he agreed that they should both be called "activists."

In commercial television news there are many things that stand in the way of ethics. The greatest come from financial considerations: the concern for ratings, the need to attract advertising and cut costs, for instance. This often clouds the ability to make ethical decisions. Some stories don't get covered because it's just too expensive. Why cover Rwanda and not Angola? Less expensive? More interest? Easier access? There are usually a combination of factors but the battle between covering stories (especially international) and covering costs is a daily one.

I think these other major ethical issues need to be addressed in broadcast journalism:

- Should we broadcast trials at all or does that convict the accused and destroy the chance for a fair trial?
- Should we devote so much air time to sensational stories involving movie stars and celebrities?
- Is the fact that another major news agency has reported a story enough justification to put it on our air even if we don't have independent confirmation?

Having said all that, I believe CNN does an excellent job on ethical issues. I wouldn't be working here if I didn't feel that ethical behavior was a crucial part of the philosophy of the company. Time and again I have found my superiors listen and truly consider issues I raise, no matter what level I have been at in the hierarchy. CNN has a whole department devoted to viewer comments on coverage. Cultural representation corrections, factual errors or misrepresentations, and suggestions for story ideas are taken very seriously. These comments are tallied and summarized for all staff on a weekly basis. I have never personally observed or heard of anyone reporting incorrect information intentionally or suppressing information for some malicious reason.

The problem with gauging ethics in television journalism lies in the fact that I believe true objectivity is impossible. Everyone has a perspective, differing interests, various education levels, and many times they influence decisions in very subtle ways. Like the wording on the abortion issue, which may seem very minor. Or decisions on running one story versus another. The key then is fairness and presenting as many different angles/perspectives on a story as possible.

So what is it, exactly, that enables me to make ethical decisions? The two primary influences on me are my Christian faith and my family. They gave me the fundamentals for my morals and sense of fairness and the concept of treating others the way I would want to be treated. I have relatives I am close to and love who are staunchly opposed to abortions and I respect their perspective on the issue, even if I may not completely agree with it. The same situation applies to issues involving Republicans and Democrats because my family is also split on that issue. My education also played a strong role. My interest in issues of diversity, human rights, and Africa specifically was influenced by my university studies.

Finally, I believe that values and ethics can be developed in the absence of a strong family unit—with a significant intervening factor. In my opinion the most powerful and essential of those would be religious faith. But beyond that, someone—a parent, priest, teacher, coach, friend—has to instill true love and respect for yourself and others into your life. Without that, there is no reason to care and, I believe, no ability to make ethical decisions. In sum, your concern for ethics is relative to the intensity of your family, religious, educational and others' influence on values and ethics.

❈ **EDITOR'S NOTE**: *Dan Horn was on an internship at a large city newspaper when he was assigned to interview the parents and sisters of a high school student who committed suicide. At the time, Horn believed the assignment might win him an award or a position upon graduation at the* Cleveland Plain Dealer. *However, while interviewing the family, he had to deal with his own emotions and influences, confront the concepts of right and wrong, and begin enhancing a value system to guide him in his career. He wrote the following* *piece in an ethics class at Ohio University and published it in* Editor & Publisher, *a newspaper trade magazine. Soon after, Horn was hired by the* Cincinnati Post.

Easy Street

Dan Horn, Reporter, *The Cincinnati Post*

I had already spent most of my Wednesday morning writing about dead people when I first heard about an 18-year-old kid named John.

It was the second week of my winter reporting internship, about two weeks before Christmas, and I was doing the only thing I liked less than writing stories about harried shoppers, Christmas trees and Cabbage Patch Dolls: obituaries.

The sweet lady who usually wrote obituaries called in sick that morning, forcing my editor to assign the thankless chore to someone else. She gave it to the winter intern who was trying to look busy.

Every funeral director in the city waited until about 30 minutes before deadline to phone in obituaries. The so-called "stiff list" quickly swelled to almost 20 names that morning, and I spent most of the time wondering aloud why these people just couldn't hold out for one more day. When I thought I could kick back and grab a doughnut, a funeral director called and introduced me to John.

He was a high school junior. He had two sisters, a divorced mom and dad and, apparently, a lot of problems. The funeral director told me the coroner would rule on the cause of death. That's funeral director "code" for suicide, and it meant I had to find out if the coroner had decided how John killed himself.

The secretary at the coroner's office performed her job perfectly that morning. She put me on hold. My deadline was five minutes away, and I was listening to Muzak on the county coroner's telephone line. Somebody ate the last jelly doughnut.

I hated my job, I hated the sweet lady who usually wrote obituaries and, on this day, I hated John.

About a week later, John's mother walked into the newsroom and handed my editor her son's suicide note. She wanted it published.

My editor looked over her VDT and noticed the winter intern was the first person back at his desk after the staff Christmas party. Silly boy. She gave me the note, told me to call a few relatives, and write a nice little tearjerker about a family grieving at Christmas time. I figured it had to be better than another story about the amazing number of people who were buying blue spruces that Christmas.

I read the note. It was sloppily written on two sheets of notebook paper with what looked like a leaking ball-point pen: "I hope nobody is mad at me for what I'm going to do. I don't want to die, but I don't know how I can go on living."

It read like the plot of an ABC *After School Special* or a gag letter college kids send off to Ann Landers. It would have been funny if John hadn't been so damn serious about it.

After talking to John's mother and father for a little while, I knew the story was far too complicated to throw together in one day. His life was more confusing than his death. He was a punk rocker who wore makeup and colored his hair, but he liked to go to prayer group meetings with his grandmother. He ran away at least seven times after his parents divorced in 1979, but his mother and father each had separate versions of the same story.

He had tried to kill himself before but he was getting professional help. It wasn't supposed to happen again. His mother told me how much she wanted the story written and his father told me how much he didn't.

His dad finally agreed to talk to me but made sure I understood that if screwed anything up, "We were gonna have words."

I decided to talk to my editor.

She told me to take my time, but said I should call John's mom back just to make sure our competition wouldn't get the story before we did. I hated my job again, but I did it. I like to think I didn't know any better.

Friends in the newsroom told me good things happened to reporters who landed stories like this one—you could win an award and get famous—and, by God, good things were going to happen to me, too.

"I know a reporter who wrote a story about suicide once," someone said.

"No kidding?"

"The *Plain Dealer* gave her a job a week later."

"The *Plain Dealer*?"

"She's on Easy Street now. Set for life. Sitting pretty."

I liked the sound of that. I was going to work straight through Christmas on this story if that's what it took to get me to Easy Street. Visions of happy editors and blue-chip internships danced in my head. I loved my job.

But before I could expect a call from the *Washington Post* I had to make sense of teen suicide. I was baffled. There was little doubt John had problems, but none of them seemed worse than anything I or anyone else had gone through as teenagers. Puberty was hell, finding a prom date was worse, and getting edged out of the big track meet made me sick for a week, but not once did I consider going into the medicine chest, grabbing a bottle of antidepressants and swallowing every pill.

John did.

Two days after his eighteenth birthday, John decided life was just too hard to handle. I wanted to know why.

I started to think less about being famous and more about why the hell I was even writing the story when I met with family members a few days after Christmas. I sat next to a dried-out Christmas tree in the living room and talked to relatives about why an 18-year-old member of their family killed himself. John's mom looked tired and worn, his father apologized for his first phone conversation, I spent most of the afternoon squirming on the sofa.

They were all in pain and I had no right to be there. John's obituary was neatly taped to a wall next to a photograph of the family. His grandmother searched through a scrapbook for homecoming photos and any other dog-eared memories she could find. His father slouched in a chair and his sisters talked as if their brother was alive. Some of them wanted me to tell John's story and some of them didn't.

For the first time, I started to think about right and wrong. I told them I felt uncomfortable and I didn't want to hurt the family more by dragging their dirty laundry—a divorce, broken home, a suicidal son—across the front page of the newspaper.

I figured my editor would kill me and I'd never get a call from the *Plain Dealer*. I didn't care. I wanted them to decide what to do as a family before they told a stranger on break from college for the winter about how their home life may have made their kid miserable.

I drove away convinced I would never hear from John's family again. I was wrong. John's mother called me that night and told me she wanted me to write the story. She said if her son's story could "save just one kid," it would all be worthwhile. She said she trusted me.

I didn't sleep that night. I stared at the ceiling thinking about how nice my break would have been if I had spent more time writing about blue spruces.

During the next few days, I started to piece together the puzzle of John's suicide. Friends who promised to go out with him on his birthday never showed up. He was having girl-trouble. Sometimes he and his grandfather argued about his haircut and clothing. His punk outfits aroused the type of brutal ridicule that high school students everywhere inflict on an one who dares to be different. As one friend said, "He took it pretty hard sometimes . . . he never said much of anything to anybody, but you could tell it got under his skin. Now they have to live with themselves."

I didn't want to hear any more.

Every teen-age boy gets stood up by his friends, breaks up with a girl, gets teased in school for stupid superficial reasons and disagrees with his elders once in a while. Every teen-age boy doesn't commit suicide because of it, and the whole world doesn't need to make judgments about what pushed John over the edge.

I wasn't going to tell John's grandfather that an argument he had with his grandson triggered the suicide, I wasn't going to tell a 17-year-old girl that John killed himself because she wouldn't go out with him, and I wasn't going to tell a bunch of high school students who didn't know any better that their name-calling may have convinced John to swallow a bottle full of pills.

The story ran a few months ago; I still haven't heard from the *Plain Dealer*. I'm not holding my breath. The story was dry, boring, and far less interesting than I first expected.

My friends, parents and editors liked the story—which doesn't make me feel any better—but John taught me something about journalism I'll always value more than a clip I can dangle in front of prospective employers. He showed me that sometimes stuffy textbooks don't have all the answers and sometimes reporters must do what they think is right, not just what they think will win them an award or get them an interview with the *Washington Post*.

As reporters, we tell ourselves all too often that we can print whatever we're allowed to print and do whatever we're allowed to do. Every once in a while, somebody comes along and reminds us that is isn't always so simple.

❋ EDITOR'S NOTE: *Lady Borton is a nationally known book author and colum-nist for the* Akron Beacon Journal. *She served with the American Friends Service Committee during the Vietnam War and now is a field director for that Quaker organization. She has been interviewed by or worked with such news programs as* USA Today *and* 60 Minutes *and has done or produced pieces for National Public Radio and American Public Radio. Her latest book is* After Sorrow *(Viking 1995), which is about "the ordinary people we fought against and their stories." In the following interview, she responds to the question, What influences or social mores, if any, do you think still affect media coverage of Vietnam?*

Still Fighting the War

Lady Borton, Field Director, *American Friends Service Committee*

In my current position, I and others do rural development work, assisting ethnic minority people in two provinces: Son La, up near the Laos border, and Thanh Hoa, south of Hanoi. We help with clean drinking water systems, education, and health care for ethnic minorities. In Vietnam there are about 50 Vietnamese ethnic groups with their own cultures, languages, customs. We do what I call "hyphen" work, making connections for people. Right now Vietnam is opening up, looking at the challenges and dangers that come with the switch to the free market system, capitalism, the World Bank and things like that.

When I've been in Hanoi, journalists have come through and they get my name because I'm one of the few expatriates who speak Vietnamese and the only one who has been involved with Vietnam since the war. I would say these journalists come with the same insight that they had 25 years ago, so particularly on the first visit there, the tendency is for people to continue to refight the war. Recently one prize-winning reporter for a major newspaper actually used the phrase "Hanoi is stuck in time." No one who lives there now feels that. The changes are so rapid that no one there can keep up with them. But the problem is that *we Americans are stuck in time.* And we tend to be stuck at whatever time we left the country. And the Vietnamese have gone on. It may be hard for us as a society to acknowledge that they have done quite well without us and that the changes that they've made might be because *they* have decided to make those changes.

Some examples of this include huge changes in basic freedoms. The freedom to be rich, to make as much money as you want. To practice religion. For instance, there is a big change in care of altars in the family and the money spent on altars and funerals and other ceremonies. People are going to the pagoda.

We all have our biases. I put my biases out there as a writer with a strong value system. Perhaps that's the difference between a writer and a [news] journalist. Journalists have their biases but often disguise them or fail to take them into account.

You saw this especially during the Vietnam War. Journalists almost never talked to the Vietnamese because they couldn't speak the language. Once I took a reporter from a news magazine out to Son My (cite of the My Lai massacre, 16 March 1968, in which U.S. soldiers shot to death 347 unarmed men, women, and children). The story broke in the fall of 1969. We had had patients who came from there. I lent this reporter my typewriter and paper. He ran out and didn't thank me. He wasn't interested in the massacres that just happened. For instance, 50 people had been fishing and helicopters massacred them about two days before that. When he finished his story, I pulled the carbons out and read them and I remember filing them away and being surprised that he was in such a hurry, because for me, this wasn't news. Things like this happened all the time—not to the extent of My Lai—but they happened. Yet these incidents never made it into the news because reporters had little contact with the Vietnamese and didn't understand the language. This lack of reporting affected how society back home perceived the war.

EDITOR'S NOTE: *Jared Lazarus was a full-time intern at the* Tennessean *when he shot this photo. He was a senior at the University of Florida at Gainesville when the case study "The Non-Choice" was written and published in* Six Shooters, *a photojournalism trade publication. An interview with Lazarus follows the case study.*

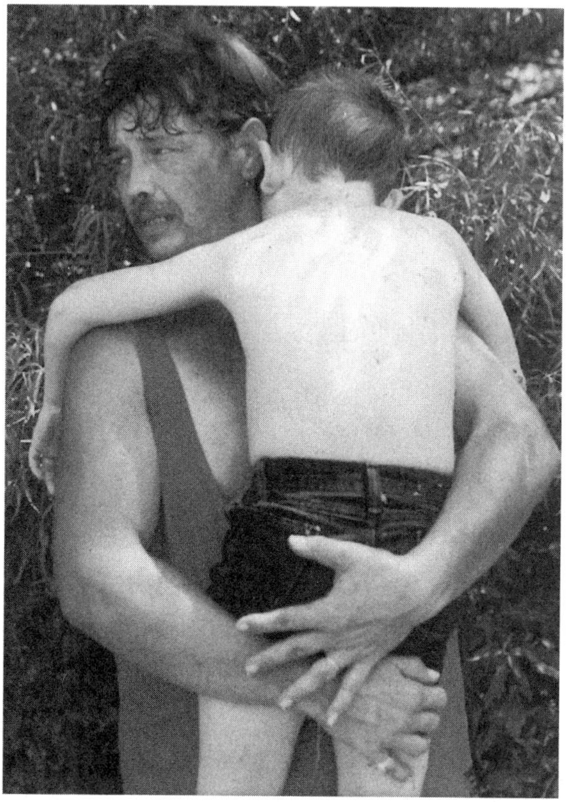

The Non-Choice

Jared Lazarus, Intern, *The Tennessean*

Several kids charged at me, frantically waving their arms for me to stop as I drove by a lake, looking for a holiday feature photo on July 3.

I heard the words, "Help!" and "Drown!"

Excited and nervous, I ran to the lake bed and saw a father leaning over his child, trying to revive him. The stepmother was right beside him, terrified and crying hysterically.

The father looked up and said, "Call an ambulance."

I never thought to take a picture.

I bolted for my car, drove quickly to the ranger's station and told him to call 911 for a drowning victim.

As I returned to the lake to let the family know an ambulance was on the way, I thought, what a picture I just missed!

The father had been kneeling over his pale, listless child, the mother crying for help, the lake inches behind—all so storytelling. What an incredible moment I had just failed to document, I thought. I began seriously doubting myself, my competence as a photojournalist, my future career in the newspaper business.

When I returned, the father was holding the ghost-white child in his arms. Eight frames later the ambulance arrived. I didn't think I had anything the paper would want. But I asked the mother for her name and number, just in case.

I called the paper because I needed just to talk to a photographer, to anyone about what I had experienced. I wasn't clear-headed at all and certainly wasn't ready to go and shoot a feature photo.

I was assured I had done the right thing by photographer Rex Perry and later by reporters and editors. I think I knew deep down I had definitely done the right thing, but part of me kept conjuring up the prizewinner image.

Since then I've talked with the boy's father, Danny Hargis. He told me that his boy is "110 percent recovered" and he bought seven copies of the paper.

I feel at peace with myself, content that I had made the right choice, the only choice, the non-choice.

One year later, Lazarus reflects on the aftermath of the incident in the following interview, responding to the question, Did any lesson on objectivity prepare you for what you encountered that day?

As far as acting on anything I had learned in class, I don't think this was the case. I never consciously made a decision to call for help and not take a picture. I suppose my actions were ethical.

When I drove by the lake, and the children ran to my car screaming for help, I didn't grab my cameras laying in the trunk. Didn't think of it. And how many times had I heard these words from professors, colleagues, and professionals: "Don't go anywhere without your camera," "Always be prepared," and "Shoot first, ask questions later"? But at that moment of confusion, fear, and excitement, all these admonitions had escaped me. And I consider myself calmer than most under stressful situations.

I acted on instinct. So when I reached the lake bed, and the father told me to call an ambulance, that's what I did. I didn't run to my car cursing myself for the incredible picture I would miss because it didn't occur to me then. That was later, even though I knew I did the right thing. If a camera was hanging around my neck, I am sure I would have forgotten its presence.

When I got back to the paper, an editor walked up to me and asked if I got a picture of the father rescuing the boy. When I shook my head and tried to explain, he said, "Your job is to take pictures of people, not save them." A reporter who overheard this told me not to listen to him.

V A L U E S   E X E R C I S E S

1. Make a list of mottoes, phrases, or sentences that a parent or relative has repeated often enough to have become part of your family lore. Include in your list any phrase or sentence that a friend, coworker, superior, teacher, or other person has said often enough for you to remember and record. Try to list at least 10 examples, and do not identify the person who passed along each motto. Now analyze each motto as objectively as possible and ascertain whether you think it is true, part true and part false, or false. Explain why in a sentence or paragraph. Schedule an interview with a person whose judgment you trust and show him or her your mottoes and analyses. Ask that person for his or her analyses and record them for the mottoes. Later compare analyses and note any significant differences. Finally, without violating your own or another person's privacy, discuss these differences and relate them to basic influences.

2. Analyze the advertisements in at least six magazines. Photocopy at least 12 ads that you believe reflect some kind of social more in the slogan, photograph, illustration, or copy. On the back of each ad, type a brief statement identifying any operative word(s) in the slogan or copy or any symbolism in the photo or illustration that indicates a specific social more, such as "Women should be concerned about their appearance" or "Men should drive rugged trucks." On a separate sheet of paper, discuss each message and ascertain how it might influence the beliefs or behaviors of certain people or groups.

3. Make a list of 10 proper nouns that trigger reactions, feelings, or opinions within you. Without violating your own or another person's privacy, explain why each specific word causes you to respond this way. Then state how you will adjust for each word when you become a practicing journalist, thereby enhancing your objectivity.

2

Responsibility

Basic Concepts

The last chapter introduced the concepts of right and wrong via family mottoes such as "Treat everyone equally" and "Pick your enemies as carefully as you pick your friends." Some of these mottoes are true; others, such as "Respect your elders," are only part true; and are some false, such as "Stealing is okay as long as you don't get caught!" When it comes to ethics, there is another motto passed down by recent generations that is, at best, only part true: "If it feels good, do it!" You see variations of this motto in popular songs and advertisements. No other saying has done more harm to values in particular and ethics in general than this one.

The motto muddles the concepts of right and wrong versus good and bad. It throws our ethical compasses off course. The fact is that doing the right thing can feel good or bad—just like doing the wrong thing can feel good or bad. The terms often are used interchangeably but have distinct definitions. Right and wrong are *choices* over which an individual has control. Good and bad are *outcomes* over which an individual has little, if any, control. Right and wrong are functions of *your* behavior. Good and bad are functions of *events* that affect others and that you help set into motion by your behavior. The concepts of right and wrong are *internal*. The concepts of good and bad are *external*. The more a person follows the motto—"If it feels good, do it!"—the more he or she is controlled by outside forces, succumbing to ethical shortcuts that temporarily ease the pressure those forces exert on our lives.

A person who lives by the concepts of right and wrong learns to accept *consequences*. This is key if we hope to lead ethical lives. Accepting consequences is a two-step process: A person takes time to reflect on the possible moral outcomes of an action before deciding to take that action. Depending on the issue at hand, a person asks such questions as: Will I be able to live with such a decision? How will it affect others? What is the worst-case scenario? Is the decision legal? Unprofessional? Unfair? Then the person decides to make, postpone, or reject the decision and assumes responsibility for that choice—*regardless of whether the outcome is good or bad*. But how does a journalist take time to reflect on actions when many on-the-job decisions must be made in a split second (covering a story, or interacting with a client, or meeting a deadline)? That is the *value* of a value system. It helps a person access situations quickly so that he or she can respond ethically.

The unethical journalist lacks a value system. Because of this, he or she believes that assessing each situation takes too much time and does nothing to alleviate immediate pressures. So the person follows the concepts of good and bad: "If it feels good, do it; if it feels bad, don't." Depending on the situation at hand, the unethical journalist asks such questions as: How will I profit from such a decision? How will it affect me? What is the best-case scenario? Will my action go undetected? If it is detected, what steps can I take or excuses can I make to blame someone else or escape punishment? Instead of becoming adept at predicting consequences and learning to accept them, the unethical journalist becomes skilled at *justifying* his or her actions.

Let's stop at this point and compare the two systems of behavior. The concept of justification is aligned with the concept of good and bad. The unethical journalist has keen interest in outcomes and only passing interest in value systems. Conversely, accepting consequences is aligned with right and wrong. The ethical journalist has passing interest in the outcomes of his or her actions and keen interest in whether those actions are right and wrong, according to his or her value system.

You have already encountered journalists in case studies who emphasized the latter tenets. Remember Eli Flournoy, the CNN producer who questioned whether he should do a story about a 1992 riot in Zaire because he thought it would be misinterpreted by the American audience? His assessment of the situation was overruled. "Anyway," he notes, "the story ran." Flournoy knew that his ethical obligation was to tell his superiors that he believed the story should be killed because he lacked the time to broadcast it ethically. He accepted the consequences of that assessment, without worrying whether his superiors would think that he was a slow or difficult writer. Flournoy also knew the specific reasons to explain his decision on the Zaire story: He majored in African Studies at Indiana University and had distinct values concerning this topic. Those particular values required Flournoy to voice his opinion on this story but did not require him to become angry or righteous; he knew that this is a judgment call in the newsroom. Overall, Flournoy is pleased with the ethics of CNN or else, he says,

"I wouldn't be working here." His value system has specific boundaries and limits so that he may accept consequences with a clear conscience.

Conversely, the unethical journalist does not accept consequences or even see the need to because, frankly, *that could feel bad*. If an outcome is bad to begin with—perhaps an editor questioning an anonymous quotation in a news story—such a journalist would think: Why make it feel worse by admitting the quote is a fabrication? Better to justify my actions to myself by saying the deadline was inhuman to begin with and the editor who suspects the infraction is an ogre; better to justify my actions to the editor by claiming the fabrication was not a fabrication at all. After all, the editor has no real way of checking. And if the quote is challenged by readers or sources, then tomorrow I'll just have to invent some other scenario.

As you can see, justification is a complicated process. It feels bad to miss a deadline or be beaten by a competitor. It feels worse to tell that to an editor. But the ethical journalist simply admits defeat and vows to try harder next time, which is all a person can do; thus, he or she accepts the consequences. The editor might become angry. So what? The ethical journalist accepts that challenge and will attempt to work out a solution—learning better time-management skills or agreeing to a progress plan that will determine his or her future with the company. These consequences might feel bad in the short term but they are *liberating* choices in the long term. First, they are choices over which the employee has control: learning new skills or improving performance. Second, they indicate to the editor that the employee realizes the values of hard work, determination, and honor.

As you also learned in the first chapter, Helen Thomas, UPI's White House correspondent, places great emphasis on the value of honor. Here is how she defines that word as it applies to "reporting, public relations, advertising or any aspect of media":

> You have to be guided by honesty, ethical behavior—"Do unto others as you would like done unto you." In everything you do, greed should not dominate your actions. No money on earth is worth your honor. The dollar says, "In God we trust," and in any profession, you will win if people trust you. If you can be trusted, you will go forward as a journalist. If you want to be somebody in this world, you should hold the banner on honor. To be morally on the right side is more important than anything else. You might win a few by being unethical but you'll never lose by being honest and trustworthy.

The unethical journalist does not care about values such as honor or honesty. To be honorable or honest can involve apologies or candor that might feel bad on occasion. The unethical journalist wants to avoid bad feelings at all costs and so becomes a slave to outside forces over which he or she has limited control. The person exerts more and more energy to influence those outside forces; soon, his or her actions are dictated by them.

Eventually, as you will learn in other chapters, the unethical journalist loses credibility (upon which every media job is based). But the person also loses something equally as precious: *perception.* Because the focus is on the external world, inviting or avoiding good and bad outcomes and then justifying questionable actions, the person stops trying to view reality as it might exist. Instead, the person views reality only as it relates to his or her ego or purposes. This is self-defeating. No person can control outcomes, so the unethical journalist adopts a motto such as "Everyone gets fired" or "My newspaper is bogus anyway."

Eventually those mottoes come to justify *lives.*

"A couple of decades ago we became confused with something called 'situational ethics,'" says Ben Blackstock, director of the Oklahoma Press Association. "Simply put, 'situational ethics' means if it feels good, do it. Do that which is the least painful and hope that not very many people find out about it."

A colleague of Blackstock's—Bob Haring, executive editor of the *Tulsa World*—learned about responsibility early in his career from mentors who gave him useful mottoes.

> My first newspaper general manager was Bill Dougherty, in Carbondale, Illinois. Bill was a fascinating man, and he gets smarter every year I stay in the business.
>
> He never second-guessed a decision I made, even as a brash youngster who made a lot of mistakes. He would back up my decisions. But he had a kindly way of letting me know how to make a better decision the next time.
>
> My most telling anecdote stems from the day I returned to the newspaper, the *Southern Illinoisan*, from Army service. The managing editor, Bill Boyne (himself a major influence on my journalistic life) was on vacation. The sports editor, Merle Jones, had been running the paper. Jones made some comment about being relieved that I was back and took off, leaving me to put out that day's paper.
>
> Something came up that required a re-make after the press started. I ordered it done. The composing room foreman, Harold McAdamis, objected. Only Bill Boyne or Merle Jones could order a re-make, he said. That was the order from Bill Dougherty.
>
> We argued. Eventually I prevailed. McAdamis re-made the page, but said, "We'll settle this as soon as Bill Dougherty gets back." Dougherty, bless him, was absent at the time for an extended lunch.
>
> I had the advantage, because I could see Dougherty's office from my desk. The minute Bill returned I was in the office.
>
> I recounted the crisis. Dougherty asked, "What's your question?" I said, "I just want to know if I have the authority." Dougherty replied, "McAdamis did it, didn't he?" Then he added: *"You make your own authority."*
>
> This became a major caveat for me: *You have all the authority you are willing to take responsibility for.*

Haring says he has retold that story many times during his 40-year career as a journalist for the Associated Press and later the *Tulsa World*. "I've tried to use it to teach people to make their own decisions, to be willing to take on authority and to take the risks of responsibility.

"Too many young people want authority without responsibility," Haring adds. "They want to give orders but want someone else to accept responsibility for the consequence of those orders. It doesn't work that way."

Haring learned about accepting consequences from another colleague, David L. Bowen, then a vice president for the Associated Press. "Bowen was a careful analyst," Haring recalls. "He bored into problems, took them apart and analyzed the pieces very carefully." Bowen taught Haring how to predict consequences before making a decision. "Bowen based his philosophy on the theory of 'worst-case management.' He would examine a problem and its potential solutions. Then he would ask, 'What's the worst thing that can happen if we do this?'

"His theory was that if you could live with the worst possible result of an action, then you could take it. I also refined that into a caveat: *Be prepared for the worst; that way you'll never be disappointed and will occasionally be pleasantly surprised.*"

Haring's anecdotes show the relationship between choices and consequences and the role of predicting outcomes before taking action or making a decision based on right and wrong. In a nutshell, that is the ethical process. But perhaps a more important lesson for our purposes here is *how* Haring learned the process—from role models whose advice metamorphosed into useful mottoes.

Role Models *versus* Idols

A popular Nike advertisement features basketball star Charles Barkley scowling at the camera and proclaiming, "I am not a role model." The spot was controversial because, as Jeff Jensen wrote in the trade magazine *Advertising Age*, "Marketers have traditionally used sports figures as celebrity endorsers, presenting them as super-achieving, larger-than-life figures worthy of admiration, emulation and respect."[1] But at the core of the Barkley spot is a significant truth: *He is not a role model.* What he is, is an *idol*. Many of his fans do not admire, emulate, or respect his values. (Barkley obviously has important ones, or else he never would have met the challenges of the National Basketball Association.) But these fans, even ones who aspire to play in the NBA, overlook the values that propelled Barkley into the pro league—determination, courage, discipline. Instead, they covet his lifestyle, athletic prowess, wealth, or fame. In sum, they would like to *become* Charles Barkley. They *idolize* him.

The difference between a role model and an idol is a value system. A role model has knowledge, advice, or methods that we can apply to our own lives or careers to achieve long-term success. Because a role model offers us values like determination, courage, and discipline, those values exist apart from the person. The person may fall from favor, and although we may express regret, the values—if genuine—should continue to serve us. But when an idol falls from favor—loses a lifestyle, wealth, or fame—typically fans are left with nothing but disappointment or disillusionment.

The fact is, celebrities are people who have little control over outcomes—no matter how moral their intentions. Michael Jordan, another basketball great, has been cast as role model in many advertisements. And in truth, early on he attempted to live up to expectations by trying to do the right thing, endorsing a brand of sneakers that are commonly known as Air Jordans. He had hoped that the product would inspire young people to achieve on the basketball court and in life. But a few of his fans idolized Jordan so much that they killed people to steal their Air Jordans. In a 1990 article for *Sports Illustrated*, writer Rick Telander quoted Jordan as saying, "I thought I'd be helping out others and everything would be positive. I thought people would try to emulate the good things that I do, they'd try to achieve, to be better. Nothing bad. I never thought because of my endorsement of a shoe, or any product, that people would harm each other."[2] Jordan's intentions were moral but were wasted on idolizers who missed the message; they just wanted the shoes.

When yet another basketball hero fell briefly from favor in 1991, acknowledging that he had contracted the human immunodeficiency virus (HIV), he received support from a company that stressed his values and did not abandon him. The star was Earvin "Magic" Johnson and the company was Pepsi-Cola. After the announcement, Pepsi officials acknowledged Johnson as an important product endorser, friend, and business partner. A year later, the company did not fear the public's attitude about acquired immune deficiency syndrome (AIDS) but helped establish "Magic Playrooms" for children suffering from the disease. The playrooms are specially designed therapy centers in hospitals in such cities as New York, Los Angeles, and Miami. In a release, Johnson is quoted as saying, "There's far too little we can do to ease the pain of these children. The Playrooms are a haven for them—here they can forget their illnesses for just a moment and concentrate on nothing more than being happy." In essence, Pepsi relied on Johnson's role model image instead of worrying about his public one.

The decision to handle the situation in this manner was considered controversial by some media analysts. Anne Reynolds Ward, manager of Public Affairs for Pepsi, recalls the pressure on colleagues when Johnson announced he had contracted HIV.

After basketball great Earvin "Magic" Johnson announced that he had contracted the HIV virus, his business partner Pepsi-Cola launched a pilot program to establish indoor playgrounds like this one at UCLA Medical Center for AIDS Research and Education.

At the time, corporate America had not yet begun to deal publicly with issues related to AIDS. The press and the public immediately wanted answers regarding Earvin's business associations with Pepsi and other consumer products companies. Hundreds of consumers wrote or called us to express their opinions on the controversy. Marketing pundits wrote Earvin off permanently as a celebrity endorser.

Our response was open and honest. We wanted to reflect the fact that our relationship with Earvin went beyond product endorsements and that we would respect his wishes as business partner and friend before bowing to external pressure to distance ourselves from him. We said that Pepsi and Earvin would work together to reach a decision when the time was right. Years later, Earvin is still under contract with Pepsi and works with us on many levels.

Public opinion about Earvin and the disease has clearly changed since late 1991. There was a groundswell of support for him as he went off to play with the Dream Team at the 1992 Summer Olympics. And, based on our experiences with the Magic Playroom, we've seen a change among companies and communities as it becomes more and more common for them to deal with AIDS-related issues on many fronts.

During the Johnson–AIDS controversy, public affairs employees at Pepsi countered outside pressures via a corporate value about honesty: "We will speak openly and directly, with care and compassion, and work hard to understand and resolve issues."

Moral Relativism and Absolutes

In *The Closing of the American Mind,* one of the most influential books of the 1980s, educator and author Allan Bloom argued that American culture was on the decline because students, in particular, believe that truth is relative. In other words, Bloom maintained, students think there are no real truths that apply to everyone and so assume that values are a matter of lifestyle choices. Let's clear up this issue right now as we end our discussion about personal values and responsibility and begin a broader one about journalism and social responsibility.

As you shall see here and in the next chapter, there are certain truths—called *moral absolutes*—that do apply to everyone. Educator and philosopher Christina Hoff Sommers believes "students may easily lose sight of the fact that some things are clearly right and some are clearly wrong, that some ethical truths are not subject to serious debate."[3] To show that, Sommers lists these truths as moral absolutes:

1. It is wrong to mistreat a child.
2. It is wrong to humiliate someone.
3. It is wrong to torment an animal.
4. It is wrong to think only of yourself.
5. It is wrong to steal, to lie, to break promises.
6. It is right to be considerate and respectful of others.
7. It is right to be charitable and generous.

Sommers adds, "I am aware that not everyone will agree that all of these are plain moral facts. But teachers of ethics are free to give their own list or to pare mine down. In teaching ethics, one thing should be made central and prominent: Right and wrong do exist. This should be laid down as uncontroversial lest one leave an altogether false impression that *everything* is up for grabs."[4]

I would add to Sommers's list these other absolutes:

8. It is wrong to prejudge others based on physical or racial features.
9. It is wrong to treat human beings like objects or property.

In addition to personal moral absolutes, there are also broader civic ones. The Johnson Foundation—whose report, *An American Imperative,* was cited in the previous chapter on generational influences—asserts, "There are some values, rooted in national experience, even defined in the Constitution, that Americans share. These 'constitutional' values have evolved into a set of civic virtues":

1. Respect for the individual and commitment to equal opportunity
2. The belief that our common interests exceed our individual differences
3. Concern for those who come after us
4. Support for the freedoms enunciated in the Bill of Rights, including freedom of religion, of the press, of speech, and of the right to assemble
5. The belief that individual rights and privileges are to be exercised responsibly
6. The conviction that no one is above the law
7. Respect for the views of others[5]

Respect for the views of others is a particularly important value in journalism. Despite the few moral absolutes listed earlier, there *are* many truths that you will encounter in your career. It is entirely possible for two ethical, moral people to hold opposite opinions about the same topic.

As you will learn in other chapters, truths sometimes clash. You may condemn "hate speech" (ethnic- or gender-based slurs) but also believe in free speech afforded by the First Amendment. As long as the two truths do not collide, you can believe fervently in both. But the responsible journalist also prepares for the worst-case scenario: a situation that forces him or her to favor one or the other truth, establishing a value to reflect that choice. The hate speech/free speech dilemma pertains to all sequences, by the way. You could be a reporter or magazine writer covering a hate crime, for instance; or a photojournalist or TV camera person documenting a demonstration and shooting a sign that contains a hate word; or an agency employee handling the account of a politician who condemns a racist opponent in a series of news releases or public service announcements. In each case, the journalist will have to decide on a specific truth and then accept the consequences associated therewith.

Here are two possible responses to the preceding issue:

Reporter 1

I'm not an absolutist when it comes to the First Amendment. Just as I believe it is wrong to cry "Fire" in a crowded theater, I believe it is wrong to use certain derogatory ethnic terms—no matter what the context—because of the potential of those words to hurt readers of my newspaper. Consequently, unless there is a very compelling reason—the president telling an offensive joke, for example—I would use a euphemism (as in the phrase "racial slur") rather than the particular hate word.

As for consequences, I might work for an editor who is a First Amendment absolutist, in which case I can be disciplined for my belief. If we disagreed to the extent that I could be fired, I would allow the editor to insert the offensive word in my copy but request that he or she remove my byline from the story. A larger consequence could be that in protecting some of my readers from hate speech, I may not be fully communicating the seriousness of an offense or the reality of a news story. But I accept that, too, because most people can read a euphemism and imagine the seriousness or reality of a news story.

Reporter 2

I'm an absolutist when it comes to the First Amendment. It is not my responsibility to censor myself or protect my readers from hate speech but to present that speech in the proper context so that they can gauge the seriousness or reality of the news.

As for consequences, I might work for an editor who is not a First Amendment absolutist, in which case I can be disciplined for my belief. If we disagreed to the extent that I could be fired, I would let him or her fire me rather than censor me. I feel that strongly about free speech and so I will have to choose my employer carefully upon graduation, working for a newspaper whose policies are similar to my beliefs. A larger consequence could be that in exercising free speech by including offensive words in proper context in my stories, I may insult or hurt a handful of readers. I accept that responsibility and trust that most readers will not condemn the reporter but the perpetuators of hate speech.

Both of these responses, on opposite sides of the hate speech/free speech debate, are inherently moral. They reflect different truths and values but avoid relativism because the journalists in question ponder and accept consequences associated with their beliefs. That process—pondering and accepting consequences—is necessary if journalists hope to cover or target segments of society ethically and responsibly.

Broader Responsibilities

Journalists operate within a press theory called *social responsibility*. This and other press theories—including *libertarian, authoritarian,* and *communist*—are described in the watershed text *Four Theories of the Press* by Fred S. Siebert,

Theodore Peterson, and Wilbur Schramm. In the following excerpt, the authors delineate similarities and differences between libertarian and social responsibility theories, which have made the greatest impact on American journalism.

> The functions of the press under social responsibility theory are basically the same as those under libertarian theory. Six tasks came to be ascribed to the press as traditional theory evolved: (1) servicing the political system by providing information, discussion, and debate on public affairs; (2) enlightening the public so as to make it capable of self-government; (3) safeguarding the rights of the individual by serving as a watchdog against government; (4) servicing the economic system, primarily by bringing together the buyers and sellers of goods and services through the medium of advertising; (5) providing entertainment; (6) maintaining its own financial self-sufficiency so as to be free from the pressures of special interests.
>
> The social responsibility theory in general accepts those six functions. But it reflects a dissatisfaction with the interpretation of those functions by some media owners and operators and with the way in which the press has carried them out. Social responsibility theory accepts the role of the press in serving the political system, in enlightening the public, in safeguarding the liberties of the individual; but it represents the opinion that the press has been deficient in performing those tasks. It accepts the role of the press in servicing the economic system, but it would not have this task take precedence over such other functions as promoting the democratic processes or enlightening the public. It accepts the role of the press in furnishing entertainment but with the proviso that the entertainment be "good" entertainment. It accepts the need for the press as an institution to remain financially self-supporting, but if necessary it would exempt certain individual media from having to earn their way in the market place.[6]

That view of media responsibility is still widely held by employees of newspapers, magazines, and broadcast news outlets. Advertising and public relations employees play important roles in the process, too, providing information to these outlets and their respective readers, viewers, listeners and customers. The theory also implies that individual journalists have a basic obligation to accept responsibility for messages they disseminate to the public. Following is a sampling of principles relating to social responsibility from journalism associations representing all sequences.

The National Press Photographers Association code of ethics states that its members show:

> Concern and respect for the public's natural-law right to freedom in searching for the truth and the right to be informed truthfully and completely about public events and the world in which we live.

The Society of Professional Journalists states under its first principle, "Responsibility":

> The public's right to know of events of public importance and interest is the overriding mission of the mass media. The purpose of distributing news and enlightened opinion is to serve the general welfare.

The Radio-Television News Directors Association code of ethics states:

> The responsibility of radio and television journalists is to gather and report information of importance and interest to the public accurately, honestly and impartially.

This "Declaration of Principles" is from the Code of Professional Standards for the Practice of Public Relations:

> Members of the Public Relations Society of America base their professional principles on the fundamental value and dignity of the individual, holding that the free exercise of human rights, especially freedom of speech, freedom of assembly, and freedom of the press, is essential to the practice of public relations.
>
> In serving the interests of clients and employers, we dedicate ourselves to the goals of better communication, understanding, and cooperation among the diverse individuals, groups and institutions of society, and of equal opportunity of employment in the public relations profession.

The Advertising Principles of American Business, adopted by the American Advertising Federation Board of Directors, states:

> Advertising shall tell the truth, and shall reveal significant facts, the omission of which would mislead the public.

It is important to acknowledge that although the various media serve segments of society in different ways, they all aspire to do so responsibly, emphasizing the public interest or the public's right to know or be informed in a truthful manner. Equally as important are the individual journalists who aspire to live up to these standards, earning the public's trust.

"As journalists, we all have a joint responsibility to create trust," says John Kaplan, Pulitzer Prize–winning photographer and founder and director of Media Alliance, a broad-based consulting group. Kaplan is concerned about the tabloid media undermining the theory of social responsibility.

"Sometimes what gets reported as a lead story on the networks originated from tabloid sources," he remarks. "The media of lower credibility are wagging the tail of the supposedly more ethical (mainstream) media because of competitive pressures."

Kaplan thinks that news is blurring with entertainment, an ethical concern that dates back to the 1950s with the advent of television. "At the beginning of '90s, a lot of news programs followed a trend started by programs like *America's Most Wanted* and *Unsolved Mysteries* by creating scenes or recreating them, when viewers often didn't realize it. Right now local television news all over the country is adding sound effects to news stories much like you'd see on *A Current Affair*. You see local reporters doing recreations. How it all ties in is that what's presented to the public as news in whatever medium it happens to be is becoming more and more a facet of entertainment."

Kaplan attributes the trend to hiring practices. "There are not enough people in reporting and management trained in journalism," he says, so ethical issues are not emphasized. "Television producers, for instance, are unfortunately geared more toward ratings than credibility. That all filters down to the print media trying to maintain circulation, trying to present lively news, often making mistakes trying to hold on to a market share." Kaplan believes that the media should set a high cultural standard for the public. "Then," he concludes, "the public will rise to that standard and expect high quality coverage."

Pam Noles, a reporter for the *Tampa Tribune,* believes the theory of social responsibility is only as moral as the society in question. If that society is prejudiced, she maintains, then ethical codes to serve the public will apply to some rather than all citizens.

> We are journalists, but also products of our society. American culture still does not want to deal with issues of race unless they are historical. Keep in mind I am saying this in the summer of 1994, the 30th-year anniversary of Freedom Summer, when over a thousand young people came to the deep South to help black people claim their right to vote. As for me, I am preparing myself to revel in the glories of the past. I'm ready for the double-trucks in the newspapers, the lead articles in the magazines, the touching black-and-white images on television. I hope that, like all news, it will seem old by late June or maybe mid-July. Then I can stop shaking.

Nonetheless, Noles says she appreciates the sacrifices that journalists of all races have made trying to inform the public about prejudice. "I am grateful for those who fought and sometimes died so that my generation could have opportunities that they could only dream of. But I live in this time, and everything now is not fine. I'm tired of journalists who are concerned about race issues but seem to have trouble connecting empathy and action. That is our job."

Although Noles is a newspaper reporter, her role model is Edward R. Murrow, a World War II radio correspondent and later vice president for CBS in charge of news, education, and discussion programs. Noles has memorized a Murrow edict pertaining to social responsibility: "The right to information is not an abstract right." Murrow believed that the media needed to provide as much information as possible to voters so that they could make intelligent choices and that a poorly informed electorate could invite disaster or calamity. Noles says she realizes that Murrow was not speaking about racial issues,

> but his truth has everything to do with what is not happening in the news today. We should be observing what goes on in our individual communities and reporting those facts without apologies, especially when it comes to racial issues. We write about the uncomfortable things everyday—rape, murder, abuse of varied kinds. Our newspapers do not approve of these things, and yet they are a staple of our stories. But when it comes to the most uncomfortable issues separating the hues, our copy is blank.
>
> Every once in a while, a report from the American Society of Newspaper Editors will flash across the industry wire tracking the state of minority representation in the newsroom. Or an alert about declining readership or trust among minorities or women or youth. Or another focus group. Another extensive survey. And I cannot understand why we spend all this money slashing and burning down the forest looking for answers while ignoring the stumps we leave, smoldering, behind.

Ideally, magazines should inform readers on a more personal level than newspapers or broadcast outlets. Magazine journalists do not write for an eclectic or general audience, but a narrowly defined one. This is due, in part, to readers being targeted by circulation managers via computer lists compiled and sold to publishers. For instance, every time an individual purchases goods by mail or sends in warranties or applies for credit, his or her name is logged in a computer program and filed under specific categories, such as "Affluent Californians" or "African American Educators." This establishes an advertising or subscriber base but it also profiles readers so that editors know them intimately and can satisfy their expectations. In turn, those readers come to think of the magazine as a friend and often flood editorial newsrooms with letters.

One of the most ethical magazines in the industry is *Highlights for Children,* founded in 1946 on Main Street in Honesdale, Pennsylvania. Its mission statement contains a prominent section on "Values":

Highlights' stories and articles do not "teach" or "preach," but they embody time-tested values of fairness, honesty, and regard for others. While *Highlights* is nonsectarian, it reflects spiritual values, the tolerance of all religious beliefs, and friendship among the races of humankind. . . . The founders intended that, while not moralizing—something youngsters are quick to spot and reject— *Highlights* would inevitably deposit what they termed a "moral residue" of admiration for worthy role models and an ambition to be like them.

The founders of the magazine were Garry Cleveland Myers and Caroline Clark Myers—grandparents of the current editor, Kent L. Brown. Brown says his grandparents "valued greatly the comments, suggestions and questions they received from their readers." In its first year, the magazine had a press run of 20,000. Every letter was answered. Now the magazine has a circulation approaching 3 million. "Today we receive about 1,000 letters a month," Brown observes. "We still answer every one of them individually."

Brown notes that letters vary from suggestions about the magazine, to problems with family and friends, to concerns about alcoholism and drug abuse. "We have a staff of full-time and part-time employees who answer these letters. If we think the letters are sufficiently serious, we may consult a professional. For the vast majority, however, we depend on our judgment and common sense. We believe that what our readers want is an honest, sincere and thoughtful answer. That's what we try to give them. We try to avoid both counseling through the mail and trivializing their concerns."

Here's an example of a typical letter to an 8-year-old reader on the subject of friendship:

> Thank you for writing to HIGHLIGHTS. You wrote that a girl told you that she was your best friend. Then she told you that she was only pretending to be your friend. You asked if you should give her another chance.
>
> Whether or not you decide to give this girl another chance is really up to you. Perhaps you could discuss things with her. Choose a time when you can talk by yourselves and let her know how her behavior made you feel. You could tell her that it hurt your feelings when she told you that she was only pretending to be your friend. Then listen to what she has to say.
>
> After talking, you will probably be able to determine if you want to give her another chance for friendship.
>
> Friendships should be based on respect for each other, similar interests, and enjoyment of one another's company. If things don't work out between you and this girl, try not to be too disappointed. Instead, why not spend time with other friends who share your interests and values?
>
> I hope this is helpful. Good luck and best wishes from all of us here.
>
> Sincerely,
>
> KENT L. BROWN
> Editor

Brown realizes that readers appreciate personal replies like this one. But he also has noticed a significant change in letter-writing trends. "In the last five years letters from our readers have more than tripled while our circulation has stayed about the same. We're not exactly sure what to attribute to that surge. It may be word has gotten around that we answer the letters we receive. Or maybe kids just feel more of a need to write to someone." At least some of those writers feel that they cannot learn about values in the home or from role models in their neighborhoods. Brown added, "I do know this. As long as they write to us, their letters will be answered by a human being and not a machine, because what they're writing about is important to them, and they are important to us."

Readers, viewers, clients, and consumers should be important to you, too. Journalists who win Pulitzers (such as John Kaplan), or who have role models (such as Pam Noles), or who embrace values (such as Kent L. Brown) do not believe that social responsibility is a theory. In their minds, it is a *duty*.

ENDNOTES

1. Jeff Jensen, "Bad role model can make good ad," *Advertising Age*, 27 September 1993, p. 10.

2. Rick Telander, "Senseless," *Sports Illustrated* reprint *Your Sneakers or Your Life*, 14 May 1990, p. 2.

3. Christina Hoff Sommers, "Teaching the virtues," *Chicago Tribune Magazine* reprint, 12 September 1993, p. 16.

4. Sommers, p. 16.

5. *An American Imperative: Higher Expectations for Higher Education*, multiple authors (Racine, WI: The Johnson Foundation, 1993), p. 14.

6. Fred Siebert, Theodore Peterson, and Wilbur Schramm, *Four Theories of the Press* (Urbana: University of Illinois Press, 1974), p. 74.

L I V I N G   E T H I C S

Read the following articles and record your reactions in your ethics journal and/or discuss them with peers or mentors.

✹ **EDITOR'S NOTE:** *Chris Perry is chairman and CEO of Meldrum & Fewsmith Communications, Cleveland. His article, about basic responsibilities in advertising, was published in the trade magazine* Advertising Age. *Perry adds, "While I do consider providing information as a primary role of adver-*

tising, I believe in today's highly charged media environment, it also is imperative to deliver that information in a compelling, arresting and tasteful manner." The emphasis, Perry thinks, should be on substance as much as style.

Nothing But Net

Chris Perry, Chairman and CEO, *Meldrum & Fewsmith Communications*

Somewhere between Bill Bernbach and the Saatchis, the advertising business jumped the track. In the name of such noble goals as breaking through the clutter, respecting the intelligence of our audience, and improving the quality of our product, the advertising we created became more important than the brands for which we created it. We began measuring the worthiness of our ads and commercials by how much applause they earned from consumers, the media, and our peers.

This was brought to my attention again recently, after reading a *Wall Street Journal* article on the latest survey by Video Story Board Tests (VST). For those who may not know, VST annually measures the industry's most popular and best remembered commercials. According to VST, "A startling 40% of 20,000 consumers surveyed each year are unable to think of a single outstanding commercial."

Well, with all due respect to the folks at VST, the only thing startling about such a statistic is that as an industry, we actually think it's important. Come on! Our role as creators of advertising isn't getting people to remember our ads and commercials, it's getting them to remember what our ads and commercials say about our clients' brands. It's getting people to remember the message, not the messenger.

Now certainly I'm not implying that advertising shouldn't be likable. Nor am I advocating a return to those pre-Bernbach days, when inane characters like Bucky Beaver were encouraging people to "brush-a, brush-a, brush-a, with new Ipana toothpaste."

But something is seriously wrong when, in this same journal article, we find ad executives making comments like this: "(Advertising) can make you feel better about choosing a brand, but . . . it can't accompany you to the store and steer you to the brand."

Call me a bleeping idealist, but I've always thought steering people to brands is what advertising was supposed to do. If not, then we'd all better close up shop and get on with our life's work.

Consider this for a moment. Could it be that the reason so many marketers believe advertising isn't as effective as it once was is that (heaven forbid) most of it really isn't? And maybe the reason it isn't as effective is that we have become more concerned with the style of our advertising than the substance of it. More concerned with making people "feel good" about a brand than giving them a compelling reason to purchase it. And maybe a tactical alternative like the infomercial hasn't become the passing fad many of us hoped, because consumers really do want ads and commercials to tell them something meaningful, not merely entertain them.

Too much advertising these days is woefully deficient at imparting meaningful messages to its audiences. Goodness knows that's not how it used to be.

As an industry, we constantly parade ads from our glorious past, as icons to "creative excellence." Two of the more frequently mentioned are the Avis and Volkswagen campaigns. By today's standards, both of these celebrated examples were not very stylish or entertaining. But man, they sure did communicate a powerful message about each brand. And they sure did give the consumer some meaningful reasons to consider purchase. And they sure did steer a heck of a lot of people to Avis and Volkswagen.

Even the way people refer to these campaigns is testimony to the difference between advertising then and now. For instance, most people tend to describe the Avis campaign in terms of the advertising's message, not the advertising itself: "Avis tried harder" or "They were No. 2, so they had to do everything a little better."

Yet, if you asked someone to describe the McDonald's advertising that appeared during last year's Super Bowl, chances are you'd hear: "A game of horse between Bird and Jordan" or "Nothing but net!"

Now, I loved that McDonald's spot as most everyone else did. And no doubt McDonald's is pleased, since "Nothing but net" has become part of America's popular lexicon. But you've got to admit, compared to the meaningful brand message in Avis advertising, "Nothing but net" is "nothing but an airball."

It's time both advertisers and agencies took a long, hard look at where advertising has been and where it's going. With the incoming tide of interactive communications upon us, people will soon be making more buying decisions right in their own homes. More than ever, the advertising we create and approve will have to help with those decisions, by providing more information and more compelling reasons to buy our brands.

In that regard, we all could learn a few things from the past. Not merely from campaigns like Avis, but from people like Bill Bernbach, who spawned advertising's "creative revolution." Years ago, when he exhorted our entire industry to reach for higher and higher levels of creativity, he never intended for us to lose sight of what advertising was all about. In his own words, "Our job is to sell our clients' merchandise . . . not ourselves. Our job is to kill the cleverness that makes us shine instead of the product. Our job is to . . . pluck out the weeds that are smothering the product message."

Hey, Bill! Nothing but net!

✤ **EDITOR'S NOTE:** *David Finn is chairman and CEO of Ruder-Finn, a New York City communications agency known for high ethical standards. The following article about basic responsibilities in public relations originally appeared in the trade magazine* Public Relations Journal.

Critical Choices

David Finn, Chairman and CEO, *Ruder-Finn*

We have come to believe in our time that appearances are as important as reality, sometimes even more so. It may well be true that the appearance of virtue is as important as virtue itself and that a good rule of ethics is: Never do anything that you would not like to see on the front page of tomorrow's newspaper. But it is not true that the false appearance of virtue is the best way to deal with evil, or that good publicity anywhere gives one license to do harm.

The poet Emily Dickinson made one of her characteristically penetrating observations when she wrote: "Tell all the truth but tell it slant/Success in circuit lies."

Her point was that you can take the edge off an uncomfortable truth by telling it circuitously. That way, your audience will not realize quite what you are saying. You won't actually be telling a lie if you follow her advice, but you may be fooling those who are listening to you into thinking that your slant of the truth is in fact the whole, unbiased truth.

With those lines, Emily Dickinson could be the poet laureate of the public relations field. She put her finger on an aspect of our business that leads to twisting the truth to suit our ends and makes us accomplices in trying to mislead our audiences.

The problem in public relations is that we can twist—or slant—information in many ways to rationalize a given point of view. Emily Dickinson saw it as a universal tendency, but I'm afraid we public relations people do it more than other professionals, since that is often the nature of our job.

Sometimes this involves a sleight of hand that distracts the attention of the observer from what is taking place behind the showy performance. Thus, former Secretary of State James Baker showed up on the Turkish border right after the Gulf War to visit a Kurdish camp site. He stayed long enough to be photographed and then left. Cynics called it no more than a "public relations photo-op." They said that nothing of substance was accomplished. It was all for show.

This falls into the category of what is popularly called *hype*. I hate that word because it suggests that the business of public relations people is to pump up a product—any kind of product but particularly one which has little value—by gimmicky promotions that make it seem much better than it is.

I object to the word used in connection with public relations, just as I objected 30 years ago to the word *image* when it first became popular in the field. Neither represents an aspect of public relations of which I am particularly proud. One suggests that artificially created images can be a substitute for reality, and the other that inferior products or insignificant events or unimpressive individuals can be hyped to look better than they are. However, I admit that both hype and image have won a place in the public relations lexicon because they describe what sometimes seems to be our assignment.

The unfortunate aspect of this tendency can be seen when a company that is not doing well is more concerned about what people think than what is actually happening. Suppliers worry about being paid. Customers worry about the company's ability to fill orders. Bankers worry about extending credit. Shareholders worry that the price of their stock will fall.

What does management do to cope with these negative attitudes? Retain a public relations firm to counteract the negative impressions.

And what does the public relations firm do? Develop articles by the president. Arrange speeches for top executives. Organize seminars or conferences. Encourage making a generous contribution to a community cause. If something is basically wrong with the company, sales and earnings will continue to slip and people will continue to lose their jobs.

Public relations may not be able to redress the real problem. Practitioners are often asked to create positive impressions that will offset the negative ones and thereby deflect attention away from whatever is causing difficulties. It is the perception of the problem that is being addressed, not the reality.

There is no doubt that there are occasions when an improved image of a company is a valid goal, particularly when real achievements are not recognized or when negative impressions are exaggerated. But to worry about a company's image without regard to its substance does not bode well for the company's future.

This brings us to an examination of the unfortunate phrase *cover-up*. The transcript of the Watergate tapes includes a short passage in which President Nixon tells his subordinates that the time has come to call in the public relations people. The crisis would get out of hand unless a way could be found to shut off the news. This was the ultimate example of the role public relations people are supposed to play in covering up the truth. It is not simply slanting the truth, or creating perceptions that may not be consistent with the truth; it is telling a lie and making people believe it.

There are many examples of cover-ups in recent times. The investigation of President Kennedy's assassination has been called a cover-up. The body counts of the Vietnam War were called a cover-up. Some of the financial scandals of the '80s were thought to have been kept from the public eye through cover-ups. To what extent any of these involved the active participation of public relations people is irrelevant. It's the sort of thing public relations people are supposed to be experts at, and they are, in fact, often called in to counsel clients who have something to hide.

Most of the famous attempts to cover up potential scandals didn't work, and eventually the truth became known. That usually turns out to be the case with lesser-known attempts to keep the public in the dark, largely because we have such a vigilant press. But since public relations people are the ones who are brought in as advisors in such circumstances, this has become one of its more widely criticized functions.

These days this role is often called *damage control* or even more popularly *crisis management.* I find these phrases as worrisome as *image* and *hype.* We don't know how to manage crises or control damage. All we can really do is prepare a communications plan and help communicate when there is a crisis. There are times when our clients would be happy if we could figure out a way to cover up the facts, and I'm afraid that that's what some of them have in mind when they retain us to help out in a difficult situation. To the extent that we permit them to believe we can do so, we are casting our business in a very poor light.

But there is an aspect of our business which I, as a writer and communicator, find more disturbing than all of these concerns. For I believe that worse than slanting the truth, worse than deceiving the public, and worse than trying to cover up ugly facts, is the excuse public relations may give our leaders to abdicate their leadership responsibilities.

There was a time not long ago when leaders of society were articulate, thoughtful individuals who had the capacity to inspire their followers with great ideas and ideals. George Washington may have had help from Thomas Jefferson for his famous farewell address, but there is plenty of evidence that he was expressing his own ideas.

Unfortunately, many top corporate and government leaders have come to rely on their public relations experts not only to write their speeches and their public statements, but often to decide what the substance of those speeches and statements should be.

Business executives today, along with other key figures in our society, feel they are "too busy" to do their own writing. In a world that places a premium on time, particularly for highly paid executives, it is considered a responsibility that can be delegated. It is also a convenience for executives who may be good managers, but poor (or lazy) writers, as well as those who have little to say. In many cases, the responsibility is handled by public relations people who are experienced at doing research, coming up with creative ideas, and knowing how to articulate them clearly and convincingly.

The problem is that writing forces people to *think*, and delegating writing means delegating thinking. Ghostwriting means ghost-thinking. A society that is managed by people who don't take the time to think is leaderless. The millions of words that are spoken or written in the name of those managers are bland generalities, often vapid and vacuous statements written to please, not to inspire or excite or even challenge. It they are more than that, they are probably the invention of the ghost.

I know one top public relations writer who was both proud and scared that his CEO always used his speeches without changing a word. He was proud that he had proven to be so accomplished, and scared because he was creating policy statements without any input from the CEO himself.

Since I have done my share of writing for executives, I know how pleased one can be that one's words prove to be acceptable to a client. It's also not hard to agree with an outstanding writer such as Bill Safire, who himself had a distinguished career as a ghostwriter, that a legitimate role can be played by gifted writers who help leaders have an impact on their audiences. But the practice has gotten out of hand.

It would be an exaggeration to say that no executive or politician spends time on what he or she will state publicly, or even that most leaders of society leave it entirely up to their public relations specialists to choose their words for them. Often there is a blend between what the executive wants to say and the skill of the public relations specialist to say it well.

But when leaders begin to depend too heavily on their speechwriters to do their thinking as well as choose their words, minds begin to stagnate and mental resources become diminished. I fear that, in too many assignments, public relations plays a role that contributes to this trend. It doesn't do society much good if, in the interests of helping our clients put on a good show, we substitute our ideas for their vision of where they are going and why, and deprive their constituents of the benefits that come from real leadership.

Everyone who has a legitimate story to tell, a valuable product to promote, or an important idea to promulgate can benefit from the sound and responsible practice of public relations. We each have to make critical choices about the way we practice public relations as we look to the future. If we are prepared to recognize the shortcomings of the past, we may be able to avoid them when we make these choices.

If we should fail to choose wisely in the way we conduct ourselves and do our job, public relations will become increasingly suspect as one of the more untrustworthy and unworthy consequences of an out-of-control communications environment. If we apply ourselves wisely and responsibly as professionals who honestly believe in the worthiness of the causes we represent, then public relations will be—and be known as—a respected, respectable, and valued enterprise as we move into the twenty-first century.

EDITOR'S NOTE: *Dan Rather, co-anchor of* The CBS Evening News, *delivered this speech about basic responsibilities in news-gathering to the Radio and Television News Directors Association (RTNDA) convention. In discussing the value of courage, Rather harkens one of his role models—the great CBS broadcaster Edward R. Murrow.*

Call It Courage

Dan Rather, Co-Anchor, *CBS Evening News*

It is humbling to be asked to speak on this night to this group. On this night, because it is the time when the late, great Ed Murrow has a commemorative stamp issued in his name. To this group, because it was before the RTNDA that Murrow gave the best speech he ever made, the best ever made by *any* broadcaster.

Edward R. Murrow was the best. Almost sixty years after he started, almost thirty years after his death—and *still* the best.

He was the best reporter of his generation. The best reporter in broadcasting or print. He reported, he led, he made the best broadcasts of his time, both in radio and television. And those broadcasts remain, to this day, the best of all time. They include the *This Is London* broadcasts from the Battle of Britain, the radio reports from the death camp at Buchenwald, and the television programs on Joseph McCarthy and *Harvest of Shame.*

Ed Murrow was not only the patron and founding saint of electronic news and the best-ever practitioner of it, he also set standards for excellence and courage that remain the standards, the world over. And, along the way, he made the best speech ever by anyone in our business.

Murrow was, in short, a hero. No wonder they have issued a stamp in his name.

But we should, we must remember this: He was a real, flesh-and-blood, flawed, vulnerable, mistake-making hero.

With all of his triumphs, many and mighty, he also fought some fights he should not have fought, and he sometimes, often times, lost. Including losing at the end. In the end, his bosses and his competitors—inside as well as outside his own network—cut him up, cut him down, and finally cut him out.

And not long after that, he died. Cancer was the cause, they say.

Murrow made his memorable RTNDA speech not at the dawn, nor at midday, but in the twilight—in Chicago, October 15th, 1958.

In it, he criticized what commercial television was becoming, and challenged himself, his colleagues—and us, all of us—to do better.

Ed Murrow said of television: "This instrument can teach, it can illuminate; yes, and it can even inspire. But it can do so only to the extent that humans are determined to use it to those ends. Otherwise it is merely wires and lights in a box. There is a great and perhaps decisive battle to be fought against ignorance, intolerance, and indifference. This weapon of television could be useful."

The speech Ed Murrow gave at the RTNDA convention in Chicago, 1958, was a risky speech, and he knew it. It was a bold shot, and he knew it. That was part of the Murrow style, and part of what has made the Murrow mystique: the bold, brave shot.

He began that speech with the modest speculation that, and I quote, "This just might do nobody any good." I don't think Ed Murrow believed that. It was a call to arms—the most quoted line is the one about "wires and lights in a box," but the more important line is "this weapon of television." Ed Murrow had seen all kinds of battles, and if *he* lifted his voice in a battle cry, surely some of his own colleagues would hear him and heed him.

As with many television and radio news people of my generation, that speech has crisscrossed the back-roads of my memory through a lifetime in the business.

I wasn't in Chicago that night. I was in Houston, serving my apprenticeship in news, a beginner in radio and television. I hadn't met Murrow yet. I could only read about his speech in the newspapers, but I absorbed every word. In my own little Texas bayou and pine-tree world of journalism dreams, Murrow became protean, titanic, huge. (I still think that.) There were other great ones: William L. Shirer, Eric Sevareid and Charles Collingwood and Douglas Edwards; and later Walter Cronkite—men of courage and accomplishment, of great skill and great intelligence. But Murrow was *their* leader.

As he had been for many others, Murrow had been my hero when I was just a boy. Across the radio, across the Atlantic and across half the United States, his voice came, the deep rumble and the dramatic pause just when he said, "THIS . . . is London." I never got that voice out of my head. It was like a piece of music that has never stopped playing for me. Murrow told me tales of bravery in time of war, tales more thrilling than "Captain Midnight" or "Jack Armstrong" because these were *true.*

He talked about the bravery of soldiers and citizens. He never made a big fuss about his own bravery. But even as a little boy, I knew it took bravery just to stand on that rooftop, with the bombs raining down thunder and lightning all around him, or to go up in that plane—"D-for-Dog"—with the *ack-ack* and the messerschmidts all about. And I never forgot that Murrow did all this because he wanted me and my family, and all of us back home in America, to know . . . the truth. *For that,* for our knowledge of the truth, he risked his life.

In my mind, then and now, neither Achilles nor King Arthur—not Pecos Bill or Davy Crockett—surpassed a hero like that.

The Murrow I met years later—person to person, if you will—the real Ed Murrow was everything I wanted that hero to be. He was a quiet man: tall, strong, steady-eyed, not afraid of silence.

What separated Ed Murrow from the rest of the pack was courage.

I know what you're thinking. I've gotten in trouble before for using the word. Probably deserved it. Maybe I used it inappropriately. Maybe I'm a poor person to talk about it because I have so little myself. But I want to hear the word. I want to hear it praised, and the men and women who have courage elevated.

Ed Murrow had courage. He had the physical courage to face the Blitzkrieg in London and to ride "D-for-Dog." He had the professional courage to tell the truth about McCarthyism. And he had the courage to stand before the Radio and Television News Directors Association and to say some things those good people didn't want to hear but needed to hear.

In our comfort and complacency, in our (dare we say it?) cowardice, we, none of us, want to hear the battle cry. Murrow had the courage to sound it anyway. And thirty-five years later, however uncomfortable, it's worth pausing to ask—*How goes the battle?*

In the constant scratching and scrambling for ever better ratings and money and the boss' praise and a better job, it is worth pausing to ask—how goes the real war, the really important battle of our professional lives? How goes the battle for quality, for truth, and justice, for programs worthy of the *best* within ourselves and the audience? How goes the battle against "ignorance, intolerance, and indifference"? The battle *not* to be merely "wires and lights in a box," the battle to make television not just entertaining but also, at least some little of the time, *useful* for higher, better things? How goes the battle?

The answer we know is "Not very well." In too many important ways, we have allowed this great instrument, this resource, this weapon for good, to be squandered and cheapened. About this, the best among us hang their heads in embarrassment, even shame. We all should be ashamed of what we have and have not done, measured against what we could do—ashamed of many of the things we have allowed our craft, our profession, our life's work to become.

Our reputations have been reduced, our credibility cracked, justifiably. This has happened because too often for too long we have answered to the worst, not to the best, within ourselves and within our audience. We are less because of this. Our audience is less, and so is our country.

Ed Murrow had faith in our country, and in our country's decision to emphasize, from the beginning, *commercial* broadcasting. He recognized commercial broadcasting's potential, and its superiority over other possibilities. But even as he believed in the strength of market values and the freedom of commercial radio and television, Ed Murrow feared the rise of a cult that worshipped at the shrine of the implacable idol: ratings. He feared that the drive to sell, sell, sell—and nothing but sell—was overwhelming the potential for good, the potential for *service* of radio and television.

He decried the hours of prime-time as being full of (quote) "decadence, escapism, and insulation from the realities of the world in which we live." As you let that sink in, let's remember that he was talking about programs like *I Love Lucy* and *The Honeymooners,* that are now esteemed on a par with the best comedies of Plautus and Moliere; Murrow singled out *The Ed Sullivan Show,* which is now studied and praised as a modern-day School of Athens, peopled by all the best minds and talents of the time. These are the programs that had Ed Murrow worried.

He wasn't worried about, didn't live to see *Full House* or *America's Funniest Home Videos* or *Fish Police.* He wasn't worried about, didn't live to see the glut of inanities now in "access" time. He never lived to see the cynicism and greed that go into the decisions to put on much of that junk.

In 1958, Murrow was worried because he saw a trend setting in—avoiding the unpleasant or controversial or challenging—shortening newscasts and jamming them with ever-increasing numbers of commercials—throwing out background, context, and analysis, and relying just on headlines—going for entertainment values over the values of good journalism—all in the belief that the public must be shielded, wouldn't accept anything other than the safe, the serene, and the self-evident.

Murrow knew that belief was wrong and contrary to the principles on which this country was founded. He'd seen how honest, mature, and responsible American listeners and viewers could be when programming itself was honest, mature, and responsible. Reducing the amount of real-world reality on television, Murrow argued, was unconscionable.

But Murrow did not just offer criticism. He also offered solutions. Importantly, Murrow proposed that news divisions and departments not be held to the same standards of ratings and profits as entertainment and sports. He recognized that news operations couldn't be run as philanthropies. But, he added: "I can find nothing in the Bill of Rights or the Communications Act which says that [news divisions] must increase their net profits each year, lest the Republic collapse."

Murrow saw turmoil, danger, and opportunity in the world; and the best means of communicating the realities to the public—the communications innovation called television—was increasingly ignoring the realities. And those few Americans who had been given the privilege of owning and operating television stations and networks, the privilege of making great wealth from them, were beginning to reduce if not downright eliminate their responsibilities to public service.

Private profit from television is fine, but there *should be* a responsibility to news and public service that goes with it; this was the core of Murrow's case.

These were words which needed to be heard. Then, and now.

I thought about coming here tonight—and you might have been better enlightened if I'd done this—to read you verbatim the text of Murrow's speech from 1958. It's a hell of a speech. Much of it is more true, more dire, more needed than it was when Murrow said it.

When Murrow spoke to your predecessors at RTNDA, he knew that *they* were not his problem. The people he wanted most to hear and heed his speech were not in that Chicago ballroom. They worked in boardrooms, not newsrooms. Murrow's Chicago speech was a brave, bold bid to persuade corporate executives, both at stations and networks and at the advertising agencies and corporate sponsors.

He failed. Not long afterward, his position inside his own network was diminished. And not long after that, he was out.

Little has changed since Murrow gave that report from the battlefield and issued that call to arms. And much of what *has* changed has not been for the better. More people in television now than then are doing things that deny the public service of television, that ensure that the mighty weapon of television remains nothing more than wires and lights in a box.

Even the best among decision-makers in television freely take an hour that might have been used for a documentary, and hand it over to a quote-unquote "entertainment special" about the discovery of Noah's Ark—that turns out to be a one-hundred percent *hoax*.

And the worst among the decision-makers have got us all so afraid of our own independence and integrity that at least one news director recently planned to have all his hirings reviewed by radical ideological and highly partisan political groups. (And he bragged about it.)

They've got another news director telling his staff that he didn't want stories on the Pope's visit. He wanted stories—plural—on Madonna's Sex Book. It's the ratings, stupid.

And they've got us putting more and more fuzz and wuzz on the air, cop-shop stuff, so as to compete not with other news programs but with entertainment programs (including those posing as news programs) for dead bodies, mayhem, and lurid tales.

They tell us international news doesn't get ratings, doesn't sell, and, besides, it's too expensive. "Foreign news" is considered an expletive best deleted at most local station newsrooms and has fallen from favor even among networks.

Thoughtfully written analysis is out, "live pops" are in. "Action, Jackson" is the cry. Hire lookers, not writers. Do powderpuff, not probing, interviews. Stay away from controversial subjects. Kiss ass, move with the mass, and for heaven and the ratings' sake don't make anybody mad—certainly not anybody that you're covering, and especially not the mayor, the governor, the senator, the president or vice-president *or anybody* in a position of power. Make nice, not news.

This has become the new mantra. These have become the new rules. The post-Murrow generation of owners and managers have made them so. These people are, in some cases, our friends. They are, in all cases, our bosses. They aren't venal—they're afraid. They've got education and taste and good sense, they care about their country, but you'd never know it from the things that fear makes them do—from the things that fear makes them make *us do.*

It is fear of ratings slippage if not failure, fear that this quarter's bottom line will not be better than last quarter's—and a whole lot better than the same quarter's a year ago.

A climate of fear, at all levels, has been created, without a fight. We—you and I—have allowed them to do it, and even *helped* them to do it.

The climate is now such that, when a few people at one news organization rig the results of a test to get better pictures (and are caught and rightly criticized)—there's no rejoicing—that a terrible, unusual journalistic practice has been caught, punished, and eradicated. Because we all know that, with only a slight relaxation of vigilance and a slight increase of fear, those journalistic sins could be visited upon us—we know that, as honorable and sensible as we, our friends and our colleagues try to be—it could happen to us.

Now you would be absolutely justified in saying to me right now, "Excuse me, Mister Big Shot Anchor Man, but what the hell do you expect me to do about it? If I go to my boss and talk about television as a weapon, and why don't you take *Current Affair* or *Hard Copy* or *Inside Edition* off the air next week and let me put on a tell-it-like-it-is documentary about race relations—I *know* they're gone put me on the unemployment line, and I'll be *lucky* if they don't put me on the funny farm."

Well, none of us is immune to self-preservation and opportunities for advancement. I'm not asking you for the kind of courage that risks your job, much less your whole career. Ed Murrow had that kind of courage, and took that kind of risk several times. But you and I, reaching deep down inside ourselves, are unlikely to muster that kind rage often, if ever.

But there are specific things we can *do.* They won't cost us our jobs. But they will make a difference—a start—a warning shot that the battle is about to be joined.

Number one: Make a little noise. At least question (though protest would be better) when something, anything, incompatible with your journalistic conscience is proposed. When it comes to ethics and the practice of journalism, silence is a killer.

No, you won't always be heeded or heard. And yes, even to question may be a risk. But it is a wee, small risk, and a tiny price to pay to be worthy of the name "American journalist." To be a journalist is to ask questions. All the time. Even of the people we work for.

Number two: In any showdown between quality and substance on the one hand, and sleaze and glitz on the other, go with quality and substance. You know the difference. Every one of us in this room knows the difference because we've been there. We've all gone Hollywood—we've all succumbed to the Hollywoodization of the news—because we were afraid not to. We trivialize important subjects. We put videotape through a Cuisinart trying to come up with high-speed, MTV-style cross-cuts. And just to cover our asses, we give the best slots to gossip and prurience.

But we can say, "No more." We can fight the fear that leads to Showbizzification. We can act on our knowledge. You know that serious news—local and regional, national and international—doesn't have to be *dull,* not for one second. People will watch serious news, well written and well produced. The proof—it's all around, but I'll give you two examples. Look at *Sunday Morning* and *Nightline.* No glitz, no gossip. Just compelling information. You can produce your own *Nightline* or *Sunday Morning*—all that's required of you is determination and thought, taste and imagination. That's what Tom Bettag and Ted Koppel, that's what Linda Mason, Missie Rennie, Charles Kuralt and their teams bring to work.

Number three: Try harder to get and keep minorities on the air *and* in off-camera, decision-making jobs. Try—and be determined to succeed.

I know that there are market survey researchers who will bring you confusing numbers and tell you they add up to one thing: Your audience wants to see Ken and Barbie, and your audience *doesn't* want to see African Americans, or Arab Americans, or Latinos, or Asian Americans, or Gays or Lesbians, or Older Americans or Americans with Disabilities. So we give our audience plenty of Ken and Barbie, and we make the minorities we *have* hired so *uncomfortable* that they hold back on the perspective, the experience, the intelligence, the talent that they could have offered to make us wiser and stronger.

Those market researchers, with their surveys and focus groups, are playing games with you and me and with this entire country. We actually pay them money to fool us—money that I submit to you could be better spent on news coverage. Their so-called samples of opinion are no more accurate or reliable than my grandmother's big toe was when it came to predicting the weather. Your own knowledge of news and human nature, your own idealism and professionalism will guide you more surely than any market researcher ever will. You and I know that market research can and often does cripple a newscast—pronto. But the market researchers will keep getting away with their games so long as you and I and the people we work for let them.

If we change the voice and the face of broadcasting, honestly and fairly, on the basis of excellence and ethics, talent and intelligence, we can shatter false and cheap notions about news, we can *prove* that our audience wants electronic journalism that is ethical, responsible, and of high quality—and that is as diverse, as different, as dynamic as America itself.

There is another thing we all can do, a difference we can make. One Word. *More.* Let's do more to think more. Let's bring all the brilliance and imagination this industry has to bear. *That's* what Ed Murrow was talking about. Let's phase out fear. If we've got an idea, let's not hide it out of fear—the fear of doing things differently, the fear that says, "Stay low, stay silent. They can't fire you if they don't know you're there." That fear runs rampant through the corridors of radio and television today.

The people we work for are more fearful than we are. Fear leads them to depend on thoughtless, lifeless numbers to tell them what fear convinces them are facts. "American audiences won't put up with news from other countries. Americans won't put up with economic news. Americans won't put up with serious, substantive news of any kind."

Bull-feathers. We've gone on too long believing this nonsense. We've bought the lie that Information Is Bad for News. We are told, and we are afraid to disbelieve, that people only want to be entertained. And we have gone so far down the Info-Tainment Trail that we'll be a long time getting back to where we started—if ever.

The more the people we work for believe this kind of nonsense, the less inclined we have been to prove them wrong. We go about our days, going along to get along. The fear factor freezes us.

The greatest shortage on every beat, in every newsroom in America, is courage. I believe, as Ed Murrow did, that the vast majority of the owners—and executives and managers—we work for are good people, responsible citizens, and patriotic Americans. I believe that the vast majority of the people in this room also fit that description. We all know what's at stake. We know that our beloved United States of America depends on the decisions we make in our newsrooms every day.

In the end, Morrow could not bring himself to believe that the battle about which he spoke so eloquently could be won. He left the electronic journalism he helped to create—believing that most, if not all, was already lost, that electronic news in America was doomed to be completely and forever overwhelmed by commercialism and entertainment values.

About that, I hope, I believe Murrow was wrong. What is happening to us and our chosen field of work does not have to continue happening. The battle is dark and the odds against. But it is not irreversible, not—not yet. To prevent it from being so requires courage.

A few, just a few, good men and women with courage—the courage to practice the idealism that attracted most of us to the craft in the first place—can make a decisive difference. We need a few good men and women—with the courage of their convictions—to turn it around. We can be those men and women. If the people in this room tonight simply agreed, starting tomorrow, to turn it around—we would turn it around.

What is required is courage.

But I don't have to tell you, you already know, but it is important for me to say it to you anyway—I haven't always had that courage. I said earlier that to talk about Ed Murrow before you tonight was *humbling*. And perhaps that's true most of all in this respect: It is humbling to realize how little courage I have, compared to Murrow, who had so much, and how many opportunities I have already wasted.

But tomorrow is a new day. We toil and are proud to be in this craft, because of the way Edward R. Murrow brought it into being. We can be worthy of him—*we can share his courage.*

Copyright by Dan Rather.

VALUES EXERCISES

1. Make a list of "wrong" and "right" items that you feel are moral absolutes.

   Example: *It is wrong to mistreat a child. It is wrong to humiliate someone. It is right to keep promises. It is right to be charitable.*

2. Identify someone on campus who you believe is a moral person and ask him or her to make similar lists of moral absolutes. Compare your list with this person's and, in a 100-word statement, note any similarities or differences.

3. Without violating your own or someone else's privacy, make a list of all the courageous acts that you have done in your life. Note whether your sense of right and wrong was involved in the incident.

4. Arrange an interview with a practicing journalist (any sequence) and tell him or her before you arrive to make a list of courageous acts that he or she has done during the course of his or her career. Has the person ever questioned the ethics of a superior, for instance? Has the person ever challenged authority? Quit a job? Refused an assignment? During the interview, ask the person whether his or her sense of right and wrong was involved in the incident.

5. Compare your list of courageous acts with the journalist's list and note any similarities or differences. Comment on the relationship between right and wrong and the concept of courage.

3

Truth

Fonts of Truth

Truth is the cornerstone on which a journalist should base a value system. But truth, as we have observed so far, can be a function of influence or perception. No doubt you have heard the motto, "Truth is relative," which implies that each person holds different truths about the same topic, and so the exercise of ascertaining truth is therefore impossible. If you believe in the motto, the best you can do as a journalist is interview sources or make pitches to clients and customers, reporting or acknowledging *their* truths. Of course, to do even this, you will have to adjust for your own influences to interpret your sources, clients, and customers accurately.

Truth *is* elusive. Often it is relative. Occasionally it is absolute. But these distinctions, which you will encounter in this chapter, are less important than your reaction to the motto "Truth is relative." You can throw up your hands and bow to that oracle, relieving yourself of responsibility. You can complain, Why study truth if it cannot be completely or at best rarely ascertained? Or you can view that motto as a challenge. You can say, Why *not* study truth? vowing to track down and clarify elusive truths and base your reports, campaigns, and photographs on some aspect of everyday or absolute truths.

Consider the ramifications of believing that truth is relative and therefore not worth analyzing or pursuing. Would you admit this to a personnel manager interviewing you for your first job in journalism? Or would you lie? These are not rhetorical questions. If you would lie, then truth is not as relative as you might think because you are anticipating that personnel directors share remarkably similar views about the topic. But let's say that you go ahead and admit your belief to the personnel director. How would you respond if he or she inquired, What is the difference between the words *truth* and *belief?*

If truth is entirely relative, it is also synonymous with belief—but that can't be. The 2214-page unabridged *Random House Dictionary of the English Language* defines *truth* as "the actual state of a matter" or "conformity with fact or reality" or "a verified or indisputable fact." It defines *belief* as "an opinion or conviction: a belief that the world is flat" or "confidence in the truth or existence of something not immediately susceptible to rigorous proof." There are subtle but important distinctions between the two terms: *truth* hinges on *reality,* whereas *belief* hinges on *opinion.*

Because truth is subject to proof, it is more laborious than belief. It is one thing for an advertiser to *believe* there is a need for a product and another to prove that *true* via marketing studies. It is one thing for a reporter to believe a politician is corrupt and another to verify that in an investigative piece. It is one thing for a public relations specialist to believe that he or she can represent a client better than a competitor and another to document that in a business meeting. Beliefs may be true or false, deep or shallow, depending on the individual. Truths have to hold up under scrutiny.

You do not need a bulky dictionary to understand the difference between truth and opinion. All you have to do is read a front-page story in the *New York Times* or *Wall Street Journal* and an editorial in the opinions section. One informs by fact and the other persuades by conviction. One is verifiable and the other is subject to debate in the letters section. That is not to say that reporters of these newspapers are fonts of truth who always inform accurately and without slant. It does acknowledge, however, that the reporting—occasionally inaccurate and/or slanted—is *close enough for credibility.*

Truth is relative by degrees. You may not know 100 percent of the truth 100 percent of the time. But it is possible to convey a significant percentage of a truth, depending on the subject, and to strive to convey more on your next assignment. To deny that truth exists because you cannot completely discern it is, in the end, a self-serving argument.

"Have we not learned a thing or two over the past several thousand years of civilization?" asks philosopher Christina Hoff Sommers. "Why should we be the first society in history that finds itself hamstrung in the vital task of passing along its moral tradition to the next generation?"[1] Truth, as Sommers attests, is the vehicle of any value system. While no person can know every truth, *every* person can know *one* truth upon which to base such a system.

The first step in that process is acknowledging the significance of truth in the workplace. Ethical questions concerning truth arise every day on Madison Avenue, says Grant Castle, president of the Castle Underwood advertising agency. "They range, for example, from rather minor situations such as explaining to one client why you can't be at their meeting (should you admit you are at another meeting?) to much more substantial ones" concerning strategies and competition. "To me," Castle says, "the issue is pretty clear. Tell the truth. Nothing goes farther in this business than trust. It is a mix between commerce and art and maybe a bit of magic. The moment that trust is broken, even if over a relatively minor incident, the relationship begins to deteriorate."

The relationship with the consumer also is important in any discussion about advertising and truth, says Harold Levine, founder of Levine, Huntley, Schmidt and Beaver. When Levine and his partners created the agency, they made a pact.

> We agreed that we would not handle accounts if we didn't feel the product was one that we would buy for ourselves. Thus, we never solicited a tobacco account.
>
> Beyond that, ethics in the advertising business becomes a critical issue when a client gives *you* information for an ad campaign. Should you accept the facts as given or demand proof of all claims? This can put you in a difficult position with the client, so rather than get into a hassle with a client we always insisted that all advertising copy be submitted to our attorney for clearance. And we insisted that the attorney look at the copy from the standpoint of the consumer. Finally, we recognized that a large number of consumers are skeptical of all advertising, and therefore an ad agency has a special responsibility to present an advertising message in a warm, human, believable context.

This entails:

- *Accurate information.* "No overstatements, no playing with the truth."
- *Accurate images.* "In TV spots, no trick photography to mislead the viewer."
- *Credibility.* "Our creative staff was directed to produce advertising that the consumer would enjoy seeing or hearing, but that also would reflect favorably on the advertiser."

Credibility is a priority in public relations, too. Linda Percefull, PR director at Littlefield Marketing and Advertising, cites two reasons for journalists to tell the truth: "First of all, it's the right thing to do. Once you've lost your credibility, it's extremely difficult to get it back. Second, telling the truth is easier. No worrying about remembering what you've said and to whom."

Telling the truth appeals to pragmatists, Percefull says. "My personal and professional style is to tell the truth and tell it quickly. I counsel clients to do the same, particularly in a crisis. My most frustrating and rewarding work has been in counseling clients through a crisis—frustrating when they won't take the leap of faith and rewarding when they tough it out and do the right thing."

Truth should be proved whenever possible, says Mary Jo Nelson, 40-year veteran reporter and editor for the *Oklahoman* and *Times* newspapers in Oklahoma City. "You do this by documentation, ample eyewitness—including personal observation—or all of these." Truth, she adds, also is associated with:

- *Discernment.* "The ability to more readily distinguish smooth charm from sincerity."
- *Hard work.* "Adopt the single-mindedness of an ant in tracking information."
- *Sacrifice.* "Kill a story if it means wrongfully hurting or slandering someone, even when the reporter knows a competitor is working on the same story."
- *Accepting consequences.* "Learn from honest mistakes."

Adopting as a motto the title of the text you are reading—*Living Ethics*—is all anyone needs to base a value system on truth, Nelson says: "Live ethics. Live right and you'll be honest in your occupation. Of course," she adds, "anybody knows that's not simple now and never was."

Let's clarify the process.

Basic Concepts

There are two avenues to truth in mass media—objectivity and subjectivity. Curiously, each requires the same commitment of the journalist:

- To determine and adjust for influences that affect how the journalist perceives the world
- To seek out information or other viewpoints via research, interviews, or consultations to gain a clearer perspective about an assignment
- To keep an open mind

Objectivity was discussed in the first chapter. The goal is to cover the world as it actually exists without allowing basic influences to color perception. Employees of newspapers and radio and television outlets usually report to a general or eclectic audience; consequently, their stories or segments must do two things: disseminate information the public needs to know and to do so factually and impartially. Moreover, the assertions in those documents must present all sides of an issue and stand up to outside scrutiny. Ideally, a reader, viewer, or listener should be able to verify facts without finding errors or omissions in these reports. Facts and images become pieces of a mosaic pertaining to a certain topic, issue, situation, incident, event, or person. When a story or segment is truthful, the individual facts and images should complete the mosaic for a clear picture. Because each newspaper and broadcast outlet will cover the same assignment with the same objective goal, the stories or segments should vary *only by degrees.* The best report will contain the most information and the clearest picture.

Subjectivity takes a different route. The goal is to cover the world as it actually exists for targeted groups of people. Employees of magazines and advertising and public relations agencies usually report to a select or narrow audience; consequently, their stories or campaigns must do two things: disseminate information that targeted groups want or should know and to do so personally and selectively. The assertions in stories or campaigns can present one side of a truth but that slant still must stand up to outside scrutiny. Ideally, a reader, viewer, or listener should be able to verify facts associated with narrow truths without finding errors or omissions. Because each magazine or agency targets a narrow audience, its objectives vary. Each will have a different slant on the same truth involving a topic, issue, situation, incident, event, or person. However, when the slants of each magazine or agency are considered *collectively,* the truth once again should vary *only by degrees.*

You will see that more clearly after a few concepts are defined. For the moment, however, the focus will be on commonalties between objective and subjective journalists. The objective journalist has to determine and adjust for personal influences that affect how he or she perceives the world so that assignments mirror reality as closely as possible. Likewise, the subjective journalist has to determine and adjust for personal influences so that he or she can perceive the world the same way as the client or targeted audience does. The objective journalist has to seek out information or other viewpoints via research, interviews, or consultations to gain a clearer perspective about an assignment. The subjective journalist also relies on research, interviews, or consultations to target and supply information to select groups of people. The objective journalist must keep an open mind to understand all aspects of reality on *each* assignment; thus, the goal of each assignment is the same: Uncover the whole truth or as close to that truth as possible. The subjective journalist must keep an open mind to understand each *slant* or *slice* of reality; thus, the goal of each magazine or campaign may vary. However, the subjective journalist moves from narrow truth to narrow truth so many times for different employers or clients that he or she usually ends up covering the *whole* truth over the course of a typical career.

As you can see, the commonalties require the journalist to commit to truth. The differences in approach apply to how objective and subjective journalists fulfill their commitments via *fact accuracy* and *impression accuracy.*

- *Fact accuracy.* Fact accuracy is otherwise known as "partial disclosure" in a report, segment, or campaign. Journalists disseminate selected facts and conclusions *viewed apart from other facts and conclusions.* In other words, specific facts are truthful but may suggest a certain slant or be taken out of context to imply something other than the complete truth.
- *Impression accuracy.* Impression accuracy is otherwise known as "full disclosure" in a report, segment, or campaign that includes *all available facts* with the goal of providing fair, objective, and complete truth. In other words, impression accuracy includes fact accuracy from all slants so that little, if anything, can be taken out of context.

Although it depends on the mission of each medium, fact accuracy usually applies to subjective journalism, and impression accuracy generally applies to objective journalism.

As any reporter knows, a newspaper or station should cover reality as closely as possible. Disseminating isolated facts violates a basic trust. Readers, listeners, and viewers anticipate full disclosure—all available facts—about newsworthy topics. Partial disclosure leaves an inaccurate impression on the audience.

Sue Porter, editor of *Scripps Howard News* and vice president of the Scripps Howard Foundation, recalls an incident involving partial disclosure in the newsroom. The editor of a daily Cincinnati newspaper assigned a story about northern Kentucky and southern Ohio business and political leaders competing to develop industrial complexes on their respective sides of the Ohio River. "The assignment was given to me with a distinct slant: expose the Kentuckians' unethical dealings," Porter recalls. "After months of research, I told my editor that I couldn't give him exactly what he wanted. We debated my findings. I was told to use information that supported the premise.

"I did that but not without presenting information that also disputed those facts."

Porter adds that the story was returned to her for revision 16 times. "'Change a verb here,' the editor told me. 'Drop a paragraph there.' Slowly my editor, the surgeon, was crafting the story *he* wanted and I was sick about it.

" 'This is it. No byline, please,' I declared as I placed the story on his desk for the seventeenth time." Porter told the editor if he wanted any more revisions or reporting on the story that "someone else will have to do it."

Porter recalls, "I can still see the anger on my editor's face as he rewrote my story—page after page. It was published without a byline and it was a long time before I got another 'big story.'" Years later, after the editor retired, Porter discussed the matter with him over lunch.

> He said he was determined to give his boss what he wanted, and that he really didn't feel he was compromising reality by presenting only a portion of the facts. The bottom line was that he felt the newspaper needed to sound an alarm. . . . In his mind, the end justified the means. Telling the story his way was a higher calling.
>
> Or was it?
>
> The answer lies in what we consider the mission of our news pages individually and our newspapers overall. I still maintain that the correct way to have addressed the topic would have been a balanced story on the news pages and a commentary on the editorial page that sounded the same alarm.

Porter makes important points. Note that she displayed courage in her dealings with the editor. She accepted the consequences of his becoming angry and not assigning her another "big story" for a while. Note as well that Porter was more concerned about remaining true to her values rather than impressing her editor. Nonetheless, Porter continued to succeed and achieve as a journalist, rising eventually to an executive position at Scripps Howard Company. Finally, note that she understands the unethical nature of partial disclosure in a newspaper and distinguishes between truth and belief, recommending editors publish "belief" on the opinion page.

"For me, the bottom-line value for any journalist should be [impression] accuracy," Porter adds. "If a writer or editor is concerned enough about accuracy, then fairness will follow. And so will complete coverage of any question."

Jack Bickham, author of more than 60 books and a journalism professor at the University of Oklahoma, is a chief proponent of impression accuracy. This value, he says, led to his success as a writer, reporter, and teacher. "Accuracy involves more than getting the known facts right—right 100 percent. The journalist obsessed with the need for accuracy will not only check and double-check to make sure his material—data, quotes, and history—is totally factual. He will also make sure he has *all* the information possibly available. This means checking back with sources, searching for other sources, always asking oneself if there is another angle, another viewpoint, another factual source, to be mined before the story is written."

Bickham believes that the objective journalist who is passionate about accuracy "is automatically fair and won't miss anything crucial. Sometimes this isn't easy, and sometimes it leads to writing or editing a story that you know will hurt someone, perhaps even someone you admire." Bickham admits that he is an idealist about impression accuracy but adds, "Without good reporting and editing, there can be no informed electorate. And without an informed electorate, our system of government cannot possibly work. Given this view, total accuracy in reporting and editing becomes a sacred duty not only to oneself and his readers, but to our country."

Subjective journalists should be as passionate about their narrow truths. But they also know that their objective media counterparts are responsible, by and large, for the informed electorate. Subjective journalists serve the public in different ways. Magazine writers and advertisers satisfy perceived needs of readers and consumers, and public relations specialists resolve problems or promote interests of clients.

Consider the role of magazines. Each magazine targets a different audience or *niche*. Writers must appeal to the needs or perceived needs of that niche. That is why it is a subjective medium, apart from newspapering or broadcasting, where employees basically perform the same tasks in every city. For instance, reporters at the *Athens (Ohio) Messenger* and the local public radio WOUB-FM essentially do what their counterparts do at the *Washington Post* and National Public Radio—only the *Post* and NPR do it better or more completely because of talent or resources. Conversely, writers for political magazines, say, have specific agendas associated with their readerships. For instance, editors of the *New Republic* may take a liberal slant on legislation to restrict the sale of automatic weapons, knowing full well that their counterparts at the *National Review* will take a conservative slant and that *Newsweek, Time,* and *U.S. News & World Report* will report mainstream slants, varying from slightly liberal to slightly conservative. All of these truths are available on the newsstand and so provide impression accuracy on current affairs—only one out of thousands of topics upon which a specific magazine may be based.

The same holds true for narrow claims in advertising. Honda may have a bigger wheelbase than a competing Toyota model that features a smoother ride or more luxury options. And the General Motors model may offer all of these amenities at lower cost but at lower overall reliability. And so on. If the fact accuracy of ads representing these and other competing models are taken into account, the consumer will make the right choice for his or her lifestyle. All of these ads are available at the newsstand or on the radio or on the TV dial and so provide impression accuracy on auto making—only one out of thousands of accounts that advertising agencies handle.

To a certain extent, this also applies to public relations. Each agency will resolve problems or promote interests of specific clients so that those problems and interests, considered collectively, provide an accurate impression to the public. For instance, the views of the Tobacco Institute are countered by practitioners representing insurance or health concerns or disseminating information via public service announcements. This is only one out of thousands of topics that practitioners handle. But the issue of public relations is more complex than that of magazine journalism or advertising because practitioners also deal directly on a continuing basis with the objective news media.

Public relations and news rely on each other and have a special relationship dating back to the founder of public relations, Ivy Ledbetter Lee, who began his career as a newspaper reporter in New York City from 1899 to 1903. Thereafter, he began representing coal miners and later the Pennsylvania Railroad Company and other powerful clients, improving their image in the news and adding another dimension—supplying information to reporters about companies and their special interests or projects. In his day, Lee was known for candor and openness when dealing with the press but he also emphasized fact accuracy with a particular, persuasive flare.

"Sometimes he presented only facts and arguments that favored his clients," according to Hugh Culbertson, nationally known researcher and public relations expert. That was Lee's right as a subjective journalist. However, as Culbertson notes, "Critics sometimes accuse him of going to great lengths to suppress or deny opponents a fair hearing."

This second practice is subject to ethical debate. It is one thing for a PR practitioner representing a petroleum company to decide which facts to release and which to withhold about a tanker leaking oil after colliding with a reef. But it is another thing for the practitioner to suppress information by providing fabricated rebuttals or inaccurate data or to mislead the media, sending reporters on false trails. As Culbertson puts it, "Perhaps a practitioner need not 'shout from the house tops' that his or her client got drunk and did embarrassing things. . . . [But] he or she has no ethical right to prevent that story from being told."

There are two major consequences related to suppressing information or misleading the news media. If a cover-up becomes known, the practitioner will cause immeasurable embarrassment to the client. He or she will compound the original problem and undermine the client's image or special interests. Worse, the practitioner will lose credibility so that the media and public will question those facts that *do* support the client.

This leads us to another basic concept about truth that applies to all journalism sequences: appropriate and inappropriate disclosure. So far, you have been reading about the virtues of truth in this chapter. We noted its importance to all sequences, introduced journalists who embraced truth as a value, and defined the ethics of fact and impression accuracy. But disclosing the whole truth or all facts to the *wrong audience* or to the right one on the *wrong occasion* can be just as unethical as lying.

Here are definitions and illustrations of appropriate and inappropriate disclosure:

- *Appropriate disclosure.* Appropriate disclosure is fact or impression accuracy that provides details or data that the intended audience needs or perceives to need within the established boundaries of privacy and taste associated with individual media outlets.
- *Inappropriate disclosure.* Inappropriate disclosure is fact or impression accuracy that provides details or data that the intended audience needs or perceives to need *in addition to other details or data that violate privacy or are inherently distasteful.*

For instance, a broadcaster may be privy to all available facts relating to a murder but he or she does not need to disseminate ones that the audience might find distasteful—data from the coroner's report, say—or that might violate someone's privacy, such as images of grief by family members viewing the body.

These are aspects of truth related to discretion. You should know the concept of appropriate and inappropriate disclosure intuitively because you interact with other people on a daily basis. If a teacher asks you why you missed class, for example, you should tell the truth: "My housemate had a serious personal problem last night and needed me this morning, so I could not attend." Depending on the teacher, he or she will accept that. Depending on the student, he or she will accept the consequences. The disclosure was truthful and appropriate. But it would be distasteful and a violation of privacy to tell the teacher: "My housemate Jane Doe was assaulted on a date last night so I missed class to visit her at the student health center."

In Chapter 9, you will learn more about taste and privacy concerns. Let's end our discussion on disclosure with an anecdote by magazine writer Rita Schweitz, who freelances as a work-for-hire author, or "ghostwriter." She tells about a tricky situation she encountered in front of an audience that had specific opinions about the role of women in society:

> Because I had ghostwritten books for a conservative Christian publisher, I was invited to attend their authors' banquet sponsored by the Christian Booksellers Association. I enjoyed the meal until the announcement that beginning at a table near mine, and going around the room, writers would stand and say a few words about the book each had written. Now I was on the spot. As a ghostwriter, it is not ethical to steal the thunder for a book with someone else's name on it or to violate the confidentiality of the ghosting agreement—especially when the author is sitting one table away! Worse, the other books I had written in my own name were with a rival company.
>
> What to do?
>
> When it came to my turn, I stood at my chair and announced, "My name is Rita Schweitz. And I'm the woman writer behind some of the men's books you might have read."

People all around the room burst out laughing, caught off guard by my comment. Given the fundamentalist views of male/female roles, and the authority attached to male leaders and teachers, it took some nerve to poke fun at that banquet. But the humor diffused a potentially awkward situation regarding the ethics of taking credit for work-for-hire words.

Moreover, it was discrete given the occasion, appropriate given the audience, and truthful given the assignment.

A Word about Satire

In any discussion about truth, it would be inappropriate to exclude satire. Satire is found in every medium, from columns and cartoons in newspapers and magazines, to radio and television talk and entertainment shows, to advertisements and public service announcements. Most journalists think that satire is humorous, but it doesn't have to be. The two key ingredients are truth and unreliability (commonly known as a *double message*). Without truth, satire becomes *sarcasm*—achieving humor at the expense of another person or group. Without unreliability, satire becomes *vulgarity*—conveying distasteful or offensive ideas. Be forewarned: These considerations make satire particularly difficult to execute because sarcasm and vulgarity usually are unethical in mass media.

The touchstone for modern day satire is "A Modest Proposal," composed in 1729 by Irish-born writer Jonathan Swift. In that piece, Swift attacked English landlords for exploiting the Irish. Instead of using an angry tone of voice, he used an upper-class legislative voice—as one might find in the House of Lords—resolving to end Irish overpopulation and famine and improve the economy via cannibalism.

Titles are particularly important in satire because they usually convey irony and enhance the double message. Swift's "A *Modest* Proposal" does that nicely because the proposal is anything but modest. Moreover, Swift added this subtitle: "For Preventing the Children of Poor People in Ireland from Being a Burden to Their Parents or Country, and for Making Them Beneficial to the Public." The subtitle prepares the reader to anticipate a helpful solution:

> It is a melancholy object to those who walk though this great town or travel in the country, when they see the streets, the roads, and cabin doors, crowded with beggars of the female sex, followed by three, four, or six children, all in rags and importuning every passenger for an alms. These mothers, instead of being able to work for their honest livelihood, are forced to employ all their time in strolling to beg sustenance for their helpless infants: who as they grow up either turn thieves for want of work or leave their dear native country. . . .

The reader soon realizes the solution is satiric:

I have been assured by a very knowing American of my acquaintance in London that a young healthy child well nursed is at a year old a most delicious, nourishing, and wholesome food, whether stewed, roasted, baked, or boiled; and I make no doubt that it will equally serve in a fricassee or a ragout. . . .

I grant this food will be somewhat dear, and therefore very proper for landlords, who, as they have already devoured most of the parents, seem to have the best title to the children.

Infants' flesh will be in season throughout the year, but more plentiful in March, and a little before and after; for we are told . . . that fish being a prolific diet, there are more children born in Roman Catholic countries about nine months after Lent than at any other season; therefore, reckoning a year after Lent, the markets will be more glutted than usual, because the number of popish infants is at least three to one in this kingdom: and therefore it will have one other collateral advantage, by lessening the number of papists among us.

As you can see, Swift's satire was not humorous. But it does contain truth and unreliability. At the time, the English ruling class was doing little to end Irish famine and hardship. So the attack was not sarcastic but true. The double message is obvious, too—otherwise, the idea of cannibalizing children would be vulgar.

Swift's satire and standards still hold up today. As he knew, satire has great power to make people see what they don't want to see. But it is risky, too. If done poorly, without a grain of truth and a *clear* double message, attempts at satire wound or offend the audience because they come off as sarcasm or vulgarity.

Satire uses irony to expose or attack human vices such as greed or vanity, says Henry Payne, award-winning editorial cartoonist for Scripps Howard News in Washington, DC. "The key word here is 'expose,'" says Payne. "Like an inquisitive police investigator, the serious satirist will find his opponent's flaw and hang him with it. But if the satirist is only a jealous adversary, he will substitute spite for proper investigation, leaving his own methods vulnerable to exposure." Payne adds, "It is not enough, then, for the satirist to be a skilled marksman. He must first do the necessary legwork to ensure he has the right mark."

Satire can boomerang and focus attention on its creator, depending on how the audience perceives the work. An interesting case study occurred at a New York campus-based newspaper. The editor reprinted what he thought was a satire on astrology. In the entry for Aquarius, the horoscope suggested people born under that sign relieve stress with "a good old-fashioned lynching." Horoscopes for other signs also contained racial content. The piece originated at a Wisconsin campus and was published in the news-

DOONESBURY, F.O.B.

DOONESBURY, F.O.B.

© 1994 Scripps Howard

Editorial cartoonists are used to taking on presidents, celebrities, and other news- and image-makers. But Henry Payne of Scripps Howard News Service in Washington, DC, took on fellow satirist G. B. Trudeau and his famous Doonesbury character in these panels concerning the Whitewater real estate conflict that involved President Clinton in 1993–94.

paper there; readers reportedly did not complain. But at the New York campus, protests about the piece played a role in the editor's being ousted. In an article about the controversy, a journalism professor is quoted as saying the horoscope "was clearly a satire. But no one should satirize lynching. Just as no one should satirize the Holocaust."[2]

The horoscope was not *clearly* a satire. Nonetheless, the professor is correct about not satirizing lynching or the Holocaust, because such comments—however truthful—make their points at the expense of African Americans and Jews. People who believe in astrology are commonly known as "New Age" types; if you wanted to satirize them, you would include content associated with that lifestyle under each sign: "Still unemployed? When an interviewer asks you about experience, don't reply, 'Out of body.'" In fact, all the creator of the original horoscope had to do was change the title from "Your *Real* Horoscope" to "Your *KKK* Horoscope." Then the piece would have been clearly satirical. As noted earlier, titles are especially important in that regard. So, satirists who use the same title as a concept for each regularly scheduled piece or panel have to be especially careful in executing their satires. At best, given the content in this instance, the title "Your Real Horoscope" may satirize inherent racist feelings shared by everyone. At worst, it may come off as sarcasm.

"My feeling is that the best cartoons reveal some aspect of the truth and at the same time convey a message," says Jim Borgman, Pulitzer Prize–winning syndicated cartoonist for the *Cincinnati Enquirer*. "Sometimes we lose our way when we are doing five or six cartoons a week. Often as a cartoonist you are trying to be a humorous illustrator of world news, which is what our profession suffers from most right now. At your best, you're trying to reveal something new, state and stir up opinions, provoke debate—unpeel the onions—all those things. And it's wonderful when one can break out of the woods and remember that that's what the point of all this is."

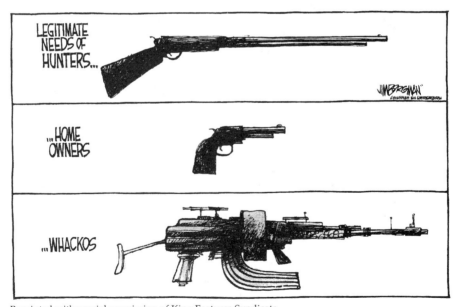

Reprinted with special permission of King Features Syndicate.

Editorial cartoonist Jim Borgman emphasizes truth by illustrating "legitimate needs" of hunters (rifles) and home owners (handguns). The double message concerns "legitimate needs" of whackos. Obviously, Borgman is not proposing that serial killers have a right to own automatic weapons. Thus, his panel contains the two key ingredients of ethical satire: truth and unreliability.

Borgman believes that the influence of syndicated cartoonists Pat Oliphant and Jeff MacNelly—two artists who inspired him, by the way—have been misinterpreted by too many aspiring satirists. "Oliphant and MacNelly draw so brilliantly and integrate humor so well," Borgman says. "But we have ended up with a lot of young cartoonists who only caught the humor part. We have too many cartoonists who really are stand-up comedians doing funny, pithy comments on that day's news, much as Dave Letterman does or Johnny Carson might have done." Borgman adds, "I always struggle to do cartoons that none of these late-night entertainers would say on their shows."

Higher Concepts

Higher truths are known as *archetypes* (from the Greek *archetypos* or "beginning pattern"). The word usually is associated with the doctrines of psychologist Carl Jung who wrote about the collective unconscious, or the passing along of myths—symbols, stories, images—from generation to generation. For our purposes, *archetype* is defined as universal truth. Whether these ideas are "higher" or even "true" is not important. You may disagree with or rebut them. However, as a journalist, you must be aware that people around the world view these truths with similar respect as if, indeed, they *have* been passed along generation to generation.

In his groundbreaking book, *The Hero with a Thousand Faces*, mythologist Joseph Campbell describes the prototype—or "monomyth"—upon which cultures around the world have based values or beliefs: "A hero ventures forth from the world of common day into a region of supernatural wonder: fabulous forces are there encountered and a decisive victory is won: the hero comes back from this mysterious adventure with the power to bestow boons on his fellow man."[3]

With variations, most societies have a story in their cultural canon that features the following:

- A hero or messiah is identified and provides new hope, as spring does after winter.
- The hero or messiah has special powers, celebrated in summer.
- The hero or messiah falls from favor, symbolized by autumn and approaching death.
- The hero or messiah is defeated or executed, ending hope, as in winter.
- The hero or messiah is resurrected with new power, inspiring higher hopes.
- The cycle begins again.

Don't confuse the word *myth* with the word *lie,* as when someone tells you, "Oh, that's just a 'myth.'" As the works of Joseph Campbell document, myth is a higher truth on which many moral values can be based. The monomyth, incidentally, does not pertain only to ancient religious narratives but also to modern pop-cultural ones, as in comic books concerning the death and resurrection of Superman in the early 1990s.

The monomyth is based on a pattern like the seasons. Cultures also articulate higher truths on a totem or stepladder or "Great Chain of Being":

Deity	Supreme Power
Angels	Supernatural Beings
Mortals	Humans
Animals	Nonhuman Lifeforms
Vegetation	Tree and Plant Life
Minerals	Rocks, Gems, Earth

From reading this list you may be tempted to think about ancient religious stories as found in American, Native American, European, Middle Eastern, African, or Asian holy books. Instead, let's analyze the Great Chain of Being in *The Wizard of Oz,* a 1900 children's story by L. Frank Baum. The book was popularized in a 1939 movie starring Judy Garland and has come to represent American values about the importance of family and home:

Deity	Wizard
Angels	Good and Bad Witches
Mortals	Munchkins, Dorothy
Animals	The Lion, Flying Monkeys, Toto
Vegetation	The Straw Man, Talking Apple Trees, Poppies
Minerals	The Tin Man, Emerald City, Yellowbrick Road, Ruby Slippers

The Wizard of Oz is a powerful story because it not only incorporates a Great Chain but it also is based on the monomyth:

Dorothy ventures forth from the world of common day in Kansas into a region of supernatural wonder: Oz. The munchkins believe she is their messiah and celebrate her. Dorothy follows the yellowbrick road to meet a great spiritual leader. On her journey she encounters fabulous forces—talking straw, lion and tin men along with good and bad witches—and wins a decisive victory over the Wicked Witch who wants the ruby slippers. When Dorothy realizes the power of those slippers, she returns from this mysterious adventure bestowing boons on Munchkins in Oz and love on her family and fellow Kansans.

The higher truth of *The Wizard of Oz* is not that the so-called wizard is a hoaxster but that Dorothy only needed to click her heels three times and say "Home" to tap the power within her. That, alas, is the archetype.

Universal truths are not only found in religious or literary works. These works have great impact because they are tapping something inside you. The following monomyth may sound familiar:

> In spring, a boy or girl blossoms into adulthood. In summer, he or she celebrates and ventures forth from the world of common day into a region of supernatural wonder: first love. Fabulous forces are there encountered and the hero or heroine wins a mate. The mate betrays him or her in the fall, and the hero or heroine suffers a kind of death. Life is cold and still. Then spring returns, and the hero or heroine resurrects, wiser now with new power or maturity as the cycle begins again.

Life is a great teacher of truth. It challenges us with situations that require us to fall back on *epiphanies* and *peak experiences*.

- *Epiphany.* You are experiencing an epiphany when your *mind* seems at one with the universe. You understand an important truth that bestows meaning in your life. For instance, you realize the significance of circumstances or events that led to your parents' or your divorce, a friend's or relative's death, a successful or unsuccessful relationship, or your own mortality, talents, shortcomings, and opportunities.
- *Peak experience.* You are feeling a peak experience when your *body* seems at one with the universe. The feeling is encountered during sex, or winning a race, or scoring the winning point in a competitive game, or surviving a dangerous accident or a close call, or giving birth. But a peak moment also may come when you master a difficult song on an instrument so that your fingers convey emotions or when you command a powerful machine such as a plane so that your body seems to have wings.

Undoubtedly, you have experienced several epiphanies and peak moments in your life. Inside you is a storehouse of truth upon which you can analyze your current values or build a new system. Epiphanies and peak experiences usually occur during or following high points, low points, and turning points in your life. Make a list of high points—for example, births; successful personal, familial, and professional relationships or achievements; and academic, athletic, or artistic successes. Make a list of low points—for example, deaths; unsuccessful personal, familial, and professional relationships or achievements; and academic, athletic, or artistic failures. Next, make a list of turning points—for example journeys, accidents, diseases, or reversals (failures that became successes and vice versa). Evaluate each item, as you learned to do in Chapter 1, to determine whether you may have to adjust your perception. Determine whether you have accepted the consequences associated with each item, as you learned to do in Chapter 2. Finally, ascertain the lesson you learned from each experience. These are your "truths" and the foundation of your current value system.

Chances are your lessons will relate to consequences involving falsehood, manipulation, temptation, unfairness, fairness, and power, and will somehow involve trust, control, cowardice, fear, courage, and authority. In upcoming chapters, you will learn about these concepts and how they relate to journalism. At this point, we have noted influences that may affect your perception and identified the concepts of right, wrong, and truth. After you have read the Living Ethics items that follow and complete the exercises at the end of the chapter, you should be able to base a value system on truth. In the next section, we will test it.

ENDNOTES

1. Christina Hoff Sommers, "Teaching the virtues," *Chicago Tribune Magazine* reprint, 12 September 1993, p. 18.

2. Allan Wolper, "Impeaching a student editor," *Editor & Publisher,* 25 December 1993, p. 17.

3. Joseph Campbell, *The Hero with a Thousand Faces* (Princeton, NJ: Princeton University Press, 1973), p. 30.

L I V I N G   E T H I C S

Read the following interviews and essays and record your reactions in your ethics journal and/or discuss them with peers or mentors.

❉ EDITOR'S NOTE: *Greg Bustin, president of a Dallas public relations firm, originally published the following essay in the regional trade magazine* Dallas Business Review. *He documents that telling the truth is not only moral but is also practical, attainable, and effective in the business world. "If nothing else," he says, "the piece shows that public relations people should take very seriously the notion of serving as the moral conscience of those we represent." You'll find several mottoes in Bustin's piece along with lessons about consequences covered in the previous chapter. As the anecdote that begins his piece illustrates, Bustin had to rely on his conscience when facing a turning point in his career. In a word, Bustin knows that ethics are meant to be lived on an everyday basis because "truth eventually will prevail."*

Truth Eventually Will Prevail

Greg Bustin, President, *Bustin & Company*

It was moments before the press conference was scheduled to begin, and only a handful of reporters were seated, pen and pad in hand. My clients, the top executives of a major U.S. company, were visibly upset at the empty seats in the room. It is one of the many risks of my chosen profession—public relations—that even the best-laid plans to stage a major news announcement can be preempted by unanticipated breaking news. As it turned out, this was precisely what had happened.

As the rankled commander of this debacle, I marched into a phone booth and called my office to learn if any calls had come in that would explain the absence of media at the event. I also marched into an ethical dilemma that I'll never forget.

"Can we round up a few staffers to pose as reporters?" I asked my colleague back at the office. "The clients will never know, and just a few additional bodies in the room would make a difference."

After all, I was confident we would be successful in generating publicity for the clients, regardless of the low media attendance. It was the *appearance* of disinterest in the event that was upsetting to them.

If you've never once been tempted to manipulate a situation wrongly and for your own advantage, this article is not for you. For the rest of us, we all will agree that in the heat of battle it doesn't take two blinks of an eye to make even a small unethical decision that we—and those who rely on us for leadership—may regret for the rest of our lives.

Surveys show that an alarmingly high percentage of people stretch the truth on their resumés. But a lie is a lie is a lie. Small untruths make it easier to tell larger lies next time. The man who's cheating on his test today may be cheating on his taxes tomorrow. The woman who promotes herself beyond her abilities today may next be trumpeting attributes that a product doesn't have.

Therefore, even those of us who consider ourselves to be ethical and honorable people can benefit from considering preventive measures that will keep us out of trouble, out of the tabloids and, most important, out of danger from violating our own consciences.

Anyone who thinks it dubious for a public relations person to offer commentary on the subject of ethics should consider that this is a profession where ethical issues and concerns figure prominently in the day-to-day practice of our business. Not only must we live up to our own professional society's code of ethics, but we are often called into situations where we must—sometimes by request and sometimes despite management's desires—serve as the corporate conscience.

The ill-fated press conference that served as a seminal moment in my professional career took place seven years ago. I'm pleased to report that we did not stack the room with warm bodies to ease the clients' discomfort. Though we lost the account, we could look at ourselves in the mirror the next day.

I still have the crystal-clear realization that I am capable of making an unethical decision—a point that reverberates on a daily basis. I have come to appreciate the Chinese proverb that says, "There are two perfect men—one dead and the other unborn."

We need to calibrate our own moral compass against timeless principles that will keep us properly aimed, especially when we're marching in unfamiliar territory or under duress. Or both. If we don't, we risk treading where the now-incarcerated executive of a multimillion-dollar enterprise strayed into dangerous ethical terrain: "First I began to see a few bear tracks, but I kept going. Then I started to see claw marks on the trees. Still I pushed ahead. Then I began to small fresh bear dung. But that still didn't convince me to turn around. Before I knew it, I was face to face with the bear and it was too late to run."

Calibrating our own moral compass is good. But it isn't good enough. We must have people around us—both inside and outside the company—who have the courage to disagree with us on logical and ethical grounds. As the saying goes, if two men agree on everything, then one of them is superfluous. Yes-men don't add value to the leader's decisions.

And sometimes they can be dangerous. As an example, one of my clients, a middle manager of a publicly traded concern, once made a disturbing demand. The day before a large contract was to be awarded, this manager learned from inside sources that his company was not to be the winner. To soften the blow that the disappointing news would have on his investors, the manager demanded, on orders from his president, that one of my employees distribute immediately a news release saying the company had "withdrawn from the bidding process."

Fortunately, my employee had the wherewithal to discover the truth and confer with me about how to handle the situation. In the end, we convinced my client and his president to await the decision from media and investors. It was clear that the president of that company had a manager who would tell him his new clothes were magnificent, while I had an employee with the courage to reveal the naked truth.

But what about all the companies that not only get away with, but seem to benefit from, unethical behavior? Well, if you ever doubt the axiom that truth eventually will prevail, don't underestimate the ability of technology to root it out of the past.

As a case in point, consider the real estate concern that believed, to a fault, in the great American principle that the only line that counts is the one that goes up. To keep that line on an incline, the company tended to "round up" on its traffic and occupancy rates. On the occasion of the company's anniversary, as reporters researched the company's record to write then-and-now articles, they discovered several contradictions in the data. In the midst of celebrating, company executives also had some explaining to do.

Today, if you lie in business, you're going to get flattened by the facts on the information highway. All the more reason to have managers and friends who can help us navigate ethical mine fields and keep us on track.

In the trenches, it's difficult to think years down the road. But time has a way of clarifying right and wrong. History is full of men and women who would have enjoyed rethinking some of their moral predicaments. It also records those who acted heroically.

Don't you know those Johnson & Johnson executives say a prayer of thanks every day for their now-famous decision to prevent further cyanide poisonings by pulling Tylenol from the shelves—even though it could have devastated the company and their own careers?

Perhaps in our work we should practice the Native American philosophy of "generational thinking." The idea is simple, but the execution is difficult: Every decision we make must withstand seven generations previous and seven generations hence. That is, each must be rooted in the experience of the past and able to weather the scrutiny of the future.

Here's hoping the great majority of our decisions stand the test of time.

❋ **EDITOR'S NOTE:** *Mara Bovsun was a public relations executive in a competitive market that sometimes put more emphasis on pleasing the client than on truth. In the following essay, originally published in* Utne Reader, *Bovsun uses a satiric tone of voice (note such phrases as "no problem," "the Big Idea," and "the Publicist's Smile") to recount a turning point that led to a career switch. Bovsun now edits two biotechnology newsletters for McGraw-Hill in New York City. Juxtapose lessons of this piece with ones cited in the previous article by Greg Bustin. Bovsun's satire makes its points at the expense of* *public relations in general and tabloid reporting in particular. It is included here to show how it feels to experience success without values—a lesson that applies to all.*

The Silly Side of PR

Mara Bovsun, Former Public Relations Practitioner

My name is Mara and I am a recovering public relations executive. It's been four years since I left the business but from time to time I still have this recurring nightmare: In my dream I see a parade of old clients, dancing around me shrieking demands that I heard over my decade in PR:

"I want to you to get Liz Taylor, holding a can of Weight-Begone, on the cover of *Time.*"

"I want you to explain why passive smoke never hurt anyone."

"I wanna put the NFL on a diet."

After each one, I moan over and over, "Can I take you to lunch? Can I take you to lunch?"

Lunch is where we took clients to "brainstorm." Over pâtés and poached salmon, we'd toss around Big Ideas—such as a cookie-shaped hovercraft for a cookie company. After dessert, the highest-ranking person would flash the Publicist's Smile and we would then agree to do anything the client wanted. Roll an orange the size of a Manhattan apartment over the Brooklyn Bridge? Build a carousel of fabric softener boxes? Get Sylvester Stallone's mother to work out with talking dumbbells? No problem.

It was after one of these feedings that I came to the beginning of the end—the sad saga of the artificial penis.

The product addressed a real medical problem—impotence. At the time, the only option for afflicted men was implantation of a solid silicone rod, which gave erections—permanent ones. But this particular artificial penis had a series of chambers that let guys inflate and deflate at will.

It would have been easy to publicize this with a letter, at most a press kit. But the client wanted a Big Idea. So we came up with a press conference, featuring a World-Famous Sex Therapist and a panel of urologists to pump up the product. Nearly every local medical reporter planned to attend. But it all wasn't big enough for the client.

"I want major media. I want television cameras. I want networks. I wanna make history," he yelled into the phone. He later showed up at the office with a book about the sex secrets of famous people, and after a 15-minute brainstorming session we produced the following "teaser" (PRese for an invitation too titillating to resist). It said:

Napoleon
Vincent van Gogh
Jack London
Dwight Eisenhower

What did these historical figures have in common with 10,000,000 American men?

IMPOTENCE.

We knew this silly release was an invitation to disaster, so we printed 100, but delivered only one, just to be able to tell the client we did it. That evening in a bar I handed it to some tabloid reporters I knew. We all had a good laugh, another beer, and that was the end of that, or so we thought.

But on the day of the Big Idea conference, a reporter from the tabloid—a reporter I did not know—showed up. Through the long, technical presentations, he sat head in hands, seeming barely awake, not taking a single note. At the end, he sprang to life, pulled the "teaser" from his pocket, and asked the World-Famous Sex Therapist, "How do you know that Napoleon was impotent?"

The client, surrounded by his bosses, grabbed the invitation from the reporter's hand, charged over to us, and said, "I wanna know just whose idea this was."

It was his idea, of course, but there was no telling anyone that now.

At 6 A.M. the next day, a coworker was on the phone. "Did you see the morning *Daily News?*" he moaned.

There on page four, the *top* of page four, was a witty attack on the invitation, the company, and the entire pharmaceutical industry for shameless self-promotion. We were fired by the client immediately. I think we were actually fired four times, but I was too numb from alcohol, humiliation, and maintaining the Publicist's Smile to know for sure.

But that's not the end of the saga. The next day, the artificial penis showed up on the editorial page of the same paper as a cartoon with Napoleon standing on a cloud, shaking his fist, and Eisenhower, London, and van Gogh in the background. God is telling them, "Don't worry, boys. It's just a drug company trying to sell another infernal contraption."

After that, I kept at it for several years, smiling, always smiling.

I might still be there had it not been for the spaghetti account. I was asked to come up with a Big Idea for a pasta company's big problem. Homemakers could not cope with the many different pasta shapes they produced, and so some shapes were losing market share. Our solution? A Celebration of Pasta.

Having recently lost a close relative to cancer, I didn't feel like celebrating and the last thing I really cared about was the shape or the price of rigatoni. But I was presenting the program, smiling, when, during the part about a black-tie gala (feting bow-tie-shaped noodles), a woman with huge teeth stopped me. "Excuse me," she said. "What color will you make the sauce?"

For some reason, that was the question that sent me over the edge. I nearly blacked out, and could see nothing except for the woman's teeth, glowing alone in the darkened room. An associate had to finish the presentation.

My life in PR was over.

Bovsun has specific ethical recommendations for public relations majors. The following was in response to the question, Based on your experience, what can you tell students about maintaining values in the workplace?

Try to avoid actions that will kill or cripple your career. Lie to the press, for example, and you'll end up having a bad reputation, no media outlets, and no income. Don't participate in an event that shows bad taste, faulty judgment, or insensitivity.

Don't allow clients to twist your arm by using that time-honored tactic: "Do you want to keep our business?" All you will end up with is humiliation, a shoulder splint, and a client who is trying to skip on paying the bill. Another good tip: Make sure that you and your clients agree on what you will and won't do at the outset. Get it in writing, in a contract. A client who will not consider such a contract is no doubt up to no good, and you should run.

After a few years in the business, you'll be able to distinguish honorable clients who want you to communicate a message (yes, they do exist) from sleaze balls who want to hide behind you while they do some dirty work.

EDITOR'S NOTE: *Jean Cochran, anchor for National Public Radio's* Morning Edition, *describes the efforts that she and colleague Carl Kasell make trying to present true and balanced information in their weekday broadcasts. She notes that she was a student of veteran CBS editor Ed Bliss at American University. She adds, "I owe most of what I know about journalist standards to him."*

The Serious Side of NPR

Jean Cochran, Anchor, *National Public Radio*

My colleague Carl Kasell and I are responsible for writing and delivering our "product." We each must make all the decisions that go into putting the newscasts together. A producer works at pulling in reports and actualities (interview segments), organizing the sound to be used in each newscast. But then the newscaster decides where it will be placed and what else to write to make up the five full minutes. No commercials!

As I go over the wires, beginning at 3 A.M. each morning, I look for relevant stories—what's happening that day or strong enough to be reported on a continuing basis. My news standards have evolved over the years, beyond the basics I brought to the job to begin with. Carl and I often discuss stories, air our thoughts and questions about them. Neither of us cares for celebrity news or news of the weird. And we try to exercise some good taste, remembering that people are eating their Corn Flakes while listening to *Morning Edition*.

Perhaps as I decide what is "not appropriate," I belie some personal bias. But another way to put it is: We each bring our own set of sensibilities to the job and we should use them.

So many factors enter in during the decision-making process. The questions we ask ourselves include: *Who cares? Should we care, and if so, why? Is there another side to this story?* And sometimes, *How on earth can I tell this entire story fairly in less than a minute?*

There has definitely been a trend toward tabloid journalism among the general media. I suppose it sells, but I am thankful that the news organization I'm with is concerned only with putting out a quality product and not selling deodorant. This gives us the freedom at National Public Radio to concentrate on pure, basic journalism.

A newswriter has to maintain objectivity, but true objectivity is impossible. You don't check your "humanity" at the door when you come to work. Quite the opposite, I believe you must apply it.

EDITOR'S NOTE: *In the following piece, Teena Holland—former broadcaster, college spokesperson, and now a reporter—recounts the lesson she learned about humanity from a low point in her career.*

The Fatality

Teena Holland, Reporter, *The Canton (Ohio) Repository*

I hate working on Sundays. The 2 P.M. to 11 P.M. shift is a pain. Only one person works Sunday to cover general news and cop stuff. It's up to that person to cover all of the death, plague, and destruction that has happened since midnight. Either the shift is *so* busy that I spend most of the time scurrying to gather facts and find quotable sources or it's so boring that I could read *War and Peace* by 8 P.M.

This day was leaning towards boring. The only item of interest to write about was a traffic fatality involving two cars and six people. The dispatcher from the Ohio Highway Patrol, my official source, said the driver of the first car was killed and the driver and four passengers of the second car had minor injuries and were treated and released from local hospitals.

There was my story. That was the way I wrote it.

Walking into the newsroom the next day was like walking into a lion's den, and I was a fresh-cooked slab of ribs. There were messages posted to my terminal, posted on my phone, my voice mail, and E-mail. Editors wanted to talk. Evidently, something was drastically wrong with my fatality story.

The person reported to be dead was actually dead. Don't get me wrong. I wouldn't wish death upon anyone. (Let's not even think about a lawsuit filed by John Doe's friends and relatives seeking punitive damages for unnecessary emotional turmoil.)

Unfortunately, my mistake was equally as serious. The driver and passengers in the other car weren't "treated and released," as I had written. All but one were still in the hospital in guarded condition with various serious injuries. A mother and her twin teenage daughters were in guarded condition. A third teenager was also in pretty bad shape. To make matters worse, they were all driving to church on that dreaded Sunday morning. So the church, the daughter's classmates, and let's face it, everyone who knew them, had it out for the reporter who couldn't get her facts straight.

What went wrong? After doing some serious head-hunting, I found out that the Highway Patrol reports classify all victims by the extent of their injuries. A person either has "visible injuries" or "minor visible injuries" or are simply "dead." Obviously, a highway patrolman isn't a doctor, so an internal injury is a "minor visible injury" in his eyes. Therefore, when the dispatcher told me victims had "minor visible injuries," I should have checked with the hospital just to be sure. Also, it's not the Highway Patrol's job to follow up on accident victims, so the dispatcher was just speculating that they were treated and released.

After pounding out a correction and listing the conditions of the four people, I scowled through the rest of the day and prayed that I could put this issue behind me. Quietly I sat in the next morning's staff meeting, hoping no one would mention the course of events that led me to this low point in my career. I leafed through the paper, wondering if my new story was buried on page G-12 or if it had run on the front page, where the original, inaccurate fatality story had run just the day before. The story was in the front of the local news section. Good. The ending jumped to the next page— just two columns away from a photo of a high school couple heading off to their prom. There, in black and white, was a girl whose name looked all too familiar.

I rechecked the accident update and, yep, it was the same girl. The photo was just supposed to be one of those happy pictures we run to show the public that even a big, important newspaper has room enough to cover proms and kids and duckies in a pond. *Why did this picture have to run today?* This good-looking, all-American girl in the photo taken just a few days before was now lying in guarded condition with multiple skull fractures.

I put my head down on the table and choked back a scream.

The moral to be learned from my painful experience, if it's not already obvious, is to double check facts and make sure you contact the right source. Only a firefighter or investigator can give you the cause of a fire, only a coroner knows the cause of death, and only a hospital spokesperson can give you the condition of a patient.

As for the unfortunate photo mishap, what can I say? It wasn't my fault, but it taught me that names in the news are not only facts. They are people, too.

❧ **EDITOR'S NOTE:** *Free-lance writer Robert Neuwirth discusses a turning point in his career that led to stronger values about truth versus belief. His essay originally appeared in the trade magazine* Editor & Publisher *and makes reference to the libel case of* Jeffrey M. Masson *versus* Janet Malcolm, *a writer for the* New Yorker. *The suit, which went through several appeals, concerns a profile of Masson in a two-part 1983 article titled "Trouble in the Archives." Malcolm was accused of fabricating quotations—a charge she has called "ludicrous." Neuwirth also makes reference to a Malcolm book,* The Journalist and the Murderer *(Vintage, 1990), which she wrote about a fraud and breach of contract suit filed by a convicted murderer, seeking to clear his name, against journalist Joe McGinniss.*

The Journalist and the Joyrider

Robert Neuwirth, Free-Lance Writer

All reporters, deep down, love good stories. I admit, I love murder. I love tragedy. I love sexy trials. I love political corruption. I love exposing the emperor's new clothes.

Working on a good story is like joyriding in a sports car after having spent your life in a sedan—you want to floor it, patch out, thrash the transmission, put the beast through its paces.

Janet Malcolm undoubtedly saw Jeffrey Masson as a good story. Her profile in the *New Yorker* was devastating. At issue in court and appeals has been whether Malcolm libeled Masson by using quotes that were not backed up by her notes or tapes. Certainly, all journalists should take note of the case. However, there is another concern, one that has not gotten much attention—except, ironically, from Malcolm herself: the issue of bad faith.

I know all about bad faith. I have been guilty of it many times. So have most reporters I know.

I have paid for stories when I knew my money was being used to buy drugs the minute I left the scene. I have deliberately misled people I was interviewing—sometimes putting on a show of sympathy to get juicier quotes.

I have delayed calling people I was writing about until the last possible moment, trying to catch them off guard. I have hidden scoops from my competitors and lied to them about it.

I am not proud about any of this, but I can assure you that, in each case, I thought I was doing my job.

A few years ago, though, that all changed. An editor put me in touch with a man who had had a stroke. He talked haltingly, with a stutter. He could take 15 minutes to find one word. However, this was a big improvement. For almost a year after his stroke, he had been unable to speak at all.

I spent hours with him to make sure I had his story right: He believed the corrupt leaders of his municipal union had poisoned him.

I began to check his account. It was all circumstantial. He had been a member of a dissident union faction. The union president had been accused of corruption, but none of the other dissidents had come down with a mysterious illness, and there was no known drug that could have caused his symptoms.

As I worked, I decided to pursue a different, more compelling story— the story of a man who had made the arduous journey back from a stroke and was now trying to make sense of his illness.

I told him, over and over, that I was not going to write the story he wanted me to write. He always agreed and then returned to his central theme: This happened to him. It was fact. All I had to do was write it down the way he rehearsed it.

I realized then the difference between his goal and mine. He came to me for vindication. If I told his story, his ideas would be legitimized, his world affirmed. I came to him looking for a good story. I wanted to joyride.

Ultimately, I decided not to write about his case. No story is more important than the person it is about. I am not saying that journalists should cover up for corrupt politicians because an article might hurt their feelings. But I do believe that if we are going to expose someone in print, we have an obligation to tell them what we think— face to face if possible. We do not let them hide in their houses and offices. So why should we be able to hide behind our pages?

I imagine many journalists will argue that a person who talks with a reporter knows the risks. But I think most people, even the most self-assured, talk to reporters because they want their side of events recorded. They want to be proved right and, if you treat your sources as friends, you owe it to them to tell them straight out what you think.

That is why it was wrong for Joe McGinniss not to tell Jeffrey MacDonald, the subject of his true-crime book *Fatal Vision*, that McGinniss believed MacDonald had murdered his wife and kids.

MacDonald had opened up to McGinniss, had made the author part of his life, and McGinniss had betrayed that trust, not by writing the book but by hiding his conclusions from the man he was writing about.

In her book on the McGinniss-MacDonald dispute, Malcolm says all reporters are, in essence, charlatans "preying on people's vanity, ignorance or loneliness, gaining their trust and then betraying them without remorse."

She suggests that we should feel "some compunction about the exploitative character of the journalist-subject relationship."

Indeed we should. So should she. Malcolm spent hours talking with Masson, even putting him up at her house, as if she were his friend.

Ultimately, she concluded that Masson was, in some of her nicer words, "impudent," "complicated," and "unruly," but she never told him. To Masson, it appeared that Malcolm had hooked him in and then, with no warning, vilified him. I am sure he felt it was an unprovoked attack.

Certainly, fabricating quotes is wrong. Stitching them together in a dishonest way is wrong. But I am afraid that most journalists will dismiss the Malcolm-Masson case as a simple matter of libel and lose sight of the ethical point: *Being a journalist does not mean you stop being a person.*

✖ **EDITOR'S NOTE:** *John Kaplan, Pulitzer Prize–winning photographer, documented Police Officer Victor "Kojak" Balsamico being consoled by a motorcycle policeman moments after "Kojak"—his preferred name—had to kill a suspect in a Pittsburgh office building. The following interviews with Kaplan and Balsamico focus on the friendship that resulted between the men because of that photograph.*

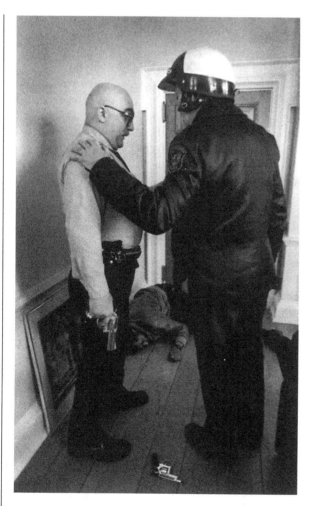

Compassionate Cop

Friends Ever Since

John Kaplan, Photojournalist

We heard on the scanner that there had been a shooting in a Pittsburgh office building. When we got there, a man had shot his estranged wife in the leg and she had run out of the room, screaming. Then the man holed himself up in a back room. Kojak decided to go in and confront the man, and a second officer stayed behind for backup. Kojak says that the gunman raised his weapon and began to pull the trigger. We heard the shot but didn't know who had shot whom until Kojak yelled to the other officer, "Get in here, he's down." This picture was taken just 15 seconds after the shooting. You can see that Kojak is literally in shock. The other photographer with me was shooting from a different angle, and you can actually see the gunman's eyes closing on one of his frames. That evening, Kojak actually went to visit the mother of the man he killed. He's a very caring and moral person. We've been friends ever since.

Victor "Kojak" Balsamico, Police Officer

The sad truth is that there are police officers who are good and bad, just as there are good and bad bankers, lawyers [and journalists]. But people respond to stereotypes about police. As for journalists, they have been forced by competition to focus on tragedies, rather than showing this side of tragedy. Compassion. It's society, too. Today we have people at home with camcorders waiting to witness someone failing out a window. On that day, God put John Kaplan on the spot to take that photo. Finally I had the courage to look at it and I still thank God for what this photo reflected about me. The only tragedy is that I didn't go immediately to see the man's mother. But that evening, our meeting was the most beautiful thing. The woman actually comforted me, and this was her son that died.

V A L U E S E X E R C I S E S

1. Make a list of your highs, lows, and turning points in life. Next to each item on that list—a minimum of 10—write a 50- to 100-word statement about a peak experience or epiphany associated with that incident. (Or write a statement about your lack of a peak experience or epiphany—that is, an incident with which you are still coming to terms.)

   Example: Turning Point: *Cancer. Someone I care about was diagnosed with skin cancer. I took her to some of her treatments.* Epiphany: *I should stop worrying about small hassles in my life and set some priorities.*

2. Write another 50- to 100-word statement pertaining to each item on your list of highs, lows, and turning points. Discuss whether the experience has influenced your perception and whether you have accepted the consequences thereof.

   Example: The person who had skin cancer recovered fully. I tend to think that people can overcome the ravages of disease if they catch it in time and seek treatment. Of course, in an age of AIDS, I realize that this turning point may have overinfluenced me in this regard. As for consequences, I will have to adjust for this bias by not blaming individuals who become ill but by informing them about symptoms and treatments.

3. Finally, under each item, write a short statement articulating the lesson you learned from the experience.

Example: Lesson: *Live life to the fullest because it is short and precious.*

Note: In formulating your responses, keep in mind the concepts of appropriate or inappropriate disclosures. In other words, as shown in the preceding examples, be discrete and do not violate your own or someone else's privacy for the purpose of completing homework. If you find that you cannot do this assignment without violating your own or someone else's privacy, do it for your own development rather than as homework or share only those items you feel *are* appropriate.

Part II

Testing Your
Ethical Base

In this section you will read about concepts and encounter situations to test your value system. Only then will you know how well your principles will serve you in the workplace. You will study several types of falsehoods, from seemingly innocent white lies in everyday dealings to global ones in propaganda. You will learn about different types of hoaxes and methods to defuse them, and you will confront issues such as plagiarism and racism that may tempt or repel you. As in the last section, each chapter contains advice from, interviews with, and essays by working professionals from all sequences, whose views may challenge your awareness and strengthen your values.

4

Lies

Everyday Lies

As noted in the last chapter, truth is the foundation on which to build a value system. Lies, however, undermine that foundation so that it cannot support other values, such as honor or honesty, and taint perception, compelling us to control instead of analyze outside forces. Journalists lead pressure-packed lives because of competition and conflicts of interest and sometimes take ethical shortcuts, such as lying, to fulfill obligations. Yet they have a moral obligation to serve the public, as you learned in Chapter 2. Some media critics argue that journalists are losing sight of that responsibility and blame them in part for disseminating lies to the populace and contributing to social problems instead of helping to solve them.

A lie is damaging enough when one person deceives another. However, that same lie communicated to millions by mass media has much greater impact. It can undermine American values. On a good day, 99 percent of what a person reads in the newspaper or hears on radio or television news *may have been said* by officials, lawyers, experts, and other sources. It is accurate in that regard. But what percentage of these quotations is actually true? Magazines, advertising, and public relations agencies may be directing their slanted truths at targeted audiences, but what percentage of those messages—circulated to households via subscription or direct mail or broadcast over public airwaves—reach the *wrong* audience?

What happens to a society that hears its president say, "I am not a crook," as Richard M. Nixon did shortly before he resigned in 1974 because of knowledge about the Watergate break-in? What happens to a society that hears its evangelists condemn pornography and adultery and then be scandalized, such as Jimmy Swaggart of Jimmy Swaggart Ministries in 1988 (for associating with alleged prostitutes) and Jim Bakker of the PTL Network in

101

1989 (for funneling hush money to Jessica Hahn)? What happens to a society that hears its idols passionately maintain innocence only to admit wrongdoing later, as Olympic skater Tonya Harding did in 1993, disavowing knowledge of the attack on rival Nancy Kerrigan? What happens to a society that hears talk- and tab-shows sensationalize gossip and celebrate rumormongers, presenting opinions as fact?

Charles E. Shepard, Pulitzer Prize–winning reporter for the *Charlotte Observer*, has attempted to explain why public figures sometimes behave in such fashion. In his 1989 book on Jim Bakker, *Forgiven*, Shepard writes:

> I believe the answer can be found in a psychological profile with remarkable parallels to Bakker's conduct and life story: the narcissistic personality disorder. . . . A person of this personality type is self-centered and grandiose. He has a remarkable lack of interest in and empathy for others even though he is eager to win their love and admiration. Typically, his value system is corruptible and his relationships with others exploitative, sometimes even parasitic, although the individual may not recognize it. "It is as if they feel they have the right to control and possess others and to exploit them without guilt."[1]

What are the social consequences when media idols such as Jim Bakker lie and reporters and writers disseminate those lies? When advertising uses sex to sell toothpaste or beer? When public relations launches campaigns promoting harmful products or evading liability? When photojournalists stage pictures? The power of the lie has increased multifold in the past 30 years. Communication has advanced from magnetic tape, three networks, and antennas to CD-ROMs, cable conglomerates, and Internet, reaching billions of people worldwide. Could it be that citizens are so bombarded by questionable or misdirected messages or influenced by value systems of fallen heroes that they no longer can distinguish between truth and falsehood?

That is the opinion of scholar and writer Hayden Carruth:

> Constantly we are told that this or that commercial product or service, or even this or that candidate for office, is "better," when we know it cannot be true. . . . Children today are taught, in lessons compounded every five minutes, that untruth may be uttered with impunity, even with approval. Lying has become a way of life, very nearly now *the* way of life, in our society. The average adult American of average :intelligence and average education believes almost nothing communicated to him in language, and the disbelief has become so ingrained that he or she does not even notice it.[2]

Carruth's assertion was tested in an ethics class at Ohio University. The standard attendance policy was changed. Students used to be allowed a maximum of three excused absences associated with illness, student-group travel, or emergencies, as defined in the student handbook. Now students are allowed to miss as many classes as they like, as long as they deliver a written excuse explaining the reason *truthfully* and *appropriately*. All excuses are accepted as long as they are presented in such manner. Consequences for lying, however, are stiff. A student caught in a lie regarding an absence could fail the course.

As soon as the attendance policy was instituted, reasons for missing class changed dramatically. Under the old policy, with enrollment approaching 100, "illness" accounted for almost 70 percent of some 200 absences per quarter (with class travel, scheduling conflicts, and unexcused absences making up most of the remaining 30 percent.) Here are results from the winter 1992 class, the first to use the new policy:

Career-related conflicts	32%	(Interviewing for jobs or writing, reporting)
Academic-related conflicts	24%	(Homework for other classes)
Family-related conflicts	14%	(Emergencies, weddings, reunions)
Romance-related conflicts	10%	(Valentine's Day, rendezvous)
Health-related conflicts	10%	(Sickness, medical/dental appointments)
Death in immediate family	4%	(Parents, siblings, uncles/aunts, grandparents)
Other	4%	

These excerpts from students' notes explain *real* reasons for missing class:

- "Tomorrow is the 19th anniversary of *Roe* v. *Wade*, and I am trying to put together a story tying that in with the possibility of the Supreme Court overturning the decision."
- "I missed class today because I had an interview with Thomson Newspapers!"
- "I won't be in class today because being the incredibly disorganized person I am, I lost notes on a paper I have due today, and I have to redo my research!"
- "I am a bridesmaid in my cousin's wedding. . . . *If* I attended class, I would miss the rehearsal."
- "I am going out of town to a bed and breakfast for the weekend. I planned this getaway long ago. It's something I've always wanted to do: enjoy a quiet weekend in a cozy 19th-century home with 12-foot-high ceilings, poster beds, and fireplaces in every bedroom. And snow outside adds extra romance to the weekend."

- "I will not be attending class today because my buddies and I are going to Lansing, Michigan, to drink beer, kiss boys, and engage in general collegiate merrymaking."
- "I've got to pack to go home for the weekend. . . . I'm going home because it's Valentine's Day and I can't stand my boyfriend. How's that for honesty?"

Not bad.

Students who missed class because of illness also wrote honest-sounding letters, brief and matter of fact. Ones who lost family members wrote letters or notes too private to share. The experimental policy was adopted officially because as soon as students started telling the truth, their attendance also increased—by as much as 50 percent in one class. Data for subsequent classes vary only by a few percentage points, depending on such factors as holidays (e.g., Valentine's Day) and special events (e.g., job conferences). A few conclusions can be drawn. When students are mindful about telling the truth, they begin to realize their priorities: too much emphasis on romance, perhaps, and not enough on academics. For our purposes, however, the experiment shows how easily students under the old policy lied about illness—to an ethics teacher, no less—because they felt the system demanded it. As Hayden Carruth indicated in his earlier citation, many of these aspiring journalists probably told their white lies without even realizing they were doing so.

Concepts and Consequences

Just as there are several types of truths, from facts to archetypes, there are several types of lies:

- *White lies.* White lies are untrue statements about seemingly minor topics told to flatter or spare the liar or another person or group of persons pain, embarrassment, or some other uncomfortable feeling.
- *Half-truths.* Half-truths are statements that contain a mix of falsehoods and truths meant to mislead the listener or provide the liar with an escape route, if challenged.
- *Exaggerations.* Exaggerations inflate out of proportion a small truth, not for the social good—as satire intends—but to make the journalist's job or assignment easier or more significant.
- *Falsehoods.* Falsehoods are complete lies or fabrications masquerading as truth.[3]

Each type of lie has its own set of consequences, depending on the lie in question and the person(s) it deceives or affects. The liar has to face consequences, too, depending on his or her conscience and whether he or she is exposed. In her book *Lying: Moral Choice in Public and Private Life,* philosopher Sissela Bok states: "Most lies *do* have negative consequences for liars, dupes, all those affected, and for the social trust. And when liars evaluate these consequences, they are peculiarly likely to be biased; their calculations frequently go astray."[4]

As Bok notes in her book, a person who tells or condones white lies usually believes they are harmless. However, because liars usually fail to foresee consequences, their views about white lies often are flawed. Nonetheless, many people condone white lies, deeming them well intended or compassionate. For example, a friend who relies on you for homework puts you on the spot one day and asks, "Do you think I am lazy?" You might feel tempted to respond with a white lie: "Not at all." But friendship should be based on truth. If you are uncomfortable with that question, you can respond, "What I think doesn't matter, what *you* think *does*," or "I don't like to answer questions like that," or "I wish you wouldn't rely on me to help with homework," or some other prudent, discrete, or truthful reply. Some people would justify telling a white lie in this instance because they might feel a truthful comment could hurt the friend's feelings. But there are consequences for that.

Hugh Culbertson, researcher and public relations expert, says, "If our friends come to realize that we have complimented them insincerely, they may put little stock in future compliments. As a result, the compliments may lose their meaning. And friendships may even be endangered."

White lies also occur at the workplace. Journalists tell white lies to each other and to sources and clients every day, depending on the circumstances. In an *Inc.* magazine poll of businesspeople, 37 percent of respondents thought that the following white lie was acceptable: "Pretending your company has divisions to make it look bigger to clients and suppliers."[5] The view is widely held. For instance, a popular advertisement for a chain of photocopying outlets features a harried businesswoman and male colleague using services and then allowing a potential client to believe their staff is larger than it actually is. What would be the consequences if the client learned later about such a deception in a billing statement? What would happen if the client believed the company in question was as large as the liars indicated? Would the client increase the order so that a bid or contract have to be changed and hours spent preparing the old one written off as a loss? Would the small staff or division have to put in unpaid overtime to meet commitments? Of course, the advertisement doesn't address such scenarios. It just wants businesspeople to use its services when they are in a bind in a strange city. In doing so, it also communicates a white lie to millions of *non*businesspeople watching network television and it sets an example.

Sometimes marketers communicate white lies to guise other problems. In the publishing business, this often results in preselling an imaginary product. "One of the constant struggles for me as a writer is the ethics, or lack of ethics, concerning illusions that foster sales," says Rita Schweitz, magazine writer and book author. She relates an incident that happened at a booksellers' convention while waiting to meet a senior acquisitions editor for a major publisher: "On the display floor, I noticed an attractive book display—a hardcover title by a big-name expert in his field. Since the editor had often given me sample copies of books, I took the liberty to pick up a copy from the display to browse while I waited. But when I removed the shrink wrapping and opened the book, the text was on an altogether different subject. Only the dust jacket was new—the book itself was an overstocked backlist title used for the mock-up display."

Preselling titles before they have been printed is common practice, Schweitz acknowledges, "so I wasn't totally shocked that the publishing house was selling an imaginary product." But she adds that this particular manuscript hadn't even been delivered yet to the publisher. Schweitz followed up on the book's progress. "Two months later," she notes, "the editor mentioned that he was under the pressure of a tight deadline. Referring to the book, he said, 'The manuscript came in weak, so I'm having to beef it up.'"

In this case, one white lie led to another. "The publisher first sold the surface illusion of a significant book," Schweitz says, "then filled it with content written by someone other than the expert whose name was used to generate sales. The book received a tremendous marketing push, but I found the final product repetitive and sensationalized."

Consequences in this case also are obvious. The editor might justify the practice as a harmless lie because the new book was not yet written but on the way. Then that white lie was compounded by others: promoting the book as significant when it actually was weak and working against a tight deadline to produce the book when sellers thought it was in stock and available. Moreover, authors who know about such practices may have less respect for the publishing house and either bargain more aggressively or sign with a rival, putting the emphasis on marketing instead of writing. That can have a serious impact on future acquisitions and profit margins.

Like white lies, half-truths might seem innocent or occur in the most innocent-sounding stories. Pam Noles, reporter for the *Tampa Tribune*, recalls a story about a grocer decorating his yard for Halloween. "His display featured a black effigy hanging from the oak tree in his front yard. Next to the hanged man stood a figure in a white robe and a hood. A reporter was dispatched, collected quotations from the man about the mongrelization of America caused by 'niggers, the Zionist threat, and the need for whites to be proud and ready to fight.' That story was written, cleared by the bureau editor, and sent up the chain. But it ran the next morning with all the racial overtones removed. An editor in the main office decided the racial angle had nothing to do with the story and would only upset people."

Noles adds, "Sometimes we can only tell part of the truth."

Consider the impact of such a lie on African American reporters. The whole truth about the grocer's yard display might have angered racist readers or distracted from the Halloween angle of the assignment. But it also dampened spirit, at least temporarily, in the newsroom. Says Noles, "I entered journalism with the dream of gathering facts and, in the telling, exposing truth. But often I have no power as a reporter." Beyond morale, half-truths can set an example for reporters and editors about how to cover future related stories and eventually lead to loss of credibility.

Half-truths involve withholding information, providing a partial picture. Exaggeration involves inflating truth, providing a full but imaginary picture. Both misrepresent reality. In the *Inc.* magazine poll cited earlier, 34 percent of business employees under age 35 said they told the truth *all of the time*, compared with 54 percent of those over age 45. The study also quotes a participant who says, "Sometimes you gotta do what you gotta do to get started."[6] The comment implies that it is all right for a beginning professional to exaggerate skills or experience to become established in the business world.

Let's test that notion in a case study: You are an advertiser making a pitch to a potential client concerned about your lack of experience. You need her account. But the potential client says that she won't give her business to any agency that hasn't conducted a half dozen successful similar campaigns. You have handled only two such accounts. So you can show her the quality of your work but you will have to exaggerate it to get her business. Moreover, you can justify exaggerating your experience because you have done three campaigns for local appliance dealers. Do you exaggerate or tell the truth?

"Come clean and admit that you have limited experience," recommends Grant Castle, president of Castle Underwood agency in New York City. "It usually takes getting caught in an exaggeration or lie early in a career to cause sleepless nights and dysfunctional days. Hopefully it happens early enough in a career to be written off as 'youthful enthusiasm.'" Castle notes that the consequences of being caught in an exaggeration outweigh the immediate benefits. "You're going to be in the business a long time. Every new business meeting you have may not be a win, but you have the chance to impress people in the pitch who will remember you later on, perhaps after they have moved to another company. That's really how you get into pitches." Clients have long memories. "Making a 'cooked' presentation won't set you up well for the future," Castle adds.

Public relations practitioners must be especially mindful about credibility because they work on a continuing basis with the news media. Caught in a fabrication, practitioners can face dire consequences. Reporters who work with such individuals may no longer trust basic information and may suspect or reject every release instead of disseminating it on good faith in a rewrite. Reporters may feel they have to cover events themselves and are not likely to make time when the practitioner beckons.

Lisa Richwine, a reporter for States News Service in Washington, DC, writes for newspapers in southern and western states and often relies on press secretaries for information and story leads about Congress. She questions the credibility of staff workers "who issue statements from members of Congress with completely fabricated quotes." According to Richwine, "Often the lawmakers don't even see the words attributed to them."

Richwine recalls an incident involving the press secretary of a congressman on her beat. A group of local officials from the congressman's district came to Washington, and the press secretary issued a release quoting him and the officials. The release implied that "the delegation had come to Washington and were working with each other and the congressman to bring economic benefits to the district," Richwine says. "What actually happened was the five or six officials came to town for the same convention but refused to work together and were fighting," trying to arrange separate meetings with the congressman and other officials. "It's a constant problem in their area," Richwine notes. "Local officials have such big egos that they frequently forsake progress for the sake of pride."

The congressman and his staff were frustrated with the officials.

> So the press secretary issued the press release hoping that I would write a story saying they were working together and that they [local officials] would get the hint that this was what the congressman wanted. The funniest thing about the whole incident is that the press secretary, with whom I have a very friendly relationship, told me, off the record of course, that she fabricated the whole release. But she didn't appear to think it was wrong. She told me, "Just so I would know what was going on," but still thought I would write the story the way she wanted it. There wasn't much of a dilemma for me. I decided I wouldn't write anything unless I could talk to the officials myself.

In the end, Richwine decided she didn't have time for that assignment.

All these lies come with consequences that affect or influence society or the practice of journalism. White lies lead to more significant ones. Half-truths hurt. Exaggerations can taint a career and falsehoods can destroy credibility. Moreover, as Sissela Bok writes, there are "risks to the liar himself of personal discomfort and loss of integrity, of a greater likelihood, however slight, of having to lie again to shore up the first lie; and of a somewhat diminished resistance to lying for causes he may wish to further in the future."[7]

Visual Lies

People make photographs. Photographs lie in all the ways people do. With modern technology, a photographer can remove a distracting diploma in a dentist's office and convey the white lie of a blank wall for background. The photographer can digitally remove a boy from the dentist's chair and place a girl there instead, conveying a half-truth as the dentist hovers over the wrong patient. Or the photographer can fabricate the entire shot, asking the dentist to pretend she is pulling a tooth and the boy to pretend he is crying.

"In the 1950s, because of slow film, newspaper photographers began setting up photographs the way magazines were doing it, following the example of *Life* and other publications," says Terry Eiler, photojournalism professor with 16 years' experience shooting assignments for *National Geographic*.[8]

> Some photographers at these magazines back then made pictures that just were too good to be true. For example, I remember one of a parent chasing a bare-assed child down the hallway. The parent was just coming into focus in the right-hand corner and the kid was in the upper left corner turning down and right into a second hallway. The kid was multiple-strobe-lit (or flashed) and was turning to a cross-lit-strobe (or flash). It seemed set up the same way Norman Rockwell would set up a portrait. The kid actually may have done that, but this was a picture that *illustrated* the story when it was supposed to *document* it.

Therein is the deception. The picture suggests that the photographer spent the day observing the mother and child for a good shot when the photographer may simply have orchestrated the shot because the editor wanted to illustrate a story with a Rockwellian motif. "These types of pictures still exist and are set up to illustrate text or a theme," Eiler says. "Some leading newspapers have said that they won't illustrate documentary journalism, and if they do, they'll note that it is an illustration for their readers."

CROSSING THE LINE IN PHOTOJOURNALISM

The above picture was taken by photojournalist Terry Eiler as a documentary photo. He came upon the cowboy, horse, and bus, and shot the picture as a documentary. Ethically, he could use it as a portrait of the particular cowboy or as an illustration to accompany text. On the line below, there are three types of photographs: documentary, portraiture, illustration. Documentary photos can move from left to right without an explanatory note. Portraiture is the fulcrum or center between documentary and illustration and contains elements of both. Illustration cannot move to the left and masquerade as a documentary without an explanatory note; neither can illustration move to the left and masquerade as portraiture if it has been digitally altered without an explanatory note.

| Documentary | Portraiture | Illustration |

One of those newspapers is the *Los Angeles Times*. In 1994, a photographer there shot a documentary of a Los Angeles firefighter splashing his head with water from an in-ground swimming pool during a firestorm that consumed a luxury home behind him. The *Times* was planning to enter the shot for a Pulitzer Prize when the authenticity of the photograph was questioned. After an editor investigated rumors, the photographer was accused of fabricating the photograph—a charge that he denied. Nonetheless, the photographer was suspended without pay for one week. In an article about the suspension by Howard Kurtz, published in the *Washington Post*, the photographer said, "I deny categorically asking or telling any fireman to pose for me in front of a pool. I may have been guilty of saying this would make a nice shot, but to the best of my recollection, I did not directly ask him to do that. . . . I've been doing breaking news stories for years and years and I've never in my life set up a picture."[9]

The lesson in this case does not concern whether the photographer did or did not set up the shot, nor does it concern whether he lied or told the truth about the circumstances surrounding the picture. The example merely shows the consequences that can accompany suspected set-ups. The photographer was in the process of being nominated for a Pulitzer Prize when the allegations arose. Instead of receiving the acclaim that comes with such an honor, he was disciplined. Moreover, the *Times* asked the Associated Press to notify its clients nationwide that the photograph should not be used again.

"Photojournalists take these issues very seriously," says Terry Eiler, who teaches in the School of Visual Communications at Ohio University. Any student who knowingly sets up a shot and passes it off as a documentary can be suspended or expelled. "Once we had a student who was covering a dancer and followed him into the bathroom," Eiler recalls. "The photographer staged a shot, asking the dancer to practice in the bathroom in front of the mirror. We found out it was a set-up. We could have thrown him out of school." But Eiler did not take action because nobody had told the student that this was a visual lie. On another assignment, the same student was overheard telling a railroad worker to walk past a train after a derailment. "When I asked him about it, he said, 'No, No. It happened. I just missed the frame.' I told the student, '*Stop right there,*'" Eiler recalls. Again, he did not suspend the photographer because the student did not know that even this was unethical. "Thereafter the student took a real interest in ethics," Eiler says. "Twelve years later he won the Pulitzer Prize, is one of our prized graduates, and a leading voice about ethics in our profession." That student was John Kaplan whose comments and photo (Compassionate Cop) appear in the previous chapter.

"In my case," Kaplan says, "I set up what I thought was an innocuous picture and I learned from that experience the consequences of that mistake. But I never knew it was a mistake because nobody taught me. I had learned about photojournalism from some very talented successful people. In those days, 20 years ago, it was more acceptable to pose a picture. I actually was taught that if a situation isn't quite pleasing enough to help create it to make it so. Then I got to college and realized that this is a serious ethical problem." Kaplan says the derailment photo is a good case study for aspiring photojournalists. "Even though it doesn't seem like a serious crime, it might make people who witnessed me doing that question the credibility of any picture I would take."

"It was a hard lesson," he adds. "But I'm glad I learned it in college."

Questionable Lies

Should the U.S. government lie to the news media and disseminate propaganda to save lives? Should a reporter ever lie to get a story if that story saves lives? These so-called questionable lies test value systems of otherwise moral people who tell them in the name of the national interest or the public's right to know. Some ethicists are absolutists when it comes to lying, believing—as did the eighteenth-century philosopher Immanuel Kant—that any lie for any reason, however noble, is immoral and destroys a person's dignity.[10]

Contemporary philosopher Sissela Bok says in rare instances—ones that people seldom face—lying can be considered as ethical as self-defense. She analyzes this case study: "A captain of a ship transporting fugitives from Nazi Germany, if asked by a patrolling vessel whether there were any Jews on board would, for Kant's critics, have been justified in answering No. His duty to the fugitives, they claim, would then have conflicted with the duty to speak the truth and would have far outweighed it. In fact, in times of such crisis, those who share Kant's opposition to lying clearly put innocent persons at the mercy of wrongdoers."[11] Bok, in essence, suggests that such lies are rare but can be told providing they contribute to an important moral goal that cannot be attained without lying.

Some government officials use that logic to justify propaganda. For instance, telling the truth to the media about the Allied invasion at Normandy in 1944 would have been disastrous because Germans would have learned about and prepared for the assault. But this historic incident is the exception, not the rule; as in personal life, nations seldom face such crises as the Allies did on D-Day, so that lying can be considered a moral "self-defense."

This leads to a more recent and disputable situation. In the mid-1980s, a controversy arose about government officials practicing *disinformation* (from the Russian word *dezinformatsiya,* which means spreading false information for political gain). Eventually, the U.S. government acknowledged that it had adopted such a policy against Libyan leader Moammar Gadhafi. To justify this deception, then Secretary of State George Shultz drew parallels between Allied efforts against Nazi Germany.[12]

Many reporters did not agree with that analogy. The circumstances and stakes differed substantially, they argued, between this country's war with Germany and our undeclared one with Libya. Several reporters, including John Walcott of the *Wall Street Journal,* noted the consequences of such a policy: "By mounting a campaign of deception on Libya, and now, in effect, bragging about their ability to distort the truth to frighten Mr. Gadhafi, Secretary of State George Shultz and other top administration officials have removed world attention from Libya's own actions, even some top administration officials concede. Instead, interest now is focused on whether anyone should believe anything the administration says about Col. Gadhafi."[13]

Deceiving citizens of a democracy to protect democracy is contradictory, according to Sissela Bok. Officials who promote deception

> are always susceptible to bias. They overestimate the likelihood that the benefit will occur and that the harm will be averted; they underestimate the chances that the deceit will be discovered and ignore the effects of such a discovery on the public trust; they underrate the comprehension of the deceived citizens, as well as their ability and their right to make a reasoned choice. And, most important, such a benevolent self-righteousness disguises the many motives for political lying which could not serve as moral excuses: the need to cover up past mistakes; the vindictiveness; the desire to stay in power.[14]

Bok's analysis also applies in part to journalists who lie to get stories, interviews, sound bites, photos, accounts, clients, and free-lance or other assignments. They, too, can be susceptible to bias. They, too, can overestimate the likelihood that their efforts will benefit the public and underestimate the comprehension of the sources they deceive in the name of the public good. Worse, journalists can be as self-righteous as politicians and are just as quick to justify their behavior. Journalists who lie in the pursuit of truth usually are no better morally than politicians who deceive citizens to preserve democracy.

So-called questionable lies are rare. They happen once or twice in a typical media career. Usually there are other alternatives besides lying to resolve dilemmas involving important moral goals. Problems arise, however, when a journalist cannot perceive those alternatives because his or her perception has become skewed. Moreover, questionable lies also come with consequences, as you will learn in the Living Ethics items.

In sum, lies test values and limit choices. The common motto "Truth will set you free" underscores that notion and constitutes the essence of the First Amendment and free press.

ENDNOTES

1. Charles E. Shepard, *Forgiven* (New York: Atlantic Monthly Press, 1989), p. 554.

2. Hayden Carruth, "Poetry in a discouraging time: A symposium," *The Georgia Review*, Winter 1981, p. 739.

3. Errors of omission—suppressing or withholding facts to mislead the listener—can be a white lie, half-truth, exaggeration, or falsehood, depending on the motive: sparing someone's feelings, providing the liar with an escape route, or deceiving the listener. The topic is covered in Chapter 2 in the discussion on fact and impression accuracy.

4. Sissela Bok, *Lying: Moral Choice in Public and Private Life* (New York: Pantheon, 1978), p. 50.

5. Christopher Caggiano, "Can you afford to be ethical?" *Inc.*, December 1992, p. 16.

6. Caggiano, p. 16.

7. Bok, p. 52.

8. Terry Eiler is well aware that *National Geographic* was one of the first magazines to be accused of visual lying by altering a photograph of the pyramids on a 1982 cover. According to Eiler, "[The] editors at *National Geographic* have taken years of grief because of their cover, which shows the pyramids closer together than they are in real life. The fact is that the editors had no cover shot for this particular issue, except for this horizontal one with the pyramids. Someone in production said he could solve that problem with a new scanner, and they made a decision based on a design problem. The technology was new and it didn't occur to them that their publication stood for the accurate portrayal of geographical images, so they ran into trouble. Nonetheless, these editors are among the most ethical I know. They just were solving a technical problem at the time. The advent of computer editing of images has made us even more aware of ethical issues in photojournalism."

9. Howard Kurtz, "Photo news & issues," by Howard Kurtz, the *Washington Post*, 2 February 1994, via the Internet. © 1994, the *Washington Post*. Reprinted with permission.

10. See Immanuel Kant's "The doctrine of virtue" in *The Metaphysic Morals* (New York: Harper & Row, 1964), translated by Mary Gregor.

11. Bok, pp. 40–41.

12. See Jeff Sommer's "Shultz: We tried to jar Gadhafi" in *Long Island Newsday*, 4 October 1986, p. 12.

13. John Walcott, "U.S. Credibility on Libya is damaged by White House campaign of deception," the *Wall Street Journal*, 6 October 1986, p. 5.
14. Bok, p. 173.

LIVING ETHICS

Read the following items and record your reactions in your ethics journal and/or discuss them with peers or mentors.

EDITOR'S NOTE: *Mark Kegans, a former student of Terry Eiler's at Ohio University, believes that journalists enjoy keeping discussions about ethics theoretical. "When it comes to real life," he says, "they recoil." In the following selection, originally published as a letter titled "A Question for My Colleagues" in the photojournalism trade magazine* News Photographer, *Kegans discusses visual lies and their impact on credibility.*

Decisive Moments

Mark Kegans, Photojournalist,
Denton (Texas) Record-Chronicle

When I began making photos several years ago, I learned about this wonderful profession from many different photographers and editors. The most vital lesson to me, then and now, was in working ethically. It was a simple lesson but one that still has a powerful effect on my methods: A photographer should not manipulate, direct, or affect a situation.

There are exceptions and variables: lighting, lens selection, environmental portraits, and the unavoidable fact that the mere presence of a photographer will influence any scene. None of these, however, muddy the ethical waters for me. Given any assignment, a photographer goes in quietly, works the situation with light, film, lenses, and eye, then leaves quietly.

Like everybody else, I talk often with other photographers, swapping tales of near-clip wins and woeful assignments. More and more, though, I hear stories, some rumor, some firsthand, of photographers who act more like directors or choreographers than the "fly on the wall." The frequency of these incidents shows that these aren't just isolated incidents or aberrations in the ethical fabric.

Indeed, there must be a school of thought amongst many photojournalists that they are not merely witnesses and recorders of moments but are also creators. Wielding influence, they make life more visually interesting. Even when life is boring, which it often can be, the enterprising shooter will often lie, beg, borrow, and steal to get the frame.

Am I naive and simply not taking advantage of a golden opportunity? We all know most subjects will do anything to get themselves in the newspaper and never think they're party to a visual white lie. Or, is there anybody else out there who believes that any photographer who stages pictures should be bludgeoned with the largest lens? If you want life to be picture-perfect, do illustrations for advertising or wedding photography. It pays better.

Perhaps I am overreacting. Maybe the truth we serve and seek is the Truth, with a capital T. Then, dressed in noble reason, it is right that the shooter stretch the reality he or she is given and make a more powerful photograph. Truth and the ignorant reader cannot be served fully by anemic images. (You can't win contests with them either.)

Here is a common type of assignment every one of us faces too often: "Joe Smith is a local rancher. Please get pictures of him working at his ranch." You know what happens next. You get one hour between other assignments to photograph Joe and the story is scheduled for the next day's paper. But when you arrive at the ranch, Joe has finished working for the day. However, he does graciously ask what you want him to do for a picture. Now, the dilemma thickens. The ethical road says make an environmental portrait and get on to your next assignment. But the editor said he hates portraits. Besides, you know they're frequently a cop-out.

There are options. Try to reschedule the assignment so you will have more time and Joe will be actually working. But, then you will have to cruise for wild art because that was tomorrow's color. Or (nobody will know and Joe is willing) get the cowboy doing something picturesque in nice light. There, you have a good frame and nobody is bothered. Right?

Some shooters will say this issue is not black and white but an ocean of gray, to be navigated carefully. But I know I am not alone on this issue. Too many friends have shared with me the disgust and disillusionment for a profession whose leaders strut around marveling at the latest digital toy or foreign project. The emperor may have a computer but he is still stark naked. And he is sick, consumed by the same old cancers—newsroom powerlessness, too much emphasis on color, ethical blindness—that technology can't cure.

From subtle manipulations to outright fabrications, the question remains constant in my mind. Who or what creates the "decisive moment" that we all live for? Is it a combination of hard work, luck, and the subject? Or, if those fail to meet his or her expectations, does the photographer become Spielberg and create the moment necessary to show Truth?

The history of photography is rich in heroes who put Truth and Beauty before fact and reality. Perhaps the lesson we should take from these giants' images is about seeing beautifully. Maybe it is up to us see *honestly*. After all, isn't believability the only ground we have to stand on as journalists? What do *you* believe?

�֍ **EDITOR'S NOTE:** *S. Lee Kanner had a devastating experience applying for a journalism job. He was interviewed for a position at an Iowa newspaper when the question of his ethnicity came up. The interview abruptly ended. So when he accepted his first journalism job in Hickory, North Carolina, he lied about being Jewish. He recalls, "The lie I uttered that day in Hickory troubled me throughout my life. I had done something shameful—denied my heritage. I did not regret it. I believed I had no choice, so I did what I had to do, for myself and my family. The lie changed my life completely, but the guilt never left me. Not until I purged myself of the lie by confessing to it in the essay." As you read Kanner's essay, which originally appeared in the journalism trade magazine* Columbia Journalism Review, *note how even an ethical lie can lead to complications, troubled conscience, and nagging doubt about whether his first publisher would have accepted the truth.*

The Lie

S. Lee Kanner, Retired Editor, *The New York Times*

A long time ago I lived a lie. It turned out to be a more punishing lie than I had anticipated and the shameful memories have clung to me like leeches. I offer no apologies. The lie turned my life around and I remain convinced, despite the enduring damage to my psyche, that I had no other choice.

For seven years after my graduation from New York University, I tried to obtain a newspaper job—the only job I had dreamed about since childhood and the only one for which I was trained. Finally, in 1943, I decided to insert a situation wanted ad in *Editor & Publisher.*

This was my second try: I had placed an ad shortly after graduation in 1936—and had received one response, from a newspaper in Iowa. I was instructed to report to a room in the old Commodore Hotel in Manhattan, where I would be interviewed for a reportorial job.

The interview lasted about an hour. It went well. The interviewer described himself as a one-man Washington bureau for the paper. He told me the editors in Iowa were concerned about a New Yorker adjusting to life in a small western city, but that he envisioned no problems.

Then, rising from his chair, almost as if the interview were over, he asked casually: "Oh, yes, what is your religion?"

"Jewish."

My answer to the question seemed to surprise him. I was fair haired, fair skinned, and did not speak like a typical New Yorker. Without a word, he walked into the bedroom, closing the door quietly behind him. It took me a minute to catch on. I closed the door to the suite just as quietly behind me.

When I inserted the second ad in *Editor & Publisher*, I fudged the seven years since my graduation as best as I could. This time I received almost 60 responses. The war was at its height, journalists were scarce. I was married, the father of a daughter, and a 4-F because of a slight hearing problem. My college journalism credentials made me a desirable prospect, even with the fudging of those seven years, which I'm sure fooled no one.

One of those replies—sent by publisher of the Hickory, North Carolina, *Daily Record*—included a railroad ticket. How shrewd of him! Most of the responses came from small papers a long way from New York City; I could not afford expensive trips without a guarantee of a job. The publisher of the *Record* said he needed a sports editor in a hurry, and the job was mine.

I had to overcome the vehement opposition of my parents, who were fearful of my leaving the sanctuary of the government position I had finally obtained in 1942. They were convinced I would ruin my life if I gave up the job. I was convinced I would ruin my life if I did not. Once the war was over, I reasoned, and all the newspapermen in service returned to civilian life, I would never get an opportunity to prove I belonged in the field.

So off I went to Hickory, a small town in Catawba County, between Asheville and Charlotte. Hickory was a furniture manufacturing center then, as it still is. As I recall, the *Record* had a circulation of about 12,000, including country subscribers. The population of the town exceeded the paper's circulation by a few thousand.

The *Record* was housed in a solid, one-story red-brick building. There were five, maybe six, people at work in the city room when I entered. I was in the newspaper business; I took a deep breath to calm myself.

L. C. Gifford, the publisher—a tall, slender, courtly gentleman, busy in his small office at the rear of the city room—came out to greet me. After introducing me to the staff, he escorted me to his office, sat me down, and closed the door—the first and last time I saw it closed.

He thanked me for my quick arrival and immediately made me aware that my duties involved more than being a sports editor. I was expected, he said, to write a sports column three days a week, design the sports page six days a week (there was no paper on Sundays), edit and write the headlines on all sports stories, help write news stories and features, and fill in for the news editor in emergencies. Wire service stories were to be used when needed, but emphasis must be on local high school sports. Hickory boasted one small college, Lenoir-Rhyne, which had a naval cadet program, he explained, and a decent sports program. Attention must be paid to the college.

I assured him I could handle it, once I had settled in and made the right contacts. He was pleased; he then suggested I might want to rent a room in a good boarding house within walking distance of the office. He gave me the address and suggested the landlady was waiting for me. I took the hint and rose.

"We begin working at 6:00 A.M., go to press at 2:00 P.M., lock up shop about 3:00," he said. "I'll see you tomorrow."

I nodded, started to leave. Then I heard almost the same question asked by the man from Iowa seven years earlier, and which had haunted me ever since.

"Incidentally, what religion do you follow?"

My hand gripped the door knob. On the long train ride from New York I had thought about this moment. I never had any doubt it would happen. I didn't turn my head—I probably could never have carried it off if I had looked at him.

"Episcopalian."

I summoned the courage to face him.

"Good," he said, smiling. "Declare yourself as soon as possible. It will make it easier for you and your wife and child."

Declare yourself? What in the world did it mean? I had never heard the expression before; I would hear it again—and again.

A week flew by. I adjusted quickly to the routine of being a one-man sports editor and sports department. I found it tremendously exciting. I made a number of innovations to improve the coverage of local events. By the middle of the second week I started contributing news features, which pleased the publisher no end. By the fourth week, acting on a rumor passed on to me by Mr. Gifford, I unearthed substance underneath gossip: The North Carolina football coach was defecting to Cornell, an Ivy League pow-erhouse. Football being as endemic to the South then as it is today, the story proved to be a major break for the small Hickory *Daily Record* and I became a minor celebrity.

So when I entered the drugstore with the best soda fountain in town and asked for an egg cream, it didn't take long for the pharmacist to figure out who I was.

"That's a New York drink," he said. "I don't know how to make it, but if you tell me how I'll give it a try."

I did and he did. The drink didn't quite make the New York grade, but I congratulated him, and a few days later a large sign appeared in the front window: "New York Egg Cream, 5 cents."

The egg cream story spread, the drink became popular and focused more attention on me, which was not all good. A few days later, sitting at my typewriter trying to finish a story, I felt two strong hands on my shoulders.

"When are you going to declare yourself, son?" The voice was deep, reverberating through the city room. The noise of clattering typewriters ceased. My colleagues awaited my answer.

I twisted my head slightly, caught a glimpse of fleshy jowls and clerical garb. Even a naive Jewish wanderer from Brooklyn could figure it out: an Episcopalian priest who wanted you to declare yourself in his church.

"As soon as my family joins me," I managed to mumble. The hands left my shoulders. He patted my back, walked toward the publisher's office. I resumed writing my story.

I realized at once that living a lie would not be as easy as telling a lie. The arrival of my wife, Elsie, and my daughter, Andrea, within the next week undoubtedly would complicate the situation. I warned Elsie about "declaring yourself," so she was prepared for the question and the lecture on the importance of doing it, delivered by the landlady of the boarding house almost as soon as she arrived.

Elsie shrugged off the incident; I could not. I loved my work, loved small-town life, but I feared that the strain of living a lie—pretending to be someone I was not, denying my Jewish heritage—would grow, not diminish. At work, I turned my head constantly, trying to avoid any more surprises.

Sundays, after we settled into our new home, proved to be the best and worst of days. One of our new friends, the manager of the radio station, usually picked us up and took us for a drive with his family. That was good. What was not so good usually occurred on the trip.

Andrea, going on three, always sat on my lap in the auto crowded with two families. Invariably during the ride she would cry out at least once, often twice, "I miss my Grandma Gussie. When is she going to visit me?" When I heard my mother's name, I automatically tightened my arms around Andrea's waist and held my breath. To me, Gussie was the quintessential Jewish name. How could our gentile friends not grasp this? They didn't, but Andrea's repeated cries for her grandmother eventually brought a polite inquiry: Why did she not come down for a visit?

It was easy to put people off by saying a visit was planned in the near future, but I knew I could never permit my parents, with their Russian-Yiddish way of talking, to come to Hickory. I began to understand there was no escaping the consequences of a lie without resorting to another lie, then another, then still another. . . .

I had worked in Hickory less than six months, but it was time to move on. I could no longer live under false pretenses, could no longer deny my religion. There was a risk involved in attempting to make a change so quickly, but I was counting on war-time conditions to help me relocate.

I applied to three papers, the *Washington Post,* the *Philadelphia Record,* and *PM* in New York. The *Post* never replied, *PM* said there were no openings, the *Record* said that if I was the writer of the headlines on the sample pages included in my application, I should make arrangements to come up for a tryout on the copy desk as soon as possible.

Could it be that I was good enough for a big metropolitan daily after so short a tenure in Hickory?

This time I told Mr. Gifford the truth: Personal reasons had forced me to apply for a job up North. I needed a week off for a tryout on the *Philadelphia Record* copy desk.

His reaction stunned me. It shouldn't have; it was typical of the decency with which he had treated me since my arrival in Hickory.

"All right," he said, "take the week off. I'm so sure you won't like being a copy editor on a big-city daily, I'll pay you for the week and give you money for the train fare. You'll be back, you'll be back."

He was wrong.

I was hired after the first day of my tryout. When a strike killed the *Record* in 1946 I got a job on the Newark *Star Ledger,* where I was a copy editor, head of the copy desk, and news editor. I joined the *New York Times* in 1952 as a copy editor. After a few years I became editor of the annual financial review, news editor of the international edition and the western edition (when most of the copy was edited in New York and transmitted from there), assistant financial editor, columnist, and assistant sports editor, thus finishing my career in the same department in which I had begun it. I retired in 1984.

I mention all these recent glories only to emphasize that, without the lie that has haunted me all these years, I probably would never have managed to break into the newspaper field. I desperately needed a chance to prove myself and the lie gave me the chance.

Not long after my retirement from the *Times,* I returned to Hickory with my wife. Why? To finally come to peace with myself about the lie? If so, the trip failed to do the job. Maybe sitting in front of my old portable Olympic and putting it all down as best as I can will purge me of my guilt.

I hope so. Even so, my visit to Hickory uncovered a nagging thought long buried inside my memory cells.

Would Mr. Gifford have changed his mind if I had told him at the interview that I was Jewish?

I don't know.

✂ EDITOR'S NOTE: *The reporter who provided the following selection lied to her editor because she felt that lying served an important moral purpose and that she had no other recourse. Her anecdote also touches on the concept of appropriate and inappropriate disclosure, as studied in the Chapter 3.*

Issues of Character

Anonymous, Reporter for a Metropolitan Newspaper

A school resource officer was arrested and charged with several counts of sexually assaulting teenage boys. Not a particularly nice story or easy one to do, but one that certainly must be written. The ethical problem revolved around the officer's sexuality and it's supposed role in the story. Discreet inquiries (and gossip) from gay friends before the officer's arrest—and open discussion after the arrest by other officers—had led me to conclude that the officer was gay and in the closet.

I need not explain why a person would choose to remain in the closet these days, especially if that person works within the homophobic world of law enforcement. I might need to explain this: Gay is natural and as of this writing, still legal in this state. Pedophilia is unnatural, involves the victimization of children and a crime. They are two different things. I am still angered every time I am reminded people don't understand this.

Which is why I was extremely pissed about five minutes after I brought the story of his arrest to my editor. The first question, practically the first words out of my editor's mouth, were "Couldn't they tell?" At first, I didn't quite catch on. Hello! This person was an editor at a major newspaper, has a college degree, and years of experience—but in my editor's mind, only gay men molest boys.

Once I figured out what my editor was saying, I acted as if I didn't understand, hoping the issue would be dropped out of frustration. It wasn't. So I explained to my editor that the issue here was the officer's crime of pedophilia, not adult sexual orientation. My editor asked if there was any way I could interview the officer and confirm his sexuality. I told my editor the officer was under suicide watch at the jail and officials would not grant an interview. Then my editor, knowing how much time I spent hanging out and gossiping with cops, asked if anyone in the department knew or suspected of the officer's sexuality.

As I've said, pedophilia and homosexuality are two different things. Why fuel society's hatred and homophobia by printing allegations that the officer was gay? What does it have to do with anything? Would the officer being gay make the crime more acceptable? Would it ease the pain of the victims, their families, or, for that matter, the officer's family?

We are in the business of gathering and printing facts. Despite the stories I'd heard again and again within the law enforcement community, despite gossip from my gay friends, until that officer confirmed or denied—the sexuality angle was rumor. If we had put it in the newspaper, it would have become fact to a majority of our readers.

So I lied. I told my editor rumors of the officer's homosexuality had never come up in any conversation I was privy to. Because I knew all sorts of other personal things about many officers, my editor believed me. Thinking about it, deadline was looming and perhaps my editor knew there was no way I could nail down that angle in time. But no, my editor never brought it up again, even though there was opportunity as we followed the story through the courts to its conclusion.

I cried when I wrote the first story. (This is not uncommon, though rarely discussed, in the news business. Our emotional involvement is supposed to be aggressive. Too many of us view being touched in the heart as a sign of weakness.) These actions had destroyed this officer's life and future. I cried for the young victims. School resource officers have a special trust among children and their parents. The courage it took for these boys to come forward, risking disbelief and snickers in the hallway, was immense. I cried for myself because I felt had been duped somehow. He was such a nice guy.

I've only told one person this story, and he thinks I should have worked the gay angle in because it was part of the officer's character and thus part of the story. My friend also pointed out that if my editor discovered I had withheld that information, I could be fired. This is true. People have been fired for less. But faced with the situation again, I would repeat my actions. Sexuality is *not* an issue of "character." It is made into one by those who are fearful, and in fearing, hate. I will not be party to giving some homophobe another case to point to and say "Ah-hah!" I will not contribute to the degradation of an entire group of people based on the criminal actions of a few.

We journalists have to be aware of the big picture when we're going after our little stories. Sometimes, if all that needs to be written about are the obvious facts, go with those and keep the rest to yourself. After all, who are you trying to impress if you put those bits in? As long as the news has been covered, there's no need for anything else. In this case, the known facts, which held up in a court of law, did enough damage.

Society would not have been served by adding the rest.

✖ EDITOR'S NOTE: *Before and during the Gulf War in 1991, the public relations firm of Hill & Knowlton took on an account on behalf of the Citizens for a Free Kuwait. The agency arranged for a 14-year-old Kuwaiti girl to testify before the Congressional Human Rights Caucus and she told the panel that she witnessed Iraqi soldiers remove newborn babies from incubators. That assertion was challenged by the mainstream news media. Soon, a controversy flared with Hill & Knowlton at the center of what many believed was a lie to rally public support for war with Iraq. In 1993, Thomas Eidson, then CEO of Hill & Knowlton, delivered a speech about the matter at an Ethics in Media luncheon in New York City. Following is a condensed version of that speech illustrating how a public relations agency manages a crisis concerning its credibility, going on the offensive.*

The Crisis

Thomas Eidson, Former CEO, *Hill & Knowlton*

A year ago, if I'd been asked to speak on "new perspectives in crisis public relations," my response might have been heated:

- The *New York Times* had just run an op-ed piece accusing Hill & Knowlton of lying and worse.
- The calls for on-air interviews had already come in from *20/20* and *60 Minutes.*
- The U.S. public relations industry had joined the assault against H&K.
- And, even though my letters to the editors of the *Times* and the *Wall Street Journal* were eventually printed, they were lost in the blizzard of rumors and false charges.

I am, of course, talking about the public criticism of Hill & Knowlton for its work on behalf of the Citizens for a Free Kuwait.

Independent reports, eye-witness accounts, statements of evidence from the U.S. ambassador in Kuwait City—all put the lie to the charges. Even so, it may be useful, in light of our subject here, to revisit some of that ground.

All things considered, we should have expected some sort of look at Hill & Knowlton's Kuwait work. After all, it was a $10 million account ($5.6 million in fees and $4.4 million in out-of-pockets) and it was an international crisis that eventually led to war.

And while Monday, January 6, 1992, began like any other day, it quickly turned into the first day of a massive controversy and crisis for Hill & Knowlton . . . and I suggest, for the public relations industry and the news media as a whole.

Let me set the stage:

The media had been gearing up for their retrospective look at Kuwait one year after the Gulf War when an op-ed piece appeared in the *New York Times*. In it, H&K was accused of duping the U.S. Congress, and, in effect, of orchestrating the U.S. entry into the Gulf War.

As you may recall, we arranged for a 14-year-old girl by the name Nayirah al-Sabah, daughter of Kuwait's Ambassador to the United States, to testify before the Congressional Human Rights Caucus.

We submitted to Congress her full name. But because she had relatives in Kuwait (including her grandmother and an aunt who was giving birth in the hospital where Nayirah had been working) and because her family was afraid of "death squads" reportedly operating around the world, she testified as others did: using only her first name.

First, however, we carried a message to . . . the Congressional Caucus and asked [members] if that was permissible. [We were told] yes; we know who she is. Other people are doing it; so she may do it, too.

You may also recall that Nayirah told members of Congress that she had seen Iraqi soldiers remove newborn babies from incubators and leave them to die. This became one of the most symbolic and repugnant images of the Iraqi occupation. It also became the basis of the challenge against H&K. In essence, Nayirah was accused of being a liar . . . of having fabricated the entire affair.

The op-ed piece in the *Times* drew a lot of very wrong conclusions. The main one was that the atrocities did not occur. The second was that H&K had helped to fabricate the incubator story. The third was that the Ambassador's daughter was a liar. And finally, the U.S. Congress has been duped by a PR firm.

Rebutting the charges was easy—stopping the wild, irresponsible press stories was impossible. Even throwing some of the best media relations talent in the United States against this challenge could not stop what had been started. What began in the op-ed page of the *Times* became a *Wall Street Journal* [second-day] story and a wire story. It was then a news story, no longer opinion.

Within days, papers as far flung as the British *Independent* and the *San Diego Union and Tribune* were carrying accusations that the incubator atrocities were a fake, and that Hill & Knowlton had lied.

Suddenly, a public relations firm—heretofore unknown to the general public—had become the source of "original darkness." It made you want to look for Hill & Knowlton's name in the Old Testament between pestilence and plague.

The fact that we had represented the Catholic Church was tossed in our face as if it, too, were some evil organization. The attacks would have been laughable if they hadn't been so damaging.

A month later the real facts began to surface from other sources.

The U.S. State Department declassified a cable from the U.S. Ambassador in Kuwait that unequivocally supported Nayirah. Eye-witnesses stepped forward—including the head nurse at the hospital where the incubator incident occurred.

Kroll Associates, the internationally respected investigative organization, issued a report that documented the atrocities and revealed official Iraqi documents ordering the removal of the incubators.

What is more, the Kroll Report placed the ambassador's daughter at the hospital where she testified she had been, at the time she testified she had been there.

At Hill & Knowlton, these reports brought a sigh but no relief. The irresponsible reporting continued. . . . In fact, this same charge against H&K aired again in Europe.

I want to read to you from an article that appeared in the *Washington Post* [in March 1993]. It quotes extensively from the Pentagon's final report on Iraqi atrocities in Kuwait, then just released, and includes the following passage:

> Some critics of the U.S.-led war against Iraq have accused Kuwaiti citizens of exaggerating Iraqi atrocities to whip up international sympathy for their cause.
>
> During the build-up to the war, for example, an anonymous young Kuwaiti woman gave a chilling, eyewitness account of the incubator episode to the Congressional Human Rights Caucus, omitting her identity as the daughter of the Kuwaiti ambassador to the United States. Her account has since been widely challenged.
>
> The report released yesterday, however, not only found that babies were taken from their incubators but concluded that human rights violations "were so widespread and methodical that they could not have occurred without the authority or knowledge of Saddam Hussein."

The article goes on to detail what it terms "a grisly catalogue of Iraqi war crimes," including "torture by amputation of or injury to various body parts . . . electric shock applied to sensitive parts of the body . . . electric drills used to penetrate chests, legs or arms . . . victims killed in acid baths" and other acts too horrifying to relate here.

Soon after the *Post* article appeared, Hill & Knowlton obtained a copy of the Pentagon's report. Under the heading "Deaths Attributable to Iraqi Torture and Execution" is the following line item: "Premature babies removed from incubators . . . 120."

End of story. Or almost: There are still the lessons to be learned from this sorry episode.

While seeds of controversy can be found in any debate that leads to war, in this case, they did not sprout from a violation of ethical conduct by Hill &

Knowlton, but from irresponsible and sloppy journalism. This is a strong charge—and one that is risky for me to make—given the industry saying, "Don't start a fight with people who buy ink by the barrel."

[Nonetheless] what specific lessons do we come away from this with?

First and foremost, the media ground rules are changing, and with frightening speed. The great newspapers and network television news organizations are, for the most part, hard working and honest, but increasingly susceptible to the ratings and readership power of a controversial story.

There is also an increasing number of organizations willing to violate long-standing journalistic ground rules in the name of building audiences. . . . Today, serious issues and social questions are being "cooked" by the media to deliver ratings points at sweeps week or to boost circulation, as fewer and fewer people read newspapers and television blurs the line between informing and entertaining.

In a parallel trend, the media are increasingly avoiding stories that might offend advertisers. . . . At the other end of the spectrum, advertisers are beginning to pressure newspapers to not run articles that might harm sales or sales practices. In the U.S. there are reports that automobile dealers are using ad dollars to stop stories about the in's and out's of bargaining for the price of a new car.

These trends are a warning flag to all of us in the business of communications. For those of us in public relations, we must make certain that an irresponsible press does not begin to dictate to firms who will be allowed to hire counsel to help them be heard in a free society.

This is the undercurrent to the attack on Hill & Knowlton's work for the Citizens for a Free Kuwait, and, by extension, on everyone in this business.

We felt the attack deeply, because at Hill and Knowlton—like most of us in this field—we take pride in doing our jobs well and with integrity.

We continue to be proud of the work we did on Kuwait. But we paid a severe price for it. Our reputation was assaulted publicly for an entire year . . . even when the facts that exonerated us were readily available.

Every agency has to decide for itself the bounds of moral and ethical behavior. Contrary to the news media reports, H&K makes that decision every day, as it has for close to 70 years.

VALUES EXERCISES

1. Keep a weekly journal of all the white lies, half-truths, and falsehoods that you say or indicate to others. Without violating your own privacy or the privacy of others, summarize them incident by incident, item by item. Under each incident or item, briefly note the immediate, future, or possible consequences of the lie.

2. Keep a weekly journal of all the white lies, half-truths, and falsehoods that others say or indicate to you. Without violating your own privacy or the privacy of others, summarize them incident by incident, item by item. Under each incident or item, briefly note the immediate, future, or possible consequences of the lie.

3. Keep a weekly journal of times when you *wanted* to tell a white lie, half-truth, or falsehood, but caught yourself and told the truth or declined to answer the question (doing so in a polite, discreet, or otherwise appropriate way). Without violating your own privacy or the privacy of others, briefly summarize these incidents and items and note the immediate, future, or possible consequences of telling the truth.

5

Manipulation

Redefining the Hoax

The *hoax* is considered a rare occurrence by journalists, so few have bothered to define it, assuming everyone knows the standard meaning of the word: "a trick or fraud, especially one meant as a practical joke" (*Webster's New World*). A more journalistic definition would be: *manipulation by a person or group making a false claim to program the media for personal gain, exposure, or some other motive.*

The definition applies to all journalists. However, public relations and advertising educators and practitioners usually pay little attention to the topic, assuming it pertains only to reporters, photographers, and magazine writers. For the most part, the topic has been relegated to news-editing texts. However, because of communications technology, editorial duties involve more emphasis on production and less on content. These attitudes and practices have increased opportunities for hoaxsters. Even though most journalists are not trained to recognize and defuse a hoax, they are held liable because consequences can be quite severe. Only two other situations are powerful enough to destroy credibility for *both* the individual and the company:

- *Plagiarism,* or the passing off of someone else's work as your own (to be covered in Chapter 6)
- *Litigation,* usually involving libel or discrimination (the latter to be covered in Chapter 7)

Plagiarism and media law are important journalism topics covered extensively in classrooms and textbooks. No studies exist to explain why the hoax is underemphasized. Yet most educators and professionals will agree that successful hoaxes are intensely embarrassing for the employee and his or her company. That embarrassment may explain why journalists are reluctant to discuss the topic.[1]

Embarrassment often is associated with a hoax because it:

- *Jeopardizes personal credibility.* The primary job of a journalist is to disseminate information according to precepts of social responsibility, as discussed in Chapter 2. A hoaxster usurps that fundamental duty and programs the media by making false claims.
- *Jeopardizes corporate credibility.* A journalist generally wants to contribute to the good name of his or her employer, not detract therefrom, calling into question the competence of coworkers and/or the entire company.
- *Exposes personal beliefs.* The hoaxster preys on the fears, desires, and convictions—as well as the values—of the journalist, revealing them for all to see.
- *Exposes cultural beliefs.* The hoaxster humiliates the audience, clients, or consumers, who may cancel subscriptions or change channels, agencies, or products.

These matters will be explored in depth later in the chapter.

Moreover, the hoax is not as rare as many journalists in this tabloid and multimedia era want to believe. The proliferation of talk shows, scandal sheets, and cable and computer networks has increased the demand for sources with good or sensational-sounding stories. There are more avenues of access for the hoaxster via modems, faxes, and 1-900 call-in numbers. So as incidents of manipulation increase, so should awareness about the hoax. Make no mistake. Journalists manipulate sources, clients, and consumers every day. They can lie to get an account or a story, go undercover or use a hidden camera, alter photographs or images, plagiarize copy, invent quotes or testimonials, deceive a competitor, and discriminate or exert undue authority.[2] These issues involve values of the individual journalist and therefore are covered in other chapters on falsehood, temptation, bias and power. A hoax, however, relies on manipulation by outside sources whose sole goal is to program the media.

That is a critical difference.

Let's illustrate it with an anecdote by a photojournalist who knew how to recognize and defuse attempts to manipulate him. Chuck Scott, former picture editor for the *Milwaukee Journal* and the *Chicago Tribune*, recalls an incident that happened early in his career when he took pictures for the *Champaign-Urbana Courier*: "I was walking in the police garage in City Hall when I observed a young woman prisoner being escorted between two male deputies. She caught sight of me with my camera and suddenly started struggling with the deputies. She probably thought the photo might win her a little sympathy [from readers]. It would have been an interesting picture, but I wanted an honest one, and so just started walking away."

The incident in the police garage underscores several key points:

- *Frequency of hoaxes.* The prisoner's attempt to perform in front of the camera shows how subtle and common a hoax can be, as defined earlier in this chapter.
- *Outside manipulation.* As explained in Chapter 3, visual lies involve set-ups and/or altering of images by *photographers* in which manipulation may have occurred to achieve some other goal—for instance, a prize-winning or front-page shot. In this case, the manipulation came from the *source* attempting to program the picture.
- *Ethical choice.* If Scott did not realize the woman was only feigning to struggle with the officers and took the picture, that would *not* be a moral issue, as discussed in Chapter 1. If, however, he recognized the hoax but went along with it to get a front-page photo, that would be "wrong" and an action for which he would have to accept consequences, as discussed in Chapter 2. However, by recognizing the hoax and refusing to take the bait and the picture, Scott made the "right" ethical decision.

As you can see, hoaxes take many forms and hoaxsters wear many masks. That makes the topic seem complex, but it actually is not. Now that we have redefined hoaxes, let's see what other commonalties they share.

Analyzing the Hoax

One of the greatest (though unintentional) hoaxes of all time occurred on the eve of All Saints' Day, 1938, when Orson Welles broadcast his script of *The War of the Worlds.* The script was based on the 1898 novel by H. G. Wells, a journalist and free-lance writer, depicting a cosmic event that shook the whole of England.

"A MESSAGE RECEIVED FROM MARS"

"Remarkable Story From Woking"

It was a tabloid headline then as now. Welles, an actor who founded the Mercury Theater, set the script adaptation in "Grover's Mill," New Jersey, and broadcast it via the Columbia Broadcasting Company nationwide over

151 stations. The adaption contained disclaimers, noting the nature of the broadcast. Nonetheless, panic ensued, precisely as it had in Wells's novel, with scholars heading out to find the Martians, members of religious congregations proclaiming Doomsday, and citizens offering their services to combat the threat.[3] One of the most-telling articles about the broadcast was written by George M. Mahawinney of the *Philadelphia Inquirer* who is said to have composed the round-up story in one hour after being deluged with calls.[4] Here is his lead:

> Terror struck at the hearts of hundreds of thousands of persons in the length and breadth of the United States last night as crisp words of what they believed to be a news broadcast leaped from their radio sets, telling of catastrophe from the skies visited on this country.

The story goes on to quote several terrified motorists. One said: "All creation's busted loose, I'm getting out of Jersey." A teenage girl allegedly phoned the Princeton Press Club with an on-the-scene report: "You can't imagine the horror of it! It's hell!" A woman in a church screamed: "New York is destroyed; it's the end of the world. You might as well go home to die." By the time such messages reached Atlanta, Mahawinney reported, between 40 and 7,000 New Jersians were said to have perished. Heart attacks were said to have occurred in Kansas City hospitals.

Orson Welles proved that mass media could spark mass hysteria. There is another important lesson about the hoax, however: *timing*. The broadcast happened on Halloween Eve, known as Mischief Night in New Jersey; moreover, the Germans were mobilizing against their enemies in Europe, threatening world war. Though written at the turn of the century, Wells's *The War of the Worlds* contains prophetic images of holocaust and mass destruction, playing off public fears in 1938.

In July 1953, another hoax occurred in a large southern city, according to Dan Lynch, managing editor of the *Albany (New York) Times Union*.[5] He writes that three men entered a newsroom claiming to have run over an extraterrestrial with their pick-up truck. They showed an editor the body of a small, red humanoid-looking creature. The newspaper ran a story—"Hairless critter killed, two escape"—and the men became celebrities. The creature, as it turned out, was a shaved, mutilated rhesus monkey. The men perpetuated the hoax because of a $50 bet that they could get their names on the front page of the newspaper.

Nonetheless, July 1953 is as important a date as October 1938. The Korean War was about to end in a stalemate, calling into question America's military dominance. Uncertainty reigned. Stalin, Soviet dictator responsible for mass executions in his country toward the end of his rule, had just died.

Joseph McCarthy, U.S. senator, was making sensational accusations against alleged "Communist" Americans. On June 19, Julius and Ethel Rosenberg, alleged spies convicted on questionable evidence, were executed for selling nuclear secrets to the Soviet Union. Everyone seemed suspect and fearful as the Cold War intensified. A UFO story coincided with the fear and uncertainty of 1953 as nicely as the Martian one did in 1938.

In 1994, UFO hoaxes had less impact on the populace. The publication of Budd Hopkins's *Missing Time* (Marek, 1981) and *Intruders* (Ballantine, 1987)—along with dozens of other UFO abduction books by other authors—already had flooded the bookstores, tabloids, and talkshow circuits. An insect-eyed alien with a hairless, bulbous head had become an icon of pop culture, appearing in everything from credit card ads to beer commercials. In sum, E.T. had become one of us. But we feared another type of abduction related to 1990s' street crime and violence: carjacking.

In Union, South Carolina, a mother of two toddlers reported to police that a Black man had carjacked her 1990 Mazda Protege, forced her from the vehicle, and abducted her sons from the backseat. The report stunned the nation with as much impact as the Orson Welles hoax and surpassed it as the greatest hoax of all time, given its length and the millions that it affected via modern mass media technology. For nine days, Susan Smith, age 23, stuck to her story as police and citizens nationwide searched for 3-year-old Michael and 14-month-old Alexander. Smith gave tearful interview upon interview to network news and morning talk shows. Citizens prayed and searched for the boys as law officers mobilized across the country. When no evidence turned up to support Smith's story, detectives focused on her, searched her home, and found a letter from a boyfriend who said he was not ready for the responsibilities of fatherhood. Finally, Smith confessed. With her two boys strapped in the backseat, she had put her car into gear on a boat ramp and watched it plunge into a lake.

Smith's hoax also employed a racial element: the description of a Black man in his late 20s to early 30s wearing a knit cap and a plaid jacket. In Chapter 7, you will read more about mass media's stereotyping of African Americans as criminals. At this point, the lesson relates to manipulation. Smith's invention was similar to that of Charles Stuart, who shot his pregnant wife Carol in his car in Boston in 1989 and blamed it on an attack by a Black man. (Stuart later took his life by jumping from a bridge.) Sadiki Kambom, director of the Black Community Information Center in Boston, commented on the racial element of both hoaxes in an Associated Press report distributed shortly after Smith's confession: "If you portray the black man as being the perpetrator, you have the chance to divert attention away from you who may be the guilty party."[6] The same AP report quotes Hester Booker of Union, South Carolina, who notes that during the nine-day ordeal, "The whites acted so different. They wouldn't speak, they'd look at you and then reach over and lock their doors. And all because that lady lied."

All of these hoaxes preyed on social mores involving fear and/or uncertainty. But timing was key, as it is in any attempt to program mass media. Here are 10 common elements indicating times that hoaxes are most apt to occur:[7]

- When information about a sensational story, client, or product seems to have reached a standstill
- When information about an event, incident, client, or product threatens or supports a person's or a group's interests
- When a political candidate is running for office or an issue is being debated or considered for legislative action
- When society is consumed by a widespread fear or desire
- When society searches for a missing link, cure, or other piece of evidence to advance learning, science, or technology
- When a hoaxster needs the exposure or publicity
- When a media outlet has recently run a promotions campaign soliciting reader or viewer participation or feedback
- When a deadline or production schedule does not allow for research
- When the media outlet has a need for a certain type of story, client, or product line
- When a story, client, or product line is linked to a specific season, holiday, or occasion

These time elements can be combined, of course. For instance, a hoax can concern a sensational story at a standstill, play on a fear, and be perpetuated near a deadline to circumvent research. There is no way to predict when a hoax will occur, but you can predict when one is *likely* to occur and thus be more apt to recognize it when it arrives.

In addition to sharing common time elements, hoaxes fall into specific categories. As noted earlier, the motive of the hoaxster is to program the media, but his or her methods and goals may vary (along with consequences for the journalist). Let's summarize all these particulars and illustrate them with examples of successful hoaxes.

Activist Hoax

Method: Relying on the journalist to operate under predictable rules and modes of behavior.

Goal: To prove to the audience the bias/incompetence of the journalist and/or his or her story, product, or client.

Example: In Boulder, Colorado, peace activists promoted and staged a phony beauty pageant—The Miss Patriot of Boulder—during the Gulf War in March 1991. One person was quoted as telling the media that the pageant was a morale booster and an opportunity for "girls" to promote the war. Some 80 people showed up to protest the event because they believed the pageant was inappropriate and objectified women. The activists used the opportunity to criticize the media for condoning the war instead of questioning it.[8]

Probable Time Elements:
1. When information about an event, incident, client, or product threatens or supports a person's or a group's interests
2. When a political candidate is running for office or an issue is being debated or considered for legislative action
3. When a hoaxster needs the exposure or publicity

Consequences: The journalist or his or her product or client will be exposed as unreliable, often resulting in limited future coverage or promotion and/or loss of image or sales.

Impersonator Hoax

Method: Relying on the media's need to:
1. Be informed or tipped about new stories.
2. Use names, quotes, pictures, and/or testimonials for developing stories or products.
3. Accept information without verification as long as a name is associated therewith.

Goal: To become part of the news or campaign, to feel momentarily worthy or validated as a human being.

Example: An impersonator hoax involves someone claiming to be a celebrity, expert, eyewitness, victim, or newsmaker. For instance, more than 50 people claimed to be eyewitnesses or victims finding syringes in the so-called Pepsi Scare in 1993. (See "What Went Right?" in the Living Ethics section at the end of this chapter.) A telemarketer for Journal/Sentinel Inc. in Milwaukee claimed to have discovered such a syringe in a can of Pepsi purchased from a vending machine at a local K mart. She opened the can in the newspapers' TV lounge and screamed. Later she admitted the hoax was "a quiet plea for attention."[9]

Probable Time Elements:

1. When information about a sensational story, client, or product seems to have reached a standstill
2. When information about an event, incident, client, or product threatens or supports a person's or a group's interests
3. When society is consumed by a widespread fear or desire
4. When a hoaxster needs the exposure or publicity
5. When a media outlet has recently run a promotions campaign soliciting reader or viewer participation or feedback
6. When a deadline or production schedule does not allow for research
7. When a story, client, or product line is linked to a specific season, holiday, or occasion
8. When a political candidate is running for office or an issue is being debated or considered for legislative action

Consequences: The journalist can be viewed as an opportunist or sensationalist, undermining credibility for the entire media outlet.

Personal Hoax

Method: Relying on the media's need to:

1. Be informed or tipped about new stories.
2. Use names, quotes, pictures, and/ or testimonials for developing stories or products.
3. Accept information without verification as long as a name is associated therewith.

Goal: To generate evidence, bolster an alibi.

Example: In 1992, a man claiming to be a pregnant hermaphrodite (born with both sets of genitals) was interviewed by Bryant Gumbel on the *Today Show* and included in reports by such news agencies as Reuters and the *Washington Post.* Reporters and a gynecologist who felt the man's belly claimed to have sensed fetal movement. In truth, the man was a homosexual living in a southern Philippine town who wanted the media to document his case so that he could legally change his name and gender and marry his lover.[10]

Probable Time Elements:
1. When information about an event, incident, client, or product threatens or supports a person's or a group's interests
2. When a hoaxster needs the exposure or publicity
3. When a deadline or production schedule does not allow for research

Consequences: In addition to loss of credibility, the journalist risks being ensnared in the hoaxster's legal or personal problems.

Political Hoax

Method: Relying on the media's need to cover politics or public affairs, especially if individual outlets do so in an advocacy or adversarial manner.

Goal: To manipulate public opinion or focus attention on an already newsworthy person, topic, or group.

Example: A man who over the years has tried to publicize evidence about the existence of living MIAs (Missing in Action) in Vietnam came up with a photo of a specific Army captain said to be held captive in Laos. The picture was shown at a news conference covered by the national media and culminating in a *Washington Times* editorial claiming the photo seemed authentic. The "captain" in the photo turned out to be a German national arrested on bird-smuggling charges.[11]

Probable Time Elements:
1. When information about an event, incident, client, or product threatens or supports a person's or a group's interests
2. When a political candidate is running for office or an issue is being debated or considered for legislative action
3. When society is consumed by a widespread fear or desire
4. When a hoaxster needs the exposure or publicity
5. When the media outlet has a continual need for a certain type of story, client, or product line
6. When a story, client, or product line is linked to a specific season, holiday, or occasion

Consequences: The journalist loses control of the message and risks becoming associated with the cause of the hoaxster and/or his or her personal problems and political agendas.

Sensational Hoax

Method: Relying on the media's need to provide blockbuster stories, products, services, or testimonials.

Goal: To shock or wildly entertain, gaining exposure or sales.

Examples: The legendary Loch Ness monster photo published in the April 21, 1934, issue of the *London Daily Mail* was actually an altered toy submarine from Woolworth's Department Store. Three men were in on the hoax, and in 1993, the surviving one confessed shortly before his death at age 90.[12]

Probable Time Elements:
1. When information about a sensational story, client, or product seems to have reached a standstill
2. When society is consumed by a widespread fear or desire
3. When society searches for a missing link, cure, or other piece of evidence to advance learning, science, or technology
4. When a media outlet has recently run a promotions campaign soliciting reader or viewer participation or feedback

Consequences: The journalist loses control of the message; he or she (and/or the employer, product, or client) is exposed as unreliable, unintelligent, fraudulent, or unworthy.

Stunt Hoax

Method: Relying on the media's need to cover celebrities, scandals, oddities, and wonder drugs/products.

Goal: To generate publicity, outwit the journalist, or cause general havoc.

Example: Well-known stunt hoaxster Alan Abel spoofed the *New York Times, Daily News, Newsday, Post,* and several metropolitan broadcast stations by doctoring a fake Lotto ticket and calling a press conference at a posh hotel. He hired an actress to pose as the sole owner of a $35 million jackpot ticket. Some TV reporters carried the session "live" from the suite of the "winner." A *Daily News* reporter uncovered the hoax by recognizing Abel as a lecturer in an adult-education class she attended on the art of practical jokes.[13]

Probable Time Elements:

1. When information about a sensational story, client, or product seems to have reached a standstill
2. When information about an event, incident, client, or product threatens or supports a person's or a group's interests
3. When society is consumed by a widespread fear or desire
4. When society searches for a missing link, cure, or other piece of evidence to advance learning, science, or technology
5. When a hoaxster needs the exposure or publicity
6. When a deadline or production schedule does not allow for research
7. When the media outlet has a continual need for a certain type of story, client, or product line
8. When a story, client, or product line is linked to a specific season, holiday, or occasion

Consequences: The journalist not only is made to look the fool by the hoaxster but also must generate more attention to the stunt by acknowledging, disavowing, and discrediting it.

A well-timed hoax can be subtle or elaborate. But because its success relies on manipulation, you can take steps to defuse it by acknowledging your fears, desires, convictions, and values.

Defusing the Hoax

A few famous hoaxes have been so sophisticated that scientists have had to defuse them. These hoaxes include the forged diaries of Adolf Hitler, excerpts of which were published in 1983 in *Newsweek* and the *Sunday Times of London,* and the 500,000-year-old Piltdown man found with extinct animal fossils in England in 1912, confusing anthropologists and evolution theories until 1953. Paper analysis exposed the Hitler hoax and fluoride tests exposed the Piltdown one.[14] But these hoaxes are the exception, not the rule. Most attempts at duping the media are easily defused. Before a journalist can analyze and defuse a hoax, he or she has to analyze himself or herself and acknowledge the fears, desires, convictions, and values that might invite outside manipulation.

Here is a quick example. In 1994, two psychology graduate students hoaxed more than dozen reporters by claiming a southern preacher believed that public television's *Barney,* a children's show, was a Satanic plot con-

FRAME: 08:32:15
An opened can of Diet Pepsi, held by a Colorado woman, appears to be lowered behind the counter of a convenience store, out of the clerk's line of sight.

FRAME: 08:32:27
The woman fumbles with her purse and pulls out what appears to be a syringe.

FRAME: 08:32:34
The woman appears to place the syringe in the opened can of Diet Pepsi while keeping it behind the counter.

FRAME: 08:32:39
The woman places the can back on the counter then asks the clerk for a cup into which she pours the Diet Pepsi and allegedly discovers the syringe.

nected to drug use and New Age spiritualism.[15] Predictably, they gave the preacher a name and invented a group to support his fundamentalist accusations: Citizens Concerned About Barney. They wrote about the preacher and the group in a letter and sent it to a radio station that aired the story. Now the hoax was "fair game" for rival media looking to match it. The hoax spread like a virus to major metropolitan newspapers and radio stations across the country.

Why?

Could it be that these reporters already believed the worst about fundamentalist preachers and so swallowed the bait without bothering to verify the existence of the preacher, "Luscious Bromley," and his so-called anti-

Barney citizens group? A survey by the Williamsburg Charter Foundation showed 0 percent of the media elite identified themselves as fundamentalist, born-again, or evangelical, although roughly 20 percent of American citizens do.[16] "Conservative Christians are politically suspect," writes Laurence I. Barrett, who covers politics for *Time* magazine. "After all, their agenda includes boycotting publications and TV shows they find objectionable, banning abortion, censoring ostensibly liberal textbooks, locking gays in the closet and feminists in the kitchen, and elevating creationism to legitimate academic science. For the overwhelming majority of mainstream journalists . . . this is frightening stuff."[17]

Hoaxsters prey on such fears, especially when they are held by journalists who claim to be fair and objective. As discussed in Chapter 1, a journalist needs to analyze his or her beliefs because a hoaxster uses them as highways to publication. Such beliefs are usually private. Here are two examples from anonymous reporters working for the same newspaper:

- *Reporter A:* "I don't believe abortion is right and I tend to pass harsh judgment on people who have gotten ones, even though I don't know their circumstances. Someone could hoax me easily by telling me a terrible story about a woman getting abortions as a means of contraception."
- *Reporter B:* "I feel people who are not pro-choice are not as good as I am. If someone came to me saying a leader of a pro-life group had committed a crime such as income tax fraud, I would be very likely to believe the story, especially if I believed the source was reliable and a disenchanted member of the pro-life organization."

In both cases, Reporter A or B would have to acknowledge and adjust for his or her belief to be objective and then investigate the hoax as he or she would any story.

Here are common fears, desires, convictions, and values that offer hoaxsters opportunities to manipulate media:

- Belief that a certain ethnic or social-class group is lazy or intelligent (An activist hoaxster can feed you a story about "inferior" Mexicans or "superior" Japanese.)
- Belief in or skepticism about UFOs (A hoaxster can provide fabricated FBI documents that prove once and for all that UFOs exist or do not exist, the product, say, of some hitherto unrecognized psychological disorder.)
- Belief or skepticism about the number of incest survivors (A hoaxster can invent or disavow an incest story to validate the journalist's view.)

- Belief that most Black men are violent and/or most White men are deceitful (A hoaxster can claim that a Black man assaulted her when it really was her White abusive husband, or that a White male employer discriminated against a Black applicant when he really didn't have a job opening, the target of the applicant's outrage at social injustice.)
- Belief that all overweight people are responsible for their appearance or that there is no medical risk associated with obesity (A company can persuade a journalist to handle the account of a gimmicky or unhealthy weight-loss program or the journalist can target a dangerous food or exercise product at obese people.)

As you can see from these examples, some of the beliefs are morally wrong (e.g., ones about prejudice) and others are morally defensible (e.g., ones about incest). That is not important when it comes to the hoax. The point is, no matter how you feel about these and other topics, you need to acknowledge your fears, desires, convictions, and values to defend against and defuse a hoax.

Here are some pointers:

1. *Always question the motive of the source.* Nothing frightens a manipulator more than questions about motive. In fact, use that word in your questions. Time your motive-based questions to catch the source off guard. Space those questions out during the interview so that you can analyze the source's answers later to determine any wavering or inconsistent data.

   Warning Signs
   - Does the source seem visibly uneasy or nervous upon being questioned on motive?
   - How, if at all, is the voice or eyes of the source affected each time you return to the issue of motive?
   - Does the source's answers to motive-based questions vary with each response?

2. *Always question your own needs.* Determine whether the source knows how your media outlet operates. In fact, ask a question using a jargon word related to your outlet or newsroom. Assess your own eagerness to pursue the story. Find out if your media outlet has run a recent promotion soliciting a certain type of story, client, or product.

   Warning Signs
   - Does the source seem to know too much about media procedure for his or her occupation?

- Is the story, client, or product falling into your lap precisely when you need it?
- Is the story, client, or product coming to you so close to deadline that you must use it without doing the necessary research?

3. *Always question the impact on audience.* Determine how the source's story, problem, discovery, or product will affect your readers, viewers, or customers. Assess how much the audience desires or fears what the source is peddling. Predict the reaction of audience if the story, indeed, turns out to be a hoax.

Warning Signs
- Does the source's story, problem, discovery, or product have the potential to harm or otherwise falsely raise the hopes of your audience?
- Is the source empowering a case by playing off desires or fears of the audience?
- How vehemently will your audience respond if the story is a hoax and what will this mean to your media outlet?

4. *Always assess your own fears, desires, convictions, or values.* Ultimately, hoaxsters rely on *you*, not your outlet, as the medium for manipulation. The more your beliefs go unacknowledged, the easier it will be for the hoaxster to prey on them to achieve his or her goal.

Warning Signs
- Do you want to believe the source because of any fear, desire, conviction, or value?
- In your past stories, press releases, or campaigns, have you in any way communicated any such belief?
- Is the source the kind of person that you secretly loath or admire, fear or feel attracted to, or a perfect example to support what you fervently believe in already?

Finally, the journalist who outwits a hoaxster *enhances* his or her credibility, along with that of the employer. Public relations and advertising executives who defuse and expose a hoax often distribute news releases or promotional literature about the incident, gaining respect and attracting clients. News journalists who defuse and expose hoaxsters usually end up with bigger stories than the original suspect ones. Consider the 1953 UFO hoax cited earlier about the men who entered a newsroom with a shaved, mutilated rhesus monkey. Imagine if that story happened today and the charges that might ensue against the hoaxsters, especially if they tormented, killed, and mutilated the animal. Consider the 1994 carjacking hoax by Susan Smith and calculate the costs, physical and emotional, involved in the futile nine-day national search. A brave reporter could have shortened the lifespan of that hoax in an investigative piece that called attention to the peculiarities involved in the case (including the racial element, the theft of an inexpensive vehicle containing two children, and the marital troubles of the Smiths).

In sum, the best defense against a hoax is to recognize, research, investigate, and defuse it. The best offense is to recognize, research, investigate, and *expose* it.

A Word about the Unexplained

As shown thus far in this chapter, a journalist has to be vigilant to guard against the hoax. That vigilance sometimes causes journalists to become cynical about hoax-sounding stories that just may be unexplainable or inherently mysterious. It is the challenge of explaining the unexplainable and solving the mysterious that enticed many young people to enter journalism in the first place. Even the most hardened professionals, at one time or other, were struck by the allure of the world or awe of the universe. You should hold fast to such feelings, if you have them, because they will help you excel in journalism without suffering burnout from cynicism or overwork.

Learn to distinguish between the hoax and the hoax's topic. If a celebrity pulls off a stunt, claiming to have had a near-death experience (NDE), and is later exposed as a fraud, that does not mean that the NDE phenomenon is fabricated. It means the celebrity fabricated the NDE. If a person claims to have videotaped a flying saucer but you learn that the tape has been set up and altered, that does not disprove the existence of extraterrestrials. It disproves the so-called sighting.

In the course of their careers, many journalists encounter an odd-sounding story that cannot be defused or exposed. Moreover, they have lived long enough to know that the world changes, sometimes dramatically, because of historic events, inventions, or discoveries. Based on those two observations, here are some odd-sounding or dramatic stories that you might encounter during *your* career, not predicted by psychics, but by journalism professors, professionals, and ethicists interviewed anonymously in an *Editor & Publisher* article:[18]

- *Afterlife.* "Through advances in medical technology, discovery of a spiritual realm after death."
- *Discovery of intergalactic life.* "Not necessary via UFOs, but via science."
- *Longevity.* "Increasingly we are going to discover ways to preserve the human body. It will influence how we live, from the products we buy to the very definition of childhood."

- *Discovery of animal intelligence.* "The beasts we kill, eat or rear as pets are as cognizant as we are and feel the full range of emotions, thoughts."
- *Global politics.* "We no longer will identify ourselves as members of nation-states, but as members of a species on the planet. This will go a long way to erase such issues as racism, sexism, and nationalism."
- *Legalized euthanasia.* "The concept of life as we know it will change."
- *End of reliance on oil.* "New technology will revitalize mass transit. Machines will have even more control over our lives."

The first thing that you might note about these observations is how most would fit the format of the *National Enquirer:* afterlife, aliens, long life spans, smart animals, utopia, killer-doctors, and smart gadgets. But as the quotations also indicate, intelligent people are pondering them. These journalists know how to distinguish between a hoax- and an odd-sounding topic and, after decades of experience, still anticipate big stories on the horizon that are as yet mysterious or unexplained.

Finally, you should not abandon your values because a hoaxster might manipulate them. For instance, you might fervently believe in pro-choice or pro-life for good reasons. If a hoaxster deceives you because of those beliefs, that does not imply that your beliefs are wrong. However, it *may* imply that you have yet to acknowledge and adjust for your beliefs and should do so before you become a practicing journalist.

ENDNOTES

1. More than a dozen journalists were contacted to discuss how it feels to be taken in by a hoax and only three who personally know the author of this text agreed to go on record about the topic. Their accounts appear in the Living Ethics section at the end of this chapter. A case in point involves the *Milwaukee Sentinel,* a newspaper that enjoys a good ethical reputation. In its June 17, 1993, edition, the *Sentinel* featured a front-page story about and testimonial by an *employee* who claimed to have found a syringe in a can of Pepsi. (Pepsi officials discuss how they helped defuse the nationwide Pepsi hoax in "What Went Right?" in the Living Ethics section.) Two editors at the *Sentinel* were contacted nine times by fax and phone message for comment about the incident. One said "no comment" and the other declined to return calls or answer faxes.

2. Some alternative newspapers willingly collaborate with hoaxsters to satirize public officials or call attention to controversial topics. See *A.A.N. News,* a quarterly newsletter for the Association of Alternative Newsweeklies, reporting on this trend. In the Fall 1993 edition, the newsletter discusses a spoof perpetuated by the *Phoenix New Times.* An escaped convict bragged that officials overseeing the work-furlough program were so incompetent that he could sell hot dogs in front of the county jail "and they wouldn't catch me" (p. 8). The newspaper arranged for a photo opportu-

nity with the attorney general, posing him with the convict in front of a hot dog stand, as part of a "Best of *Phoenix*" supplement. The escaped convict proved his point, left the scene, and was still at large after the newspaper published the photo and the newsletter published its account.

3. Similarities between H. G. Wells's novel and the calamity sparked by Orson Welles's broadcast are discussed at length in "The big hoax" by Michael J. Bugeja in *Culture's Sleeping Beauty* (Troy, NY: Whitston, 1993).

4. Donald McQuade and Robert Atwan, *Popular Writing in America* (New York: Oxford University Press), p. 127.

5. Dan Lynch does not identify the city but discusses the incident at length in "Guarding against hoaxes," *Editor & Publisher*, 29 February 1992, p. 44.

6. "Blacks felt the heat in Dixie Town as alleged carjack suspect was sought," AP report, in the *Newark Star-Ledger*, 5 November 1994, p. 4.

7. Based on content analysis by the author of some 100 case studies of hoaxes.

8. Moyra Knight, "Pageant turns out to be a hoax," *Daily Boulder (Colorado) Camera,* 16 March 1991, p. 1.

9. Cary Spivak et al., "Woman admits story a hoax," *Milwaukee Sentinel*, 19 June 1993, p. 1.

10. Howard Kurtz, "Yes, sir, that's no baby, 'Pregnant' man gave birth to hoax," the *Washington Post,* 10 June 1992, sec 8, p. B1-2.

11. Susan Katz Keating, "Exposing a P.O.W. hoax," *Reader's Digest*, December 1993, pp. 53–58.

12. "Fake in the lake," *People*, 28 March 1994, p. 109.

13. Rocco Parascandola and Bill Hoffman, "A lotto B.S.," the *New York Post*, 9 January 1990, p. 1.

14. See John Berendt, "The hoax," *Esquire*, April 1994, p. 60.

15. "Comedians hoax papers with preacher bashing Barney," *Editor & Publisher*, 2 April 1994.

16. Laurence I. Barrett, "The 'religious right' and the pagan press," *Columbia Journalism Review,* July/August 1993, p. 33.

17. Barrett, p. 33.

18. "Michael J. Bugeja, "Guarding against hoaxes, Part II: The untold story," *Editor & Publisher,* 16 May 1992, pp. 56, 43.

LIVING   ETHICS

Read the following articles and interviews and record your reactions in your ethics journal and/or discuss them with peers or mentors.

✖ **EDITOR'S NOTE:** *George Plimpton is known as a preeminent author, publisher, literary figure—and April Fool's Day celebrant. The latter distinction led to his being "hired" to spoof* Sports Illustrated *readers in an April 1985* *article that has become a classic in hoax studies. Titled "The Curious Case of Sidd Finch," Plimpton's stunt hoax took in hundreds of avid baseball fans who desperately wanted to believe that a horn-playing, 28-year-old, Harvard-educated, yogi recluse could fire a baseball 168 miles per hour. Like Orson Welles's 1938 broadcast of* The War of the Worlds, *Plimpton left many clues indicating the hoax-like nature of his piece. But the article was brilliantly illustrated with photos of the elusive Finch alongside Mets players who were in on the hoax. Moreover, a copy of the New York Mets "Free Agent Player Report" was featured, stating that Hayden "Sidd" Finch never played baseball before, had "weird" off-field habits, was asking for "0?" dollars, and could be "The Phenom of All Time." In the following* Esquire *excerpt from an essay titled "Welcome to the Dynamite Museum"—a supposed "anarchist" organization whose purpose is to keep "the electorate on edge"—Plimpton recounts responses to his hoax.*

The Saga of Sidd in *SI*

George Plimpton, Writer

The magazine happened to have an issue coming up with the date April 1 on the cover. I was called in—the editors aware, I presumed, of my background at the *Harvard Lampoon*. . . .

I eventually wrote a spoof about an English-born aspiring monk named Sidd Finch (Sidd for Siddhartha), who had learned in a Tibetan monastery, mind over matter, to throw a baseball 168 miles per hour (the record was 101, held by Nolan Ryan) with absolute accuracy, and who ended up at the Mets training camp in St. Petersburg for a tryout. I never thought many readers would fall for the spoof. Sidd Finch had so many idiosyncrasies—playing the French horn, pitching with one foot bare ("for balance")—that it didn't seem anyone could take him seriously. But then I saw the photographs taken to accompany the article: compelling pictures of a gangling, gawky pitcher (a schoolteacher friend of the photographer's) who looked exactly like the man in my mind's eye when I wrote the article. There he was in uniform, standing around with his teammates (the Mets were in on the gag), and I began to wonder. It seemed so authentic.

At 3 A.M. on the day *Sports Illustrated* appeared on the newsstands, the phone rang in my motel room in Chapel Hill, North Carolina, where I was to lecture that morning. A reporter from the *New York Times* was on the other end. "It's not true, is it?" he asked. . . . "How did you guess?" I replied, something like that, and I lost my chance.

Nonetheless, nearly two thousand letters came into *Sports Illustrated* following the article's appearance. Many included the phrase "hook, line, and sinker" and described in detail the embarrassment of being duped. The accounts were often joyous, vindicating the curious appeal in being victimized by a harmless hoax. About forty subscribers, however, canceled their subscriptions, feeling that thereafter they could never "trust" the magazine.

How did I feel about this? Mark Twain, despite the fact that his work is rife with pranks and hoaxes, held the practical joker "in limitless contempt . . . the reflection that I have been a practical joker myself seems to increase my bitterness rather than to modify it." How odd. I found myself quite exhilarated by the experience and by the effect it caused. Not long after, a man who recognized me from across a street in Providence, Rhode Island, stuck a forefinger in his mouth and pulled himself along like a hooked fish . . . and I grinned and shouted at him that Sidd Finch had signed with the Boston Red Sox.

I feel I have done the Dynamite Museum proud.

❊ EDITOR'S NOTE: *After the Martin Luther King holiday in 1993, an Ohio University professor, attempting to call order before lecturing a huge class, reportedly expressed a dislike for the King holiday—and all holidays in general. A few African American students walked out. Jeff Howe, a reporter for the* Post, *OU's campus newspaper, wrote about the incident and the controversy escalated until it dominated the news for a month. As it happened, Howe and five other* Post *reporters were students in the ethics class of the author of this text. During a lecture about hoaxes, Howe was warned that a hoax was imminent because of the politically charged topic. Students brainstormed about the forms such a hoax could take as the controversy reached a breaking point with calls for the professor to resign or be de-tenured.*

Suddenly posters appeared on campus announcing a rally with the following message: "Who Cares What Happened? It is time to take the offensive against offensive speech. Get the racists out of OU!! Demonstrate against OU's complicity with racism! This Friday, 12 noon, at the Civil War Monument. Be there & take a stand! Sponsored by People United to Stop Hatred." Letters soliciting support for the rally were published in the Post *and the community newspaper the* Athens News.

When reporters went to cover the event, they quickly realized it was an activist hoax organized by supporters of the professor who meant to put a stop to the story. One activist said letters sent to newspapers under a fictitious name were meant to "spoof the media, since the media has been the cause of all of this. With one phone call, it could have been determined that it was a fictitious name. Instead, the media picks it up and runs with it. We proved our point." In the following written interviews, Jeff Howe explains why he and other Post *reporters were caught off guard after being warned in class;* Post *reporter Heather Bainbridge explains how it feels to have contributed to the hoax by writing an article announcing the planned rally; and the editor of the* Athens News, *Terry Smith, discusses double standards of hoax activists.*

Hoax Rally

Jeff Howe, Ethics Student and Reporter, *The (Ohio University) Post*

You asked why no one in your Winter Quarter Ethics class understood the hoax waged against an uncomprehending (and-oh-so-exploitable) student body. After all, who else but reporters in a journalism class—being taught the nature of such media abuse (use?)—could pluck the sham while still ripe?

Well, I'm not sure, because after you specifically—by *name*, no less—prepared me for an upcoming hoax, I still neglected to respond adequately to the situation. What should I have done? How many times have I kicked myself in the ass for missing such an opportunity? I should have (a) predicted the nature of the ruse after the first letter—the antagonizing faction's position was unwarrantedly, unbelievably extreme; and (b) written a review of the "performance at the monument," because, of course, this is what it was. It was art at its most enticingly reductive element: it made people think (or it damn well should have).

Why did *we*, collectively, miss the boat? Because, I think, we are students still and detached from the day-to-day applications of our lessons. We are generally a group of media-saturated, affluent KIDS and perfectly susceptible to "the media hoax." A lesson for our fathers, our mothers, our educators: We ingest unwittingly the visual, oral, verbal information surrounding us. Our perceptions have formed as no other generation has through the oft-obscured eyepiece of mass media. In short, we are saturated—but at new, unregistered levels.

You "over-saturated" us. You fed us extra helpings, and we have grown fat and we eat what we're fed.

Heather Bainbridge, Reporter, *The (Ohio University) Post*

I had been a newspaper reporter for less than six months. I didn't take ethics class yet. In fact, I was only a second-year student of journalism. I never thought that sources might lie to me, but they did.

I can remember everything about gathering information for that story. It was about 7 P.M. when my editor Chris handed me a news release and said to start working on a story about the new organization, People United to Stop Hatred. I remember reading the release and thinking the people were making wild remarks and blowing a situation out of proportion, but I also thought that happens a lot and I should keep an open mind.

When I got off the phone with the first source, I told my roommate how strange I thought the person had been. He said the group had been monitoring the professor's classes and could not believe OU had not "removed this racist person from the campus." But he also had information on how many people were in the organization, what prompted them to organize, and what they planned to do at the rally. They even had titles for the executive staff. All of these remarks made sense. Why would someone lie about that stuff?

My first clue should have been when Joel Rudy, dean of students, told me he recognized one of the organizer's names from actions in the past. And then, when he told me no one from the organization had talked to anyone in the administration about the university's actions, I should have questioned the people again but I didn't. I talked to two members of the "new" organization, two members of the administration, and even the organizer of another rally scheduled for the College Green at the same time on the same day. I then wrote what I thought was a good article that covered both sides of the issue fairly. I was proud of myself—but all that pride changed the next day.

When I hurried to College Green so I could get to the Friday noontime rally and I saw the absurd actions of this "new" organization, I did not know what to do. The *Post's* office was across the street, so I went there to find out what the editors wanted me to do. They told me to get some reaction from the crowd. I did that for about 20 minutes and then went back to tell them what I had (about the hoax). They told me to forget it. Even though almost every *Post* photographer had run over to take pictures, we were not going to run anything about it. They apologized for getting me involved and then Chris handed me another news release about another activist's recent actions and asked me to have the story for Monday's paper.

I went home, started to cut out all the information written in the *Post* and the *Athens News* about the group and began making calls for my next story. I kept all the clippings and then sent them to my parents to show them how their little girl was tricked for the first time as a journalist. I still have all of them as a reminder of something that I hope never happens again. But I know it will, if not to me, then to someone else. The lesson? Anyone can get into the newspaper if they make it sound like they are doing something newsworthy, especially it they know how the process works and use it to their advantage.

Terry Smith, Editor, *The Athens (Ohio) News*

The *Athens News*, which I edit, was one of the media victims of the hoax, a phony protest rally that was publicized as the real thing.

The controversy that set up the hoax involved an art professor [reportedly] disparaging the Martin Luther King holiday in front of a packed lecture hall, which prompted outrage on campus, particularly from Black students. (For those who don't know him, [the professor] is widely recognized as OU's resident eccentric—which is really saying something in this town!)

The *Athens News* learned of the demonstration via a letter to the editor—and if I recall correctly, a mailed-in press release. The rally, set for the College Green on a Friday, was described as an anti-[professor] affair, in which he would be condemned as a racist. We printed the letter after I followed normal procedure and phoned the listed author for verification. (This procedure obviously has flaws; if a person lied in a letter, then he'll go ahead and lie on the phone.)

Our reporter and photographer went to cover the supposed rally and right away figured out it was phony. The professor's motley assortment of supporters—some of them notorious campus tricksters and others campus activists—held ersatz anti-racism signs and pretended to stone [the professor], who participated in all his goofy glory. They intended to turn the tables on the local media, who they apparently felt had blown the controversy out of proportion. I heard later that . . . a longtime campus activist said something to the effect that the media, the *Athens News* included, were idiots for being taken in by the hoax.

Needless to say, I was pissed off. On every hot political issue that's hit the OU campus in recent memory, from the Contras to South Africa to the CIA to Desert Storm, [this activist] has attacked government policy. He and some of the other hoaxsters can be depended upon to castigate the establishment for a variety of sins. Usually, dishonesty is at the top of the list.

Yet to set up their hoax, the [activists] deliberately deceived local newspapers and their readers. Then they laughed about it.

These are the kind of people who can disgustedly hold up a *Wall Street Journal* and snarl, "Lies, lies, lies," and then turn around and cheerfully lie through their teeth to further their own agenda. It's like, "We're right, so everybody in our little circle is allowed to lie—but nobody else can." This, of course, is hypocrisy of the worst sort. . . . TV evangelists also are good at this. It's wrong no matter who's doing it.

Let me make that point a little differently. Lying is wrong. In order to hoax somebody, you've got to lie. Therefore, hoaxing is wrong.

Typically, a successful hoaxster is gleeful about succeeding in his trickery, and [this activist] and his fellow hoaxsters were no different. They positively reveled in their successful prank—how could the newspapers be so stupid as to believe them?

Presumably, somebody who sets out to pull a media hoax intends to be successful. Otherwise, why bother? The whole process seems awfully cynical. Like with any con, the hoaxsters start off with the assumption that people are stupid enough to be taken in by their prank. Then they go out and prove their assumption. Then they congratulate themselves on their success. *People really are stupid!*

It's apparently an ego thing. . . .

In the aftermath of the [professor] hoax, I tried to decide whether we could have handled things any differently at the *Athens News*. And whether I really was stupid. I thought about it till my poor little brain hurt, and then decided that I wasn't necessarily dumb. I just didn't have the time or inclination to verify every piece of mail that gets dumped in my box. We'd never get the paper out. I decided I'd rather risk the occasional smartass hoax than become so paranoid and cynical that every letter holds a potential exploding cigar. (What an image!)

And finally, I decided, if you have to choose between flaws, better gullible than dishonest.

✜ EDITOR'S NOTE: *Guido H. Stempel III, distinguished professor at Ohio University, is nationally recognized as a leader in journalism research. He is the co-author and editor of such works as* Research Methods in Mass Communication *and* The Media in the 1984 and 1988 Presidential Campaigns. *He also is widely known as a magazine columnist for the newspaper trade publication* Presstime. *In the following piece, Stempel discusses how hoaxes affect the highest levels of government and how journalists have an ethical duty to verify information and defuse hoaxes.*

Snowballs and Three-Dollar Bills

Guido H. Stempel III, Columnist, *Presstime*

A. J. Leibling, press critic for the *New Yorker* for many years, once wrote, "By not reporting there are a lot of things you can avoid finding out." In so stating the issue, Liebling made it an ethical one. We all know that reporting raises ethical concerns, but Liebling is telling us that the *failure* to report also raises ethical concerns.

It is not, however, merely that by not reporting we fail to inform; it is that we misinform. When Janet Cooke wrote a series for the *Washington Post* about Jimmy, the 8-year-old heroin addict, and it turned out that Jimmy was a composite, we were outraged. This was clearly a breach of ethics. It was a hoax.

Yet, by failing to report completely, we offer the American public more serious hoaxes all the time. Worse yet, our society ends up making policy on the basis of these hoaxes.

For example, there has been circulating for some years now a "survey" that said the most serious problems in our schools are drug abuse, alcohol abuse, pregnancy, suicide, rape, robbery, and assault. It made the *New York Times* six times, including once in Anna Quindlan's column. It was in the *Wall Street Journal*, "Dear Abby" and "Ann Landers," and George Will's column. It was reported by CBS News and Rush Limbaugh. It was in an article by William Bennett in *Reader's Digest*.

There's only one problem with the survey—it's as phony as a three-dollar bill. It never happened. Barry O'Neill, a faculty member at Yale, tracked it down with the help of electronic data bases. (Barry O'Neill, "History of a Hoax," *New York Times Magazine,* March 6, 1994, pp. 46–49.) He found it was the work of a disgruntled Texan, T. Cullen Davis. Davis admitted he simply had made up the list. He passed it on to other people, and it snowballed.

Is it ethical for a columnist to use information from other sources without verifying it? Is it ethical or sensible to assume that everything you see in print is true?

The worst part of this story is that for years the education fraternity Phi Delta Kappa has commissioned a survey on school problems by the Gallup Organization. That survey is always published in the organization's magazine, which is available in many libraries. Anyone who bothered to look at it would have recognized that the Davis survey was a hoax. The Phi Delta Kappa polls in recent years indicate that the American public thinks lack of financial support is the biggest problem in education.

Then there is the claim that 6 percent of the criminals commit 70 percent of the crime. This widely repeated claim was picked up by President Clinton in his 1994 State of the Union message in which he was promoting "three strikes and you're out"—that is, lifetime jail sentences for persons convicted three times. William Raspberry, Pulitzer Prize–winning columnist for the *Washington Post*, called the FBI and asked for reports and statistics in support of this claim of 6 percent committing 70 percent of the crimes. The FBI said they had no such report, no information that would support this claim. Exactly where the figure came from is unknown. What we do know is that it is not true. Again, is it ethical to pick up material and publish it without any effort to verify it, even if the President of the United States said it?

In the controversy about cigarette smoking, it has been standard procedure when a study is announced documenting the harmful effects of smoking to get the Tobacco Institute to respond to it. The Tobacco Institute has never seen a study on harmful effects of smoking that it liked. It constantly insists that smoking isn't harmful and nicotine isn't addictive. The media, by continually airing their views on these studies, are promoting a false view on smoking and health. Is that ethical journalism?

In the summer of 1994, one of the tobacco companies bought a series of full-page ads in major newspapers proclaiming that the studies of secondhand smoke were inconclusive. Most were not "statistically significant." In other words they were chance findings. Yet, anyone familiar with statistics would know that having 24 of 30 studies find that secondhand smoke is harmful is not a matter of chance. However, not only did the ads with this misleading claim run; the media covered the ads and did not correct the misinformation. Is it ethical to repeat statistical claims without understanding enough about statistics to know whether the claims are valid?

Coverage of health care has been long on opinions from vested interests and short on facts. We have to have a Democrat and a Republican in every story. The point of view of the insurance industry seems more welcome than the public perspective on how health insurance is working. Myths about health care seem more welcome than facts, perhaps because they're more readily available. It is, of course, easy to find a politician who will comment on health care. It is also easy to find an insurance industry spokesperson who will assure us that there really isn't a health-care crisis. In the process, we reduce a complex issue to simplistic nonsense.

What we're saying here is that too often we lose sight of the truth. We accept what we can get easily on a given subject. We assume that everyone who is willing to speak for publication knows what he or she is talking about and is telling the truth. It is fairly evident now that such an assumption is not warranted in many cases. If journalists continue to operate on that assumption, they are, as Leibling says, not reporting and therefore not finding out. Worse than that, we are misleading our readers and listeners because of our failure to do the job of reporting completely.

Journalists also need to recognize that they are jeopardizing their own credibility and that of all journalism when they offer such hoaxes to the public. A lot of readers and listeners will question things like the education survey and the crime statistic mentioned above. A lot of Americans know from personal experience that what they are reading about health care is off target. The media risk becoming like the fabled boy who cried wolf—that is, not being believed when they're right on an important matter.

❈ **EDITOR'S NOTE:** *Craig Weatherup, president and CEO of Pepsi-Cola North America, published the following comments in a booklet about how his company successfully defused a nationwide hoax commonly known as "The Pepsi Scare." Note how the image of a syringe in a food product plays on the populace's fears about infection and tampering and how Pepsi's values about "honesty" and "openness" serve the company during the crisis. Weatherup's comments introduce a day-by-day drama chronicled in the booklet and excerpted here.*

What Went Right?

Craig Weatherup, President and CEO, *Pepsi-Cola North America*

Just about every American knows what went wrong for Pepsi the week of June 13, 1993. News that a Seattle family might have discovered a syringe in a can of Diet Pepsi launched a nationwide scare that generated hundreds of copycat claims across the country.

Now that the infamous "Pepsi Hoax" has been consigned to a bizarre chapter in corporate history, it's important and more revealing to ask: What went right? How did a company with billions of soda cans on store shelves across America ensure consumer safety and security while protecting its 95-year-old trademark? And how did we maintain a positive image amidst a blitz of often negative media attention?

These are questions worth asking. As Congressman Hamilton Fish stated in an address to the House of Representatives, "This was no simple scam, but a challenge against the security of the nation's food supply."

Despite the situation's complexities, our response was basic and straightforward. Reacting to the very first complaints, we mobilized our crisis management team and began working in tandem with FDA investigators to dissect our production process and address consumer concerns under the hot media spotlight.

Meanwhile, 50,000 people who make and sell Pepsi products across the U.S. kept the faith. Their ability to get the job done while bombarded with questions from the press, customers, and consumers was key to weathering the storm.

Above all, public safety was paramount to all other concerns. From the very beginning, we maintained an unshakable belief in the safety and security of our manufacturing process. That faith was confirmed as time went on. We also drew on a good mix of preparedness, teamwork, cooperation with government agencies, and openness with the public.

Our strongest allies during the crisis were honesty and openness. We believed that if we invited America inside a Pepsi plant—via video—and showed them a behind-the-scenes look at the speed and safety of our production processes, as well as other key events that shaped the crisis, their good judgment and reason would prevail—and the scare would end.

The voice of our consumers came through loud and clear—in thousands of supportive phone calls, letters, conversations with Pepsi salespeople, and at the cash register. The week of the hoax, sales dipped only 3–4%. Afterwards, millions of American families voted their confidence by putting Pepsi in their carts—just in time for the Fourth of July weekend.

The details of this case and our lessons from it follow. We're happy to share them with you in the hopes that the underlying principles will be as useful to you in a crisis situation as they have been to us.

Thursday, June 10

It all began at noon on Thursday, June 10, 1993, when a Seattle TV station informed Alpac Corporation, Pepsi's local franchise bottler, that an 82-year-old Tacoma man claimed to have found a syringe in a can of Diet Pepsi.

Alpac was unable to reach the man's attorney and caught more details on the evening news.

Alpac's well-rehearsed crisis management team swung into action. Although Alpac was convinced of the safety of its operations, Carl Behnke, Alpac's president and CEO, said, "We had to operate under the premise that the tampering could have happened in our plant until we could prove differently."

At the outset, the claim was bizarre, for the contaminant—a syringe similar to those used for insulin injections—is not an object used in any aspect of Pepsi's manufacturing or quality control processes.

To manage this unique and extraordinary case, a crisis team was established. Alpac's manufacturing staff worked round the clock with regulatory officials to investigate all aspects of the complaint. Alpac's management, supported by the Pepsi national crisis team, personally responded to all press, customer, and consumer inquiries and issued updates as soon as they were available.

Alpac drew on the investigative expertise of the FDA, which began a thorough examination of the plant, its production records, and its personnel. As media calls poured in, Alpac's approach was total openness and honesty with the public. TV crews toured the plant to witness firsthand how its production and quality assurance processes made product contamination or infiltration virtually impossible.

Yet, within 12 hours, a report of another syringe turning up in yet another can of Diet Pepsi hit the airwaves. Alpac and FDA released a series of consumer advisories. The FDA's alert recommended that consumers take the precaution of pouring their Diet Pepsi into a glass before drinking. The warning was issued to areas supplied by Alpac in Washington state, Oregon, Hawaii, Alaska, and Guam, but it commanded news attention nationwide.

At that point, the so-called Pepsi Scare would be the nation's top story for the next 96 hours.

Monday, June 14

As news reports of syringe sightings came in from different parts of the country, the national crisis team at Pepsi's Somas, New York, headquarters mobilized to manage the scare.

With clearly defined roles, team members focused on the most critical needs: responding to the press, coordinating with regulatory officials, and giving customers, consumers, and employees the facts.

As head of the team, Craig Weatherup, Pepsi president and CEO, conferred with parent company PepsiCo and FDA Commissioner David Kessler, and prepared to speak to the American public on network television.

The crisis coordinator directed the team's actions and coordinated communications to ensure a single voice inside and outside the company. Other key groups on Pepsi's crisis team included:

- *Public Affairs*, where a press team of six prepared to meet the onslaught of press calls and handle hundreds of radio, television, and print interviews. Others formed a production team to write and develop the right communication tools for the media, including video news releases, audiotapes, press releases, charts, and photos. Six government affairs managers helped disseminate facts to Pepsi's 400 bottlers.
- *Consumer Relations*, where two dozen specialists manned Pepsi's toll-free telephone line 24 hours a day to allay consumers' fears with the facts and gauge public attitudes.
- *Scientific and Regulatory Affairs*, where technical and product safety experts served as the link to the FDA's Office of Criminal Investigation and tracked each syringe complaint.
- *Sales and Marketing Personnel*, who relayed key facts to Pepsi customers, supermarkets, restaurants, convenience stores, and others who sell Pepsi products—and who helped to keep their businesses running smoothly.
- *Manufacturing Experts*, who assisted in local FDA investigations and in developing effective explanations of the production and quality control processes for the press and public.
- *The Law Department*, where in-house legal counsel coached the crisis team on communications and reporting issues.

Information was channeled through a clearinghouse before it went to Pepsi bottlers, 50,000 employees, and hundreds of thousands of Pepsi customers. The clearinghouse served as the resource for up-to-date communications from the crisis team.

Tuesday, June 15

Secure in its grasp of the facts, and backed by the FDA, Pepsi went on the offensive in the form of a bold, no-nonsense statement. "A can is the most tamper-proof packaging in the food supply," Pepsi President Craig Weatherup said repeatedly. "We are 99.99% certain that this didn't happen in Pepsi's plants."

To disseminate its message visually, the team needed to produce video footage that would clearly show how safe Pepsi cans really were. To get its message across, the team spent much of Tuesday creating footage that would show, rather than tell, how safe Pepsi's canning process is. The image that would overpower the picture of a syringe next to a soda can was found right in its bottling plants, where high-tech, high-speed equipment turns each empty can upside down, cleans it with a powerful jet of air or water, inverts it, fills it, and closes it—all within nine-tenths of a second.

On Tuesday afternoon, video footage of the canning process was beamed by satellite to hundreds of TV stations across the country. During the next 48 hours, 296 million viewers—almost triple the number of people who watch the Super Bowl—went inside a Pepsi canning facility and saw cans whirling by at a rate of 1,200 per minute.

"In a communications age, where video images can sear instant, lasting impressions into the public consciousness, the company that fails to understand how the image-making machinery works may live to regret it," reported Thomas K. Grose, a media analyst. "[Pepsi] instinctively knew it had to fight videotape with videotape."

That videotape, and three others issued by Pepsi over the next three days, illustrated the company's position that its products were safe. By the end of the week, Weatherup had appeared in person on a dozen network TV news shows and Pepsi spokespersons had conducted more than 2,000 interviews with newspaper, magazine, TV, and radio reporters.

"Our strategy was to reassure the public that this was not a manufacturing crisis," said crisis coordinator Madeira. "What was happening with syringes was not occurring inside our plants."

Wednesday, June 16

It was 4:00 in the morning, and the entrance to Pepsi's Somers, New York, headquarters looked like the site of a moon landing. Crews from ABC, NBC, CBS, and CNN were installing satellites to beam interviews with Pepsi President Craig Weatherup as he explained the company's rationale for no recall for the morning news programs.

Meanwhile, the crisis team was preparing a third videotape with an image that was unforgettable —an in-store surveillance camera had filmed a shopper, in the middle of a store, slipping a syringe into an open Diet Pepsi can while the cashier's back was turned.

While it was legally acceptable to use the material, the FDA asked Pepsi not to release the tape until an arrest was made, and Pepsi agreed. "Wednesday was pivotal," crisis coordinator Rebecca Madeira recalled. "The media understood our production integrity message, and we were gaining support as the day went on. We were hopeful that the FDA would announce more arrests as reports of hoaxes and recantations poured in from police across the country."

That evening, Weatherup appeared on the *MacNeil Lehrer News Hour* and on *Larry King Live.* Viewers who called in questions were overwhelmingly supportive of Pepsi.

Thursday, June 17

There was an air of expectation at Pepsi Headquarters on Thursday. An FDA press conference announcing more arrests was scheduled for that afternoon.

This time, FDA Commissioner Kessler did more than announce arrests. He strongly exonerated Pepsi by reassuring the public that Diet Pepsi was safe. "On the basis of all the information we have so far, the notion that there has been a nationwide tampering of Diet Pepsi is unfounded," he said.

Kessler's declaration had added impact because "it confirmed what we'd been saying all along," product safety expert Jim Stanley noted. "Because Craig Weatherup had already laid the groundwork, the public and the media instantly accepted Kessler's statement."

To illustrate FDA's conclusion, Pepsi released the surveillance video-tape that proved that tampering could occur out in the open, in busy stores, in front of eyewitnesses. Television viewers saw for themselves a hoaxer caught in the act. Pepsi President Craig Weatherup reaffirmed the company's decision not to recall product and thanked the public for its support. "We believe in what's right and what's fair," he said. "We believe in having the freedom to bring you the highest quality products. . . . But most important, we feel that neither Pepsi, the 50,000 hard-working people who bring you Pepsi products, nor the American public can allow ourselves to be held hostage to this type of deception."

It was a moment of vindication, but as Weatherup would remind employees, it was not a time for the company to let its guard down. "Given the inevitable increase in attention to our products and processes, each of us must take every measure necessary to ensure their integrity, including enhanced security," he said. "No compromise of that integrity, intended or otherwise, can be tolerated."

Friday, June 18

Friday was a day to celebrate, to put a definitive end to the scare, and to move on. First, an ad was created to publicly end the crisis. It began: "Pepsi Is Pleased to Announce . . . Nothing" and ran on Monday, June 21, in newspapers across the country.

To declare the crisis over for employees, a meeting for 1,200 people was held at Pepsi headquarters. Videotapes of FDA Commissioner Kessler's announcement, Pepsi's surveillance footage, the "Pepsi Is Pleased to Announce . . . Nothing" ad, and an open statement to the American public were shipped to all employees at 400 Pepsi facilities around the country. "It's time now for us to move quickly and decisively to restore . . . our business," said Pepsi President Craig Weatherup in a personal letter to employees. Armed with the facts, employees took Pepsi's message to hundreds of thousands of customers across the country.

V A L U E S   E X E R C I S E S

1. Research the topic of hoaxes in the library and find examples of the six types presented in the text—Activist, Impersonator, Personal, Political, Sensational, and Stunt. Then synopsize each hoax in the manner presented in the text, outlining specific methods, goals, summaries, and consequences. Attach a photocopy of each example to your synopsis. (You may not use hoaxes discussed in the text.)

2. Without violating your or someone else's privacy, make four lists (5 to 10 items each) based on the subjects below. (*Note:* Be sure to phrase your items appropriately or eliminate items that you feel uncomfortable sharing.)

    *   *Personal biases, fears, and convictions.* (Are you prejudiced against any ethnic group? Do you fear a mugging or assault? Do you have a strong personal or religious belief?)
    *   *Social biases, fears, and convictions.* (Do you think that a certain ethnic group gets special treatment? Do you fear that the moral fabric of your country is eroding? Do you believe in the death penalty?)
    *   *Sensational biases, fears, and convictions.* (Do you believe that a certain ethnic group is subhuman or a super-race? Do you fear ghosts? Believe in astrology? UFOs?)
    *   *Political biases, fears, and convictions.* (Do you radically support, oppose, or fear a specific politician, party, or political issue?)

3. Choose one item from each list that you prepared from Exercise 2 and provide a brief statement about how this bias, fear, or conviction can be used against you by a hoaxster and how you might defuse it.

6

Temptation

Dealing with Temptation

Temptation is relative. What might tempt one journalist—personal use of a company car, say—might not tempt another. Thus, temptation is a matter of choice. That ties it to individual values. Simply defined, temptation is the urge to reject or change one's value system because of pressure, competition, ambition, reward, or conflict of two equally important interests. But temptation, like the hoax, can catch us off guard so that in the aftermath of a decision we often feel guilt or regret.

Why? The urge to reject or change one's value system usually is *situational* when temptation is involved. In other words, we normally would not reject or change our values but now might do so to take advantage of a *sudden opportunity* or to solve a dilemma that we had yet to foresee or prepare for—like the clash of two equal but conflicting interests. The process of changing or revising values is usually a slow and careful one, based on such concepts as influences, consequences, and truth. Typically, the core elements of temptation—sudden opportunity or unforeseen conflicts of interest—require that we make a quick decision and change or reject our values accordingly.

Howard Buford, founder and president of the New York City advertising agency Prime Access, says, "Unless you think about ethics ahead of time, when faced with pressure, you're just going to do whatever is most expedient. My experience is that over time that ethical envelope gets pushed and there are definite situations which, if you think about them, you might say to yourself—*Walk away from it*. But that's not going to happen unless you have thought about ethics ahead of time."

Without a strong value system, you are more likely to yield to temptation. There is little time in the workplace to analyze questionable situations. Because of this simple fact, journalists often get themselves into ethical trouble, as we have already seen in Chapter 5. The hoax also tempts the journalist and preys on his or her busy schedule, offering itself close to deadline when there is little time to verify information. But there is a key difference with regard to the hoax and temptation: *intent*. Initially at least, most journalists do not know that they are being hoaxed but they almost always sense when they are being tempted.

Here are situations in which temptation usually strikes:

- *Deadlines.* The journalist under pressure considers taking an ethical shortcut that entails falsehood or wrongdoing, plagiarizing a story or press release or someone else's ad campaign, compromising his or her values simply to get the job done.
- *Competition.* The journalist wants to beat the competition so desperately that he or she takes ethical shortcuts that compromise values, exaggerating a rival's bad business record or stealing stories, clients, or marketing research.
- *Ambition.* The journalist desperately wants to advance in the company or score a scoop or coup that he or she takes ethical shortcuts rather than earning a promotion or beating rivals according to the concepts of right and wrong.
- *Reward.* The journalist so desires recognition (to feel validated) or money (to purchase items or ease debts) that he or she compromises values associated with work ethic or merit, such as honesty, honor, dedication, and excellence.
- *Conflict of interest.* The journalist's political, personal, or moral interests clash with his or her employment ones, but typically the journalist foresaw no conflict until now, requiring him or her to choose one or the other interest or to compromise values or conceal intent.

Plagiarism is one of the most common types of temptation, associated with pressure, competition, ambition, and/or reward. Conflicts of interest are among the most complex, often involving the values of other people and circumstances beyond the employee's immediate control. Both will be discussed in detail later in the chapter.

At this point, it is important to note that every journalist is tempted at one time or another. You should never feel guilt or regret for contemplating ethical shortcuts because of deadlines, competition, ambition, and rewards. As any journalist knows, deadlines can be impossible and competition can be cut-throat. Ambition and reward can inspire an employee to set goals and achieve at higher levels. Contemplating shortcuts to beat deadlines and competition or to get ahead or a raise in the company is an urge you may feel to offset the pressures of employment. The issue here concerns the choices you will make because of that urge. Will you yield to or reject it, postpone a decision about it, or amend or change your values to embrace it? In sum, feeling the urge does not make you an unethical person. It does indicate, however, that your value system has a weak link. Consequently, temptation offers us opportunities to test our values and strengthen them.

As an example of how quickly temptation can strike, consider the case of a *Detroit Free Press* sportswriter covering the 1994 Winter Olympic Games in Lillehammer, Norway. At the time, Tonya Harding, a skater implicated in the beating of rival Nancy Kerrigan, was the main focus of the Games and a global story that commanded much interest. The sportswriter, witnessed by two other reporters, was not trying to violate Harding's privacy for a story but nonetheless gained access to the skater's electronic mail by chance, entering the skater's birthdate. "They were just goofing around, though we still, of course, think this was wrong," said Dave Robinson, deputy managing editor at the *Free Press*. "There was absolutely no intention to use the information for a news story. [The reporter] was at the keyboard, someone read the number, they punched it in, it worked and it said 68 unread messages on the screen, and they immediately signed off."[1]

The reporter apologized in a letter to Harding. Even though the intent in this case was to "goof around" with a computer, at Harding's expense—a wrong decision accompanied by consequences—it is doubtful that the reporter really believed the birthdate would unlock the skater's e-mail. Nonetheless, when it did, the temptation to access the unread messages must have been keen. But the reporter's values kicked in and prevented her from reading such mail. If she had read the e-mail and based a story on those messages—to beat the competition with a scoop—she knew that this would have been a firing offense. Worse, the *reporter* might have become the focus of countless tabloid stories about "Tonya's E-Mail Secrets."

Not all journalists jump at the opportunity to write or shoot an award-winning story or photograph or secure a blue-chip client or account. Everyday these people make decisions based on values to let such opportunities pass because of the consequences that might ensue. In the case of Lady Borton, writer and field director for the American Friends Service Committee in Vietnam (whom you met in Chapter 1; see "Still Fighting the War"), that meant foregoing a global scoop that could have won her national acclaim and a top job as a reporter. But she had a value about fairness that would not allow her to take advantage of the opportunity because it could have harmed innocent people. "I was in Vietnam any number of times when the country was still closed [to the American media]," she says. "I could have gone out to the streets and talked to the people about political issues and could have come back to the States or phoned in my story. I could have placed the story anywhere because no one else was there. I could have gotten my story and left but afterward those people who talked to me would have been questioned or made miserable.

"That time has passed," Borton adds. "But back then, between 1975 and 1990, I could have endangered people's lives as a reporter, and that is not fair."

According to Borton, "The great weakness of the news media is the push toward the *story* rather than the *people* of the story, and so the people often are violated. When you finally get the story, the story is not worth it. I'm not talking about investigative journalism," Borton notes. "I'm talking about day-to-day coverage. What we're looking for is sensationalism, that's the goal, and if we obliterate people in the process, it doesn't matter because the journalist leaves and the people stay behind."

Temptation does not necessarily have to involve global stories and professional values and concerns, as it did in the cases of the *Free Press* reporter in Norway and Lady Borton in Vietnam. It can be local, private, and personal, with potential serious professional ramifications, as happened to Eddith Dashiell, now a broadcasting and media law professor. The incident occurred in 1985 when Dashiell was a young news director for a public radio station in St. Louis and covered a famous actor who came to town to promote seat-belt safety. Dashiell recalls,

> I had received a public relations packet from a major corporation in the area. The company was sponsoring what I considered to be a newsworthy public service campaign. As you can see, I am avoiding mentioning the company's name or identifying the actor for ethical reasons of my own. Believe me, this actor was—and still is—well known. In 1985 he had just left a very popular prime-time television drama (which is no longer on the air). Today he has a role on a prime-time situation comedy, but for the purpose of this case study I will just refer to him as "Mr. Famous Actor."

Dashiell continues, "Because of his popularity, I thought 'Mr. Famous Actor' would be a good source for an interview." So Dashiell arranged one through the public relations director of the company sponsoring this public service campaign. "The PR director said the actor would be arriving in St. Louis that night, and if I wanted to interview him I could come to the hotel where he was staying because there was going to be a reception in his honor."

The reception turned out to be a private party. "There were about thirty guests and a lot of beer," Dashiell says. "I was the only reporter there. While the guests were in the main area drinking and laughing, I set up my recording equipment in an adjacent sitting room.

"After about half an hour, the PR director quietly guided 'Mr. Famous Actor' from the party to my microphone." The interview went well. "I thanked the actor but, to my surprise, he invited me to stay. I did not feel comfortable at this party, but I decided to stay a few more minutes to be polite and then slip out without being noticed.

"'Mr. Famous Actor' came up to me a short time later. We had polite conversation, and then he began making passes at me. . . . I have to admit I was tempted, but I politely refused his offer. He was persistent, invading my 'private space' with occasional hugs. I finally was able to make a graceful exit with my self-respect in tact."

Dashiell had to cover the actor the next day at a local school. He talked about how his sons had made him aware of seat-belt safety. "He was the dedicated father and husband in front of hundreds of St. Louis schoolchildren," she says. "We spoke to each other, but we did not talk about his advances of the night before. I doubt if he even remembered making them. To this day I am convinced that I had made the right decision to put my professional (and personal) ethics before his (or my) hormones."

Dashiell believes her personal values about relationships were key in the case study.

> But there were also serious professional ethics to consider as well. As a journalist, I had cultivated a source with the public relations director of this major company. This director was also at the party, and he would have witnessed the beginning of my one-night stand with "Mr. Famous Actor." This public relations director also had contact with potential sources for news events of a greater magnitude than just some actor promoting the wearing of seat belts. If I was pegged in the journalism and public relations community as a journalist who had non-committal sex with people she interviewed, my credibility as a good journalist would have been destroyed.

As Dashiell's anecdote illustrates, temptation involves values, consequences, short- and long-term ramifications, and sound judgment. Here is a four-step process emphasizing those elements to help you deal with issues involving temptation:

1. *Consequences.* Because temptation usually involves sudden opportunity, consequences can be greater than you initially anticipate.

   Ask Yourself:
   - What is the worst-case scenario I could suffer by yielding to the demands of deadlines, competition, ambition, or reward?
   - Am I willing to pay that price?
   - How will yielding to temptation change me as a person? as a journalist?

2. *Short- and long-term effects.* Because temptation usually offers immediate relief to a pressing urge or problem, the short- and long-term effects often differ greatly.

Ask Yourself:
- Is the relief that temptation offers worth compromising my values?
- If I yield to temptation now, what is to stop me from yielding again?
- How will my political, social, or lifestyle agendas change over the short- and long-term if I yield to temptation?

3. *Sound Judgment.* Because temptation usually involves sudden opportunity, you need to assess your current state of mind before acting.

Ask Yourself:
- Is the specter of deadlines, competition, ambition, or reward causing me to respond in a way I normally would not?
- Is the suddenness of the opportunity clouding my judgment?
- Am I imagining or overlooking consequences that are causing me to behave in a manner that I normally would not?

4. *Independent, voluntary choices.* Because temptation usually challenges basic values, you need to be sure that your choices—*yielding, postponing the decision to yield,* or *refusing to yield*—will be voluntary and of your own accord.

Ask Yourself:
- Is any other person or third party playing a role in or overinfluencing my decision?
- Is any other person or third party clouding my judgment on this matter?
- Has any other person or third party influenced how I have gone through the processes of establishing consequences, determining short- and long-term effects, and evaluating judgment?

As noted earlier, temptation offers unique opportunities to test and strengthen personal and professional values. The more you deal with such issues by analyzing them in the manner just described, the more sound your judgment will become.

Now let's confront one of the most common types of temptation so potentially damaging that we must focus on it separately.

Plagiarism

Let's begin with an anecdote about cheating, which is what plagiarism is at the base level—presenting someone else's work as your own.

Christina Hoff Sommers, philosopher and educator, once wrote about "ethics without virtue" and took an approach that a colleague disliked. As you may recall from previous chapters, Sommers maintains that ethics classes overemphasize debates on social topics such as abortion and euthanasia while students "learn almost nothing about private decency, honesty, personal responsibility or honor."[2] According to Sommers, this gives students a false impression about ethics, part of which concerns social morality (mores) and part of which concerns private morality (values).

Sommers had a confrontation about that topic with her colleague, related in her essay "Teaching the Virtues":

> She told me that in her classroom, she would continue to focus on issues of social injustice. She taught about women's oppression, corruption in big business, multinational corporations and their transgressions in the Third World—that sort of thing. She said to me, "You are not going to have moral people until you have moral institutions. You will not have moral citizens until you have a moral government." She made it clear that I was wasting time and even doing harm by promoting bourgeois virtues instead of awakening the social conscience of my students.
>
> At the end of the semester, she came into my office carrying a stack of exams and looking very upset.
>
> "What's wrong," I asked.
>
> "They cheated on their social justice take-home finals. They plagiarized!" More than half of the students in her ethics class had copied long passages from the secondary literature. "What are you going to do?" I asked her. She gave me a self-mocking smile and said, "I'd like to borrow a copy of that article you wrote on ethics without virtue."[3]

The Sommers anecdote is intriguing because the students in question had strong stances on social issues but saw no moral problem with copying someone else's opinions on those topics. Another level of irony concerns where the cheating took place: an ethics class. When aspiring journalists behave in such manner, they sacrifice their credible and trustworthy reputations. Moreover, when journalists steal from each other or outside sources and pass off that work as their own, they not only tarnish their own reputations but also that of their employers.

Plagiarism is associated with all journalism sequences. It is defined as stealing or closely imitating someone else's written, creative, electronic, photographed, taped, or promotional or research work, identifying it as your own without permission or authorization.

Often, the term *plagiarism* is confused with:

- *Invention,* or fabricating portions of or the entire journalistic work—quotations, testimonials, staged images, composites, falsehoods, statistics, and so on—and passing them off as authentic. (In sum, the category includes self-generated hoaxes by journalists whose motive is not to program the media but is related to pressure, competition, ambition, or reward—elements of temptation—rather than manipulation.)
- *Copyright infringement,* or disseminating someone else's work without permission or authorization. (Plagiarism, by its very nature, infringes on the copyright of a property in addition to passing it off under the name of another person.)
- *Matching story or assignment,* or using someone else's journalistic work as a "tip" to generate an original authentic creation.

An example of invention involves an incident that occurred in 1977 at the St. Louis bureau of United Press International. A photographer stringing for the wire service there transmitted four dramatic purse-snatching photographs that had been staged several weeks earlier. The photographer reportedly wanted to prove that spot-news photos could be fabricated and still appear authentic. In a letter to *News Photographer,* Marc Kosa explained why he invented the series of photos: "It had always bothered me that as a photojournalist I was always at the mercy of most situations. . . . Unfortunately the shots turned out even better than I anticipated and on Oct. 28 the temptation to use them became too much to resist."[4]

An example illustrating the prevalence of plagiarism and the confusion about what constitutes it involves a former dean of Boston University's journalism school. The dean resigned when the *Boston Globe* reported that he may have plagiarized a commencement speech using material from a scholarly journal that also was reprinted in *Reader's Digest.*[5] However, in trying to match the story, the *New York Times* acknowledged that its account was "improperly dependent" on the original *Globe* article, or "essentially plagiarized," according to *Editor & Publisher.*[6] In sum, matching a story or assignment must be original and authentic. That means a journalist trying to match a competitor's work may not simply "rewrite" portions of or all of that work or rely on it for facts, quotations, citations, research, testimonials, and the like, passing it off as his or her own.

As the preceding example also illustrates, any accusation of plagiarism is intensely embarrassing for both the journalist and the media outlet.[7] Michael Sweeney, a former reporter for the *Fort Worth Star-Telegram,* recalls

the case of a student editor of a campus publication who was accused of plagiarizing—not once, but twice. In 1980, Sweeney was news editor, in charge
of day-to-day operations of the *Daily Nebraskan* at the University of
Nebraska in Lincoln. Sweeney says his editor wrote most of the editorials
and "took strong stands, including advocacy of *raising* Nebraska's drinking
age from 19 to 21. You can imagine how well this went over among an audience that included many 19- and 20-year-olds." Sweeney's editor also
devoted an entire front page to promote a letter-writing campaign about the
financial future of UNL. "You can imagine how well this went over among
the news staff," Sweeney observes. But then his editor wrote an editorial
using phrases and paragraphs from the February 18, 1980, issue of *Time*. A
reader caught the plagiarism, and the editor acknowledged it and apologized in an editorial: "[T]his editor has come to grips with plagiarism and
recognizes its severity. It is one person's acknowledgment of a serious mistake and hopefully won't be carried over to the institution."[8] Two months
later, the editor composed another editorial—"Reagan Would Bring Back
America's Greatness"—and was accused of plagiarizing a March 31, 1980,
Newsweek column by George Will.

Sweeney recalls the reaction to the plagiarisms at the *Daily Nebraskan*
newsroom:

> When [the editor] plagiarized—*Time* magazine, was it?—for the first editorial in
> the middle of the semester, the reaction among the staff was of two kinds. First,
> some staffers weren't surprised that [the editor] would screw up. On the other
> hand, there was a strong feeling that "there but for the Grace of God go I." Many
> people on the staff were willing to forgive one error. We all know how quickly
> some stories are written and rammed into the paper. We realize how easy it
> would be to forget to give attribution to another source, or to fail to recognize
> the difference between quotation and paraphrase. Need a fact in 30 seconds to
> fill this hole? Here, try this. It's in *Time,* and it's perfect.
>
> Among the students and professors on campus, however, opinion was
> more strongly against [the editor]. He had angered students with his alcohol
> campaign [and other stories]. These people didn't like him and seized the first
> plagiarism case as a chance to publicly denounce him. That meant that in the
> brotherhood and sisterhood of journalism, we on the *Daily Nebraskan* staff had to
> stand up for him. After all, if the editor loses credibility and face, then the staff
> associated with him must lose a measure also. So we tried to put aside our nega-
> tive feelings about [the editor] and go about our business in the public eye while
> privately muttering about how he nearly screwed us all.
>
> Things quieted down in about a week. The publications board took no
> action against [the editor] other than to warn him that a second case of plagia-
> rism would result in his immediate dismissal. It was uncomfortable to have sto-
> ries about the *Daily Nebraskan* on the cover of the city paper for a while, but soon
> they were bumped off by other, hotter news stories.

"You'd think that one episode of plagiarism would sensitize [the editor]," Sweeney observes. But readers caught the second incident. When charges arose again, the editor tried to resign at a meeting of the publications board. Sweeney recalls, "Someone on the board—I believe it was Jim Patten, a tough-as-nails reporting professor at Nebraska—said: 'We won't accept your resignation. You're fired.'"[9] This time, Sweeney says, the staff abandoned the editor. "Here we had gone from supporting him—at least in public—to practically singing 'Ding-dong, the witch is dead' as we wrote the headlines and laid out the pages. I recall that the managing editor and I conducted a little ceremony in which we sliced [the editor]'s name and title off the top of the masthead. That left my name, as the No. 2 guy, on top of the mailer. 'Hey, look, guys, I'm on top!' I told the copy desk. I was crowing. In retrospect, I feel a bit ashamed at the levity and the exultation."

Sweeney acknowledges that the editor had been careless but adds that this is a "human trait" and wishes someone would have said a kind word to the editor upon his departure. Nonetheless, he notes, "The hard, brutal fact is that newspaper and broadcast journalists must hold themselves to high standards. They must try to rise above these all-too-human frailties they expose in others, or else they must be ready for a double portion of ridicule. I really believe that credibility is the only coin we possess, and when we lose it we as journalists are bankrupt."

In addition to loss of credibility and ridicule, plagiarists also risk lawsuits against them. According to Tom Hodson, media law expert, judge, and former clerk to the U.S. Supreme Court,

> The easiest of legal strategies involves proof of copyright infringement. All a plaintiff has to do in such circumstances is show that he or she owns the work in question and that it was used without attribution or permission. Then you can collect damages, court costs, and even reasonable attorney fees. Other legal strategies include civil and criminal actions. It is a violation of common law for someone to take property of another and appropriate it for his or her purposes and profit. The plagiarist also may be committing a fraud upon the public for indicating certain works are his or her own. Also, the violator may have taken property of the author and converted it for his or her own purposes and made money on the use of the item or gained fame as a result of the use of the item. In such case you can receive even more monetary damages.

Editors at magazines, agencies, and companies also deal with the specter of plagiarism when they publish the work of free-lancers. Kathryn Fanning, managing editor of *Byline*, a writer's magazine, says, "I'm not overstating it when I say that discovering you've printed a fraudulent manuscript grips your stomach with anxiety in the same way the discovery of a spouse's infidelity might. The editor not only feels betrayed, knowing his readers have been cheated, but he worries about the feelings of the real author."

"Of course," Fanning adds, "editors ask free-lancers to sign contracts stating that their manuscript is original (and in our case, unpublished). I shudder to think of the legal ramifications should the real author sue an editor who bought such a piece in good faith without protecting himself with a contract."

As in any theft, plagiarism wastes time and money and damages personal and professional reputations, causing emotional and financial distress. The temptation to steal another's work can be keen in the hectic atmosphere of a newsroom or an agency, but infractions are easy to prove and penalties are stiff. In essence, the plagiarist steals to relieve short-term pressure and then hopes in the long-term that nobody recognizes the theft.

The ethical lessons are obvious—don't plagiarize and underestimate the intelligence or vigilance of your audience, colleagues, competitors, or employers. However, other issues involving temptation are more complex, especially when they involve a clash of two equal but conflicting interests.

Dealing with Conflicts of Interest

Conflicts of interest are monetary or nonmonetary. The former is fairly easy to address ethically because it involves money or gifts or services given to journalists for special favors. They include:

- *Junkets,* or an expenses-paid trip so that a journalist can cover an event. Officials at a ski resort, for example, might offer a magazine editor a week at the resort to write a favorable review of the facilities.
- *Freebies,* or gifts such as free meals or tickets, to befriend or influence a journalist. Officials at a new casino might invite a reporter to a banquet or send him or her tickets to see a top-name celebrity or even provide gambling chips to "try out" the new slot machines or tables.
- *Bribes,* or an outright payment or promise to buy services or goods from a media outlet in return for some favor. For instance, a lawyer can promise to purchase advertising from a TV station whose general manager cancels an investigative consumer segment about a product manufactured by the lawyer's client.

General rule: *Journalists should not take junkets, freebies or bribes and agencies and companies should not offer them.* Keep in mind, however, that magazine and book editors, along with advertisers and public relations practitioners, often solicit authors or clients over lunches and/or distribute free samples such as back issues or promotional literature or products and host corporate visits or tours. These are typical business expenses. The best way to check the ethical nature of any suspected junket, freebie, or bribe is to determine whether the item, function, service, or tour in question is an attempt to *program media for personal profit.* If so, resist it.

An intriguing example happened to Saul Bennett, president of Robert Marston Marketing Communications in New York City. Bennett was performing a basic public relations task—informing a writer doing a story about pharmaceutical products about a client's new over-the-counter drug—to gain exposure in a national magazine. "Fortunately, the writer said I had reached him just before his deadline for submission of the article, and he said he would be happy to include material I sent about my client's product. Fine, so far," Bennett recalls. "The article appeared and my client's product was mentioned in one of the paragraphs." Then Bennett received a bill from the magazine journalist for "public relations services rendered" in connection with incorporating material into the article. "I exploded," Bennett says. "I felt terrifically deceived and called the writer for an explanation. To my dismay, he suggested that I ought to have known all along that he was wearing two hats, one as a professional writer (he was a member of a national writers' society) and the other as a public relations individual who, presumably, could do what he wished by intimidating public relations people into paying, outrageously, a 'fee' for services." Bennett protested and refused to pay and the writer told him never to contact him again. "I was so troubled by this that I contacted the head of the writers' society to get an 'ethical' reading on what had occurred. She assured me that she, too, was appalled, and that the writer had absolutely no claim on a nickel of 'public relations services' fee."

Again, the lessons are obvious. Bennett was not attempting to program the media but simply offering information that a writer might want to use. It would have been grossly unethical for a reputable practitioner such as Bennett to try to bribe the writer into incorporating material into an article for a national magazine, offering him payment. But that is exactly what the writer wanted, believing he could wear "two hats." Of course, the writer could not. His main duty was to inform the audience, and so he had the right to reject Bennett's material if it was unsuitable. Instead, by asking Bennett for a fee, the writer was programming media for personal profit. Finally, although the incident affected Bennett's and the writer's professional relationship, money was at the core.

Nonmonetary conflicts affect personal and professional relationships because of *values*. Possible conflicts are endless but mainly fall into three categories:

- *Personal vs. personal value.* This occurs when your personal value clashes with a personal value of a relative or other person outside your place of employment, such as might occur during a divorce or family upheaval. (Although this type of conflict is important to note because it may indirectly cause ethical problems at work, it is beyond the scope of this book.)
- *Professional vs. professional value.* This occurs when one of our professional values directly conflicts with another of your professional values or when one of your professional values conflicts with that of your coworker, superior, client, source, or employer.
- *Personal vs. professional value.* This occurs when one of your personal values directly conflicts with one of your professional values or when one of your personal values conflicts with the professional value of your coworker, superior, client, source, or employer.

Essentially, such conflicts arise because the journalist did not foresee or prepare for the collision of two or more values. For instance, in a professional versus professional conflict, you might be torn between a value that upholds free speech and another that respects privacy. As an editor, then, should you use the name of a father charged in an incest case because it is public record? Or should you withhold the father's name because it will identify the daughter who has the same last name? An example of a personal versus professional conflict might involve a reporter who is an active participant in gay issues and who is reassigned to the copy desk because her employee believes her activities may influence her objectivity. Now the journalist has to make a moral choice. Is it right to quit participating in issues and events that affect her lifestyle? Is it right to quit the newspaper after succeeding in or establishing a career?

In nonmonetary conflicts, you usually have three options:

- *Choosing one value over another value.* In the incest case example, the editor can choose to use or withhold the father's name. In the gay issues example, the reporter can choose lifestyle over career (or vice versa).
- *Amending one or both values so that you can tolerate the troubling situation.* In the incest case example, the editor can make an exception about disclosing names when they indirectly invade the privacy of

children. In the gay issues example, the reporter can accept the copy desk assignment but increase her social activism.

• *Coming up with one or more new values to deal with the troubling situation.* In the incest case example, the editor can adopt a value of audience participation in such issues and solicit advice from readers via an editorial or poll.[10] In the gay issues example, the reporter can adopt a value about the sanctity of free speech and litigate against her employer because of the reassignment.[11]

Common conflicts of interest often occur in day-to-day assignments or activities. Some involve a clash of two ethical values held by different employees. Some involve a clash of an ethical value by one employee and a corporate interest by another.

Let's consider the two examples. Lor'e Postman, a reporter for the *Rock Island (Illinois) News*, has strong values about rape coverage. "Rape is always a difficult subject," Postman says. "Even in the 1990s, raped children, women, or men still feel like suspects rather than victims when they take the stand. As journalists, we must think twice before writing rape stories—from the first report of the assault to the trial and on to the sentencing. We must understand the consequences of printing the defendant's name (*note:* he hasn't been convicted), be aware of linking the victim with the suspect (and identifying the victim that way), etc."

Postman was assigned to cover the sentencing of a 26-year-old man found guilty of rape—or "aggravated criminal sexual assault" in Illinois. According to testimony, the female defendant was out with friends at a bar, Postman says. "She wanted to leave, but her friends said they didn't want to go yet. A girlfriend's brother offered a ride. She said no. Later she asked her friends to leave again. Still they said no. The friend's brother again offered, this time (supposedly tired because it was late) she said yes. He drove her to a local park and raped her."

Postman's paragraph describing these details read as follows:

Ms. Donald [assistant state's attorney] said the woman had been drinking in a Moline tavern with friends, said she wanted to leave, but none of her friends were ready to go. Mr. Danner, a friend's brother, offered her a ride, but she refused, Ms. Donald said.

Later, the woman again asked her friends to leave, and again they refused. Mr. Danner again offered her a ride, and this time she accepted, Ms. Donald said.

Postman's editor changed that paragraph to read:

Ms. Donald said the woman was drinking in a tavern with friends and accepted a man's offer for a ride home after her friends were not ready to leave.

"Big difference," Postman observes. "Purely by accident I happened to check the edited story before leaving the paper. Naturally I flipped out, got on my soapbox and lectured my editor about the clear differences in our stories. He hemmed and hawed, finally agreed and let me change it back. Then he edited it again."

The new edit read:

Ms. Donald said the woman had been drinking in a Moline tavern with friends, said she wanted to leave, but none of her friends were ready to go. A friend's brother offered her a ride, but she refused. Later, the woman again asked her friends to leave, and again they refused. Mr. Danner offered the woman a ride, and she accepted.

"This time there was only a slight difference," Postman says. "The editor took out Mr. Danner's name as being the friend's brother. The editor said he didn't want to 'connect' Mr. Danner with the crime, although that changed after I argued the man had been convicted. I believe by not saying—'Mr. Danner, a friend's brother'—readers would ask: 'Why didn't she take the ride home with the friend's brother instead of the stranger who offered her a ride later?'"

The editor agreed but had one last change. "He didn't want the word *rapist* used in the text," Postman says, arguing that a person convicted of rape isn't necessarily a rapist, although a jury might think so. "We went around and around," Postman recalls, "and having won the larger battles of the night, I conceded and took the word out. . . . But greatest irony came when I opened the paper and spotted my story. The headline? 'Rapist given 26 years.'"

In this case, Postman's values about rape coverage and truth were so strong that they overpowered the editor's values about rape defendants and fairness. But some conflicts pit values over corporate interests, with serious consequences at stake.

Crompton "Hub" Burton, assistant vice president at Ohio University, worked as a sports director and public relations coordinator at major television stations in Massachusetts, North Carolina, and Arizona. He has strong values about credibility. "Over my fifteen-year career as a sportscaster, applying journalism ethics to my work was very important," Burton says, "so important that ultimately I paid a very high price" at a Massachusetts station that was experiencing financial difficulties. "Skating on thin ice would have put it mildly with ratings headed nowhere and station management searching for quick-fix easy answers," Burton recalls.

> At about this time, a salesperson approached me about doing a story on professional wrestling. When I asked why this was appropriate, the salesperson responded that the promoter of the wrestling event was a client and that airing a preview story would be valuable to the sales department.
>
> It's funny, but at the time, my answer was an immediate "no" based not so much on the merits of professional wrestling as on a sensitivity about sales departments influencing editorial judgment in the newsroom. Make no mistake. In the final few weeks of my contract, I was very much aware of ratings, sales and what elements drive commercial television. But based upon my training, allowing the station's financial gain to affect the objective and unbiased presentation of the news *crossed the line*.

Burton says this was not the first time he had to deal with such a conflict but that this particular one proved to be a turning point for him. "A short matter of weeks later, I was informed that my contract was not to be renewed." Burton was told that ratings were slipping, audience research indicated that there was a problem in sports, and the sales department had found him difficult to work with. "Accepting the first two as a part of commercial television was one thing, but responding to management's accusation that my cooperation with the sales department was inappropriate or lacking—now that was something else!

> For me, this whole experience highlighted a classic exercise in ethics—with a job on the line, with ratings in the balance. Is the most expedient avenue the one of least resistance? Does running a wrestling feature or live shot in the sportscast ultimately become important enough to lose a job over or make a stand on?
>
> For me, the answer that day was yes, and today, the answer remains the same. Balancing the objective and unbiased reporting of the news against the commercial nature of the industry is an ongoing challenge. If you allow the precedent to be set, something is lost in that newsroom that can never be recovered.

The case studies by Lor'e Postman and Hub Burton illustrate the importance of values in dealing with conflicts of interest. In the short term, Postman challenged her editor and gained respect. In the long term, Burton—despite losing that particular job—went on to great success in broadcasting, public relations, and later academe.

Here is a four-step process to help you decide what action to take in similar disputes:

1. *Consequences.* Because temptation usually involves unforeseen conflicts, consequences can be greater than you anticipate.

   Ask Yourself:
   - What is the worst-case scenario I could suffer by resolving conflicting interests or values by
     (a) Choosing one over the other?
     (b) Amending one or both?
     (c) Coming up with one or more new values?
   - In each case, am I willing to pay that price?
   - How will each resolution change me as a person? as a journalist?

2. *Short- and long-term effects.* Because temptation usually offers immediate relief to a pressing conflict, the short- and long-term effects often differ greatly.

   Ask Yourself:
   - Is the relief that resolution offers worth
     (a) Compromising one value for another?
     (b) Amending one value to keep another?
     (c) Coming up with new values to replace one or more of my old ones?
   - If I choose (a), (b), or (c), where will I draw the line the next time I have to resolve a similar conflict?
   - How will my personal or professional interests change over the short- and long-term if I choose (a), (b), or (c)?

3. *Sound judgment.* Because temptation usually involves unforeseen conflicts, you need to assess your current state of mind before acting.

   Ask Yourself:
   - Are the unforeseen aspects of the conflict causing me to respond in a way I normally would not?
   - Is the pressure of the conflict clouding my judgment?
   - Am I imagining or overlooking consequences that are causing me to behave in a manner that I normally would not?

4. *Independent, voluntary choices.* Because conflicts often pit personal and/or professional values against each other, you need to be sure that your choices—*favoring one value over another, amending one or both values to resolve the situation,* or *conceiving new values*—will be voluntary and of your own accord.

Ask Yourself:
- Is consideration for any other person or third party playing a role in my decision?
- Is any other person or third party overinfluencing my judgment on this matter?
- Has any other person or third party influenced how I have gone through the earlier processes of establishing consequences, determining short- and long-term effects, and evaluating judgment?

Finally, keep in mind that you may not be able to avoid consequences in nonmonetary conflicts. However, by going through the preceding process, you will decide issues in a manner consistent with your values and you will know that you did your best under trying circumstances according to your conscience. That alone lessens the pressure associated with temptation and wrongdoing. It also builds character.

ENDNOTES

1. Dorothy Giobble, "Unauthorized entry," *Editor & Publisher*, 5 March 1994, p. 11.

2. Christina Hoff Sommers, "Teaching the virtues," *Chicago Tribune Magazine*, 12 September, 1993, p. 14.

3. Sommers, p. 14.

4. "Marc Kosa responds," letter in *News Photographer*, March 1978, p. 38.

5. See "J-School dean resigns in plagiarism controversy," *Editor & Publisher*, 20 July 1991, p. 11.

6. *"Times* confesses: 'Improperly dependent,'" *Editor & Publisher*, 20 July 1991, p. 11.

7. Plagiarism is a serious charge and should not be made against another journalist or outlet without consulting an attorney to determine if there are sufficient grounds or losses to justify a suit.

8. *"Time* article should have been cited," the *Daily Nebraskan*, 29 February 1980, p. 4.

9. According to a story in the May 2, 1980, issue of the *Daily Nebraskan*, Patten is reported to have initiated the dismissal action against the editor, claiming that the board had warned the editor that this would occur if another plagiarism was reported.

10. This occurred at the *Spokesman-Review* in Spokane when an editor solicited advice from readers on whether the paper should identify parents who rape children. Overwhelmingly, the community recommended naming parental rapists. See "Identifying parents who rape their children" by M. L. Stein, *Editor & Publisher*, 8 January 1994, p. 14. For the record, the author of this text believes that a newspaper is

supposed to act in the best interests of the community, despite what the majority of readers feel about an issue, according to precepts of social responsibility.

11. This occurred at the *Morning News Tribune* in Tacoma when a reporter sued her newspaper in a wrongful discharge suit. See "Lesbian journalist sues over transfer" by M. L. Stein, *Editor & Publisher,* 7 August 1993, p. 10.

L I V I N G   E T H I C S

Read the following interviews and articles and record your reactions in your ethics journal and/or discuss them with peers or mentors.

�֍ **EDITOR'S NOTE:** *In 1989, substantial portions of an article by* BYTE *Magazine's senior products editor Stan Miastkowski appeared in a signed column by an editor of another computer magazine. Miatskowski's article was titled "Why I Still Don't Use a Macintosh"; the plagiarized piece was titled "Why I Don't Use a Macintosh" and condensed to fit the column format. For example, Miastkowski's last concluding paragraph in the 1988 Special Mac Edition of* BYTE *reads: "It's all more than a little ironic in a number of ways. Apple, a company that got its start with a definite counterculture thrust, has turned into a typical corporate giant. Had it played its cards differently, there might be a Mac on nearly every office desk and in every home in the U.S. Meanwhile, IBM has established the real standard by opening up the architecture and making PCs truly ubiquitous." The plagiarized column's conclusion reads identically except for the deleted phrase "in every home in the U.S."* BYTE's *editors demanded a retraction in the other computer magazine, and one of sorts appeared at the end of another signed column acknowledging that Miastkowski's article was "borrowed" from* BYTE's *Macintosh supplement. Years later, the author of this text interviewed Miastkowski—now a full-time free-lance writer and consultant—about the incident. His thoughts on the relationship between deadlines and temptation also appear here.*

PC Plagiarism

Interview with Stan Miastkowski, Former Senior Products Editor, *BYTE Magazine*

Michael J. Bugeja: "How did you feel when you read your plagiarized article in another computer magazine?"

Stan Miastkowski: "I was kind of amused. I didn't get angry about it at all, mainly because it was such a terrible job that my immediate reaction was, '*Boy this guy is du-u-u-u-mb.*' Basically, when someone takes an entire column and just about uses it word for word [with his picture and signature], well."

Bugeja: "How did you learn about the theft?"

Miastkowski: "Some *BYTE* reader picked it up and sent it to *BYTE*. I might have been more angry or upset if it [plagiarism] was subtle. But it was unbelievable. I remember laughing out loud."

Bugeja: "What can you tell readers of *Living Ethics* about the dangers of succumbing to plagiarism in the professional world?"

Miastkowski: "Plagiarism certainly can be tempting to folks who are lazy. My overall impression of people who plagiarize is that they're lazy."

Bugeja: "Are their any special dangers that journalists should be aware of concerning product reviews?"

Miastkowski: "The fine line concerns technical subjects about science, computers, medicine. For instance, when you go out and research an article, chances are you are going to read what has been written about a product by other writers. I tend to write a lot of reviews about products. . . . After writing about products for so long, I have my own list of important topics I want to cover. But when I read what someone else has written and they mention something I didn't realize about the product or that person goes beyond something I might have looked at in a cursory manner, that would lead me to take a closer look [at the product in question]. I may end up writing about this angle. *[Laughs.]* Let me ask you, an ethics teacher. Is that *un*ethical?"

Bugeja: "No, as along as that aspect of your review is in your own words and uses your own ideas and approaches. It would be similar to a matching story in newspaper journalism. The reporter interviews the same people or topic as his or her rival. The original writer gets credit for having written about the people or topic first."

Miastkowski: "Oh, good!" *[Laughs again.]*

Bugeja: "One more question: What is the greatest professional problem that might tempt someone to plagiarize in the workplace today?"

Miastkowski: "I'm a full-time freelance writer now. When I was an editor, one of the things that I saw happening and see happening throughout the computer publishing industry is the incredible deadline pressure. Smaller staffs. Smaller editorial budgets. More pressure to deliver the hottest news with no money [to gather that news] faster than ever. That's a big danger. I have talked to editors who have absolutely impossible jobs. It makes me wonder, in an environment like that, do they get tempted?"

EDITOR'S NOTE: *The following observations by three newspaper journalists represent the range of monetary and nonmonetary conflicts that are apt to occur in entry-, middle- and upper-level media posts.*

Entry-Level Conflicts

Anonymous, Daily Newspaper Reporter

Just after Christmas, I talked with an editor about doing an enterprise piece on the persistent need for charity in our community. As I undertook the piece, I was about four months into the job, working as a metro reporter for a community daily in upstate New York.

The newspaper has a 35,000 daily and 55,000 Sunday circulation in seven counties, most of which have poverty rates that rival those in Appalachia. The idea for the story/package was to illustrate the people behind the numbers.

After spending a day gathering numbers and talking to officials, who gave me all the cold facts, I needed to find a family or person who could give me a face and story to go with the statistics. My options were limited to the daily soup kitchen, just a few blocks from the paper, that served the entire county of 90,000 people.

Since the package would carry Page One the day it ran (and it was later decided to use a picture page, also), a photographer accompanied me to the kitchen one afternoon. Only organizers knew we were coming.

As soon as we entered, the photographer with his thousands of dollars of equipment and I with my pen poised in one hand and notebook in the other, row after row of "clients" turned away. In that moment, we had a decision to make. No one trusted us, and many already felt shame.

Our newspaper's ethics policy is quite clear. Every employee signs a sheet promising not to accept *anything* free, from a source or agency, because of position. There are to be no exceptions. Knowing that—but also knowing we were headed for a brick wall—the photographer and I made the decision to lay down our professional selves, grab a tray of food, and ask if we could sit down with some people.

An hour later (and, I might add, after one heck of a good, hot meal—far better than I make in my microwave), enough people were convinced that by talking to us, they could make a difference. More importantly, everyone I talked to agreed to be photographed. It's hard enough to convince someone you want his or her photo in the paper. Imagine the struggle when you are sitting in front of people who are embarrassed about their need.

Being able to talk to about 35 people, including whole families, made the difference in my story. Good reporting like that means you can select the best story to tell, not just accept what comes at you. The story ran a week later, during a bitter cold spell. With the thermometer dipping to 20 below zero, and schools and businesses all around us closing because of the cold and snow, our readers got to know about a 5-month-old baby who was being carried to the soup kitchen three times a week because her father, who lost his job, had no other way to feed her.

The story ran as a Page One enterprise, with two photos on the front page, too. The jump included sidebars on more people and their needs, a volunteer and why she helped, and several other photos. Short items on what needs the kitchen had to keep serving the community were included, along with the statistics.

Because of that story, I found out when writing a follow-up piece that more people were volunteering to help, the kitchen had been called by local residents and businesses willing to donate items needed (including a heating lamp to keep the meals hot as the lines got long).

Later that spring, I ran into one of the men I interviewed but did not use in my story. He had found a job a month after the story ran by telling a personnel director he no longer wanted to resort to the kitchen. The director knew about the kitchen from our story. None of that would have happened if we had followed our ethics policy to the letter. I am convinced of that, as is the photographer. We didn't really know what could happen to us if we were caught, but I assume the punishment would have been in the form of a letter in our files.

After returning from the kitchen, I did tell my immediate editor of what we'd done. But by that time, I'd already tried to circumvent the policy by writing a check for the meals to the kitchen. That action, my editor told me, was enough. But I also was encouraged not to talk about it, since it did officially violate the very policy I had signed just about two weeks before this all happened.

When I found out I would be writing this for a book, I spoke with a top editor about it for the first time. I was told that, in his opinion, I had compensated for any conflict by paying for the meals. At the same time, there still is an attitude that I shouldn't say much about it to anyone, for fear someone "higher up" will hear of it and make an example of me.

Personally, I don't feel I made any ethical violations. I paid for the food I ate, although it was a tough call to decide how much to pay. There isn't a scale in place for people who eat at soup kitchens but can afford to eat elsewhere. And I am steadfast in my belief that without plopping down and showing I was human too that any of the people eating there would have trusted me. I'm sure what I did is what any good reporter would automatically do, especially when you consider none of these people had ever dealt with the press before we walked in the room. I'm pretty confident that presented with the same problem today, I would have done the same thing. The end result was and is worth any reprimand I might have gotten for violating the ethics policy.

Middle-Level Conflicts

Gail Taylor, Investigative Reporter,
The (Morgantown, West Virginia) Dominion Post

Ethics is about value systems. When a journalist approaches a story, he or she should do so with the assumption that the story will be accurate and truthful as well as compelling and informative. At least, those are the assumptions that I take with me when I approach a story. It always surprises me, however, to learn that not all journalists feel the same way.

For example, recently a situation arose that put an editor in a difficult position. An employee in the paper's marketing and promotions department decided to try her hand at writing a restaurant review. The editor's assistant was given the responsibility of editing the story.

When it came time to write the story, the editor's assistant received a call from the writer who asked, "What do you do when after you and your guest eat at a restaurant, you have to spend four hours at the hospital because he got food poisoning?"

Yes, it really happened. The writer said she had sampled everything her guest had eaten except for the Ranch dressing on his salad. After leaving the hospital, she telephoned the restaurant manager who admitted that sometimes the waitresses fail to put the salad dressing in the refrigerator. Also, he mentioned that sometimes they toss the salads with their hands after handling chicken.

The editor's assistant responded to the writer by saying, "Well, at a real newspaper, you would write about it, but here I'm not so sure." He then asked if the restaurant was an advertiser. Of course, the writer didn't know.

In the end, the writer and the editor decided it would be best to omit any reference to salads in the review. So telling the truth doesn't always win out, especially when a reporter works for a newspaper that is sensitive to complaints from advertisers. I must say that the assistant's comment or excuse which implied that we were not working for a "real" newspaper was also upsetting and insulting to me as a journalist. . . .

Another example relating to ethics and advertiser sensitivity involved a story that I did about the growing underground music scene in a small town. A big part of the story focused on the success a group of young entrepreneurs was having with a nonalcoholic bar. It was almost phenomenal that they managed to draw many acts popular in cities such as D.C., New York, Baltimore, and Pittsburgh. I also focused on the people who came to listen to these acts. They were part of a counterculture that had their own way of dressing, their own language, and perhaps other similarities.

In asking one of the club owners how she managed to draw such acts and their fans, she stated that rather than paid advertisements, they relied on word of mouth and fliers.

After the story was written, my editor gave it the okay, and the story ran. The next week, the associate publisher approached me, and she was extremely upset. She told me that she wanted to talk with me about my story. One statement that she made was, "You should never say that a business can survive without advertising."

Of course, I couldn't believe what I was hearing. Number one, I never said that the club could survive without advertising. Second, I thought, "shouldn't my editor have told me this?"

The associate publisher continued, "It makes our job very hard when you writers say something like that."

Well, much to my surprise or perhaps because of my surprise, I responded by telling her that I had always been taught that, as a reporter, I should tell the truth. I went on to say that I was confused as to why she was explaining her problem with my article to me rather than to my editor. I informed her that I had graduated from "one of the best journalism schools in the country," and we had always been taught that there is a wall between advertising and editorial.

"You really don't think that wall exists, do you?" she asked.

I didn't know what to say. This was my second month on the job and, until now, I had no reason to believe the wall didn't exist. I wasn't sure whom to believe—my professors at Ohio University or my employer.

I thanked the associate publisher for taking the time to talk to me. When she asked me to promise that I would never write anything like that again, I had to tell her the truth—that I could not make that promise.

Then, I went to speak to my editor-in-chief. He had already been approached by the associate publisher, but had not planned to talk with me about the story. I remember asking him, "Am I suppose to write it like I see it or am I suppose to be concerned about offending the associate publisher?"

He told me that I was supposed to write it like I see it, but that I should remember "the publisher is the publisher, and what she says goes."

As a footnote to this episode, I received a note of apology from the associate publisher the next day. I still have it. It read in part, "My conversation with you was not meant to upset you. It was simply meant to expose you to other aspects of the paper. I hope there are no hard feelings."

You might think that a newspaper that seemed governed by the will of the advertising department would never tackle something as difficult and possibly controversial as investigative journalism. But in fact, a few years ago, the newspaper hired a consultant to teach interested reporters investigative writing techniques.

The team was led by a former reporter from a large metropolitan newspaper. His techniques focused on document searches at the federal, state, and local levels and on interviewing. It was a great learning experience for a young reporter. However, early on, I noticed that, of the seven members initially involved with the project, only a couple seemed genuinely interested in contributing full time.

In fact, I was asked to participate near the middle of the first project because some of the reporters who were assigned to write stories failed to finish them on deadline. This perplexed me. Rarely do reporters miss deadlines unless they have good reason. I couldn't imagine a better opportunity than to be temporarily absolved from a regular beat so that I could learn some new skills.

It wasn't until I had spent almost six months working with what was left of the team (one other reporter and the consultant) that I learned investigative reporting is not always appreciated by your peers.

Some of the stories we wrote focused on local and county public officials as well as individuals connected to state and national politics. When we began to research the county tax system, it was agreed that we should move from the newsroom to an office downtown. As the editor-in-chief said one day, "This place leaks like a sieve." It was hard for me to believe, but it appeared that some of our colleagues were either knowingly or unknowingly tipping off subjects before we could interview them.

So, in addition to being concerned about conducting interviews that were thorough and fair, and being concerned about the quality of our writing, we had to be careful about how our reporting affected our relationship with coworkers.

Luckily, we had the full support of the editor and publisher. This was a time when having a publisher show concern for our work was beneficial. This was made clear to me when I had to interview one of his relatives about conflict of interest. Although my story had to be rewritten because the paper's attorney didn't feel comfortable with the tone, the story ran without losing any of its meaning.

When I was part of the investigative team, we never rushed to print a story—ever. We always made sure we gave our subjects ample opportunity to tell their stories.

Still, as fair as we tried to be, some people in the community perceived us as threatening. I remember that a friend of mine was getting a haircut at a local barber shop when he overheard one of the town's elected officials complain about those "evil people" writing about the tax system.

The people who seemed to be the most receptive to our stories were the men and women who tended not to be directly involved in politics. Instead, they went about their daily lives—paying bills on time, paying taxes, and not expecting special treatment. These people read our work. Sometimes they called to congratulate us when they felt we hit the nail on the head. For the most part, they did nothing about the injustices that we reported on except write a few letters to the editor.

Sometimes reporters begin to believe the "hype" that tends to surround their profession. They have a tendency to believe that they can influence public opinion, that they can lead people to make a difference. I learned that if you write stories for this reason, then that's wrong. . . . Journalists must write for the sake of writing and for the sake of truth, regardless of the conflicts they encounter.

Upper-Level Conflicts

Walter S. Friedenberg, Former Editor, *The Cincinnati Post*

When I joined the *Cincinnati Post* as editor and the first Christmas rolled around, I was astonished to see a parade of messengers and deliverymen arrive in the city room with Christmas-wrapped packages and boxes and clanking bags full of whiskey. I was told that these were gifts from businesses and newsmakers around town who were saying thanks for the coverage they had gotten in the *Post*.

I had been brought up in the don't-take-nothing-from-nobody school and accordingly made discouraging noises to the managing, city, and sports editors—remarks intended not to cause a Carrie Nation-style smashing of bottles, but to suggest that this should be the last Christmas at which these gifts are given and received.

Imagine my surprise when a couple of days before Christmas, I arrived home from work and found on the kitchen table a box containing an enormous smoked turkey—gift of a major business in town.

At that point, I spoke to my predecessor and asked him how he handled ethical challenges presented by roast turkeys, whiskey, and other Christmas gifts. His reply: "I would never accept anything I couldn't eat or drink in 24 hours." That didn't help much. I wound up keeping (and enjoying) the turkey, then writing the donor a careful note. It said: "Thank you for your kindness. However, your kindness presents me with an ethical problem. No one in the newspaper business should expect or accept any gift or benefit from anyone, especially someone who has an interest in the way the paper reports or comments on that person, or his or her business, profession, politics, and other interests."

That did the job. The next year, no turkey arrived and gifts brought to the city room dropped off to a couple from persons who had not gotten the word. By the third Christmas, we were completely out of the Christmas gift business. We had diplomatically but firmly ended an unethical practice.

Not long after becoming editor, I had a visit from about eight leaders of Cincinnati's distinguished Jewish community. There was some polite chiding of the paper's editorial views on the Middle East, which, as a former foreign correspondent and foreign affairs editorial writer, I was happy to defend.

I was then asked whether I would like to pay a visit to Israel for a couple of weeks, with all expenses paid and absolutely no limitation on where I could go, whom I could see, or what I would write. I was aware that the Israeli and South African governments were inviting editors to "expenses-paid" visits.

I explained that as a correspondent I had occasionally accepted plane and truck rides from foreign governments, but only to reach locations inaccessible by commercial or private transportation. My view was that if a visit to Israel were important or interesting enough for me, either my paper or I personally should pay all the expenses. I felt that a journalist should not accept any benefit that presents, or even appears to present, a conflict of interest. My visitors said they quite understood my view and accepted my decision, with no offense.

✖ **EDITOR'S NOTE:** *Sue O'Brien is associate dean at the School of Journalism and Mass Communication, University of Colorado at Boulder, and teaches Media Ethics and Public Affairs Reporting. She is one of the most versatile and accomplished contributors to* Living Ethics. *Her early career was in radio and television news, including stints as an anchor and political correspondent for NBC Radio in New York and as news director of Denver's KOA Radio and KOA-TV, now KCNC-TV. In 1980, O'Brien moved from observing politics and public policy to helping shape it as press secretary to Colorado Governor Dick Lamm. She spent the 1984–85 academic year earning her MPA at the John F. Kennedy School of Government at Harvard University, then returned* *to Colorado to manage Governor Roy Romer's first campaign. After Romer's election in 1986, she joined the* Denver Post, *working as an assistant city editor until 1988, when she moved to her present job at the University. In the following piece, O'Brien discusses an extraordinary conflict of interest: She was arrested for drunk driving while serving as press secretary to a governor with a tough stance on that issue.*

This Mess Was Going Public

Sue O'Brien, Former Press Secretary for
Colorado Governor Dick Lamm

With a career that's spanned being a political reporter, television news director, newspaper assistant city editor, and governor's press secretary, there's plenty of material to consider about conflicts of interest in public life.

A friend encourages me, though, to describe the time I was arrested for drunk driving and found myself serving as my own press secretary. It happened in March 1983, just weeks after Colorado had passed what was then the nation's most stringent drunk-driving law. During the legislative push, as spokesperson for a governor who fervently supported the crackdown, I had worked closely with sponsoring community groups. My arrest posed a conflict, pure and simple.

After work and an uncounted number of double scotches, I had been caught—in an alcoholic blackout—playing bumper cars with autos parked in my neighborhood. Jail and a bail bondsman followed. I woke the next morning with a chastened awareness that the booze problem that had haunted me privately was now out in the open.

What I offer here is not so much a story about me as about what the public sector calls accountability. This case confronted and tested my belief that the sovereign remedy for conflict is disclosure. In the process, I also learned to sift through what, indeed, is the public's business and what is not.

To some, I may seem to be offering a cynic's strategy for getting out of trouble. I can only assure you that I didn't have the wits that day to worry about salvaging my career. I only wanted to try to live by the same rules I had so long applied to others.

Guided by grace, I embarked on a series of disclosures, from the private to the public. The first call went to my boss, the governor, to tell him what had happened and offer to resign. I also warned him that I needed to alert the friend whose hospitality I'd abused because her home was the site of my last drink. But she also was a reporter for the *Denver Post* and would be obliged to share my story with her editors. That meant this mess was going public.

From the *Post*, the story spread, breaking first on the television station where I'd spent most of my career. For the rest of the evening the phone rang constantly. I owed an answer to each reporter who called. ("I'm sorry, Sue, my editor's making me do this.") I knew I need not confess or say anything quotable, but I also knew I needed to confirm that I'd been arrested. Yes, the charge was drunk driving, and yes, the governor knew.

The next day, the level of disclosure had to deepen. I helped the governor draft a statement saying I'd offered to resign but that, in the face of my recognition I was in trouble with alcohol and would seek treatment, he wasn't going to decide for a while. Two weeks later, another news release announced I was entering an alcohol treatment facility, that the costs were covered by my health insurance, and that I had 60 days of accrued sick leave.

Are there proper limits on this kind of disclosure? I thought so when a *Rocky Mountain News* reporter called me on the private line in the patients' lounge. What did it feel like to be in an alcohol treatment program? "Tell your editor to go to hell," I said. "I'm not on duty." That wasn't so much a breakdown in courtesy as a rediscovery of healthy boundaries between the personal and private. You don't have to projectile vomit your personal life. This is about accountability, not catharsis.

I fired my first defense lawyer for telling reporters I was going to plead not guilty. I *was* guilty and wasn't going to plead differently. Ultimately, I blessed the district attorney (recently appointed by my own governor) who chose not to reduce the charges against me. This wasn't a time to give or ask for favors. Later, the judge (recently not promoted by my own governor) sentenced me as he would have any other first-time offender—but had the decency to deliver it in chambers. For each of them, this was a study in accountability, too.

Through it all, I received unexpected sympathy—from state legislators to the mothers of MADD, who I'd worked with on the new drunk-driving bill. Their common message was that the news coverage had been unfair—that other people didn't get covered that way. But the point was that I wasn't other people. I was the governor's press secretary and I had publicly advocated for the very law I'd violated.

My instinct from the beginning was that I was fair game. I didn't need to be conveniently colorful, but I did need to acknowledge what had happened, what I was going to do about it, and what the governor was doing.

Since then, I've been permitted to manage another governor's successful campaign, work as an editor for the *Post*, and eventually teach. The arrest and my history as an alcoholic are part of my file in newspaper morgues. Everyone has stories they would rather not tell. I believe it's better to tell your own bad news. It also helps if this is more than a strategy—if you believe in what you're doing.

Today, I volunteer this story rarely and carefully, usually when a journalism ethics discussion raises questions of public-figure privacy and principles of disclosure. It's still one of the most telling conflict-of-interest stories that I know.

But it was one tough way to test a theory.

VALUES EXERCISES

1. Do two case studies based on your professional (or academic experience) involving:

   • A situation in which you were tempted to compromise your values because of deadlines, competition, ambition, or reward
   • A conflict of two professional values or personal/professional values

   For each of these case studies, write a brief summary of the situation, how you handled it, and the outcome of that situation. (*Note:* Follow previous guidelines about appropriate disclosure and do not violate your own or someone else's privacy.)

2. Run each case study from Exercise 1 through the "Four-Step Process" concerning temptation and conflicts of interest (presented earlier in this chapter). Answer questions raised in those processes and record them in your notebook or ethics journal. Do not turn in your answers but analyze them.

3. Write two more summaries, based on the case studies completed in Exercise 1, explaining how, if at all, you would handle each situation differently.

7

Bias

Exploring Racism

As we approach a new century, several ironies exist with regard to race and mass media. The first has to do with technology. On the one hand, computers and other communications tools such as scanners and satellites have brought the world into our dens and offices. For instance, textbooks in various disciplines can be completed in the author's home office equipped with computer, scanner, printer, phone, fax, and modem at the ready. The author who needs to look up a fact or reference material used to visit the local library. Now all he or she has to do is type a few commands on the computer screen and access the stacks by phone. Sources have electronic addresses so the author doesn't even have to walk to the mailbox to send letters.

Many of you will become consultants, copywriters, and free-lance journalists doing the bulk of your work and billing at home. The phenomenon of the home office or business is not limited to journalism, of course. Anyone privileged enough to own a computer can bank, pay bills, and purchase goods and services via phone or modem each day. Cable networks offer news from around the corner or the globe, both of which are becoming more diverse. By the year 2000, one in three people in the U.S. workforce will be a person of color.[1] As you can see, however, the world is becoming more diverse as it becomes more accessible electronically. To deal with racial and cultural values, journalists must be exposed to diversity but are increasingly working in narrower spaces.

This places a big responsibility on journalists in the computer era. But the first irony is compounded by another: Although journalists are able to access the world from their keyboards, many of their readers, viewers, or targeted consumers cannot because most Americans cannot afford the same technology. In other words, they still walk to mail letters or borrow books from the library, bank or pay bills in person, and drive cars to work in diverse neighborhoods. Thus, members of the audience or market may actually know the richness of diversity better than the journalist and, unless steps are taken to counter the trend, the gap between them is liable to increase.

Now we confront the final irony. The First Amendment, among other things, allows citizens to hold racist ideas. Americans have the right to be racist in the privacy of their own homes or even in public, as long as they do not break any civil rights or hate-speech laws. Journalists, more than members of any other group, are committed to protect and embrace the First Amendment. But unlike citizens holding other jobs, journalists cannot be racist because racism is, at the core, a lie that skews perception upon which all reporters and practitioners must rely.

The *Random House Dictionary of the English Language* defines *racism* as a belief or doctrine that inherent differences among the various human races determine cultural or individual achievement, usually involving the idea that one's own race is superior and has the right to rule others.

The desire to be associated with a race or ethnic group is a basic human instinct, according to Pat Shipman, author of *The Evolution of Racism: Human Differences and the Use and Misuse of Science.* "And it is in this instinct that racism is anchored," Shipman notes, "for racism is little more than a strong identification with one group, combined with fear and dislike of all others. Typically, the fear and dislike are fueled by unfavorable stereotypes, falsehoods, and half-truths, which serve to reinforce groups' boundaries."[2]

Journalists reject stereotypes, falsehoods, and half-truths and embrace objectivity, fairness, and accuracy. Consequently, those who choose journalism as a career adopt certain mandatory practices that members of other professions, such as dentistry or plumbing, for instance, do not. To succeed as a dentist or plumber, you must know how to fix teeth or lay pipe. You can be racist and accept the consequences, losing customers or contracts and circumventing civil rights laws. But you still can make a living in some neighborhoods. To succeed as a journalist, you must perceive the world as it actually exists, whether you are covering a story for a news outlet or targeting a campaign for an agency. Otherwise, you risk these dangers:

- *Mistakes.* Your report, photograph, advertisement, illustration, or campaign will contain misperceptions and inaccuracies that will tarnish your own and/or your company's reputation.
- *Problems.* Your misperceptions and inaccuracies may cause your story or campaign to fall short of expectations.

- *Embarrassment.* When your work is deemed racist, *you* become the focus of media attention and implicate your employer and coworkers by association.
- *Liability.* When your work contains race-related misperceptions and/or inaccuracies—believing allegations made by sources associated with your race, for instance, or overbilling or shunning clients not associated with your race—you or your firm can be sued, depending on factors involved in each case.
- *Morality.* Even if your work succeeds, you contribute messages to society that will cause other people—including sensitive members of your own race—pain, suffering, and humiliation.
- *Disturbances.* The pain, suffering, and humiliation caused by your report, photograph, illustration, advertisement, or campaign can lead to protests against your employer or boycotts against your product or client.

These consequences spell personal failure as a journalist. More than counterparts of any other industry, employees of mass media should know that racism is wrong. They cover or deal with aspects of it every day. They embrace objectivity, fairness, and truth as chief values and yet, because of ignorance about racial matters, sometimes fail to cover or target audiences or consumers objectively, fairly, and/or accurately. These same employees are bound by social responsibility which, in part, protects freedoms and rights of all citizens in the Republic, and yet the media still are responsible for generating stereotypes that limit these freedoms and rights for certain U.S. races and ethnic groups. Finally, media managers should know the obvious solution to race-related problems: Hire more minority employees so that the newsroom and conference room represent the true faces of America.

Yet the media fall short here, too. In the newspaper industry, with a workforce of some 53,700 in 1994, only 5,600 (10.49 percent) employees were people of color—about 2 1/2 times below the total representation of minorities in U.S. society.[3] African Americans comprised 5.4 percent of the total, with Hispanic Americans, Asian Americans, and Native Americans listed respectively at 3.0, 1.8, and 0.3 percent. The numbers for photojournalists are similar, with 4.8 percent listed as African Americans, 4.6 percent as Hispanic Americans, 3.4 percent as Asian Americans, and 0.4 percent as Native Americans.[4] Toni Laws, spokesperson for the Newspaper Association of America says that, newspapers "purport to disseminate truth" and "have a responsibility to acknowledge that white males do not have a monopoly on understanding truth. Bringing different perspectives to bear on the news will probably bring the reporting of it closer to the truth that newspapers seek."[5]

The television industry fairs somewhat better, with 18.5 percent of the professional workforce listed as minorities.[6] African Americans account for more than 9 percent of that total with Hispanic Americans, Asian Americans, and Native Americans at 6 percent, 2 percent, and 0.5 percent, respectively. Minorities make up 11.3 percent of the radio workforce, with African Americans at 4.4 percent, and Hispanic Americans, Asian Americans, and Native Americans at 3.2 percent, 2.2 percent, and 1.2 percent, respectively.

The American Society of Magazine Editors has no statistics about minority representation. Stephen Shepard, an ASME president and editor of *Business Week*, notes that although the magazine industry does not track minority representation, any percentage number would be "insignificant."[7]

The public relations industry lists 155,000 people in the profession, with 7.1 percent African American and 3.2 percent Hispanic American, according to 1993 Bureau of Labor Statistics cited by the Public Relations Society of America. No statistics were available for Asian Americans.

The American Advertising Federation and the Advertising Research Foundation had no data on minority representation in advertising. Representatives of both organizations estimated that statistics would be similar to those reported for public relations.

Lynne Choy Uyeda, founder of Asian American Advertising and Public Relations Alliance in Los Angeles, says that tallying minority representation in her fields is difficult because agencies and companies are scattered across the United States and range from small independent companies to major communications corporations. Nonetheless, she believes, the percentage of Asian Americans working in advertising and public relations would be lower than that of African Americans and Hispanic Americans. She says that cultural values are responsible, in part. "Bringing attention to ourselves is not in our culture, and working in the advertising and public relations industry is not something that is typically encouraged by Asian families." Consequently, fewer than 30 Asian-owned agencies exist, she says, mostly on the West Coast.

Uyeda was one of the first to found an agency in 1984. "When I first went into the business, nobody else was around and nobody knew there was an Asian market," she says. "Even within our industry, if we are Asian, the mainstream people tend to look at us not as real professionals. They assume that we all look alike and do not recognize the diversity within the Asian population. To them, Asian is a generic term." This attitude in advertising and public relations compounds problems associated with Asian cultural values, Uyeda notes, keeping many Asian Americans out of the business. When Asian Americans apply for jobs, many personnel directors assume "we just got off the boat yesterday," Uyeda says. "They assume we don't speak English. They assume we are non-Americans and therefore would be very hard to deal with. They assume we don't know how to do business American-style. That may be true for the new arrivals. But then these American companies forget that many of us have been here three to four generations. When interviewers speak to us, their first comment might be, 'My, you speak English so well.' They don't understand how insulting these things are."

Such attitudes may account for other, troubling statistics regarding race and mass media. According to a *USA Today*/CNN/Gallup poll, 66 percent of African Americans believe newspapers "do not pay attention" to Black interests in their coverage.[8] Newspapers were cited as the most racially inflammatory medium, with 47 percent of Black respondents claiming that coverage actually worsens race relations and only 14 percent claiming it improves such relations. Conversely, only about 25 percent of Hispanic Americans and 12 percent of Asian Americans thought coverage worsened relations. Perhaps more important are statistics concerning minority representation in mass media. When asked if having a reporter of their own race or ethnic group might improve coverage-related stories, 74 percent of African Americans, 68 percent of Hispanic Americans, and 63 percent of Asian Americans responded that it would make a "great" or "moderate" difference. Only 10 percent of White respondents said it would make a "great" difference, and 33 percent said it would make a "moderate" one.

The mass media has been aware of the problem of minority representation since the release of the Kerner Commission Report. The report grew out of race-related riots in the late 1960s and made these specific recommendations:

- Expand coverage of the Negro community and of race problems through permanent assignment of reporters familiar with urban and racial affairs, and through establishment of more and better links with the Negro community.
- Integrate Negroes and Negro activities into all aspects of coverage and content, including newspaper articles and television programming. The news media must publish newspapers and produce programs that recognize the existence and activities of Negroes as a group within the community and as part of the larger community.
- Recruit more Negroes into journalism and broadcasting and promote those who are qualified to positions of significant responsibility. Recruitment should begin in high schools and continue through college; where necessary, aid for training should be provided.
- Accelerate efforts to ensure accurate and responsible reporting of riot and racial news, through adoption by all news-gathering organizations of stringent internal guidelines.

As Sidmel Estes-Sumpter, planning manager at WAGA-TV in Atlanta, writes, "The terminology is archaic, but if you substitute the words 'people of color' for the word 'Negro' or 'Negroes,'" you get a "blueprint" that the news media has yet to follow more than a quarter century after the Kerner Report.[9] According to Estes-Sumpter, "The news media has wrestled with these issues by creating hundreds of diversity committees and task forces, year 2000 goals, tons of paperwork and reports. These efforts, though, have yielded little progress and a lot of frustration." At the core of the discontent is the issue of stereotypes that alienate and offend people of color.

Resisting Stereotypes

Another irony exists with regard to racism and media—the word *stereotype*. It is a printing term depicting the outmoded practice of making a cardboard mold of a page of type and then pouring molten metal into the mold. The word has come to mean a "set form or convention," according to the *Random House Dictionary of the English Language*. Metaphorically, journalists are still composing misperceived characteristics about certain racial and ethnic types and stamping those molds on all who belong to a particular race or group.

The issue of stereotypes is treated in a report titled *News Watch*, a publication of the Center for Integration and Improvement of Journalism at San Francisco State University. "Although they can cut both ways," the report notes, "stereotypes frequently have been used to denigrate individuals because of race or ethnicity. Broad generalizations about a racial or ethnic population rob individuals of their uniqueness. To report with accuracy and comprehensiveness, journalists must be aware of, and avoid the use of, stereotypes."[10]

The report provides many examples of stereotypes, several of which are mentioned here. One of the most common labels—the assumption that "American means white"—appeared in a July 2, 1993, story in the *San Francisco Chronicle* when a sportswriter said of tennis star Jim Courier: "For what it's worth, Courier is an American tennis force in the strictest sense. When it comes to (Pete) Sampras, Andrea Agassi, Michael Chang, Ivan Lendl, (Martina) Navratilova, Jennifer Capriati and Mary Joe Fernandez, either the player or their parents were immigrants to the United States."

The report concluded: "To stereotype U.S. citizens who emigrated to the United States as the other, or foreigners, is not only inaccurate but downright unAmerican in a nation in which immigrants have played such a large role in history."

The sportswriter in question apologized for the stereotype, saying it in no way reflected his beliefs. He is correct because that is yet another danger associated with stereotypes. These so-called molds were fashioned by others and used so many times that many have become clichés. When you use one, as the sportswriter did, you may be accused of being racist when you really are only echoing the misperceptions of the past. For example, consider these stereotypes associated with Native Americans:

- "Circle the wagons"—a phrase that appeared at least five times in headlines in the *New York Times* between October 1993 and May 1994, according to *News Watch.*
- "On the war path"—a variation of which was used in a headline in a January 15, 1994, article in the *San Francisco Examiner*: "KPIX goes on warpath."
- "Cavalry to the rescue"—a variation of which was used in a July 23, 1993, *Grand Forks Herald* story: "No cavalry coming yet: House vote on $3 billion flood assistance delayed."
- "Ugh"—used in a May 4, 1993, headline in the *New York Daily News*: "Donald Says Ugh to Indian Gambling."

These and other stereotypes—"smoking a peace pipe" or "going off the reservation"—smack of a "cowboys and Indians" mentality and, among other things, depict Native Americans as "savage" or "hostile."

Mark Trahant, executive editor of the *Salt Lake City Tribune*, cites an 1867 editorial published in the *Idaho (Boise) Statesman* that is indicative of that era. The article called for a feast to commemorate a grant treaty council of all Idaho Indians and recommended: "Then just before the big feast, put strychnine in their meat and poison to the death the last mother's son of them."

Trahant, a member of the Shoshone-Bannock Tribe in Idaho and past president of the Native American Journalists Association, writes, "This may be ancient history to some—but to me, it's part of a continuing fabric of history that has not yet found the right pattern. The majority press still writes about American Indians with this misplaced passion—now it's found on the sports pages" with reference to names of sports teams.[11]

Delmarie Cobb, writing in the trade publication *Electronic Media,* notes that African Americans watch eight hours of television each night but seldom see themselves as "anything other than entertainers, comedians, drug dealers, murderers, irresponsible fathers and husbands, or mothers with babies out of wedlock. The strength of television is its unique ability to project pictures—and images can have a searing effect on people's psyches."[12]

An illustration of that assessment is a comparison between portrayals of African Americans in two covers of major magazines in August 1993. The White-owned *Newsweek*'s title read "A World Without Fathers, The Struggle to Save the Black Family"; the Black-owned *Ebony*'s read "The New Black Family, Determined, Dynamic and Diverse."

News Watch states, "The chasm between the two perspectives illustrates the criticism most often voiced about the way mainstream American journalism covers African Americans: It focuses on the downside rather than the more everyday—and representative—side of black life, thought and culture."[12]

Patricia Raybon, free-lance writer and educator, discusses these and other stereotypes associated with African Americans in her essay, "A Case of Severe Bias," in the Living Ethics section at the end of this chapter.

Stereotypes associated with Hispanics include the terms *illegal* and *alien.* According to *News Watch,* "The National Association of Hispanic Journalists, among other Latino groups, has long argued that when used as nouns, the terms 'alien,' 'illegal' and 'illegal alien' are dehumanizing and inaccurate. Individuals can commit illegal acts, such as entering the United States without proper documentation, but how can a human being be deemed an 'illegal' person? The term 'alien' conjures up images of menacing, greenish creatures who are invaders from another planet."[14] Other stereotypes include barefooted, sloven, sombreoed, siesta-taking Hispanics depicted in headlines, stories, slogans, advertisements, campaigns, photographs, or illustrations.

Many Whites see Hispanic Americans as one ethnic group. However, diversity exists to such extent in the Hispanic American community that debate continues as to how, precisely, to refer to members who appear to share the same ethnicity. According to *News Watch,*

> The term Hispanic has gained wide use since it was adopted by the U.S. Census Bureau to designate Americans of Latin American ancestry, but it is shunned by some Latino leaders whose ancestry is not Spanish. Latino, the term used by the *News Watch* team, also has gained wide use, but it, too, is seen by some as inaccurate when referring to Latinos of Indian or African ancestry. Chicano was the preferred term for some Mexican Americans in decades past, and is still used by many, but it is seen as a politicized term by some Mexican Americans. Mexican or Mexican American or Cuban or Cuban American, Puerto Rican and other terms are preferred by varying numbers of people from each community.

To avoid stereotyping, *News Watch* advises, simply ask the source or client what specific term is preferred: "Regardless of the answer, the consultation would demonstrate an interest in getting it right."[15]

Diversity in the Asian American community also is rich and complex, no longer comprised mainly of Chinese, Japanese, and Filipinos, as was somewhat common before the Vietnam War. *Project Zinger,* a critical look at news media coverage of Asian Pacific Americans—also published by the Center for Integration and Improvement of Journalism—cites these common stereotypes: "Depending on who's talking, Asian Pacific Americans are clever, shrewd, sneaky, inscrutable, exotic, good in math, a model minority, China dolls, Geishas or rich. Whether positive or negative, however, a stereotype is inaccurate."[16]

Jon Funabiki, director of the Center for Integration and Improvement of Journalism, cites a blatant example of a Japanese American stereotype: a 1943 cartoon in the *San Francisco Examiner* depicting Japanese American men with buck teeth and thick eyeglasses, crossing their fingers and reciting the pledge of allegiance in a World War II concentration camp. "The cartoon is a frightening reminder of how the news media can whip up racism," Funabiki writes. "Fifty years later, the media are still promoting stereotypes and fears of a different kind of 'Asian Invasion.' Whether a story concerns automobile sales, computer chip manufacturing or real estate deals, Japanese businesses, institutions and people are often characterized as sinister marauders hell-bent on making up for their losses during the war."[17]

He cites as examples an October 9, 1989, cover of *Newsweek* on Sony's purchase of Columbia Pictures. The title warns "Japan Invades Hollywood" and portrays the Statue of Liberty as an Asian woman in a kimono. The May 1989 issue of *Atlantic* features a threatening sumo wrestler eyeing the globe under the title "Containing Japan."

Funabiki says that such stereotypes often affect the lives of Asian Americans, noting the 1982 murder of Vincent Chin, a Chinese American beaten by an autoworker in Detroit who assumed he was Japanese and blamed him for unemployment in the auto industry.

Stereotypes fuel racism and thus have great impact on people's lives. For instance, Hilary Tham, a free-lance writer based in Washington, DC, is a Malaysian Chinese who became an American in the early 1970s. A decade later, she experienced a racial encounter in the parking lot of a Texas restaurant. "My five-year-old daughter opened the door of our old car into the side of the sporty red car and provoked its blonde woman driver to leap out and scream at us, 'You Vietnamese! You think you can come here and take everything!'" Tham says that at the time local newspapers were carrying stories about resentment of Texas fishermen about relocated "Vietnamese 'Boat People'" who were arriving there and making good in a short span of time. The refugees were depicted as taking work away from locals, buying TVs within a few months, and achieving easy success after coming to the United States. I think these images from the media might have been what triggered the woman's vitriolic reaction to a simple incident. Or it could have been more personal—she may have lost a job, a boyfriend to a Vietnamese."

Stereotypes also affect relations in the workplace. In an unscientific survey sent to minority magazine practitioners and published in the trade magazine *Folio:*, a respondent writes: "A black co-worker was separating pages of financial reports and a white manager approached. He said he wanted to keep them clean, so maybe he should get her a pair of gloves." Another writes: "I get the feeling that because I'm black they [whites] can talk to me any way they want. One v.p. had the nerve to say to me once, 'Do you understand?' very seriously. I'm perfectly literate. I read and write."[18]

Avelia Crynes, a skilled public relations practitioner, was applying for a job in 1986. "The posting of each job stated that women and minorities were highly encouraged to apply," she recalls. "During each interview I would be asked if I could relate to African Americans or if I could relate to white females. After all, being a Hispanic female how could I possibly *not* relate to these individuals?

"The interviewers consistently overlooked my professional abilities," Crynes continues. "I distinctly remember one interview in which the interviewer had the audacity to ask if I could speak 'jive.' Not once did the interviewer ask if I could speak Spanish, so why did it matter if I could speak 'jive' as the interviewer so pathetically inquired?"

Crynes eventually secured a position with a major corporation based on her ability to address minority issues and to recruit African Americans, Hispanic Americans, and Native Americans. "The interviewer was impressed and surprised that I had been raised and educated in a predominantly African-American environment. In addition, he felt that my being Hispanic would enable me to recruit both Hispanic Americans and Native American students to his program. Finally," Crynes says, "I had been given the chance to prove myself. After the first year of employment, I had broken every record held within the department and developed several new public relations campaigns which were quite successful."

Crynes is an example of how people of color often have to endure stereotypes before getting a chance to succeed in media jobs and to attract other minorities to such work. Because the use of stereotypes usually causes pain and humiliation, some prospective minority applicants with as much talent as Crynes feel stymied during job searches. No statistics exist to indicate how many such applicants stop searching for jobs in journalism because the interviewers recruiting them unwittingly uttered stereotypes.

Stereotypes are not leveled only at people of color, as you will learn in the Living Ethics section at the end of the chapter. They affect everyone. The best way to resist stereotypes is to be able to identify them. Ask yourself:

- Is the racial or ethnic angle in my story, photograph, illustration, advertisement or campaign absolutely necessary?
- If so, is it appropriate?
- If I am unsure, can I check with a member of that racial or ethnic group to determine appropriateness?
- Do I or my company have a resource list of experts on minority relations with whom I can regularly consult?
- Do I have access to handbooks that note offensive racial or ethnic terms?
- Am I reinforcing stereotypes by omission, eliminating people of color as sources for or subjects of nonracial stories, photographs, illustrations, advertisements, or campaigns?

- Do I know enough about a particular culture to cover or target that culture without resorting to clichés or labels?
- Can the views, words, or images in my work be misconstrued by people who do not share my own racial or ethnic type?
- Do the views, words, or images in my work reflect my true beliefs or do they suggest a false racist or ethnic bias for which I may nonetheless be held accountable?
- Have I underestimated the intelligence or sensitivity of the audience, client, or consumer in any way?

Keep in mind that anyone can make an innocent mistake regarding the use of stereotypes. Mei-Mei Chan, executive editor for the *(Idaho Falls) Post Register* (who contributes an insightful essay about Asian American stereotypes in the Living Ethics section), tells a compelling anecdote:

> Even in an ideal environment, we must take care we don't stay trapped in ivory towers where we make lofty assumptions about knowing our readers. At the *Chicago Sun-Times*, a veteran, talented reporter wrote a feature about raccoons becoming a big nuisance, cleverly comparing them to gangs in the way they intimidate, move in packs, shuffle around. This story was read by a handful of editors, including myself and a black colleague. A white female editor pointed out the historical connotations of "coons" and wondered if that might be a problem. We all said no, our readers were smarter than that. We all were wrong, of course. The story was blasted as intentionally racist by our large contingent of black readers.

The moral here relates to basic journalism: *Do not make assumptions.* If you suspect a stereotype in a story, photograph, illustration, advertisement, or campaign, eliminate it and revise more originally. If you are still accused of generating a stereotype, learn from the experience and practice another basic journalism tenet: *Do make apologies.*

Dealing with Bias

As discussed in other chapters, appropriateness is a strong but much underemphasized value. Appropriate moral people do not appear racist to others. Their morality welcomes people of all ethnic and racial backgrounds, and their appropriateness gives them a sense of occasion. But *in*appropriate moral people sometimes do appear to be racist. Although their morality welcomes people of all ethnic and racial backgrounds, they lack a sense of occasion so that their words or actions often spark accusations of racism. Finally, they and their associates vehemently deny those accusations when the real issue is insensitivity—*or racial inappropriateness.*

An example of this occurred in 1988 when CBS Sports fired commentator Jimmy "The Greek" Snyder for making what many felt were racist remarks about African American athletes. Snyder was approached in a restaurant by a reporter for WRC-TV in Washington and asked to comment about the progress of Blacks in society, to commemorate the upcoming Martin Luther King holiday. Snyder began talking about the difference between Black and White athletes, claiming it "goes all the way back to the Civil War when, during the slave period, the slave owner would breed his big black [man] with his big woman so that he could have a big black kid—that's where it all started."[19]

This, of course, is a stereotype. Pat Shipman, expert on race and science, writes, "From a biological perspective, the genetic variability among humans is trivial: after all, we share 99 percent of our genes with chimpanzees. And yet this mild genetic divergence is not wholly insignificant, for it arose in part as a means of adapting to different environments."[20] Those differences—hair, eye and skin color, height, shape of nose, and so on—vary not only from continent to continent but country to country *within* continents. Snyder's comment assumes that African Americans are tall, agile, fleet—yet another stereotype—assuming all Black people look alike. As everyone knows, Africa is an immense continent with hundreds of ethnic types with distinct physical features. We do an injustice to people of African descent—not to mention those of Hispanic, Asian, and Native American descent—when we lump them into one category. How would Americans of European descent respond if Scandinavians, English, Irish, Germans, French, Spanish, Italians, and Slavs—along with other continental peoples—were lumped into one Swisslike group?

In addition to other factors, athletic prowess is a function of hard work and determination: values. To Synder's credit, he mentioned this; but again inappropriateness tainted the remark: "There's ten players on a basketball court. If you find two whites, you're lucky. Four of five or nine out of ten are black. Now that's because they practice and they play and practice and play. They're not lazy like the white athlete is."[21]

For the most part, the media did little to address the specter of stereotypes or the question of Black athletic prowess. Months after his firing, Snyder was still inquiring, "What did I say wrong?"[22] Some journalists were asking the same question. Steven Goldberg, writing in the cultural magazine *Chronicles*, states that Synder's comments may have lacked tact but adds that "most of what he said was basically correct, and none of it was insulting to blacks."[23]

In a word, the lack of tact was as insulting to Blacks as the stereotypes—given the occasion of Martin Luther King Day. People anticipated one message from a famous commentator and received another so inappropriate that shock ensued. Consider the following:

ANTICIPATED VERSUS RECEIVED MESSAGE

Occasion: **Martin Luther King Day**

X^1: *Anticipated message*: "African Americans have made great achievements in professional sports. But we need more black coaches, not to mention owners. On Martin Luther King Day, we need to acknowledge the contributions of Blacks off the playing field as well as on it."

X^2: *Received message*: "During the slave period, the slave owner would breed his big black [man] with his big woman so that he could have a big black kid— that's where it [athletic excellence] all started."

Message	X^1		X^2
	Insightful	*Ordinary*	*Inappropriate*

Response: Shock

You do not have to deal with racial issues to use the preceding chart to gauge appropriateness. Chances are, no matter what your racial or ethnic background, you have experienced the same response at one time or other. For instance, simply recall:

- An event or situation about which you felt great enthusiasm and the urge to share that enthusiasm with a significant person, group, or authority figure
- The sharing of that enthusiasm with that person, group, or figure, anticipating support or approval
- The feeling you experienced upon receiving an opposite message from that person, group, or figure.

Here are typical responses from ethics students asked to recall such events or situations:

- "You wonder why you made the attempt in the first place."
- "You feel worthless or stupid."
- "You think, 'Why dream? Why care?'"
- "You cut off ties."
- "You fight. You want to get to the bottom of it."

That is how it feels to experience bias or the pain and humiliation associated with stereotypes. Although you may not be a person of color, or experience racism every day, you can deal with it effectively as a journalist by being able to identify with it on this rudimentary level. Then contemplate and practice these other recommendations by the authors of *News Watch*, adapted to suit all journalism sequences:[24]

Appropriate Descriptions

- Apply consistent guidelines when identifying people by race. Are the terms considered offensive? Ask individual sources how they wish to be identified.
- Only refer to the ethnic or racial background of people when it is relevant. When it is, the identification needs to be sensitive.
- Consult a supervisor if you are unsure of the offensiveness or relevance of a racial or ethnic term.
- Use sensitivity in descriptions of rites and cultural events Avoid inappropriate comparisons. For example, Kwanzaa is not "African American Christmas."
- Be specific when using ethnic or racial identification of individuals. Referring to someone as Filipino American is preferred to calling that person Asian. The latter term is better applied to a group.

Appropriate Coverage

- Strive to present an accurate and full report to your readers, viewers, listeners, clients, and customers.
- Do not overemphasize issues. For example, overemphasizing crime can perpetuate stereotypes, especially if minorities are depicted as the perpetrators.
- Do cover a variety of stories about minorities, not just those related to race, and depict or quote minorities in nonrace-related photographs, advertisements, illustrations, and campaigns.
- Find out how issues affect different segments of society.
- Expand your Rolodex. Include minorities who can provide authoritative opinions for a variety of subjects.

Appropriate Relationships

- With the help of a community member, tour your city regularly, especially in unfamiliar neighborhoods.
- Journalists and their supervisors, as well as other media staff, should educate themselves about the communities of people being covered or targeted.
- Work on building relationships with someone different from yourself. It can even be a mentoring relationship.

- Ask yourself if you have allowed preconceived ideas to limit your efforts to include diversity.
- Take inventory of your circle of friends, coworkers, reading material, music, and extracurricular activities. Assess how diverse they are and make some changes if diversity is limited.

Journalists who follow such advice will have a personal edge over insensitive counterparts. The edge is twofold. As noted in the beginning of this chapter, journalists who reject racism also avoid errors associated with misperceptions. They write or document complete and accurate stories or target consumers or publics with insight and precision. Perhaps more importantly, however, they learn different ways to solve problems, approach assignments, appreciate cultures, contribute to communities, and, above all, disseminate appropriate and accurate information.

ENDNOTES

1. Marilyn Kern-Foxworth, "Minorities 2000," *Public Relations Journal*, August 1989, p. 14.

2. Pat Shipman, "Facing racial differences—Together," *Chronicle of Higher Education*, 3 August 1994, p. B2.

3. "A report on the 1994 Newspaper Newsroom Surveys," National Association of Minority Media Executives, p. 3.

4. "A report on the 1994 Newspaper Newsroom Surveys," p. 5.

5. Rodney K. English, "What newspapers can teach magazines," *Folio:*, 15 August 1993, p. 38.

6. This and other percentages are taken from RTNData compiled by Dr. Vernon Stone, University of Missouri journalism professor emeritus.

7. Pat Guy, "Magazines seek minorities," *USA Today*, 22 October 1992, p. 4B.

8. Mark Fitzgerald, "Most Blacks upset by news coverage," *Editor & Publisher*, 6 August 1994, p. 15.

9. Sidmel Estes-Sumpter, "Responding to a revolution," *Kerner Plus 25 Report*, March 1993, p. 2.

10. *News Watch*, multiple authors, Center for Integration and Improvement of Journalism, San Francisco State University, 1994, p. 8.

11. Mark Trahant, "Ethnic media an important bridge to minority communities," *Kerner Plus 25 Report*, p. 25.

12. Delmarie Cobb, "News 'fairness' must extend to Blacks," 24 September 1990, *Electronic Media*, p. 4.

13. *News Watch*, p. 36.

14. *News Watch*, p. 44.

15. *News Watch*, p. 46.

16. *Project Zinger*, multiple authors, Center for Integration and Improvement of Journalism, San Francisco State University, 1993, p. 3.

17. Jon Funabiki, "'Asian invasion' clichés recall wartime propaganda," *Extra!*, July/August 1992, p. 13.

18. Rodney K. English, "What are lily white and read all over? Mainstream American magazines," *Folio:*, 15 August 1993, p. 38.

19. "CBS fires Jimmy 'the Greek' for comments about Blacks," New York Times News Service via the *Columbus Dispatch*, 17 January 1988, p. 1.

20. Shipman, p. B2.

21. "CBS fires Jimmy 'the Greek' for comments about Blacks," p. 1.

22. Rudy Martzke, "'Greek' convinced his statements were accurate," *USA Today*, 14 April 1988, p. 3C.

23. Steven Goldberg, "What's so bad about Jimmy the Greek?" *Chronicles*, May 1988, p. 7.

24. *News Watch*, pp. 52–53.

L I V I N G   E T H I C S

Read the following interviews and articles and record your reactions in your ethics journal and/or discuss them with peers or mentors.

❊ **EDITOR'S NOTE:** *Patricia Raybon, a former editor of the* Denver Post's *Sunday Contemporary magazine, is an associate professor at the University of Colorado at Boulder. A published essayist, Raybon is writing a book about racial forgiveness and has published essays in such publications as the* New York Times *and* Newsweek, *where the following piece originally appeared.*

A Case of Severe Bias

Patricia Raybon, Journalism Educator

This is who I am not. I am not a crack addict. I am not a welfare mother. I am not illiterate. I am not a prostitute. I have never been in jail. My children are not in gangs. My husband doesn't beat me. My home is not a tenement. None of these things defines who I am, nor do they describe the other black people I've known and worked with and loved and befriended over these 40 years of my life.

Nor does it describe most of black America, period.

Yet in the eyes of the American news media, this is what black America is: poor, criminal, addicted and dysfunctional. Indeed, media coverage of black America is so one-sided, so imbalanced that the most victimized and hurting segment of the black community—a small segment, at best—is presented not as the exception but as the norm. It is an insidious practice, all the uglier for its blatancy.

Over the years I have observed a steady offering of media reports on crack babies, gang warfare, violent youth, poverty and homelessness—and in most cases, the people featured in the photos and stories were black. At the same time, articles that discuss other aspects of American life—from home buying to medicine to technology to nutrition—rarely, if ever, show blacks playing a positive role, or for that matter, any role at all.

Day after day, week after week, this message—that black America is dysfunctional and unwhole—gets transmitted across the American landscape. Sadly, as a result, America never learns the truth about what is actually a wonderful, vibrant, creative community of people. Most black Americans are *not* poor. Most black teenagers are *not* crack addicts. Most black mothers are *not* on welfare. Indeed, in sheer numbers, more *white* Americans are poor and on welfare than are black. Yet one never would deduce that by watching television or reading American newspapers and magazines.

Why do the American media insist on playing this myopic, inaccurate picture game? In this game, white America is always whole and lovely and healthy while black America is usually sick and pathetic and deficient. Rarely, indeed, is black America ever depicted in the media as functional and self-sufficient. The free press, indeed, as the main interpreter of American culture and American experience, holds the mirror on American reality—so much so that what the media say is *is,* even if it's not that way at all. The media are guilty of a severe bias and the problem screams out for correction. It is worse than simply lazy journalism, which is bad enough; it is inaccurate journalism. For black Americans like myself, this isn't just an issue of vanity—of wanting to be seen in a good light. Nor is it a matter of closing one's eyes to the very real problems of the urban underclass—which undeniably is disproportionately black. To be sure, problems besetting the black underclass deserve the utmost attention of the media, as well as the understanding and concern of the rest of American society.

But if their problems consistently are presented as the *only* reality for blacks, any other experience known to the black community ceases to have validity, or to be real. In this scenario, millions of blacks are relegated to a sort of twilight zone, where who we are and what we are isn't based on fact but on image and perception. That's what it feels like to be a black American whose lifestyle is outside of the aberrant behavior that the media present as the norm.

For many of us, life is a curious series of encounters with white people who want to know why we are "different" from other blacks—when, in fact, most of us are only "different" from the now common negative images of black life. So pervasive are these images that they aren't just perceived as the norm, they're *accepted* as the norm.

I am reminded, for example, of the controversial Spike Lee film, "Do the Right Thing," and the criticism by some movie reviewers that the film's ghetto neighborhood isn't populated by addicts and drug pushers—and thus is not a true depiction.

In fact, millions of black Americans live in neighborhoods where the most common sights are children playing and couples walking their dogs. In my own inner-city neighborhood in Denver—an area that the inaccurate local press consistently describes as "gang territory"—I have yet to see a recognizable "gang" member or any "gang" activity (drug dealing or drive-by shootings), nor have I been the victim of "gang violence."

Yet to students of American culture—in the case of Spike Lee's film, the movie reviewers—a black, inner-city neighborhood can only be one thing to be real: drug-infested and dysfunctioning. Is this my ego talking? In part, yes. For the millions of black people like myself—ordinary, hard-working, law-abiding, tax-paying Americans—the media's blindness to the fact that we even exist, let alone to our contributions to American society, is a bitter cup to drink. And as self-reliant as most black Americans are—because we've had to be self-reliant—even the strongest among us still crave affirmation.

I want that. I want it for my children. I want it for all the beautiful, healthy, funny, smart black Americans I have known and loved over the years.

And I want it for the rest of America, too.

I want America to know us—all of us—for who we really are. To see us in all of our complexity, our subtleness, our artfulness, our enterprise, our specialness, our loveliness, our American-ness. That is the real portrait of black America—that we're strong people, surviving people, capable people. That may be the best-kept secret in America. If so, it's time to let the truth be known.

❈ **EDITOR'S NOTE:** *Mei-Mei Chan, executive editor of the Idaho Falls'* Post Register, *is the only Asian woman in the United States who holds that job title at a daily newspaper. She is often quoted or cited in journalism trade magazines that cover diversity. As Chan writes in the following article, "I have become a popular token in the industry, asked to speak and make statements such as this for your ethics textbook. I willingly accept—so that someday soon, I won't be so unique."*

Asian Stereotypes

Mei-Mei Chan, Executive Editor, *The (Idaho Falls) Post Register*

I was born in Canton, China, an only child, and grew up in Chicago with the Brady Bunch as my surrogate family. How I longed to be part of that clan, one of the pretty blonde girls with the handsome brothers, manicured parents, big house and dog, whose problems were all solved in 30 minutes.

Over the years, I've been insulted because of my ethnicity—sometimes unintentionally. As a college student in Europe for the summer, an Austrian roommate said during a misunderstanding, "that sneaky Chinese." As a married adult, I walked into a grocery store in Washington, DC, and was confronted by a coupon lady who asked, "Do you speak English?" In my current job as Executive Editor of the *Post Register*, one caller quizzed me about my name. When I said I was Chinese, he paused, then said, "Oh, you must be very smart."

Stunned, how does one respond? Sometimes it's senseless cruelty. More often, it's crude ignorance. What does one know of Asians without getting to know a specific Asian? Images based in history have been perpetuated and twisted in the media and popular culture: Those Japs bombed Pearl Harbor. They're taking our jobs away from us. They're model citizens, brilliant students, nerdy engineers, obedient Geishas, restaurant and laundry workers, gangsters, gardeners.

But they're also living below the poverty line, or struggling to adapt in a foreign country—skilled professionals doing menial work, for example, because of the language barrier. And they're also integrated into every level of mainstream America, as teachers, insurance salespeople, clerks, cops, craftpeople, politicians—just average everyday citizens.

The media must be fair and accurate—that's our job. Any time a headline says "Japanese invade" or a story says "model minority," or Asians are covered only on Chinese New Year, we fail, miserably. We are perpetuating harmful images that distort reality, fuel hatred, and can—and have—resulted in physical violence. Perhaps the most widely known case is that of Vincent Chin, a Chinese American beaten to death in 1982 by an auto worker who blamed him for unemployment woes.

When news coverage centers on white middle-aged males, when that "majority" is used exclusively for sources or in pictures, that, too, is a disservice.

The Asian American Journalists Association (AAJA) has evaluated good, bad, and ugly coverage through *Project Zinger,* finding many blatant, and some more subtle, examples of bias and insensitivity. Among them were cartoons depicting Asians with buck teeth and slanted eyes; a *Newsweek* article focusing on Olympic skater Kristi Yamaguchi's ethnic ties—even though she's fourth-generation Japanese American; and the delay by the media to include Asians, particularly Korean Americans, in coverage of the Los Angeles riots following the Rodney King verdict in 1992.

AAJA offers a handbook on more accurately covering and portraying Asian communities—did you know, for example, that there are 17 distinct Asian groups and another 8 Pacific Islander groups?

Diversity is not just color. It's gender, education, age, background, religion, you name it. Your community may appear to be homogenous now, but it won't always be. Even here in Idaho, we have counties whose minority numbers have climbed fourfold since 1990. And most communities are not as homogenous as we might think.

It usually takes extra effort to discover those other stories, the less visible communities, the less vocal elements. They don't have public relations machinery, and often view the media with distrust and fear.

Those who cover the news are only beginning to understand and react to these different voices. React we must. As readership stagnates and minority numbers increase (by the year 2000, one of three Americans will be minorities), they are the newspaper industry's best hope for survival.

As the only Asian female executive editor of a daily paper, I have become a popular token in the industry, asked to speak and make statements such as this for your ethics textbook. I willingly accept—so that someday soon, I won't be so unique.

Executives and managers must fight the inclination to surround themselves with those like themselves. When you have like-minded people, you don't have conversations; you have a monologue. As the world keeps changing, who wants to hear a monologue?

Diverse voices make for richer, multidimensional discussions; what you then provide to readers and viewers is fuller and deeper, more in tune with reality. My background, your background, their background—those differences are assets in today's media.

People of color are currently in great demand in the industry—a sharp minority copy editor can just about write his or her own ticket anywhere in the country. The problem is that the pool is minuscule, compared with that of Whites. Only about 12 percent of 33,000 journalism school graduates are minorities. And only 10 percent of all graduates go into newspapers, radio, or TV. Of that minority number, somewhere around 400—there is the cream (as with any group)—are quickly scooped up by the big players. Then there is a large body of adequate journalists, whose background may be the edge that gets them hired over adequate White journalists.

It can be very difficult for smaller media companies to hire qualified minority journalists, who, like many other colleagues, long for the bright lights of the *New York Times* or *Los Angeles Times*. Although job banks exist at the minority journalism organizations, they are usually not up to date and not centralized for recruiters. I get at least one unsolicited resumé a week at the *Post Register*, with 90 percent from males (presumably white) and 10 percent from females. Despite fairly extensive efforts, I have been unable to fill a position with a person of color, though that is a top priority.

Among many media companies, Asians and Native Americans are not perceived to be as minority as Blacks and Hispanics. Ten years ago, an executive at the *Washington Post* admitted, "We had not considered Asians to be minorities."

Once hired, people of color face challenges other new hires do not. Because they stand out so visibly, they are held to higher standards. They are expected to be better than adequate, to prove they deserved being hired; "being average" is perceived by some observers as failure. Rather than taking time and effort to train minorities (and everyone else), managers are schooled in the "sink or swim" method. When a White person sinks, it's just more driftwood. When a person of color sinks, it's an indictment of the whole race. Those minorities who do rise, and who are not prepared or trained for their new tasks, are viewed as another example of affirmative action at its worst.

The traits associated with Asians are yet more obstacles. Like the inequity that dubs assertive women "bitches" and assertive men "go-getters," Asians who don't fit passive, agreeable images are soon dubbed trouble makers. I've been told by managers that I'm too aggressive—it's hard to image a male colleague being chided for that. On the other hand, I have to work at overcoming my reluctance to interrupt, to be able to barge into my publisher's office as my White male counterpart does.

Because of the stereotyped image, or the broken stereotyped image, Asians often are overlooked when it comes to promotions to top positions. And just as grass is greener on the other side of the fence, there is no more desirable employee than one someone else has—thus the frustration among, and frequent movement by, people of color.

In conclusion: All of us have biases—that's a given. We need to be aware of the more damaging ones, and be willing to overcome them. Every day, how we view the world is greatly colored and skewed by the powerful, pervasive media. That is a serious responsibility and a difficult undertaking. It is vital that the media work at accurately and fairly portraying every aspect of the world, including people of color, whose numbers continue soaring. You cannot do that without a diverse staff collaborating to make thoughtful decisions. We need more young people of color to join the journalism profession so they can be part of that brain trust, to help present what is true, and break down barriers to understanding and mutual respect.

❖ EDITOR'S NOTE: *Lynne Choy Uyeda heads Lynne Choy Uyeda & Associates, an advertising and public relations firm founded in 1984. Uyeda is considered a pioneer in the field of campaigns targeted at Asian Americans and diverse Asian immigrant groups. Her company is retained by major corporations and government entities. In 1977, she founded the Asian Business Association and served as its president in Los Angeles from 1988 to 1990. In 1992, she founded the Asian-American Advertising and Public Relations Alliance, which has about 125 members. In the following piece, Uyeda discusses stereotypes with which Asian Americans must contend and the challenges that await them in advertising and public relations.*

Gee, You Speak English!

Lynne Choy Uyeda, Founder, *Asian-American Advertising and Public Relations Alliance*

I inform the person that I speak English very well.
"Where are you from?" he asks.
"Los Angeles, California," I reply.
"Where were you born?"
"Sacramento, California."
"I mean, where were your *parents* born?"
"San Francisco."
This is a typical interrogation. It also can begin with "What's your nationality?"
"American," I say.
Sometimes former veterans and other travelers to Pacific Rim countries might say a few fractured words to me in an Asian language. I respond with a blank stare because English is my first and only language.
At about this point, such a person might attempt to draw me out by mentioning his affinity for particular Asian foods. I tell him my favorite foods are pasta and pizza.
He is confused. My perfect English throws him off. My taste for pasta and pizza doesn't tell him anything about me. Almond-shaped eyes and café au lait complexion might identify me as Native American or, in some cases, Hispanic. The interrogator's problem is that he does not know how to ask a simple question. I inform him the proper way to find out person's ancestry is to ask: "What is your ancestry?" This is not an offensive question. California's ethnic diversity, interracial marriages, and biracial offspring will soon rival Hawaii's.
This conversation takes place, on average, about twice a month. I must admit, it's less crude than how some other people have put the question: "What *are* you, besides being Oriental, that is?" I politely inform such people that "Orientals" are "things" such as objects of art, as in rugs and vases. When referring to people with ancestral roots in Asia or the Pacific Rim countries, the correct term is *Asian, Southeast Asian,* or *Pacific Islander.* The term *Oriental* has been outdated since the 1960s and was dropped by the U.S. Census Bureau as a race designation during the 1970 Census.
Nonetheless, this topic of conversation is an opportunity to share knowledge. It is also an example of how non Asians view Asians, and the

innocent curiosity that most Asians have about each other. If we cannot readily identify ourselves, we cannot expect non-Asians to understand our diversity. Unlike the diverse Hispanic population, which generally speaks Spanish, Asians do not have a unifying language as a marketing tool. Correct identification of Asians and Pacific Islanders, in addition to knowing their diverse languages and cultures, can be complex when planning a strategy to market to these groups. Until the 1960s, most Asians were either Chinese or Japanese. With increased immigration, it is not surprising that native Californians have difficulty in "sorting us out."

To the untrained eye, we all look alike. It is not surprising that mainstream advertisers are cautious when approaching these groups. It's simpler to ignore this untapped consumer base.

I confess to my own wariness in correctly identifying Asians without knowing their surnames. Their demeanor and dress may or may not identify recent newcomers from first-, second-, third- and fourth-generation Asian Americans. Also, identifying physical traits become less pronounced after being in the United States for several generations. Intermarriage among Asians and other nationalities further complicates proper identification. What about the Japanese Peruvians whose first language is Spanish? What about ethnic Chinese who consider themselves Vietnamese, Thai, or Cambodian? Or the Chinese from Malaysia who are quick to tell you they are not Malay? Or the Chinese-Brazilians who speak Portuguese? Or the Chinese from Indonesia? Or the Chinese and Japanese who settled in Australia and New Zealand?

Asian marketing specialization, still in its infancy, was pioneered by American-born Asians who started their careers at mainstream agencies and communications corporations. They recognized a niche to be filled. Projected Asian population statistics and increased immigration became the foundation for a whole new specialization within the industry. Soon, Asian Americans opened their own shops. As the Asian population grew in the United States, especially in metropolitan areas, large corporations—notably the telecommunications industry—saw the value in marketing to Asians who call long distance for business and family reasons. Effective campaigns to reach these potential customers had to be done in their languages of preference. Capturing the Asian market on the ground floor was a good business move that brought with it brand loyalty. Voila! Asian-owned shops that had been around a few years were suddenly perceived as "Asian market specialists."

The situation created a catch-22 for Asian-owned agencies perceived to be "Asian market specialists." Potential clients and mainstream agencies still find it difficult to rely on our talents to create and execute general-market campaigns. This is a double-edged sword for Asian Americans, as well as for African American and Hispanic American specialists. I suspect that our handling general-market campaigns threatens many mainstream agencies. So they rely on us as "specialists."

As professional practitioners, we have an advantage as agencies realize the importance of the Asian American market. I encourage everyone entering the profession to stay ahead of the crowd. Become knowledgeable and practice hands-on experience in the mainstream and ethnic markets so that you can offer added value to agencies and corporations in years to come. In California and major metropolitan areas with a sizable Asian population, minorities will soon be the new majority. But we have a long way to go before we reach the crest of the wave.

❖

EDITOR'S NOTE: *Andrea Tortora, an outstanding graduating senior at the E. W. Scripps School of Journalism, served as editor of the Ohio University newspaper, the* Post. *As an Italian American, she is not considered a minority but nonetheless experiences stereotypes—generated by mass media—associated with her nationality. She responds to those labels in the following editorial.*

Italian Stereotypes

Andrea Tortora, Editor, *The (Ohio University) Post*

As a child I looked forward to spring afternoons with the burst of exhilaration one gets when biting into a fresh-picked cherry tomato.

The annual planting of my family's tomato garden is one of my fondest memories. Each spring my grandfather—Vito Tortora—would guide the family in the proper way to cultivate the versatile fruit.

The day's events were always followed by a large family dinner. The meal would include an antipasto, garlic bread, meatballs, sausage, chicken and spaghetti with "gravy."

I thought this was the way everyone spent time with his or her family and felt sorry for friends who did not plant a garden.

But Grandpa died in 1986, and Grandma no longer helps us plant our garden.

I no longer think all people live as I do.

I take pride in being a full-blooded, third-generation Italian. I still enjoy watering the tomato garden in the summer, and I still look forward to four-course meals with my extended family.

But popular culture tells me to be ashamed of who and what I am. "Friends" ask me how "Uncle Vito's" business is doing. They are wary in their friendships for fear that "cousin Frankie" will gag them in their sleep, and all that will mark their passings will be a fish head on the doorstep of their homes. Many ask if I know someone in the mafia or if my father is a member.

Maybe they don't realize these questions are just as offensive to me as racial slurs.

I always have enjoyed sharing my cultural background with friends— we had more than enough food at our meals to accommodate extra guests.

But I also have encountered several instances of "unconscious" preju- dice toward people of Italian descent. For instance, people tried to imitate what they thought was a humorous example of an Italian accent. Curiosity about my family's (nonexistent) involvement in the mafia could not be sup- pressed, and I was often bombarded with questions.

I was driven to my limit when accosted by fun-loving residents at one of Ohio University's international residence halls. "Hey, Andre-a! Howa is your Mamma doin'? I bet youa missa that good paesano food, eh?"

Immediately I turned and told my fellow American I would rather have him insult me directly by calling me a "guinea" than for him to waste his breath trying to be pleasant about it.

He seemed shocked that I did not find his dialogue entertaining and said he did not think something like that would bother me. The ignorance in his attempt to be funny hurt me more than the words that fell out of his mouth.

My curiosity about the mafia is as piqued as any American's. I have watched the *Godfather* movies hoping to understand the mystique surround- ing the organization, but it remains a mystery to me.

I refuse to submit to the fallacy that all Italians belong to the mafia, and I am ashamed that such a corrupt group has besmirched my Italian back- ground. My family is peopled by barbers, teachers, hardware store owners, and accountants—professions in which all members of our nation partici- pate. Reluctantly, I tolerate the occasional mafia "joke," but like most other Italians, I have become angry with the constant slurs.

If one believes calling his Japanese friend a "Jap," her African American neighbor a "nigger," or his Hispanic roommate a "spic," is offensive, why is it humorous for one to call me a "wop" or "mafioso"?

For those still living in the era of immigration, most Italians today are not "straight off the boat." That phrase described my great-grandparents. My grandparents and parents are Italian Americans. My generation is American Italian.

I no longer possess the suitcase full of traditions my grandparents car- ried. I have become Americanized, like the Irish, Africans, Chinese, Japanese and all other ethnic groups in our multinational society.

But no matter how American I have become, my Italian background is part of my personal culture. I prize and cherish tomato gardens and extended family gatherings and will defend my heritage until the stereo- types of Italians are destroyed.

EDITOR'S NOTE: *Monica Neiporte is not a minority but nevertheless has endured media-generated stereotypes because she has long blond hair and a pale complexion. Those stereotypes cast her as soft, timid, and unintelligent—more interested in romantic relations instead of public relations—her major at Ohio University. Those stereotypes do not apply to Neiporte who, during her college career, had to be called off of an investigative crime story because her instructor felt her life could be endangered. At about this time, she applied for a job with a major retailer. Neiporte describes her experience here.*

Blonde Bias

Monica Neiporte, Reporter, *The Athens (Ohio) Messenger*

Like everyone else, I have heard the countless dumb blonde jokes but I never really thought that people believed those stereotypes to be true. That is, until I went on an interview that opened my eyes to the fact that there were people who would judge me solely by the color of my hair.

In the past, a female professor told me I should cut my shoulder-length hair and wear either a navy or black suit when it came time to interview if I wanted people to take me seriously. I thought that was the most ridiculous thing I had ever heard and I was actually insulted. I have never had short hair and didn't want to wear a navy suit like most of the other young women wore on "interview days." I thought they all looked like airline stewardesses and I felt the peach suit I was wearing was just fine. But maybe I should have taken her advice.

My senior year in college I was working part time for a department store chain that is based in Ohio. My manager kept encouraging me to interview with the company's recruiters when they came to campus because I was already an employee of the company. I was told that I would have a certain advantage over other applicants because the company's policy was to promote from within whenever possible.

I decided to go to the interview, even though the job for which I was applying had nothing to do with journalism. I majored in public relations and was told by the store manager that if I even hoped to get a public relations position with that company, I would have to hold a managerial position first.

My actual interview took a turn for the worst when the man who was interviewing me told me I could not leave the interview until I told him at least one thing that I did not like about working for the company.

I told him I liked working for the company very much but disagreed with the way our store manager handled confrontations with customers. I told him about an occasion when a customer insisted to me that an item should be on sale and then shouted a whole string of obscenities at me. I told the recruiter that in this instance I felt the manager, who was standing there during the incident, should have asked the customer to leave the store. Instead, she told me to give the customer the sale price and walked away, leaving me as the object of the customer's ranting and raving in a crowded store.

The recruiter also noticed the engagement ring on my finger, which I wore to the interview despite my father's warnings that I shouldn't, and asked when I was getting married and if I planned on starting a family right away.

The wedding wouldn't be for another year and a half and I had no plans for a family for quite a few years, I told him.

I left the interview satisfied I had answered all of his questions and feeling confident that I would at least be asked back for a second interview.

I was wrong. I received a very short letter in the mail telling me that I did not meet the company's criteria used to evaluate prospective employees. I was sure that a mistake had been made because, after all, I was already an employee of the company.

I talked to my store manager and she telephoned the recruiter who had interviewed me to ask why he felt I didn't meet his criteria at least enough to be asked back for another interview.

Later that evening she told me, in front of customers, that the recruiter felt that I was not cut out for retail. He said I was timid, unassertive, not self-motivated, unenthusiastic, was too "soft" to handle confrontational situations, and not "career oriented" enough to accept the responsibilities of a supervisory position.

I thought for sure that the recruiter had gotten me mixed up with someone else he had interviewed that day.

My journalism professor, Michael Bugeja, and I discussed the situation and he encouraged me to write a letter to the director of recruiting asking for another interview with a different recruiter. He pointed out to me that all the adjectives the recruiter used to describe me were stereotypes associated with blondes—in fact, the only thing that seemed missing from the list was "air-head."

I immediately sent a letter to the company's director of recruiting and told him that I felt I had been unfairly evaluated and requested another interview. In the letter I noted that all of the words used to describe me were stereotypes of blondes and I was confident that none of those words applied to my personality. In fact, I said, if I was so timid and soft, then why would I take the initiative to request another interview and voice my opinion that a mistake had occurred.

Weeks went by and my letter went unanswered and my phone calls went unreturned. Finally I received a letter from the director saying he stood by his recruiter's evaluation and if I wished to pursue a career with the company, he felt I should work as a clerk (for minimum wage) for another year to prove myself. Then I could interview again.

I was appalled that I should have to "prove myself" to these people when they selected other candidates who had never worked for the company or even in a retail store. I put in my notice immediately.

I work for the local newspaper now, covering murders, courts, and other hard-news events. Nonetheless, the incident with the recruiter proved how pervasive stereotypes are and how media influence everyday affairs—in my case, with images of the "soft, timid blonde."

V A L U E S   E X E R C I S E S

1. Analyze items, magazines and newspapers and isolate a minimum of four stories, photographs, illustrations, or advertisements that perpetuate what you believe is a stereotype. Photocopy each item and write a 50-word statement about each suspected bias.

2. As you did in the Values Exercises at the end of Chapter 3, make a list of at least six highs, lows, and turning points *associated with race or bias*. Next to each item on that list, write a 50- to 100-word statement (without violating your own or anyone else's privacy) about how that experience affected your perspective about race matters. Incidents can range from comments heard in the living room to the boardroom or be based on more dramatic encounters or confrontations.

3. Record in a journal what you say, hear, or experience that somehow relates to racism or bias.

4. For one week, describe friends and acquaintances by their inner or professional qualities, rather than by their racial, gender, or body types. Record reactions in your journal.

5. Choose journal selections from Exercises 3 and 4 and, using appropriate and polished language, write a 200-word summary of your experiences.

Part III

Enhancing Your Ethical Base

The concepts of fairness, power, and values have been covered or implied in the previous sections about building and testing your ethical base. For instance, the concept of fairness is treated in Chapter 1, Influence (perception and objectivity); Chapter 3, Truth (impression accuracy); Chapter 6, Temptation (dealing with conflicts); and Chapter 7, Bias (resisting stereotypes). The concept of power is treated in Chapter 1, Influence (impact of language); Chapter 3, Truth (higher concepts); Chapter 5, Manipulation (analyzing the hoax); and Chapter 7, Bias (exploring racism). The concept of values has been treated in the Introduction and each chapter, with special emphasis in Chapter 1, Influence (basic influences); Chapter 2, Responsibility (moral relativism and absolutes); and Chapter 4, Lies (concepts and consequences).

In this section, you will focus on enhancing your values via fairness by preparing for unforeseen conflicts or assessing past ones and via power by measuring your own impact on society and the messages you send or censor. In the last chapter, working professionals will name the one value that has been key in their success. You will learn the emphasis that media outlets place on values and the documents they use to ensure them in the workplace. Finally, you will turn your own values into similar documents or codes.

8

Fairness

Concepts and Cases

Before discussing basic concepts and case studies relating to fairness, a quick review of information from other chapters will be helpful. This will assist you in distinguishing between truth and fairness and between conflicts involving temptation and others involving fairness.

Ethical journalists strive to achieve fairness and then assess whether they have met or fallen short of that goal. For instance, in Chapter 3, Truth, you learned about impression accuracy or "full disclosure" of all available facts in reports, segments, or campaigns. We said that sometimes individual journalists provided these facts in objective pieces and sometimes groups of journalists provided these facts in subjective but competing advertisements or public relations campaigns. In either instance, complete truth—or impression accuracy—is a *goal* for an individual or an entire industry. Like objectivity, fairness cannot be completely achieved in every instance; it is the process that is important, as we shall see.

In Chapter 6, Temptation, we covered conflicts of interest involving two important but clashing values. We said these conflicts usually occurred unexpectedly so that the specter of temptation could entice us, providing short-term relief but eroding value systems in the process. A function of fairness is to analyze these conflicts after the fact to determine whether you were treated fairly or whether you treated others fairly. Once you make such a determination, you are better prepared to act in the next crisis or conflict. In a word, your values will have been *enhanced*.

In sum, fairness is a two-step and continual process. You strive to attain it and then evaluate whether you have, making appropriate adjustments to prepare for the next encounter. That makes fairness the most important value in any value system. It can be argued that fairness eventually ensures ethical behavior because of the continual goal of self-examination and improvement. Fair-minded people must know right from wrong to evaluate work and actions. They commit to truth and therefore do not lie. They might be manipulated or tempted by others, but because they stress preparedness, they are less apt to be tricked or enticed the next time. Fair-minded people do not discriminate because racism is a lie.

However, to embrace fairness or use it to enhance values, you must have courage. You have to accept truth as you find it, even if that truth goes against everything that you have thus far believed. You have to acknowledge, openly and freely, when you have been manipulated, tempted, or biased; pride or ambition cannot stand in the way of such disclosures. For these and other reasons, our discussion about fairness has been postponed until this point. Fairness seems simple but it subsumes all other values; thus, before embracing it, you should have a good knowledge of influence, consequences, truth, courage, honor, appropriateness, and other concepts.

Defined, *fairness* is a continual process of improvement involving the evaluation of work and behavior to determine (1) whether the work is accurate or truthful, (2) whether the behavior is honest or appropriate, and (3) whether methods or values can be enhanced to meet those goals.

Journalists who embrace fairness are respected and credible. Typically, they are known as the most reliable public relations practitioners or insightful advertisers or capable photographers, broadcasters, writers, editors, and reporters. Carolyn J. Klimczak, a regional bureau chief for the *Sandusky Register*, believes that fair-minded journalists are respected by sources—even ones they investigate or cover aggressively.

> As recently as last week, I received a thank-you note in the mail from a council president in the city I cover—Norwalk, Ohio—thanking me for being fair with him. Where I work, the winds of controversy blow fiercely, constantly, and journalists without an inner compass can get swept up in the storm. I have never been charged with bias in any of my jobs, even as I've seen charges leveled at my competitors. I protect the reputation I've gained as being fair and tough, always reminding my sources that I have a job to do, as do they.

To assess fairness, you must understand another important concept: *viewpoint*. Not only must you know or be aware of your own values and truths but you must also understand that of your coworkers, audience, sources, clients, and/or competitors. As you learned in Chapter 1, people tend to experience the world according to family morals or social mores (among other factors). However, we need not refer again to basic influences to understand *viewpoint*, defined as an event or opinion as experienced through someone else's eyes. All you have to do is attend a trial (or watch *The People's Court*) to know that the defendant and plaintiff have witnessed the same event and view it in remarkably opposite ways, according to each person's personality, morality and/or special interests.

Later you will learn methods to *estimate* another's viewpoint. You cannot completely know it, even in what appears to be the most extreme and obvious cases. Many people who assume that others' viewpoints can be identified, pinpointed, and experienced are not fair minded but arrogant. At best, someone else's viewpoint can be approximated. Fortunately, the attempt to understand and accept that viewpoint and balance it with your own is not only a function of fairness but a courtesy that relatively few people are willing to extend. Those who do extend such a courtesy do not feel morally superior to others because the only value system that interests them is their own. Thus, fair-minded journalists contribute to the profession or society by example and often become role models for others. Typically, they do this three ways:

- *Their value systems are strong enough to serve as touchstones for others.* (In the Living Ethics section at the end of this chapter you will read a piece by an advertising executive who calls on his industry to hire more minorities and a selection by a newspaper ombudsman [or reader's representative] who analyzes news coverage to ensure impartiality.)
- *They evaluate their actions, admit errors and provide access or opportunities for wronged parties to express their viewpoints or truths.* (In the Living Ethics section you will read about a student newspaper granting access to its pages in an attempt to correct a false report incriminating a basketball star.)
- *They enhance their values by (1) analyzing unforeseen conflicts of interest before those conflicts occur, (2) evaluating their performance to determine whether it meets their standards, and (3) assessing whether they have treated others fairly or whether others have treated them fairly.* (In the Living Ethics section you will read a case study involving a reporter sent to interview family members about the brutal murder of a toddler by her father—an assignment that haunted her for years—until she resolved it using the preceding process.)

One of the ways that journalists contribute to the profession is via scientific polls or studies, measuring the level of fairness practiced in the industry. One such study by Cornelius B. Pratt, a professor in the Department of Advertising at Michigan State University, asked 449 members of the Public Relations Society of America to respond to the following case study:

Frank, a senior public relations manager, was staying overnight on a business trip. He went into the hotel lounge to have a drink. He found himself seated next to another public relations manager from his leading competitor. The public relations manager, who appeared to have had several drinks, was in a talkative mood. He talked about his clients and divulged confidential information to Frank. Frank happened to handle the account of a competitive brand.

Frank did not identify himself and instead bought the other executive several more drinks, thinking that if he could not hold his liquor it was his problem. Frank received valuable confidential information about the competitor's new advertising campaign, marketing strategies and other information that could sharply increase the profits of his own client.

Please circle the number that best indicates your opinion

Definitely yes=1   Maybe yes=2   Maybe no=3   Definitely no=4

1. What Frank did was wrong.	1 2 3 4
2. Frank should, at the minimum, be promptly punished.	1 2 3 4
3. I would do just what Frank did.	1 2 3 4
4. Most corporate communicators would do what Frank did.	1 2 3 4
5. My firm/dept. has a policy, written or oral, that addresses this situation or practice.	1 2 3 4
6. In general, it is a good idea for a firm/dept. to have a policy, either written or oral, that addresses the situation or practice.[1]	1 2 3 4

You may be interested to know that Pratt and his associates found that the concept of fairness is fairly high among practitioners.[2] Of those surveyed, 71.2 percent believed "what Frank did was wrong" and 56.3 percent thought "Frank should, at the minimum, be promptly punished," answering "definitely yes" or "maybe yes" to those statements. Conversely, the study showed that 31.8 percent of respondents "would do just what Frank did" and 55.7 percent thought that "most corporate communicators" would, too. Only 28.1 percent said that their companies had a policy addressing the scenario; but 64.4 percent thought such a policy was "a good idea."

Such studies, when released and/or published, often encourage fairness in the workplace because journalists discuss or contemplate the results. For the record, what Frank did was clearly unethical. The case study is debatable up until the point that Frank began buying drinks for his competitor, taking advantage of the situation. Now Frank was an active participant in the deception. Furthermore, armed with secrets about his competitor's advertising campaign and marketing strategies, Frank would have to conceal such information from or share or lie about how he procured it with his campaign team or supervisor. In any case, Frank can suffer several potential consequences:

- Word about Frank's unethical behavior will circulate among his peers, damaging his credibility.
- Frank may be punished by his supervisor if he confides his secret or if the supervisor learns about his actions.
- Frank may conceal his secret and then be given bigger accounts on the false assumption that he has the requisite skills to manage them—risking incompetence and failure.

Lor'e Postman, reporter for the *Rock Island (Illinois) News*, wants to prepare for unforeseen conflicts involving news coverage. She does not read scientific studies like the preceding one but several local and national newspapers, pondering the ethical ramifications of an issue or event and sharing them with a colleague or mentor. This way, she can analyze other viewpoints to see if they are fairer than her own.

Here's a typical inquiry:

When should the media re-inform readers/listeners about murders that are coming to trial? We cover murders in detail when they happen and usually fill the paper/airwaves with details for days after. But months, and possibly years, pass during which little if anything is written. Should you write about the incident again the week before the trial starts? The day of the trial? The day the jury is picked? I don't mean write that this is coming to trial and a jury will be picked. I'm talking about a story which brings every tiny detail back into light.

Postman applied these concerns to a specific case: the murder of a 17-year-old high school girl by six gang members. She notes that three of the youths had already pleaded guilty to lesser charges in exchange for their testimony against the three remaining defendants. The news media in her area knew about the trial and reported when it would begin and that a jury was being picked. "Naturally," Postman continues, "we also included several nut graphs about what supposedly happened. We didn't write more because the editors and I decided it would be better to start fresh and gather all details from testimony.

"Our competitor, the *Quad-City Times*, ran a full-blown package the second day into jury selection. The package included interviews with the three defendants, their friends, the friends and family of the murdered girl, police investigators, witnesses—you name it, they interviewed them. (Granted, it was a pretty good package.)"

Postman also notes that judges in her area are concerned about change of venues, or moving trials from one country to another, to ensure impartiality.

They're worried, and understandably so, that every prospective juror is biased by media reports of the crime. In this case, jury selection started on a Monday. About 80 prospective jurors were called in. Before they were questioned about their experiences with gangs or feelings about crime and punishment, each was taken into a separate room and questioned about what he or she had read or heard about the case. This increased jury selection time by one day. On Tuesday, defense and state attorneys were to begin the second round of questioning to disqualify jurors based on their feelings about gangs, crime and punishment, etc. However, that morning, the *Times* ran their package. When Judge James Havercamp entered the courtroom Tuesday morning, he saw a dozen jurors with the *Times* in hand, and others talking about the stories. Several jurors were disqualified (and remember, many people do everything possible to get off jury duty). The process was set back another day. Now Havercamp was worried about needing to change venue.

"I don't know what the answer is," Postman admits. "If it were I, I would wait until the jury was selected and then run the stories. Granted, the *Times* may have been worried that we would beat them to the punch. That's an understandable concern. But it almost forced a change of venue, and cost taxpayers dollars."

In her assessment, Postman may overlook added taxpayer costs caused by irresponsible lawyers and political-minded judges (typical concerns of the "watchdog" media). Instead, she is interested in a common fairness conflict involving the First versus Sixth Amendments in the Bill of Rights to the U.S. Constitution. As you know, the First Amendment states: "Congress shall make no law respecting an establishment of religion, or prohibiting the free exercise thereof; or abridging the freedom of speech, or of the press; or the right of the people peaceably to assemble, and to petition the Government for a redress of grievances." The Sixth Amendment reads, in part: "In all criminal prosecutions, the accused shall enjoy the right to a speedy and public trial, by an impartial jury of the State and district wherein the crime shall have been committed."

Postman knows that free speech allows her and her competitors to republicize details about the Iowa murder trial, but feels, in all fairness, that the defendants deserve the right to be tried where the crime was committed and that taxpayers shouldn't have to pay added court costs. But the most noteworthy comment in her assessment is "I don't know what the answer is." That implies that Postman will continue to analyze the fairness issue. For the moment, however, she suggests a personal code of behavior to guide her in future incidents: "I would wait until the jury was selected and then run the stories."

Her solution honors the First and Sixth Amendments without apparent conflict. As a consequence, however, apparently she will allow competing reporters to scoop her initially—and shoulder the consequences.

Public relations practitioners sometimes deal with the same dilemma. In addition to working with supervisors and other employees, however, they also must persuade their clients to take fair and appropriate measures in crisis-management situations.

A case study involving all of these issues happened to Linda Percefull, former reporter for the *Tulsa World* and now director of public relations at Littlefield Marketing and Advertising. One of Percefull's clients was a private school. A controversy arose "when male students independently reported a popular coach-teacher had fondled them," she recalls. "The school verified the complaints and suspended the teacher. School officials called me because they were concerned the media would pick up on his suspension and do a story."

According to Percefull, the officials planned to allow the teacher to resign quietly, "thereby avoiding embarrassment and protecting the rights of the molested students." Percefull was not so sure. "This would seem to be the easiest move, but there could have been more serious consequences in the future. For example, what if the teacher moved to another district and molested students? The school would have to share some responsibility for not taking stronger action."

Percefull and her team reviewed the rights of each party, "from the accused teacher to the accusing boys and their parents to the rest of the staff and patrons of the school," she says. "The dilemma was in fairly balancing the rights of the teacher with the rights of his accusers.

> Ultimately, the school officials took the leap of faith and fired the teacher. We issued a brief news release regarding the firing without mentioning the molestation charges. School officials addressed each audience separately—talking privately to parents of the students making the accusations, meeting with teachers and issuing a statement to students.
>
> The media reported the story accurately, briefly citing "serious allegations." The parents of the accusers felt supported by the school and said they appreciated the school's decisive action. A few teachers expressed concern over the firing. However, the school responded that the teacher had the right to appeal (which he did not do).

Percefull notes, "Patrons expressed renewed faith in school officials because they took such decisive action" while protecting the privacy of students. "Within a few days, things returned to normal." She adds, "This situation represents the true value of public relations. Public relations is a management function, not a press release. Too often, we focus on saying the right thing, but the real key is *doing* the right thing. The words will follow."

Perhaps ethicists overemphasize conflicts of interest between employees. Those conflicts can be tense or dramatic and serve as good case studies, indicating consequences or questionable values. But more often than not, reporter and editor or practitioner and supervisor work together to ensure fairness. Here is a typical situation as told by Avelia Crynes, a former minority relations analyst for a large petroleum company:

> My job responsibility was to establish a rapport with Women and Minority Engineering Programs across the nation. Traditionally the field of engineering has been dominated by white males. In addition the working environment for women and minority engineers was somewhat hostile. My assignment was to devise a creative public relations plan that would give my organization credibility with the women and minority engineering students.

Crynes produced a video titled "Marketing Your Talents for Work Force 2000," designed to appeal to a diverse audience.

> The video opened with the Vice President of the company who was Native American talking about value of diversity. The video portrayed the organization as a multicultural company. I purposely selected female and minority engineers for the video: a Hispanic male who spoke in Spanish and English, a Native American female who spoke in English and Navajo, and a white female and black male.
>
> My dilemma was that the video portrayed the organization as a multicultural company that was committed to diversity. [In reality, 6 percent of the company's employees were minorities and 16 percent were female.] The company was moving very slowly toward work force diversity. So I had to ask myself, "Is this video misleading?" I knew that as students viewed the video that they might get the impression that the organization would provide them with role models and mentors of like background. I also knew that women and minority engineering students looked for organizations that employed a significant number of women and minority professionals, to avoid a hostile work environment.

Crynes decided to discuss these fairness concerns with her supervisor in the Human Relations Division. Together they reviewed the contents of the video and redefined its objectives. They determined that the video's contents illustrated how other women and minority engineers obtained their professional goals. But the real objective of the video was to educate the students on how to conduct successful job interviews and succeed in industry. "We all agreed that the video would serve as an educational tool for the college students making the transition from academia to industry. We also felt that the video would serve as an educational tool for the company's managers and employees concerning the need for a diverse work force."

By discussing her concerns with her supervisor, Crynes was able to avoid a conflict of two equal but important values: her desire to succeed in her job versus her commitment to diversity. Instead of initiating a confrontation about minority hiring at her company, Crynes was able to use the video to serve her target audience—college students—and educate managers about the positive aspects of diversity.

The academic, theoretical, and actual dilemmas presented here all have one goal in common: improving fairness. Let's take a closer look at that process so that you, too, can analyze situations and enhance your values.

Practicing Fairness

Journalists who report the news must be fair and impartial, as we have observed in several previous chapters. This section focuses primarily on advertising and public relations specialists who practice fairness in dealing with diverse or underrepresented markets or in balancing mainstream messages in public service campaigns. Before addressing those topics, however, you should know that the fundamental elements of fairness in the news media also apply to advertising and public relations. Here are three such guidelines by Phil Record, ombudsman for the *Fort Worth Star-Telegram*, who speaks at length about fairness in the Living Ethics section at the end of this chapter:

- *Seek truth and report it as fully as possible.* "The goal, of course, is to provide your readers with the information they need and expect and requires that you be honest, fair, courageous and as accurate as possible."
- *Act independently.* "You need to avoid being unduly influenced by those who would use their power or position to counter the public interest."
- *Minimize harm.* "Some people are apt to get hurt or made uncomfortable in any gathering and reporting of information. As a journalist, you should seek to minimize the harm or discomfort your truth-telling is apt to cause."

Advertising and public relations agencies also seek truth, of course. That truth may be narrower than that of the news media, as explained in Chapter 3, but is equally important because it contributes to and balances other slants and messages. In fact, it can be argued, some agencies counter stereotypes in the *news* media by handling special or underrepresented clients. As such, these practitioners also act independently and seek to minimize harm in accord with the preceding precepts by Phil Record. All of this will be illustrated by focusing on three agencies: Prime Access, a New York City advertising firm specializing in the gay and lesbian market; Brogan &

Partners, a Detroit agency reaching teen, minority, and female markets in public service campaigns; and Ann Becker and Associates, a Minnesota firm working with mainstream and diverse groups, including the National Lesbian and Gay Journalists Association.

"We want to help companies manage relationships with the gay and lesbian community," says Howard Buford, president of Prime Access, whose clients include AT&T. The agency designed a direct-mail campaign aimed at gay men, with the slogan: "It's time for a change." The letter inside the mailer does not begin with a statement about services but about corporate policies and philosophy:

> At AT&T, we believe it's important for you to feel good about the company you do business with. AT&T has always recognized personal individuality, and we respect the diversity that all people represent. In fact, AT&T has an environment in which gay, lesbian and bisexual people feel comfortable in the workplace—and has a long-standing nondiscrimination guideline regarding sexual orientation.

Buford, a graduate of Harvard Business School, has made inroads with clients such as AT&T whose representatives are sensitive to gay and lesbian issues. Buford began his career working at Burson Marsteller and UniWorld Group, specializing in marketing to African American and Hispanic American audiences. "I saw an opportunity and need to do this kind of work in the gay and lesbian market," he says, and so founded Prime Access in 1990.

As the excerpt in the mailer indicates, a commitment to fairness is not only important within Buford's agency but also within companies that his agency represents. "The gay and lesbian community is our livelihood," Buford says, "so we can't let it be ripped off." Consequently, he asks potential clients about their fairness policies regarding gays and lesbians and whether they have internal organizations for these employees. "This is partly a business question in that if you run gay-targeted advertising and a company lacks appropriate policies, then you can be vulnerable on other fronts. You may end with some serious damage control," he adds, if a client wants to sell to that community and yet does not value members of that community within its own organization. "We want to make sure the attitude is in place. If the attitude is not there, then we talk to clients. We say, 'We can do advertising for you, but at the same time, these people will be interacting with your employees,'" Buford adds. "A client really has to believe in the people we represent, or those people won't feel good about interacting with that company or buying its products or services."

Marcie Brogan founded her agency in 1984 and later formed an alliance with the Detroit office of N. W. Ayer, the well-known New York advertising agency. Brogan and her four-woman staff have established a reputation for fairness in the industry. Part of the agency's success is due to "the way we communicate to women and what we communicate about women," Brogan says. "This is probably most apparent in our work for the Michigan Department of Public Health for which we do AIDS prevention, anti-smoking, mammography screening and anti-violence messages." Brogan says her agency also seeks to change behavior and attitudes of teens and other groups designated as "high risk" in AIDS awareness campaigns. "So we need to be conscious of ethnic as well as gender values, community standards, age considerations and literacy levels of our audiences."

Sometimes the agency attempts to counter other advertising messages. For example, cigarette ads in women's magazines usually feature glamorous models smoking cigarettes in clean environments. Brogan's TV spots and print campaigns include these marketing strategies:

- Let women, especially African American women, know they are singled out by tobacco companies; counteract that smoking is glamorous.
- Maintain support stance; often it takes many times to quit for good.
- For kids, emphasize that smoking is socially undesirable.

Brogan & Partners, a Detroit agency, specializes in reaching women, teens, and minorities. Here and on the following two pages are sample TV and print ads aimed at discouraging tobacco and drug use and preventing breast cancer and AIDS.

BROGAN & PARTNERS

300 Town Center
Suite 475
Southfield, MI 48075
(313) 353-9106

CLIENT MICHIGAN DEPARTMENT OF PUBLIC HEALTH

PRODUCT AIDS PREVENTION

TITLE "FIRST TIME"

LENGTH :30 TV

TEENAGE MALE: I know drug addicts get AIDS. But I shot up just one time. So I'm not losing any sleep over it.

V/O: The first time with drugs can be the most dangerous.

That's when you're most likely to share a dirty needle

TEENAGE FEMALE: I don't know ...the first time with my boyfriend ...how can I say, "Wear a condom?"

Just this once, it'll be okay without it.

V/O: Once may be all it takes to get AIDS. And the first time you get AIDS is the last time you get AIDS.

AIDS. What you don't know can hurt you.

This commercial and concept have been copyrighted. If you wish to produce or customize, please call (313) 353-9106.

YOU'RE AT RISK OF GETTING BREAST CANCER

If you have a family history
If you have no family history
If you have had children
If you have never had children
If you're thin
If you're not thin
If you're white
If you're African American
If you're past menopause
If you're pre-menopausal
If you never eat carrots
If you always eat carrots
If you're "big up there"
If you're "small up there"
If you live in the city
If you live in the country

If you're a woman you're at risk.
Especially if you're over 40. One in eight women will get breast cancer.
Call your doctor or if you need a free or low cost mammogram
and follow up services, CALL

1-800-922-MAMM (1-800-922-6266)

Michigan Department of Public Health

To get those points across, Brogan used a "Smoking Stinks" slogan depicting mouths and lips full of ashen cigarettes. The campaign produced these results, according to her tracking research:

- After three months, 19 percent of respondents were aware of a smoking hotline providing health and quitting information.
- Some 25 percent of calls to the smoking hotline were from children, age 9 and up.
- Studies showed that 75 percent of respondents thought the campaign was effective with targeted groups among the most likely to recall the advertising.
- The Michigan ads were picked up by the National Office on Smoking and Health and the Black Entertainment Network for national use.

The ads, which also won several awards—including Caddys and Addys—show that fairness not only is a factor of content and design but also one of balance. They also show that advertising is a broad and diverse profession, offering opportunities for practitioners who want to specialize in public service campaigns promoting causes relating to gender, minority, or health awareness.

Such awareness benefits the practitioner and the agency, according to Jeneene Rydberg of Ann Becker and Associates, which specializes in public relations and meeting planning. "In these two fields you will undoubtedly come into contact with diverse groups of people," she notes. "My approach has been to try to find some basis on which to build rapport. A strong ability to empathize is helpful. Even the most unique individual has something in his or her life that one can identify with—pets, children, sports or other outside interests." Rydberg adds that she may not agree with a client's agenda or even like the person outside of the professional relationship. "But I still work very hard to find the common thread we share. It might be simply that we are both professionals and approach our work as such."

Rydberg notes that planning a conference with the National Lesbian and Gay Journalists Association "has given me some wonderful insights into the world of journalism as well as into the gay and lesbian cultures. It has also provided me with firsthand experience that I can share with others to dispel their stereotypical thinking or reactions." Rydberg observes, "You do not have to enjoy working with diverse groups. But if you can put the benefits into perspective, you will always come out ahead with more knowledge and experience on which to draw from in the future."

To help you with that process, here are guidelines to address potential conflicts involving fairness and to evaluate your own or others' work and/or behavior:

1. *Ascertaining any conflict.* To practice fairness, you have to determine what, if any, potential conflicts may influence your or others' judgment.

   Ask Yourself:
   - Am I willing to approach specific people or issues with an open mind or do I have any preconceived notions that may lead to a conflict or dispute?
   - Are others willing to approach me with an open mind or do they seem to have preconceived notions that may lead to a conflict or dispute?
   - Have both parties listened carefully to each other to dispel any such preconceived notions?

2. *Balancing viewpoints and differing interests.* To promote fairness, you should be able to identify, evaluate, and balance viewpoints and interests.

   Ask Yourself:
   - If I were the other party and held an opposite opinion or lifestyle, how would I view this particular issue or dispute?
   - How are others viewing me, based on my opinions or lifestyle?
   - Are there any misperceptions in viewpoints that need to be identified, addressed, and/or balanced by one or both parties?

3. *Seeking bonds or advice.* To ensure fairness, the parties involved should seek out common bonds or opinions and/or contact impartial advisers to resolve issues or disputes.

   Ask Yourself:
   - What experiences or values do I and the other party share so that we can identify common bonds?
   - What interests or activities do I and the other party share so that can identify like opinions?
   - What specific concerns shall we bring to the attention of impartial experts so that we can overcome basic obstacles and try one more time to reach a decision or resolution?

4. *Evaluating actions or treatment.* To enhance fairness in the future, you need to evaluate the preceding processes to determine whether you have learned anything from the issue, dispute, or resolution.

   Ask Yourself:
   - How could I have been treated more fairly?
   - How could I have treated the other party more fairly?
   - How has the process affected or enhanced my values on fairness?

At the beginning of this chapter we noted that journalists who embrace fairness usually have strong value systems because of the continual process of self-examination and improvement. Practitioners such as Jeneene Rydberg of Ann Becker and Associates affirm that belief. "Often I will work on a project for six to twelve months, a relatively short period of time in the whole scheme of things," she observes. "If I am really unhappy with a client, I keep reminding myself of how I am going to learn from this experience and, if all else fails, I fall back on the old phrase—'no pain, no gain.'

"Everyone has something to offer," Rydberg concludes. "We as individuals stop growing if we cannot see past the easy divisions in society and recognize that underneath we all share a common history and struggle for survival."

ENDNOTES

1. Cornelius B. Pratt, "Four scenarios about ethics," *Journal of Public Relations Research*, 6 (4), pp. 256–266.

2. Cornelius B. Pratt, SungHoon Im, and Scarlett B. Montague, *Investigating the Application of Deontology Among U.S. Public Relations Practitioners*, Department of Advertising, Michigan State University, abstract.

L I V I N G   E T H I C S

Read the following articles and record your reactions in your ethics journal and/or discuss them with peers or mentors.

�֍ **EDITOR'S NOTE:** *At its basic level, journalists promote fairness within their respective professions. Harold Levine, founder of Levine, Huntley, Schmidt & Beaver, entered advertising when the field was dominated by White Anglo-Saxon males with few, if any, Italians or Jews. Levine saw those groups invigorate advertising and thinks that African, Hispanic, and Asian American practitioners can do the same for the profession today. He proposes some fairness guidelines in the following selection, which originally appeared in the trade magazine* Advertising Age. *His suggestions also apply to public relations and magazine journalism which, as you learned in the previous chapter, have exceedingly poor minority representation.*

Opening Creative Doors

Harold Levine, Director of the American Association of
Advertising Agencies Institute for Advanced Studies

Recent headlines have proclaimed a "dearth of talent" and "no creative
stars, no leadership" in the agency business. Add to this picture comments
from agency executives stating, "The business lacks creative excitement"
and "The business isn't as much fun, as it used to be."

This is a sad commentary on a business that sells itself to clients as imaginative, creative, and intuitive.

My suggested solution: Open the doors of the business to all, including
African, Hispanic, and Asian American men and women. Allow their
energy, creativity, and enthusiasm to reinvigorate the advertising business
the way the Jews and Italians did in the 1950s, 1960s, and 1970s.

Let me explain: When I left college in 1939, the advertising business was
controlled by a few major agencies, and the key player was the account executive. He frequently controlled the account and all too often dictated the creative execution. The business was dominated by white Protestant males
with few, if any, Italians or Jews.

It wasn't until long after World War II, and the beginning of the civil
rights movement, that "ethnics" began making name for themselves in our
business.

A few individuals like Franklin Bruck, William Weintraub, Milton Biow,
Lawrence Valenstein, Arthur Fatt, Jack Tarcher, and Paul Gumbinner did
start their own agencies and were successful in getting a few general
accounts. However, the major agencies resisted opening their doors to
minority employees. The few that did so did not promote those individuals
to top executive positions. Along came the turbulent 1960s and the agency
business came alive with creative excitement. Doyle Dane Bernbach; Delehanty, Kurnit & Geller; Papert, Koenig, Lois; Ally & Gargano; Scali, McCabe,
Sloves; and Della Femina, Travisano & Partners were all making history
with dramatic new approaches to advertising problems.

The very people who were not welcome at the large agencies decided to
go out on their own and, by virtue of their creativity, made a significant
impact on the business. As a result, the creative department became the
engine that made the agency a success.

We need that surge of energy now in the advertising business, and I
suggest that if we were to open the doors of all agencies to African, Hispanic, and Asian Americans, we would be stimulating the advertising business with their enthusiasm and creativity.

Some industry executives I have spoken to say they have tried to hire minorities, but there just aren't any candidates. That's not true. If Sam Chisholm, Caroline Jones, and Byron Lewis can hire black and Hispanic professionals, then surely other agencies can find minority talent.

However, it's not going to happen unless there is a commitment to change. Here are a few suggestions:

- Encourage the consultants who help clients in agency reviews to include minority-owned agencies as candidates for general consumer product accounts. In this way, clients will begin to see African, Hispanic, and Asian Americans as advertising professionals, not just experts on "ethnic promotion."
- Contact the major black universities such as Howard, Spellman, and Morehouse and speak to officials about their advertising and marketing courses. Encourage agency executives to visit the schools, lecture classes, and seek talent for their agencies.
- Establish a task force of advertising professionals to meet with officials of the United Negro College Fund, as well as the leadership of the Urban League and the NAACP, to discuss the problem and seek solutions.
- Ask the American Advertising Federation to encourage ad clubs throughout the country to sponsor ad clubs in targeted inner-city high schools and provide speakers, exhibits, and agency tours for these clubs.
- Let it be known to major universities and art schools that ad agencies are open to hiring their best minority talent. Perhaps we can encourage some young people to look at advertising as a career, instead of Wall Street or the legal profession.

If Spike Lee can make great movies, and Maya Angelou can write great poetry, and Colin Powell can run the military, then surely there are talented young minority men and women who can produce great advertising and run big accounts.

I sincerely hope some agency executive will take up the challenge and begin to help make changes. Then the next Levine, Huntley, Schmidt & Beaver will come from a new group of minorities, and their enthusiasm, desire for success, and new visions of creativity will lift our business to new heights.

❧ EDITOR'S NOTE: *An important "fairness" representative works on behalf of readers and viewers at several newspapers and stations: the ombudsman. After 40 years at the* Fort Worth Star-Telegram, *Phil Record was named to that post, primarily because of his experience and moral values. Richard L. Connor, president of the* Star-Telegram, *says that Record begins each week by reciting this original prayer, affixed to the wall: "Lead me to the truth. Let me always be fair in my quest for it. Give me the wisdom to recognize the truth. And the courage to proclaim it as I find it to be, not as I wish it to be." That prayer encompasses the fundamental aspects of fairness. Here is Record's first "On the Record" column in the* Star Telegram, *explaining the role of the ombudsman.*

Spirit of Ombudsmanship

Phil Record, Ombudsman

In naming me to be the ombudsman of the *Star-Telegram,* Publisher Richard Connor has taken a step too few publishers and editors have dared to take.

In doing so, he has shown a willingness to risk exposing some of the newspaper's failures, sins, shortcomings and weaknesses to public scrutiny.

But it is a risk worth taking because it is hoped that we can make the *Star-Telegram* more accountable to you, the reader, and that this, in turn, will give you greater confidence in your newspaper.

Note the expression "your newspaper." A newspaper should, in a very real sense, belong to its readers. It should be concerned about their dreams, their fears, their hopes, their ambitions. Each newspaper should accurately reflect the community it serves. In accomplishing these objectives, a newspaper will develop its own personality.

There is a definite reluctance on the part of many newspapers to pay someone to be an in-house critic. The *Star-Telegram* is only the 33rd newspaper to become a member of the national Organization of News Ombudsmen.

But we are getting ahead of ourselves. Just what is an ombudsman (pronounced OM-buds-man)?

The term evidently originated in Sweden in the mid-1700s and was applied to an independent government official who investigated complaints aimed at the government. Once the investigation was completed, the ombudsman would recommend a punishment and/or a remedy.

The term came to be applied to the U.S. press as a result of an article written by A. H. Raskin, an assistant editor of the editorial page of the *New York Times.* The article, "What's Wrong With American Newspapers," appeared in the *New York Times Magazine* on June 11, 1967.

Raskin suggested that newspapers "establish departments of internal criticism to check on the fairness and accuracy of their coverage and comment."

"The department head ought to be given enough independence in the paper to serve as an ombudsman for the reader, armed with authority to get something done about valid complaints and to propose methods for more effective performance of all the paper's services to the community. . . ."

In less than a month, John Herchenroeder was named ombudsman of the *Courier-Journal* in Louisville, Kentucky. Interestingly, the *Courier-Journal* still has an ombudsman; the *New York Times* does not.

Obviously, the idea has not spread through the journalism community like wildfire. That is a shame.

There is not a rigid job description for a newspaper ombudsman. Most ombudsmen approach the job a little bit differently. In fact, some of those functioning in this capacity go by different titles: reader advocate, reader representative, public editor, etc.

Sometimes the person reports to the editor, in other cases he or she reports to the publisher. At the *Star-Telegram,* we have decided to retain the venerable title of ombudsman. To have greater independence, the ombudsman here will report directly to the publisher.

Why an ombudsman? Let's look at the guidelines of the Organization of Newspaper Ombudsmen, ONO.

"The objectives of a newspaper ombudsman shall be: (1) To improve the fairness, accuracy and accountability of the newspapers; (2) to enhance its credibility; (3) to strive to improve quality; (4) to make the newspaper aware of the concerns of, and the issues in, the communities served by it."

The duties of an ombudsman, as proposed by ONO, should include: "(1) Serving as in-house critic; (2) representing the reader who has complaints, suggestions, questions or complaints; (3) investigating complaints and recommending corrective action when warranted; (4) alerting the editor to complaints; (5) making speeches or writing to the public about the newspaper's policies, attitudes and operations; (6) defending the newspaper, publicly or privately, when warranted."

It is obvious that the strict definition of ombudsman has been somewhat stretched when it has been applied to the press. That's OK. What is important is that the press comes to capture what former *San Diego Union* ombudsman Al Jacoby has described as the "spirit of ombudsmanship."

Not all complaints will be handled by the ombudsman. Where a simple correction needs to be made, the person seeking the correction will be referred to the department editor involved. If this editor fails to satisfy the caller, he or she then will be referred to the ombudsman.

I hope to make this weekly column a dialogue with you, inasmuch as I will frequently be responding to your complaints, your questions and your suggestions.

I plan to deal with more than complaints. I hope to take some of the mystery out of this business by explaining how and why we do some things; we who make communications our livelihood have done a pretty lousy job of explaining the journalism profession to others.

I also will be talking about journalism ethics, the First Amendment and freedom of information. My first priority will be to listen to you, the reader, and to make your concerns and views better known in the newsroom. Next I will be listening to my colleagues here at the *Star-Telegram*, who will be voicing their own concerns and complaints about how we do things. Last, I will be voicing some of my own opinions based on more than 40 years in this business.

I know I will never be able to satisfy everyone. But I hope I will capture your interest.

�֎ EDITOR'S NOTE: *Allan Wolper, an associate professor of journalism at Rutgers University in Newark, New Jersey, covers campus journalism for the trade magazine* Editor & Publisher. *His assignments often include controversies concerning student publications, censorship, political correctness, protests and litigation. His published pieces are known for their detail and fairness. In the following article, which originally appeared in E&P, Wolper covers an incident at the University of Iowa student newspaper, which wrongly identified a former UI basketball star as having been arrested for burglary, and then tried to correct the mistake. The story includes several lessons we have already covered in Chapter 7 and ones we will cover in Chapter 9. But at the core, Wolper's piece is about fairness on three levels: (1) the way his piece is written, citing all parties in a complete and impartial report, (2) the lengths that student journalists went to make amends in the* Daily Iowan, *and (3) how those amends did not fully satisfy the wronged party, illustrating the concept of viewpoint.*

Student Newspaper Tries to Right a Wrong

Allan Wolper, Campus Correspondent, *Editor & Publisher*

At 9:30 P.M. on February 12, 1994, two watches and a television set were taken out of a home at 98-28th Eighth Ave. in Inglewood, California.

Police say an officer and his dog arrived about ten minutes later and arrested a man they say was responsible for the break-in.

The suspect was taken to the Inglewood police department, where he identified himself as James David Moses, Jr. of Iowa City, Iowa, and was charged with burglary, possessing stolen property, and carrying a concealed weapon.

Several days later, the *Daily Iowan*, the student newspaper at the University of Iowa, called the Iowa City police department to check on a drug bust.

Chris Pothoven, a student journalist, was told there was a bigger story in Inglewood, California, where James David Moses, a former University of Iowa basketball star, had been arrested on a burglary charge.

Pothoven called Inglewood and was assured by the police that they had placed James D. Moses in a holding cell and were ready to arraign him.

On February 15, the *Daily Iowan* published a brief story on the front page above the fold with a picture that said former UI basketball star Moses was being held in connection with a robbery in Inglewood.

But the police had the wrong Moses, and so did the *Daily Iowan*.

The suspect in Inglewood was Wilbert Moses, a cousin of the former University of Iowa basketball star. James Moses was in Iowa City when the burglary occurred.

"We had checked with the cops twice and each time they told us that they had James Moses," recalled Loren Keller, the editor of the *Daily Iowan*. "They even said the man they had in jail had the same middle initial as James."

But the one call the paper did not make continues to haunt them.

"They never called me," said Moses, who was finishing up the last six credits toward his degree. "The athletic department knew where I was. They should have checked with their own sportswriters. But they didn't.

"This is another example of a paper rushing to put a black athletic star in a bad light. And the people out there will say that another black athlete who didn't make it to the pros gets into trouble."

Keller concedes that the *Daily Iowan* had erred in not checking with the UI athletic department or trying to track down Moses, but denies that racism had anything to do with the way the story was handled.

"If we had made those calls the story wouldn't have run," Keller said. "But we wouldn't have handled the story any differently if a white player had been involved. We were simply given the wrong information.

"I feel so bad about the whole thing."

Tim Browne, deputy district attorney of Los Angeles County, said police tried immediately to find out whether Wilbert Moses was lying when he identified himself as his cousin, James.

"People give us false names all the time," Browne said, "and we check it out. In this case, it took a little longer because our fingerprinting equipment still wasn't working well because of [a recent] earthquake."

Meanwhile, Inglewood police punched the name James Moses into its computer and found that he had been mistakenly arrested in 1990 in Iowa City, but his arrest record had not been expunged.

Moses endured several hellish weeks of unwanted media attention before police learned he was innocent.

Inglewood police asked Iowa City for a copy of that 1990 incident.

"We sent them the report," recalled Iowa City Detective Ed Schultz. "They wanted to see if the description we had matched the man they had in custody. It didn't."

It was at this point that the *Daily Iowan* called Iowa City police and was told that James Moses was being held on burglary charges in Inglewood, California.

The *Daily Iowan* received a batch of early-morning telephone calls within an hour after the story on James Moses appeared on its front page. The situation intensified as KRNA-FM, the local commercial radio station, attributed the story to the Associated Press, indicating it was receiving national exposure.

In fact, the Des Moines AP office said that its Iowa City correspondent had "passed on the Moses story."

"I thought it had been a wire piece," said Joe Nugent, the KRNA-FM radio news editor who wrote and voiced the story on the station's early morning newscasts. "I was wrong."

The radio station continued to identify Moses as the suspect in a subsequent broadcast, and attributed his arrest to the *Daily Iowan.*

James Moses said a close friend of his called the station to report that he had been in Dunton, Iowa, with her when the burglary occurred.

"The woman who called didn't identify herself or leave a name," said Nugent.

Randy Larson, an Iowa City attorney representing Moses, had already called the *Daily Iowan* to demand a correction.

"We checked again with the police," said Keller. "We figured that maybe they had a different James Moses. But even the middle initials matched."

The tragedy of errors ended later that day when Wilbert Moses admitted at his arraignment that he had lied to the police about his identity.

The next day the *Daily Iowan* published a front-page apology to Moses in the same space that had originally contained the charges against him.

And KRNA-FM used its early-morning drive-time news programs to admit that it, too, had incorrectly named James Moses as a burglary suspect, and later wrote a format apology to him.

The journalistic mea culpa was given front-page attention in the *Iowa City Press Citizen* and prominently featured in the sports section *of* the *Cedar Rapids Gazette.*

The *Daily Iowan* also gave Moses the entire top section of its editorial page to write about his news media nightmare.

"I don't think anyone can imagine how I felt," Moses said in an article that was promoted on the front page. "Upon becoming a student athlete at the UI, you are suddenly living life in a fishbowl. Everything you do and say is open to public scrutiny.

"I have learned a valuable and unforgettable lesson. . . . The media can make your career with accolades . . . or with one quick swoop of the pen, can destroy your character as a human being.

"Not only was I so embarrassed that I was afraid to show my face in Iowa City, I have been emotionally drained. There are those who will always associate my name with the crime."

Keller apologized personally three days later with an article on the editorial page.

He noted that newspapers and media organizations make mistakes every day, some minor and annoying, and others, like the one that ensnared Moses, "truly hurtful."

"Moses has without question been embarrassed," Keller wrote. "He's been wronged in print by the *DI* and is upset. He has every right to be."

"An explanation of how and why the mistake was made isn't going to excuse what happened, but perhaps will show that we did not act with reckless disregard of the facts.

"Carelessly? Yes. But not without a reasonable amount of caution."

Keller said the *Daily Iowan* should have called the University of Iowa athletic department to help the paper locate the former basketball star.

"Moses says he has learned a valuable and unforgettable lesson from this incident," Keller said. "So have we. The power of the press is something that is easy to take for granted when you're a daily part of it.

"As enjoyable as the freedom that power allows [is], sometimes it's easier to forget the serious responsibility on the other side of the coin.

"Finally a sincere apology to James Moses. We made a mistake and we're truly sorry. It is my personal hope that our readers now understand the real story and that your name is completely cleared."

Steve Rowe, an assistant sports information director at Iowa, said none of the news organizations contacted him before the Moses story broke.

"The first we knew about it was when we saw it in the *Daily Iowan*," Rowe said. "I found out one of the assistant coaches had seen James in Iowa City. But by the time we called the paper they knew they had made a mistake.

"Unfortunately you can't take it back. But the *Daily Iowan* handled it professionally once they realized their mistake."

Rowe said that college football and basketball stars from urban areas find it difficult to play in places like Iowa. "There are no professional teams, so the athletes are very much in the limelight," he explained. "It is very difficult to play here because people know who you are."

Months after the incident, Moses said that he was still experiencing the fallout. "They defamed my character. . . . The negative perception is still out there. I don't know how it will affect my future career.

"The *Daily Iowan* gave me a weak retraction. It's what the media is doing these days. Writing about somebody's character before they get the whole story. Just like saying a guy is a child molester when it is not true.

"The media should be accountable for whatever they write."

✖ EDITOR'S NOTE: *Emily Caldwell, a former reporter at the* Biddeford (Maine) Journal Tribune, *composed the following piece to come to terms with fairness issues concerning her coverage of a family tragedy: A young father murdered his 22-month-old daughter and then committed suicide. Caldwell was asked to write a story about "family reaction"—an assignment that in part would be responsible for her quitting her job and obtaining a master's degree and a public relations position in* University News *at Ohio University. Here are issues with which Caldwell had to deal: Did she unfairly invade family members' privacy during their grief? Was her editor acting unfairly in making the assignment in the first place? Did the community have a right to know how such a tragedy could have happened? Should she have refused the assignment because the nature of it conflicted with her value of compassion? Addressing these questions took courage. Caldwell had to contact and ascertain the viewpoint of her editor years after the fact and then balance his and her viewpoints via expert advice. Nonetheless, the process helped Caldwell put the issue into perspective in this article, which eventually was published in* Editor & Publisher.

Fairness and Grief

Emily Caldwell, Free-Lance Writer

A 24-year-old father in Lebanon, Maine, slashed his 22-month-old daughter 11 times with a knife, stabbed himself in the chest and set his bedroom furniture ablaze with a cigarette lighter on a Friday night in March 1991.

I was the reporter on weekend duty when Norman and his daughter, Kristen, died. They were not the first deaths that I had covered as a newspaper writer, but the circumstances were the most tragic that I had encountered.

I was not then and am not now the kind of reporter who thrives on such stories. In fact, I dreaded death stories, and I routinely ducked away from my editor's desk when the police scanner in the newsroom indicated spot news was in the making. When I needed a story, I sought issue-oriented news or features. Death frightened me and stories about death made me emotional and uncomfortable.

Coverage of death also calls for what I feel is one of the biggest drawbacks of newspaper reporting: the pursuit of family reaction.

I half-heartedly accept seeking personal information for a story about, for example, a teenager killed in an accident—comments from a youth's parents and friends can transform a police officer's recitation of the facts into a more personal account about the person who died. But when a father kills his daughter and commits suicide, I find little about pursuit of a story in the name of good journalism that can justify a telephone call to the mother of the dead child a day after the murder.

To me, even the most compassionate reporter's approach to the story amounts to an invasion of privacy and lack of consideration for her grief.

I had worked at the *Journal Tribune* in Biddeford, Maine, for a year and a half when I was assigned to cover Norman's and Kristen's deaths. Police ruled the incident a murder-suicide Saturday afternoon, when they also reported that Norman and Kristen died of smoke inhalation; the toddler had survived the knife wounds.

My initial response was emotional—all I could think about was the fact that during the last moments of that child's life, the man whom she was supposed to be able to trust was cutting her with his knife. I didn't want to write this story. But my emotions and reluctance didn't matter. The family's reaction to the tragedy did.

Sandy, my managing editor, was filling in for the city editor that weekend. He told me to find out why Norman did what he did. I resisted. I argued that newsroom policy was to write short, no-byline stories about suicides. I didn't deny that I wanted to avoid the ask-the-family-members-how-they-feel routine. Sandy argued that the child's death called for a more meaningful story. He told me to find and talk to Jennifer, Norman's live-in girlfriend and the mother of the dead little girl. Jennifer was 19.

What Sandy didn't seem to consider was how Jennifer might feel about this intrusion. Not only would I be asking personal questions about what led to the deaths of her boyfriend and daughter, but I would be asking them at what I suspected was the most painful time in Jennifer's life. Such treatment of murder victims' families was something I frequently thought about with disdain. It's a policy I still think about and question almost three years later.

Before I tried to reach Jennifer that Sunday, I phoned Norman's sister. She called me a vulture and said I gave newspaper reporters a bad name.

I apologized and told her that a family member's input could help explain why Norman wanted to die. My persuasion led her to change her mind. She let me into her home.

She cried as she told me that her brother had needed psychological help and that he was distraught because he had lost a job six months earlier. She gave me a picture to put in the newspaper. After speaking with her, I drove to Lebanon in search of Jennifer. I hoped I wouldn't find her.

I knew Jennifer was staying at her mother's house, where she was protected by an unlisted phone number. I wandered the nameless, rural roads of Lebanon for two hours, stopping at grocery stores and houses asking for clues about where the house might be.

Some people treated me with contempt and told me to leave the family alone, reinforcing my feeling that this approach was inappropriate. I eventually found the house with help from a local restaurant owner.

Jennifer's mother greeted me as I pulled into her driveway. She thought I was lost. I had passed the house four times, agonizing over what to say when I knocked on the door. I considered telling her I was lost to avoid the request for an interview, but having found the house, my loyalty to Sandy and concern about keeping my job prevailed.

Jennifer's mother closed her eyes and shook her head when I told her who I was and why I was there. She didn't cry or get angry, but she looked like she might do both.

I asked to speak to Jennifer, telling her I had talked to Norman's side of the family and I wanted to balance the story. She actually went inside to ask Jennifer but came back to tell me that the young woman refused.

I asked Jennifer's mother if she would be interviewed, but she also refused. Then, Jennifer's mother cried. I cried. I briefly grasped her hand, and as we stood in her driveway, she told me, "We all loved that baby so much."

I apologized and drove away. And I never used that quote.

Monday morning, I wrote a story based primarily on a state trooper's account of the deaths. I also had talked to a neighbor and to Norman's father, who hadn't seen his son or granddaughter for months.

Despite my efforts, I could not provide quotes from Jennifer. I kept the details of my meeting with her mother to myself.

I felt satisfied that I had maintained my personal integrity: I had not pressed for the interview with Jennifer's mother or taken advantage of her grief by using her one heart-wrenching quote. But I maintained my integrity at my expense; I had the distinct feeling that in Sandy's mind, I had failed.

He didn't discuss the story. Deadline was over. He asked what I had lined up for the following day. A year later, for various reasons—including the hope that I never would write another death story—I quit my reporting job to attend graduate school.

Ironically enough, I recently found myself on the other side of the argument. I had a graduate assistantship to critique the *Post*, the daily student newspaper at Ohio University. The week before my first critique last year, a first-year student died after falling out of her dormitory window. Her death raised a series of questions, and the school's police spokesman offered few details to the press for several days.

During my critique, I admonished the newspaper staff for not finding out what happened to the woman through interviews with her friends, bystanders or her parents and for not placing the initial story about her death on page one.

Editors told me that initial reports hinted that the death might be a suicide and that their exhaustive efforts to speak to friends and the woman's parents had produced nothing.

It was only after my conversation with the editors that I realized my assumptions that the staff had fallen short of its duties were unfounded. Hindsight made the difference.

Similarly, Sandy tells me now, 2 1/2 years after the murder-suicide in Maine, that I didn't fail in reporting the story. He says he realized long ago that the story was complete without Jennifer's remarks. But in assigning the murder-suicide or any similar story involving death, his first consideration is gathering as much information as possible.

"You line up the people who might know something," he said. "In another sense, it's respectful of everyone involved, especially the mother of the kid, to give her a chance to say something. . . . I think you have to be gentle. There's no question about it—it's an awful thing to do. But if you're prepared to take no for an answer, how much of an invasion of privacy is it?"

Sandy also said he's not convinced that reporters' requests for interviews intensify the trauma for victims of tragedy. As long as reporters are compassionate and don't badger a subject, he said, the media's effect is minimal.

"If it's handled right, it's a fleeting moment in the most traumatic weekend in this woman's life. . . . I think it's arrogant to think we're the most important thing going on. The impact of our involvement is overshadowed by the event itself."

The only exceptions, he said, would be if survivors are suicidal or ill because of the tragedy. And no matter what the circumstances, Sandy would assign a reporter who he believes would approach the story with sensitivity.

Louis Hodges, a nationally known ethicist and professor at Washington and Lee University in Lexington, Virginia, points out arguments for and against approaching Jennifer or any victim of a similar tragedy.

Disclosing something about Norman and her relationship with him, Hodges noted, might save a life if someone else shows symptoms similar to Norman's. But asking her to discuss the tragedy could subject her to scrutiny that could further harm her and amounts to using her grief to help readers understand the deaths.

No industry standard exists for how to handle death stories, Hodges said. Editors typically assign reporters to interview the people most directly affected by the tragedy.

Without written professional standards, Hodges said, journalists are left trying to balance the moral right of people to be left alone with the effort to shed some light on an offender's state of mind when committing such a brutal crime.

"If they've got a really hot issue that's of interest to the public, they're likely to pursue it vigorously," Hodges said, referring to newspaper editors. "If they're going to err, they're likely to err on the side of telling too much."

I'm troubled by that likelihood, especially if a newspaper tells too much at the expense of a source already mourning the loss of a lover and child.

I was lucky in covering Norman's and Kristen's deaths—my contact with Jennifer's mother was brief and cordial. But the pain that I caused during that exchange still bothers me.

"I'm kind of glad reporters are that sensitive," Hodges said. "It's humanity coming through. You're under real pressure to violate your own conscience in order to keep your job. . . . If I were a reporter given the assignment, I would try to carry it out and try to keep from gagging in the process."

His suggestion to reporters facing similar stories: "Be a person first and then do the reporting bit."

VALUES EXERCISES

1. Without violating your own or someone else's privacy, recall a professional or academic situation, incident, or event in which you believe you were treated unfairly. Describe this in your journal but do not hand in the entry.

2. Without violating your own or someone else's privacy, recount a professional or academic situation, incident, or event in which you believe you treated someone else unfairly. Describe this in your journal but do not hand in the entry.

3. Again in your journal, put each example described in Execises 1 and 2 through the fairness process: ascertaining conflicts, balancing viewpoints and differing interests, and seeking bonds or advice. Finally, make a determination about whether you were treated fairly (Exercise 1) and whether you treated another fairly (Exercise 2).

4. Now that you have determined fairness in the professional or academic disputes cited in Exercises 1 and 2, explain in a 250-word statement for each example:
    - How you could have been treated more fairly
    - How you could have treated another person more fairly
    - How the process has affected or enhanced your values on fairness

9

Power

Bases and Cases

Power is not a value but a force people employ to put forth their values or the reputation they earn because of those values. So the concept is both active and passive. When we put forth our values to meet a challenge or resolve a problem, we actively tap our power, calling on our sense of right or wrong or fairness to address those situations. If, for instance, our challenge is unemployment and our problem is financial, we can look for jobs in the classified ads or rob a bank. Our values dictate choices. Once we choose, however, the concept of power takes over as we decide how much to employ to execute that choice: We can solicit a recommendation from a mentor or a bank sack from a teller. Afterward, depending on that choice, power is passive and a function of reputation; we can bask in its glow or sweat in its glare.

So defined, you can see why power is the last concept we will cover in this book. (Chapter 10 provides practical information about turning values into codes.) We have alluded to power in each chapter, from the influence our family has on values to the last essay you read by Emily Caldwell entitled "Fairness and Grief." At this point, you should be familiar with various personal and professional values and their importance at home or at work. Now you need to know how to assert those values in an appropriate manner.

Ethics has two components: values and power. Values is the numerator and power is the denominator. As in math, if the denominator is zero, you have nothing, no matter how enormous or insignificant the numerator. No action, no choice. (Deciding to take no action—ignoring a news story or overlooking harassment because you like the source or perpetuator—*is a choice.*) Likewise, the unemployed person with financial problems might have made a choice to look for a job or rob a bank; however, we cannot discuss *applied ethics*—how values dictate choices—until the person gets off the couch. Otherwise, we are dealing with *theoretical ethics*—discussing our opinions about a person's responsibility to pursue or avoid work or a society's responsibility to curb or account for crime. These may be important philosophical considerations, but they are one step removed from reality and so, as you have read earlier and often, our values are not on the line. When they are, power puts them there.

The power of the press is derived from the First Amendment. Because of it, journalists enjoy great freedoms. They have the freedom to hurt others and make mistakes in reports, campaigns, and advertisements, although consequences may ensue because of libel, liability, and obscenity laws. In general, however, reporters can investigate, document, tape, photograph, and criticize anyone, even the President; advertisers can help sell controversial products or services—handguns to palmistry—without too much government interference; and lobbyists can influence Congress or fight its proposals. Because of the First Amendment, private citizens may own media outlets and wield influence in the breaking or making of public servants. For instance, the April 20, 1992, issue of *Time* features a sinister black and white negative photo of then presidential candidate Bill Clinton with the title: "Why Voters Don't Trust Clinton." The January 4, 1993, cover features a White House portrait and heralds the President-elect as "Man of the Year." The media has the freedom to make such reversals. In essence, without the First Amendment, this textbook would be a government publication and ethics would be a matter of medals or tribunals.

Certainly the U.S. government has great powers, too. It can conceal policies from the press by labeling them top secret or restrict access to sensitive areas, especially during war, acting in the national interest. But in times of peace, censorship is primarily a concern of journalists working for U.S. companies operating in foreign countries with stricter laws regulating the media. The leaders of those countries know the common maxim—knowledge is power—and so censor their media to protect their policies. This relates not only to news coverage but to advertising and public relations campaigns as well. As David B. Ottaway has written as a State Department correspondent for the *Washington Post*, oppressive regimes often worry about their political *and* economic health, suggesting a correlation: the weaker the health, the stronger the censorship.[1] Typically, these leaders restrict markets or campaigns promoting products or services that their citizens cannot afford or might want to adopt.

"Worldwide," according to editors of the *Quill*, "press censorship is the rule, not the exception. The Divine Right of Kings is a half-forgotten, even quaint notion. But Reasons of the State is alive and well, and dwelling nearly everywhere. In much of Africa—black Africa as well as South Africa; in parts of Europe; in the Middle East; in the Far East; in Asia; in Mexico; in Central America; in South America—reasons of state are used to squeeze and channel and even shut down the flow of information."[2] The specter of censorship is like an infection in these countries; the journalist's first impulse may be to fight censorship but eventually he or she might succumb to it. According to John Tusa, an executive of the British Broadcasting Corporation (BBC), "Censorship has a thousand faces—openness only one, whichever country you are in. Of all its masks, self-censorship can be as bad as any, the willing decision not to report something you know is happening."[3]

When self-censorship arises because of government policies or media crackdowns, it is typically related to temptation, or the clash of two conflicting interests: the desire to report versus the desire to keep a license or press card in a foreign land. When self-censorship occurs in the United States, it is usually in response to an agency or editorial policy rather than a governmental one: *taste*.

Defined, *taste* is the suppression of images or messages in a specific medium by authorized representatives of that medium, usually with a goal of appropriateness in response to privacy or community and customer standards or with respect to budgetary concerns. As such, taste is an issue related to the First Amendment and the power of the press. Free speech allows for most messages and great power, as we have noted. Depending on values or corporate policies, journalists restrict or transmit images and/or messages in the interest of—or without regard to—taste.

Taste is a function of values; the decision to restrict or disseminate questionable material is a function of power. Images or messages may be powerful in and of themselves. When edited, altered, or sent by the machinery of mass media, they can hit the audience with subtle or terrific force. That can affect business and is therefore an aspect of media management. Moreover, standards of good taste vary from media outlet to media outlet, market to market, town to town, region to region, industry to industry. In other words, what one radio talk show will allow, another might not, depending on community standards; what advertisers might allow to sell movie tickets or swimwear in a metropolitan daily, a photo director might edit or crop in the same newspaper in the same city, according to industry standards. Those standards are influenced, in part, by the individual publisher, owner, or media executive. Sometimes they are influenced by financial priorities. In any case, such standards are executed by supervisors in the newsroom or conference room, usually with the audience, consumer, client, or budget in mind.

Reprinted with special permission of King Features Syndicate.

Pulitzer Prize–winning cartoonist Jim Borgman satirizes the photo-illustration of O. J. Simpson on the June 27, 1994, cover of Time. *The altered photo was appropriately labeled a "photo-illustration" on the contents page of that issue. However, the June 27, 1994, cover of* Newsweek *carried an unaltered photograph, sparking a taste-related controversy about* Time's *sensationalizing the case. Borgman's satire addresses the issue with regard to journalism ethics, depicting the cartoon character Homer Simpson of Fox TV's* The Simpsons, *indicating how low journalism standards have fallen during Simpson coverage. The covers of* Newsweek *and* Time *accompanied articles about the slow-speed freeway police chase of Simpson who, at the time, was threatening to commit suicide. Educator Eddith Dashiell discusses taste considerations concerning that chase in her Living Ethics essay "On Air with O. J."*

Public relations practitioners must adhere to the same standards and influences as other journalists, with regard to appropriateness. But certain political practitioners also must evaluate the appropriateness of their behavior as lobbyists. Some cynical practitioners believe that regardless of holds office, "the power dynamic remains the same: it's about access and influence and—at least in part—cold cash," according to the editors of *Inside PR* in a special report titled "Juice: The Future of Power and Influence in Washington."[4] The report counters that cynicism by quoting several practitioners with strong values, including Margery Kraus, president of the Washington, DC-based agency APCO & Associates, who states: "The question of ethics looms larger than ever in the past. Companies that care about their reputation do not want to be perceived to be doing anything that is ethically questionable."[5] Reputation, as you have observed, is a passive aspect of power, shaped by values and how they have been asserted. The same holds true for agencies and other media outlets: They earn reputations, too.

Appropriateness is key in building relationships with legislators, according to Charles Pucie, president of another Washington, DC-based agency, Capitoline. Pucie says that companies who operate without regard to appropriateness on a confidential basis with legislators eventually will encounter problems with the way that behavior is perceived outside of Washington; moreover, he adds, favors can be called in only once.[6] "You get access by building credibility, by building trust," says Peter Seagall, director of Dorf & Stanton's Washington office, in the *Inside PR* report. "That kind of access matters, because it means Congressmen will at least listen to what you have to say and take it seriously."[7] In the final analysis, the behavior of lobbyists may be regulated in part by Congress, but ultimately the values of agencies and their practitioners are responsible for appropriateness in legislative halls and offices.

Values also are affected by budget considerations. Money wields power, too. In corporate public relations, for instance, the marketing department often decides which PR campaigns to fund or refuse. Jerry L. Sloan, who directed public relations operations at Ford and American Motors, retired in 1992 to teach and is a fellow of the Public Relations Society of America. During his 32-year career in the automotive industry, he helped create campaigns combining truth with product enthusiasm. In the 1980s, one such campaign was the "Border-to-Border" promotion program to augment the press launch for the Jeep Cherokee. The "BtB" started in Vancouver with 10 automotive magazine journalists divided into five teams driving new Jeep Cherokees in a five-day competition to Tijuana. Teams earned extra points for driving on dirt or rocky roads rather than on paved highways.

"Press programs to launch new products always result in widespread press coverage," Sloan observes. "The expectation was that the journalists would write about their exploits and the Jeep products in their publications. It was a smash! But to fund the program, the public relations staff had to convince the marketing staff to provide the funding. Marketing was always very heavily funded, and public relations was treated like the plague when it came to the annual allocation of funds. Marketing came through, and after the program, the head of marketing thought it had been money well spent." The next year, the event gained momentum with the competition starting in Montreal and ending in New Orleans. Marketing agreed to fund the program again. "The third year was another story," Sloan notes. "Times were tough in the auto industry and particularly at American Motors.

Although everyone knew the 'BtB' was a successful program, marketing said it couldn't spare the money. PR didn't have it. No one had it."

Sloan didn't necessarily agree with this particular marketing decision, however. "The cost of the program was about a third of the cost of a one-page ad in *Time* magazine. Which would have more valuable in promoting the Jeep—the 'BtB' or $25,000 to $30,000 worth of advertising? Marketing thought advertising would be more profitable." Because that department was empowered by the budget, PR lost and the "Border-to-Border" Jeep promotion "went down the drain," Sloan recalls.

At news outlets, advertising departments can influence coverage because of budgetary concerns. This can imply that certain media corporations practice a different ethics than they espouse. For instance, executives sometimes kill or heavily edit stories because reporters are investigating advertisers or producing segments affecting an advertiser's business. Common examples include:

- Consumer stories making price comparisons for a week's worth of groceries at local supermarkets or for a year's coverage at auto insurance agencies
- Investigative stories focusing on service station repairs or price fixing
- Service articles or segments informing the audience how to negotiate with car dealers when making purchases

Typically, local supermarkets, insurance agencies, service stations, and car dealerships are top advertisers that influence profit margins and dictate the bottom line. In such cases, managing editors may want to pursue truth vigorously and responsibly—embracing strong values—but must yield to advertising considerations (instead of value-oriented taste ones) and spike those stories.

Issues of taste in news coverage can have great impact on the audience and are covered at length in essays in the Living Ethics section at the end of the chapter. One of the most mundane tasks is gathering information from police reports or court documents, often the source of taste-related privacy problems in the newsroom. The task may be mundane but the details in such reports or documents often are stark. When published, they can cause great pain to family and friends of crime victims. Such was the case with an Ohio University student whose friend was murdered along with a female acquaintance near Akron. The OU student felt the information that area newspapers published about the murders violated the privacy of the victims and their family and friends.

I know my friend's death was brutal and painful. I know Wendy suffered more horror than I can ever imagine in my life. However, thanks to the newspaper's vivid description, images of her death fill my mind. Did I need to know, let alone the public, that Wendy was found naked from the waist down, with her top pulled up and her bra torn in half? Was it necessary to print that she was raped twice, by two guys? Or that her face was covered with "inch-deep lacerations" from a knife? Or that they were "killed with a blunt instrument smashed against the right sides of their heads." Or that "the weapon crushed (Wendy's) skull" and that "both died of brain injuries."

I did not. These descriptions have caused nightmares and unnecessary horror. When I think of Wendy I no longer think of the beautiful model she was. It's hard to get the image of her bloody, mutilated body out of my mind. It's hard to stop picturing her being raped in this "field of tall cattails." And it is hard to realize that her death was slow and painful.

Did the paper have to mention that before she was beaten to death, the guys tried to kill her by strangling her with a shoelace?

The student believes newspapers should have eliminated those details from their reports in the interest of privacy and community standards. Some editors might argue otherwise, however. According to their values, they would risk hurting or offending some individuals in the name of the public good or the community's right to know. The details of the Akron murders illustrate the brutality of rape, a gross abuse of power; they may influence citizens or their representatives to take a stronger stance on crime, for instance. Nonetheless, the student's viewpoint is also legitimate because words, like images, can be inappropriately vivid or contain racial slurs, sexual objectification, or obscene overtones.

The decision to use or edit potentially inappropriate material is a function of fairness as well as taste. Racial slurs present a special challenge inasmuch as an abhorrent word such as *nigger* will offend, hurt, or humiliate certain segments of the audience but also indicate the severity of the offense or bigotry. Kenn Venit, a television news consultant, believes, "No news organizations wants to offend its audience, but no one wants to censor, either."[8] For instance, Venit says that coverage of actor Ted Danson's 1993 monologue in blackface at the Friar's Club in New York, at which he "roasted" actor and then-companion Whoopi Goldberg, was subjective, with several newspapers quoting Danson and others using "ni- - er," "- - - - - r," and "- - - - - -" instead of "nigger."[9] Sometimes an editor's impulse to protect readers from slurs or profanity undermines the primary duty to inform them, which in this case might mean using the offensive word without substituting hyphens or euphemisms. The latter can be especially confusing. Venit cites a newspaper trying to avoid the word *fuck* in a piece discussing former President Nixon's use of "the most common four-

VALUE OF HOPE

Charles Withers, an employee who escaped the shooting at the post office, consoling a friend who had waited outside for him.

Postal Survey Leaves
Violence Unaddressed

By MARTIN TOLCHIN

Ellen Lorentzson, AP photographer, was out jogging on the morning of November 14, 1991, when she heard a commotion in her neighborhood and soon after returned to shoot the picture above. Three postal workers inside the Royal Oak Post Office near Detroit had been shot to death and six wounded by a disgruntled former employee. Instead of focusing on the murders, she photographed a postal worker who survived the ordeal, reunited with his girlfriend. The photo was featured in the *New York Times.* "I generally don't see a reason to take pictures of dead bodies. That's not the story. There's another angle to tragedy," Lorentzson says. "Part of why the picture is so effective is that it shows the anguish, but also shows the hope, on that day because this man survived. And that is as much of the story as the people who were killed or injured. Hope is as powerful as tragedy."

letter barnyardism" and asked: "How am I supposed to know what barn-yardism we're talking about here?"[10]

Linda Lotridge Levin, writing in the *Quill*, conducted an informal survey of daily newspapers in New England and learned "that in an effort to remain the guardian of the public's morals and to present, as several noted, 'a family newspaper,' most had written policies on the use of—or rather the avoidance of—'dirty' language."[11] Levin's survey also asked editors whether they would quote the president of the United States verbatim if he said "fuck you" in a public place. Her results? Five editors replied "probably"; 14 said "maybe" (but only if television or radio used it first); and 10 said they would not print such an expression.[12]

Fuck, as broadcasters know, is one of the Federal Communication Commission's seven profane words generally banned from public airwaves. (The others are *cocksucker, cunt, motherfucker, piss, shit*, and *tit*.) "Magazines print some of them," Levin writes, "even the kind of magazine a junior high school student might read at home."[13]

One such magazine is *Writer's Digest*, a free-lance and creative writer periodical used in many classrooms. Its editor, Bruce Woods, encountered the term *fuck* when publishing an interview with world-renowned author Stephen King. King, discussing slow days at the typewriter, said, "I had this tense scene where there were a lot of sexual politics involved, and I wanted to do it right and I didn't know if I could. And what that means is that I dallied by the teapot, and I read the sports twice and I said to myself: "Well, you shouldn't be doing this, you shouldn't be reading anything right now, because when you read, it fucks you up."[14]

Dealing with the word *fuck* is a "balancing act," Woods says. On the one hand you try to maintain "the integrity of the piece" and on the other, make it suitable for the audience. "This is sometimes not simple," he adds. "Do you risk running an article that nobody—because of the offensive material it contains—will finish, purely in the name of editorial integrity? Do you run a piece that nobody will finish—because the life has been taken out of its voice—in order to kowtow to what you suppose are the sensitivities of your audience?" Woods decided to use *fuck* in the King interview "because it is a part of King's voice and also because, I felt, readers expect King to be a bit dangerous." Woods did eliminate one or two earlier uses of the word, however, "both to avoid chasing readers away before they could be hooked by the piece and because we felt that the impact of the remaining usage would be most dramatic in the article's conclusion."

A handful of readers objected. Woods published a letter from an anonymous reader who wrote, "Well *WD*, you finally did it. You've stooped to the low level of pornographic writing. I was shocked to see the use of an offensive four-letter word in the Stephen King interview. I will no longer purchase your periodical, and I will be sure to tell others of my reason for this decision."[15]

The vast majority of readers did not complain about the use of *fuck* in the King interview, one of the most popular pieces that year. But the reader's canceling of her subscription is the typical response and a consequence that all editors weigh before approving the use of a profanity. When hundreds of readers protest inappropriateness, a journalist can be reprimanded or worse. This happened to Matt Coker whose column was "put on sabbatical" in the *Daily Pilot*, a southern California newspaper, when he wrote about the hypocrisy in eulogies about the passing of former President Nixon in 1994. Coker's column began: "A moment of silence, please, to mourn the passing of our 37th president. Now that that's out of the way: DING DONG DICK IS DEAD!"[16] Other consequences can involve public protests and/or boycotts, as occurred after a controversial cartoon was published in the *Sacramento Bee*. The cartoon depicted a hooded Ku Klux Klan member holding a paper with this quote by Nation of Islam leader Louis Farrakhan: "You can't be a racist by talking—only by acting." The hooded KKK member says to his unhooded counterpart: "That nigger makes a lot of sense."[17] A local president of the National Association for the Advancement of Colored People (NAACP) called for a boycott of the paper, which lost about 1,400 subscriptions between February 4, when the cartoon ran, and February 12. Peter Schrag, editorial page editor, said that the cartoon was trying "to show the falsity of Farrakhan's claim" and did so "by using one of the most powerful and hateful words in our vocabulary." He added, "Sadly, the word itself proved to be so powerful that many readers never got beyond it, and for them, the cartoon failed."[18]

Editors and other executives also play a role in determining what advertisements are appropriate in their publications. In 1993, H. Mason Sizemore, president of the *Seattle Times*, banned all tobacco ads. "These ads were designed to kill our readers," he says, "so we decided to refuse them."[19] Other products typically banned by newspapers and other media outlets include mail-order merchandise, vending machines, X-rated movies, fortune tellers, 1-900 number services, firearms, work-at-home jobs, certain financial schemes, adoption services, abortion services, certain medical products, and escort services.[20]

Taste, with regard to advertising, concerns the message as much as the product. An ad has two goals: to inform and to influence. When it informs, it sends a manifest (or obvious) message: "Buy this toothpaste because it prevents tooth decay." When an ad influences, it sends a latent (or subtle) message: "Buy this toothpaste and experience love because a beautiful woman or handsome man will kiss you." Taste can involve one or both messages or how those messages are used in tandem with images or illustrations.

It is easy to spot questionable taste in a manifest message. Typically, the product may violate social mores or community standards. As previously stated, certain products and services—pyramid schemes and escort services,

This drawing was made by textbook author Michael J. Bugeja's daughter Erin at age 6. It is, in essence, an advertisement with a manifest and latent message: "Wear Lee Jeans/Experience Joy." The drawing illustrates the influence that advertising can have on children.

for instance—usually are banned by mainstream outlets. Questionable taste in latent messages can be easy to spot, too. One such message was published in an ad in the *Minneapolis Star Tribune* at the height of the controversy involving Tonya Harding's role in the baton beating of rival Olympic skater Nancy Kerrigan. The product, a self-defense device, was billed as "The Tonya Tapper" with the slogan: "You've Seen How It Works/ Now Get One for Your Protection." In this case, the manifest message was: "Buy this product to protect yourself against crime." The latent message was "You've Seen How It Works." What the audience saw on television news was Nancy Kerrigan doubled up and crying from pain on a rink floor after being beaten by a baton. That makes the latent message questionable. After the ad ran, the *Star Tribune* received about 20 calls from readers who thought it was in poor taste; nonetheless, it met in-house standards because the product was legal.

"The ad didn't say anything about [Harding's] guilt or innocence," a newspaper spokesperson said. "If it had, it would have changed the way we looked at it."[21]

In some cases, the manifest and latent messages are fine but become questionable in tandem with an image or illustration. For instance, an advertisement for a gas chlorinator in a trade magazine informs the audience that "it's simpler—it works better—it costs less." The latent message states that the product is "built right (half the story)/ and backed right (the other half)." The ad seems in poor taste, however, because the main photograph illustrating it has nothing to do with the product: an apparently naked blond model with her hand on the chlorinator. Ad copy in the bubble covering her breasts and pubic area inquires whether the reader plans to buy or shop for a chlorinator within the next year. The reader can check a "yes" or "no" box. Another box states: "I want photo only."

Sometimes ad copy alone can be controversial. For instance, a hair styling ad in a mass market women's magazine contains copy that may cause a woman to feel unnecessarily bad about her body: "Your thighs may be too thunderous, too saddle-baggy, too thin, too jiggly, too cottage-cheesy (large curd), too hereditary or just too much like the 'Before' in a 'Before/After' ad." The apparent goal is to convince women so labeled that they still can feel good about their hair.

At times, slogan, copy, and image combine with latent and manifest message in such a way that all elements seem objectionable, as in an ad about a home entertainment system. The ad, published in a lifestyle magazine, bears the slogan "I Remember When He Couldn't Keep His Hands Off Me!" It features a blond model in a negligee and her male lover, fully clothed, playing a TV game with the controls at his crotch and a phallic-looking monster in a suggestive location on the screen. Part of the copy reads, "I scream but he doesn't hear me above 15 channels of pure pulsating stereo sound with 7 dedicated to real voice speech. . . . I'll show him. I'll play that [game] and beat the pants off him!" Again, the idle blond as sex object seems in poor taste, along with the positioning of the man and the pun-like copy describing their romantic plight.

Of course, men can be objectified, too, in so-called trendy ads. A popular and much debated advertisement for Bodyslimmers in 1993 depicted a headless shapely female model (intentionally objectified in an undergarment) with the following slogan: "While you don't necessarily dress for men, it doesn't hurt, on occasion, to see one drool like the pathetic dog that he is."[22]

Some might find these advertisements clever, crude, or coy but fundamentally *harmless*. Keep in mind, however, that the proliferation of such messages in a culture adds up like bytes in the hard drive of your computer until the culture is full of such ideas. Thus, they shape mores and influence values, as you learned in the very first chapter of this book. Also keep in mind that although these ads might be targeted at specific markets, the inherent messages and images can be read or viewed by any age group. When a message goes out on newsstands or airwaves, the advertiser loses control of his or her target audience—an often overlooked consideration in debates about the goal of advertising versus the ethics of taste.

Author and feminist Betty Friedan has been at the forefront of such debates for more than three decades. Specifically, she has researched the role advertising plays in the perception of women in society. In an article in the trade magazine *Advertising Age,* Friedan recalls when corporate officials asked her to be a consultant to Band-Aid in the early 1960s. "They sent me the ads, and this was a rather fuddy-duddy group then," she says. "Like so many ads, they showed women's great sacrifice and attention to the child. I told them to let the child put on his own Band-Aid—he's independent. That would appeal to the modern woman. Don't just show the woman living through the child."

Friedan's research and views have been the subject of many theses and dissertations. One such thesis by Nilanjana Roy Bardhan at Ohio University states that Friedan discovered "that advertisers promote the stereotypes of women and try to make them feel good about household chores in order to augment the selling of home products." Bardhan's research, however, found that "women's depiction in magazine advertisements as homemakers has decreased through the late 70's and 80's but the portrayal of women as sex objects or as being obsessed with personal appearance has increased."[23]

Advertising, along with other media, is responsible in part for that stereotype.

The First Amendment protects the democratic process, as the original framers of the U.S. Constitution intended. But the power of the press is so great that it also can shape the perceptions or mores of the same citizens whose freedom it is supposed to protect. That's a heady responsibility. As you have learned, most journalists want to serve their audience, clients, or customers and so make tough decisions based on taste considerations and values. If you haven't already, you will participate soon enough in that decision-making process. To do so effectively, however, you must realize the power that *you* possess and learn how to apply it appropriately.

Empowerment

The word *empower* is more elusive than it seems at first glance. You can empower another person by relinquishing your own authority or abilities, as in this sentence taken from *The Random House Dictionary of the English Language*: "I empowered my agent to make the deal for me." Or the word can mean "to enable," as in another sentence from the same dictionary: "Wealth empowered him to lead a comfortable life." The word *empowerment,* often associated with gender equity, is based on both meanings, implying that one should not blindly relinquish authority or abilities and instead claim them for one's self.

In this book, that definition is extended to all journalists because empowerment is important in the workplace.

As we have observed, power is associated with the force you employ to express your values or the confidence you gain because of them. When so defined, it is impossible to be powerless because everyone has values and everyone aspires to have confidence in his or her abilities. People who claim otherwise may not be aware of or have made a choice not to acknowledge their power. Conversely, you may not realize how much power you actually possess, especially if you have decided to practice or pursue a career in journalism. Such an aspiration assumes that you like to communicate with others via words or images or already are working in or studying mass media. That means you are more powerful than ordinary citizens because you have been entrusted with techniques and technology to reach an audience via words and/or images.

Add to this the incidentals of your life or your background that enhance your power base. Perhaps you were reared in an affluent family and have access to powerful individuals who can promote your interests or advise you. Or perhaps you were reared in a less fortunate environment and have encountered challenges along the way, sharpening your awareness or independence. There are simply too many variables to address theoretically when it comes to establishing the scope of each person's power. To exercise it, however, each person has to analyze those variables. Otherwise, you may be too apt to empower others, sacrificing your values or beliefs, or too uncertain about how to apply them in a crisis. Remember that power is a force, not a value. Too little force, and your values or beliefs will be trodden or overlooked. Too much force, and they will offend or oppress. In either case, your values or beliefs will not serve you in your personal or professional life.

Let's illustrate that with the power base of a typical journalism professor. In most cases, the person:

- Will have had a good education in the United States or abroad
- Will have had professional media experience
- Owns computer and camera equipment and can send or transmit messages or images instantaneously
- Influences readers, viewers, or listeners with published works, papers, or talks

- Has access to powerful people in publishing, education, and journalism
- Is a member of influential academic/professional associations
- Is employed and earns a decent wage
- Has tenure and so cannot easily jeopardize his or her job
- Can exert authority over children and spouses
- Can exert authority over students and staff

As you can see, there is real potential for abuse here. If the professor wanted, he or she could take advantage of less educated people, to feel superior, or he or she could use experience or contacts cynically, to dull the dreams of others. He or she could tell aspiring journalists that they will fail, thereby making the professor feel more gifted, or use skills unethically, thus advancing causes that serve his or her financial interests. The professor could prevent the hiring or promotion of others to lessen the competition in his or her discipline. The person could hack his or her way down the information highway. He or she could use professional contacts and associations to find jobs for ingratiating graduates and could practice favoritism to boost ego. He or she could abuse children or a spouse, to control their behavior, or abuse students and staff, to make teaching less demanding. Better yet, as a journalist and professor, the person could claim the First Amendment or academic freedom to take on any challengers.

But if the professor resists those self-serving temptations, he or she can add one more item—more powerful than the sum total of all others—to his or her power list: *credibility*. The same applies, of course, to anyone who does not abuse power. In fact, when several of these journalists work at the same media outlet, that company enjoys a reputation for credibility because its employees practice *restraint*. Defined, *restraint* means postponing the decision to respond with an appropriate amount of power to a perceived threat until you can ascertain whether that threat actually exists and, if so, whether it is potentially minor, significant, or catastrophic.

In Chapter 2, Responsibility, we discussed courage—bravely responding to a challenge or an opportunity while honoring your values in an attempt to do the right thing. Dan Rather, co-anchor for *CBS Evening News*, wrote at length about the concept in "Call It Courage" in the Living Ethics section of that chapter. Now it is time to consider the term's antonym, *cowardice*, or fearfully responding to a challenge or an opportunity without honoring traditional values or moral rightness.

The term *coward* is a strong word. True cowards are rare, and sometimes people seem cowardly because they are dealing with serious psychological problems or histories that are beyond the scope of this text. Sometimes people unjustly accuse themselves (or are accused by others) of cowardice because they responded fearfully in a situation that ended unhappily. As any war veteran will tell you, fear is a natural or logical response when confronting a potentially significant or catastrophic threat. In fact, fear lends meaning and substance to the words *courage* and *bravery* because a courageous or brave act suggests that a person did not succumb to fear *when the stakes or consequences warranted.*

Everyone has acted cowardly, including the author of this book, at one time or another. True cowards respond in predictable ways in almost every situation and blame others or justify actions when criticized for their behavior. Ethical people try to analyze their behavior and make adjustments that strengthen values. Finally, they do not easily call others cowards, especially in power situations. Nonetheless, cowards do exist in the workplace and can destroy lives or careers. For that reason, it would be irresponsible to omit a discussion about cowards in a chapter on power. Such people realize that they are abusing or betraying others but have made a choice not to seek help or correct their behavior.

All cowards share two traits and one feeling. The traits are fear and disregard or contempt for moral values. The feeling is lack of self-worth. Cowards fall into two camps: the Abuser and the Betrayer. To understand each of the following profiles, remember the two meanings associated with the term *empowerment:* to relinquish power or claim it for one's self.

The Abuser

This type of coward wields power without restraint and seeks out people willing to relinquish authority. The Abuser not only claims his or her own power base but also the base of any person who will surrender moral territory. The motive usually is related to ego, personal gain, or control of others. The Abuser fears people so much that he or she must hurt or intimidate them or reduce them to objects (so as to work his or her will without guilt or remorse). The more abusive this person becomes, the more puffed up he or she feels and confuses that feeling with confidence (a by-product of strong values). That confusion is responsible for continuing cycles of abuse and oppression as the person tries to feel superior and compensate for lack of self-worth.

The Betrayer

This type of coward cannot determine whether a threat is real, minor, significant, or catastrophic. Consequently, the person does not practice restraint, avoiding challenges and problems at all costs, even ones that could harm his or her life or the lives of others close to him or her. The Betrayer relinquishes power blindly and surrenders moral rightness in the process. The motive usually is related to self-protection, self-interest, or self-control. This Betrayer fears people so much that he or she inflates their power to justify the relinquishing of his or her own (and thus avoid confrontations). The more challenges and problems this person circumvents, the fewer duties he or she will have and the more he or she will confuse that feeling with relief (also a by-product of strong values, knowing you have done the right thing). That confusion is responsible for continuing cycles of betrayal and surrender as the person tries to be left alone and compensate for lack of self-worth.

As mentioned earlier, journalists who use power judiciously earn credibility for themselves and their media outlet. The opposite occurs at those outlets when management is cowardly or employs one too many cowardly employees. You suspect as much at scandal sheets or tabshows that "tell all" without regard to propriety or privacy or at community weeklies or stations that "tell nothing" even when the stakes or consequences warrant. You suspect as much at advertising agencies that stereotype people to sell products because they see minorities or women as objects or at ones that shun all race- or gender-related accounts because they fear diverse or new ideas. You suspect as much at public relations agencies that manipulate news during crises because their clients are culpable or at ones that shun media—even when their clients are falsely accused—because they fear public opinion.

Just as true cowards are rare, so too are cowardly media outlets. Professional associations that oversee each industry, such as the Public Relations Society of America (and others whose codes are reprinted in this book's appendix), set standards that deal with improper behavior. For instance, Susan Fry Bovet, editor of *Public Relations Journal,* has taken a strong stance against sexual harassment. (You will encounter three incidents of sexual harassment in the Living Ethics section.) According to Bovet, writing in the ethics section of her magazine:

> Public relations practitioners have a duty to protect their organizations and clients from sexual harassment charges by establishing policies and procedures for dealing with such incidents in the workplace. . . . Sexual harassment is really about power, rather than sex. Its tactics and goals vary, but it usually involves the threat of job or account lose. Often, women who leave jobs that have become "impossible" or are fired or forced out before retirement don't even realize they have been victims of sexual harassment, which is covered in the discrimination provisions of Title VII of the Civil Rights Act of 1964.[24]

As Frye notes, the Civil Rights Act of 1991 imposes stiff penalties in sexual harassment cases when the employer knows about but does not correct behavior or take adequate steps to remove the abuse. In sum, the act now targets cowardly managers along with employees who abuse others in such manner at work.

Conversely, it is important to practice restraint until you are sure that another employee or manager has harassed you. Amy Pyle, an assistant city editor in the Valley edition of the *Los Angeles Times,* suspected that she may have been treated unfairly when, on her first day at work, an editor called her "kiddo." Pyle is quoted as saying, "It upset me but then I learned he called everyone kiddo. It was just his way of speaking. It's important not to overreact. The key for women is to recognize when something is important enough to take action."[25]

To determine how to use your power effectively when a situation is important enough to take action, follow these guidelines:

1. *Ascertain your personal and professional power.* Ethical journalists acknowledge their power so they can tap or restrain it during suspected challenges or crises. To acknowledge your power base, make a list of items.

   Ask Yourself:
   • Am I intellectually or physically powerful?
   • Do I have access to powerful tools or technology such as cameras or computers?
   • Can I communicate powerful ideas?
   • Do I know or have access to powerful people?
   • Do I supervise or have authority over others?

2. *Evaluate your personal or professional power.* After you have acknowledged your power base, determine how you have been employing that power. Analyze each item on your list.

   Ask Yourself:
   • Do I usually abuse this type of power when I have the opportunity?
   • Do I usually exert the appropriate amount of this power to meet each challenge or problem? Or do I usually over- or underestimate situations?
   • Do I usually avoid using this type of power at all costs?

3. *Take prudent action or practice restraint.* Identify items on your power list that are realible or need improvement. The goal is to meet each challenge or problem with the appropriate amount of power to suit the occasion. Each time you exert power, record the results in your journal.

   Ask Yourself:
   • When I feel the urge to take action, do I usually (a) suppress that urge when the stakes or consequences warrant a response, (b) act on

behalf of others for whom I have no responsibility, or (c) act in my own interests?

> **Note:** *If (a) or (b), seek advice from a mentor or role model whose judgment you trust to determine how to proceed or whether your participation is really required.*

- What are the usual results of my taking action: (a) bigger or more complex problems, (b) symbolic but important participation, (c) compromise to resolve a situation or dispute, or (d) total resolution of a situation or dispute?

> **Note:** *If (a), practice restraint until you can determine how your participation will be beneficial.*

- If I take action, who else might be affected: (a) innocent individuals or groups, (b) individuals or groups indirectly associated with the situation, or (c) only those directly associated with the situation?

> **Note:** *If (a) or (b), practice restraint until you can determine whether your interests are greater than the effect your actions may have on other innocent or indirectly related persons or parties.*

4. *Take responsibility for your actions.* Once you have ascertained and evaluated your power, you need to accept consequences for your actions. This will help you maintain or restore your personal integrity and/or professional credibility.

Ask Yourself:

- Do I have anything to apologize for or correct? For instance, did I misperceive a threat or make a hasty judgment based on faulty information?

> **Note:** *If so, apologize or correct errors to match the degree of misperceptions or mistakes—without unduly damaging your own or other parties' interests.*

- Does another party have anything to apologize to me for or correct? For instance, did someone else misperceive a threat by you or make a hasty judgment based on faulty information?

> **Note:** *If so, you may decide to demand an apology or a correction or some other resolution to offset the misperception or mistake.*

- Are the consequences a direct result of (a) my actions, (b) part my and part someone else's actions over which I had no influence or control, or (c) someone else's actions over which I had no influence or control?

> **Note:** *If (b) or (c), assume responsibility for your part in the situation and/or inform other affected parties about the actions over which you had no influence or control.*

As you learned in Chapter 8, it is difficult to estimate another's viewpoint, motive or intents. Viewpoints, motives, and intents are part of the power process, too. So it may take time before you learn how to apply the appropriate amount of power to meet each challenge or solve each problem. However, the more you go through the process as previously outlined, the greater your perception and sense of fair play will be. Your reputation will be enhanced, along with your values. In the next chapter, you will learn to create a document to showcase those values to employers.

ENDNOTES

1. David B. Ottaway, "Gathering string," *The Quill,* March 1987, p. 29.

2. "Censored, by reasons of the state," no author, *The Quill,* March 1987, p. 23.

3. John Tusa, "When donkeys are tractors," *The Quill,* March 1987, p. 25.

4. "Juice: The future of power and influence in Washington," special report, *Inside PR,* May 1992, p. 15.

5. "Juice," p. 16.

6. "Juice," p. 16.

7. "Juice," p. 16.

8. Tony Case, "Publishing profanities," *Editor & Publisher,* 6 November 1993, p. 11.

9. The controversy about the remark focused on racism, despite the fact that Goldberg was Danson's love interest at the time and supported him throughout the controversy at the Friars Club. As you have learned in Chapter 7, the use of *nigger* was inappropriate for the occasion, "roast" notwithstanding.

10. Case, p. 11.

11. Linda Lotridge Levin, "Dirty words and blushing editors," *The Quill,* September 1986, p. 25.

12. Linda Lotridge Levin, "F-word contortions," *The Quill,* September 1986, p. 25.

13. Levin, "Dirty words," p. 24.

14. W. C. Stroby, "Interview with Stephen King," *Writer's Digest,* March 1992, p. 27.

15. "Digging at the king," anonymous letter, *Writer's Digest,* June 1992, p. 4.

16. M. L. Stein, "Column killed after critical words about Nixon," *Editor & Publisher,* 14 May 1994, p. 14.

17. M. L. Stein, "Cartoon's message backfires in California," *Editor & Publisher,* 19 February 1994, p. 9.

18. Stein, "Cartoon's message," p. 9.

19. Dan Bischoff, "Smokeless in Seattle," *American Journalism Review,* October 1993, p. 36.

20. Margaret G. Carter, "When is an ad not an ad," *Presstime,* October 1993, p. 31.

21. Dorothy Giobble, "'Tonya Tapper' ad creates a stir," *Editor & Publisher,* 26 February 1994.

22. For other such campaigns, see "Men now fair game for in-your-face ads" by Jaime Trapp in *Advertising Age*, 4 October 1993, p. S-12.
23. Nilanjana Roy Bardhan, *Ms. Magazine (1972–93): The Relationship Between Editorial and Advertising*, thesis manuscript, 19 November 1993, p. 6.
24. Susan Fry Bovet, "Sexual harassment," *Public Relations Journal*, November 1993, p. 26.
25. M. L. Stein, "Unwelcome gender politics," *Editor & Publisher*, 11 September 1993, p. 13.

LIVING ETHICS

Read the following interviews and articles and record your reactions in your ethics journal and/or discuss them with peers or mentors.

EDITOR'S NOTE: *One of the most prevalent abuses of power in the workplace is sexual harassment. The three incidents described here were taken from written interviews with a magazine colleague, a former student, and a news director/professor at Ohio University. Their accounts illustrate the humiliation that sexual harassment causes and the lessons that each woman has learned about power, including the most important aspect thereof: her own.*

Three Incidents of Sexual Harassment

Anonymous, Free-Lance Writer

I spent Friday morning working alone in my motel room. That afternoon, I went to stay overnight with Jane, the head of a department at a major university who had a book idea she wanted to shape into a proposal. When Jane and I returned on Saturday around 4:30 P.M. to the motel, Conrad joined us to go out for pizza. Conrad is a colleague of Jane's in his early 50s who is accustomed to power, wealth, and prestige. He also had a book proposal. When Jane left for her home, Conrad wanted to show me a few things about his proposal because the evening was still early. Intuitively, I felt uncomfortable going to his home office and suggested working in the motel. But Conrad said he needed things that were at his flat, so I agreed even though I felt uneasy.

After we arrived at his apartment, we worked hard on his project—totally legit, no problems—then reached a stopping point for the evening. He asked if I would like something to drink. I said yes, assuming he meant Coke or ice tea. He returned from the kitchen with two goblets of wine. He set them on the table, lit a candle, turned off the overhead light, and shut the shades.

I stared at him in disbelief, but was caught so off guard I said nothing.

Conrad continued our conversation on political issues, asking what I thought about abortion. When I said I was against it, he responded, "Well, I know this isn't supposed to happen, but let's just say you and I had an affair and you found out you were pregnant in the first trimester. What would you do then?"

It felt clear that there were two levels to the comment, and I was being propositioned. I looked him straight in the eye and said firmly, "I wouldn't get myself in that position in the first place." He continued, unfazed. "Well suppose your daughter was dating someone she liked and things got out of hand and she got raped—that's how a lot of these things happen, you know."

My mouth went dry. I slid my hand under the table and began fingering the can of mace I carry in my briefcase. I felt scared and stupid. I didn't know my way around the city or anyone else in the city whom I could call. I didn't even know which way to run if it came to that. I summoned my courage and bluffed an assertiveness I didn't feel. I ignored his "rape/abortion" comment and told him I wanted to return to my motel *now* and gathered things to go.

Conrad paused a second, then nodded. On the way out, he hugged me—I stiffened and pulled away. He then took me to my motel. On the short drive back, he talked about business matters as if nothing had happened, but the air was brittle with tension and the conversation bristling with incident.

Conrad didn't press the matter. He didn't push for sexual contact when I gave clear signals that I wanted nothing to do with an affair, but his suggestive behaviors and comments were out of line and harassing. I felt angry. The thing that hurt most was the loss of our genuine friendship. I trusted him completely; now I no longer can. I consider it unethical and unwise for me to continue to work with him, and have severed our business relationship.

Looking back, it seems incredibly stupid for me to have gone to his home office alone in an unfamiliar city. And I never should have accepted a ride with him back to the motel. Next time, before I work in a strange city, I'll research it, take maps, and know whom to call in case of emergencies.

Anonymous, Former Account Executive

My first position out of college was as an advertising account executive with a small-town daily newspaper. My responsibilities included selling and designing advertising campaigns for local businesses. One of my accounts was a jewelery store owned and operated by a father and son team. The father became a problem.

The trouble began almost immediately. The father would tell me dirty jokes and make lewd comments. He would comment on the way I dressed and eye me up and down. Needless to say, the situation was uncomfortable, but as a very green salesperson I was at a loss what to do. Because he was my client, and I very much needed his business, I was wary about telling him how I felt. Besides, it was not as if I had never heard dirty jokes or off-color remarks before. I found myself laughing self-consciously at his remarks and then vainly trying to change the subject back to the business at hand.

The situation did not improve. In fact, it went from bad to worse. I became so uncomfortable that I started to avoid the father completely, which was difficult because he ran the show. At the very least, I tried never to be alone with him in the store. Unfortunately, this strategy did not always work either.

One day, I walked into the jewelry store and the father was by himself. I was there to pick up an ad. He told me it was in his office and asked me to follow him. I did. Once inside the small room, he stepped behind me, closed the door, turned off the light, and grabbed me. I was in shock. I remember feeling his lips on my face, searching for my mouth. His whiskers were rough on my skin. He was not gentle. I finally got my wits about me enough to push him away and scream. He let me go and I lunged for the lightswitch. I will never forget the humiliation I felt standing in that office staring into the face that moments ago had been smashed against my own. The first thing that entered my mind was that somehow I was at fault. If only I had not laughed at his jokes and remarks, I kept thinking. If only I had had the courage to tell him his comments embarrassed me. I felt completely ashamed.

He began mumbling that he was sorry and didn't mean anything. He said he thought it would be best if we didn't mention the incident—just pretend it didn't happen.

I never did mention it, until years later to very good friends. In fact, I continued on as his account executive, although our relationship was definitely different after that episode—but forget it I never will.

I learned from that experience, as I should have. I learned never to compromise my values for fear of hurting someone's feelings. I learned that professionalism is the most important aspect of a working relationship. Once an individual steps outside of the bounds of professionalism, everything changes and it is very difficult to go back. Most importantly, I learned not to be ashamed. What occurred in that man's office was not my fault. He was a womanizer and would have treated any woman the way he treated me. Perhaps a more experienced person would have had the courage to stand up to him sooner. I know if anything similar happens again, I will behave much differently. But he did not close the door to that office and attack me because of the clothes I wore or the person I am. He did it because he had no respect for women and probably never will.

Nancy Burton, Radio News Director, *WOUB-FM*

My experience with sexual harassment goes all the way back to 1986. I was a full-time consumer reporter at a network affiliate; it was my first job in broadcasting. I had been out of school for two years. I thought at that time I had learned a lot about reporting, getting information out of tight-lipped assistant attorney generals and helping consumers get their money back from no-good contractors. I could even handle the three live shots a week that were expected of me. What I couldn't handle the was the second news director of my broadcasting career. When the general manager hired him, the GM thought he was the answer. The GM thought this man was the person to make us Number 1.

He was wrong.

I remember the afternoon. I went into the news director's office to get my script checked before editing. That is standard operating procedure, especially at small- to medium-sized markets. Someone, usually the news director, checks the script. As I was leaving, the news director asked if I could meet him later to talk about signing a contract. My gut reaction: *Why can't we just talk about it after my piece is edited?* At the same time, he appealed to my ego. I had been at the station two years and no one had ever mentioned a contract to me, so he was the first sure sign—*they liked me*. When I voiced my concern about meeting later, he said it would be easier if we talked away from the station, over dinner. I was hesitant, but this was my first job. I was 23 years old. He was new. I wanted to make a good impression. I agreed. That was my first mistake.

Instead of eating in town at a restaurant, he opted for an inn over 20 miles north of the city. It's ironic, but as I recall this story for you, I remember as the news director and I were driving up the highway, we passed a reporter and photographer in another news car headed to a story. I was later told I had a real strange look on my face. The person looking back at me from the news car was my boyfriend at the time. He's now my husband.

At any rate, dinner was fine. The news director talked about my work. He told me the company wanted to make sure I would stick around for awhile. We talked about what the station might be able to offer, but I was also very honest with him. I told him I had been at the station for two years and I really wanted to move on to a larger market. While I was not unhappy at the station, I was ready for a new challenge. I had no family in the area. I was single with no real responsibilities except to myself, so I wanted to move on. That's when the conversation suddenly turned personal. He started talking about how he missed his wife and children; I felt awkward. Then he said we would not leave the restaurant/inn until I signed a contact. He said he was willing to get a *room* if that is what it took. I can't remember exactly what I said, but I refused and told him I thought it was a good idea if we left immediately. I think I made some excuse about someone/something in town expecting me. It was a lie, but I had to get out of there.

Needless to say, the car ride back to town was quiet. I got into my car back at the station parking lot, drove immediately home, and didn't say a word to anyone. I was embarrassed, ashamed, and more convinced than ever that I was looking for a new job.

The incident didn't come up again until several months later. I was out on a story and when the photographer and I got back, the newsroom was abuzz. The news director had resigned and it was effective immediately. He was gone. The general manager called a mandatory station meeting in the afternoon. He said personal reasons forced the news director to take off. The GM was very upset and thought it was a real setback for the station, specifically the newsroom.

A short time later, several women in the newsroom started talking. We weren't so upset that the news director was gone. Then it came out. I recalled the whole incident that had taken place several months ago. Another woman, the 11 o'clock producer, said, "He once asked me what kind of underwear I was wearing." Another reporter remarked, "He used to flirt with me all the time."

Once the shock wore off, we, at least six of us, went to the general manager to tell him what this news director had done. Needless to say, the expression on the GM's face said it all. He couldn't believe it. He said he would deal with it later, although nothing ever happened, but in the meantime, he knew he had to find a news director quick. He brought this grandfather-type back. He had been the news director forever and the station had replaced him against his wishes. Now they were begging him to help us out. He was a great teacher. He had been my first news director, and now he was back.

Was it courageous to go to the GM and tell him what this horrible news director did? I think maybe it would have been more courageous if I had gone into the GM's office the next day and reported what happened. I guess fear prevented me from doing that. I think I also thought, deep down inside, maybe I had done something to provoke him. Maybe I thought somehow it was my fault.

We did hear that the news director moved on to another job down South. It was there that he got caught on the job. I guess some woman there was very courageous. One other thing—there are a lot of sleazy news directors who harass their staff. Friends in the business have told me horror stories. But I don't want to single out broadcast news. Harassment is something that happens in boardrooms and factories as well as newsrooms.

EDITOR'S NOTE: *Eddith A. Dashiell has produced or reported for several radio and television stations, including WSMV-TV in Nashville, National Public Radio, and the Associated Press Radio Network. Before teaching broadcasting at Ohio University, she was a professor at Middle Tennessee State University and a lecturer at Indiana University and the University of Missouri–St. Louis.*

On Air with O. J.

Eddith A. Dashiell, Journalism Professor, *Ohio University*

Satellite news gathering gives the television media the ability to get news and information to their audiences instantaneously. Television news no longer has to rely entirely on electronic news gathering, which requires the time-consuming editing of videotape before a story can be aired. With a microwave truck and a camera, reporters can broadcast live from almost any location at any time of day or night.

The instantaneous coverage of news also demands instantaneous decision making on how to cover breaking events. The television news media have become so blinded by the glitz of the live technology that they have allowed that technology to dictate how the news should be covered while ignoring some important ethical issues. In 1994, the ethics of reporting a potential suicide was one such issue when the networks decided to do live coverage of the police pursuit of O. J. Simpson, wanted on murder charges in the killing of his wife and her male companion.

On Friday, June 17, Americans—via mobile news units and news helicopters—witnessed the drama of the Los Angeles police trying to apprehend Simpson. The five-hour search for O. J. dominated Friday-night television. News reports said Simpson was riding in the back of a white Ford Bronco with a gun pointed at his head. Based on the contents of a letter Simpson had left behind, his attorney was afraid he would try to kill himself. News helicopters and mobile units followed O. J. as he and his friend, A. C. Cowlings, traveled 50 miles along Los Angeles freeways to the driveway of Simpson's Brentwood home. The scene was set for the first nationwide, live coverage of a suicide. Americans watched and wondered whether O. J. would take his own life.

I watched the coverage in disgust and disappointment. As a broadcast journalist, I am concerned about a growing trend. The television media seems so obsessed with the technology of satellite news gathering that they do not take the time to carefully weigh any ethical considerations of good taste, sensitivity, or fairness.

From a journalist's point of view, I agree that the Simpson case was of significant public interest to cover nationally and aggressively because of O. J.'s national reputation and popularity. What I find to be in poor journalistic taste was the decision by the television media to interrupt programming to air *continuous* live coverage of Simpson riding in the back of a white Bronco while he was reportedly contemplating suicide.

The networks apparently had only one goal: to use their technology to give viewers live coverage of the "manhunt" for O. J. Simpson, even if it meant possibly airing the suicide of a celebrity. The coverage of O. J. reminded me of a suicide several years ago that was captured on camera and prompted serious debates among media organizations about the ethics of using graphic visuals of a suicide.

In January 1987, Pennsylvania state treasurer R. Budd Dwyer was facing 55 years in prison for mail fraud, racketeering, perjury, and bribery convictions. He put a pistol in his mouth and publicly took his life at a Harrisburg news conference. The media had no prior knowledge that Dwyer was suicidal. The media had expected Dwyer to resign during the news conference, not kill himself in front of reporters. With Dwyer's suicide recorded on video and film, the media had to make some important ethical decisions on how much—if any—of the video or photographs of Dwyer's death should be used.

Some television news directors agreed that airing the entire episode of Dwyer pulling the trigger and his body slumping to the floor was "just pushing things too far." They argued that the news value of Dwyer's suicide was that a public official had decided to kill himself on camera and not the physical act of a person bleeding and dying. These news directors decided to air tastefully edited versions of the news conference. Other news directors, however, decided to air the entire suicide with Dwyer firing the pistol and falling. They argued that television lives by the camera, and the entire video was needed to complete the story. They argued that it was not up to the news media to "sugarcoat reality." Seven years later, the networks and cable stations that provided uninterrupted live coverage of the police pursuit of O. J. Simpson apparently supported this philosophy.

The impression the television media gave viewers on June 17, 1994, was that if O. J. did pull the trigger, they wanted to make sure they had live coverage of his death. Have the networks and cable stations become so competitive for rating points that they have been reduced to following a reportedly suicidal former football star in hopes of attracting viewers by allowing them the opportunity to witness a real-life suicide?

Fortunately, O. J. Simpson did not pull the trigger that day, and viewers did not have to witness his death on live television. But what if he had shot himself? How would the television news media have handled the situation? Would they have immediately gone "to black" or to a commercial? Or would they have kept the cameras on Simpson's body?

The stations that covered the suicide of Budd Dwyer in 1987 had the advantage of being able to view the video before their viewers did. They were able to decide whether the video was suitable to air in its entirety, in an edited form, or not at all. They had ethical and editorial control over how the video of Dwyer's suicide should be handled. The stations that decided to air the entire, unedited footage of the Dwyer suicide also aired warnings before the videotape rolled—another example of the ethical decision making. If O. J. Simpson had pulled the trigger during live television coverage, there would have been no time for warnings and no time for ethical decision making.

Handling suicides has always been a sensitive issue in the media. In general, it has been the policy of the media not to cover suicides unless the suicide is linked to other newsworthy circumstances. The suicide of a celebrity always gets a great deal of media coverage, and in recent years, there have been some high-profile suicides: Vincent Foster, former White House counsel to President Bill Clinton, in July 1993; and Kurt Cobain, lead singer of the rock group Nirvana, in April 1994.

There has been the concern that by covering a suicide or a suicide attempt, the media would be showing other distressed individuals—especially teenagers—the way to successfully take their own lives. Suicide is the third leading cause of death (following accident and homocide) of teenagers between the ages of 15 and 19. According to the National Center for Health Statistics, between 1960 and 1988, the suicide rate among adolescents increased by 200 percent.

Researchers have linked this drastic increase in teenage suicides—in part—to the media. The teenage suicides tend to occur in "clusters," a series of deaths occurring in a short amount of time, and those clusters have been found to occur shortly after extensive or sensational media coverage of a suicide. Researchers believe these teenagers are imitating the suicides they learn about from the media.

For example, in the month following Marilyn Monroe's suicide, there was a 12 percent increase of suicides nationwide, particularly among young women. In 1977, researchers found a significant increase in gunshot wound suicides in Los Angeles County in the 7 days following comedian Freddie Prinz's suicide by a gunshot wound. Following Kurt Cobain's suicide, mental health experts feared that some teenagers would take their own lives, copying the rock idol. Two days after Budd Dwyer shot himself in Harrisburg, a teenager in nearby York, Pennsylvania, took his life by reportedly firing a gun into his mouth. While no one can be sure Dwyer's suicide influenced the 17-year-old, his death raised important ethical questions about how much of a public suicide should be shown to tell the story. If O. J. Simpson had committed suicide during the television media's live coverage of him, would there have been any copy-cat suicides—distressed people who believed that if suicide was the answer to O. J.'s problems, then suicide was a good choice for them as well?

Mental health professionals advocate that the media be educated about the social imitation effect of suicide and that this effect should included in the ethical decision-making process. These professionals are not calling for censorship of suicide coverage—they just want a more aware and sensitive media that understand the danger in the irresponsible reporting of suicides. As a journalism educator, I feel it is vital for broadcast journalists to consider the negative impact live coverage of a person firing a gun at his or her head or jumping off a building will have on their audience. If the television media must cover suicides, then those suicides should be covered in a responsible and tasteful manner, without the abusive use of graphic video or live reports.

The live coverage of O. J. Simpson amid concerns that he would commit suicide rather than surrender to police went against everything journalism educators teach about responsible, ethical, and professional journalism. The situation was too unpredictable and volatile to have unedited, uncensored coverage of the police pursuit of Simpson. With live coverage comes a loss of editorial control. The networks could not predict what Simpson would do. If he had pulled the trigger, the television media would not have been able to control how the immediate sequence of events would have played themselves out on the screen.

Journalists should take the time from their daily deadline pressure to reflect on how the live coverage of Simpson on June 17, 1994, could have ended if he had followed through with plans to end his life. Are news directors willing to accept the social responsibility of airing live coverage of a sensitive story when they have prior knowledge that they could be airing the graphic depiction of a suicide and no means to view the material before it airs?

The coverage of O. J. Simpson emphasized an overall neglect of ethics and responsibility on the part of the television media in how they use new technology to cover news. Ethics and responsibility have gotten trampled in the mad rush by news organizations to be first with the story—*live*. If the credibility of the news product is to be preserved, then the technology should be used to enhance the message—not overpower it.

Immediately after Budd Dwyer committed suicide in front of two dozen reporters, the media had some serious discussions about the ethics of covering suicides. With the technical capability of airing a suicide, live with no prior review—as could have been the case with O. J. Simpson— these discussions need to resume. I recommend that broadcast news organizations conduct "ethical fire drills"—working through the possible scenarios of live coverage of sensitive stories (such as suicides) *before* these events actually occur. By working through the potential problems and the ethical concerns of covering these types of stories, reporters would be able to use their fine technology to enhance the content of their news coverage without becoming sensational and irresponsible.

EDITOR'S NOTE: *Virginia Mansfield Richardson worked for the* Washington Post *as a staff writer, editor, and editorial aide for 11 years, covering such beats as government, education, finance, and science. Her piece here does not concern a story at the* Post *but one that happened in 1992 at a small suburban daily newspaper in Virginia. She deals with ethical issues (such as those covered in Chapters 3, 5, and 8), but ultimately her essay is about power involved in documenting the death of a child. In addition, it emphasizes the concept of restraint being tested to its elements. Typically, journalists deal with reluctant sources who try to withhold information or ones who protect their privacy. These journalists ask, "How can we gather more facts or persuade someone to permit a picture?" In the following case, Mansfield Richardson and her editors confronted the exact opposite issue—parents who not only agreed to go on record about their tragedy but who also volunteered to photograph the death of their child when hospital representatives refused to allow a photojournalist to do so. The questions for the newsroom eventually became, "How can we protect the parents' and child's privacy and how much should we publish in the interest of good taste?"*

Death of a Child

Virginia Mansfield Richardson, Former Writer,
The Washington Post

A young, uneducated, poor couple called an editor at a suburban daily newspaper to say they had decided to end life support measures for their daughter Tina, 5, who had multiple handicaps. The couple offered to let a reporter follow them through the entire process, including the funeral and burial, if the newspaper would ask in the articles for donations to be sent to the couple to help pay for funeral expenses. The couple also said they were partially motivated because they wanted to document their daughter's life in some way.

The editor jumped at the opportunity and immediately assigned the story to me. From a journalist's perspective, no editor in his or her right mind would turn such an opportunity down because it's a rare chance to cover a human drama which also happens to deal with the current debate over whether terminally ill patients should be kept alive on life support.

The first of several ethical and moral issues arises here. Was it right to expose for mass public consumption the extremely private emotional issues that this couple faced, even though they agreed to it? Were they so desperate for money to bury their daughter that they did something they would not do under normal circumstances? Was the newspaper taking advantage of this couple's serious financial woes?

None of these questions was ever discussed between me and my editors in the course of covering this story. The key ethical question that was discussed from day one of the story was how to deal with the agreement that the newspaper run a request for donations at the end of the story. The editor-in-chief called me into his office the day I was assigned the story to talk about how we should handle this. No one had a problem with running the donation request; after all, it was part of a verbal agreement. The editor could not decide if we should tell the readers up front that this was the main motivation for the couple allowing the newspaper to cover their tragedy. After an hour-long discussion of the situation—defining the problem, discussing at length values and principles, and determining that our main loyalty was to our readers—my editor decided the proper thing would be to tell the readers the truth high up in the story.

However, when the desk editors got wind of his decision, they hit the roof. They saw the main loyalty as presenting an untarnished view of this human drama to the readers. The readers were still the main loyalty, but these editors justified their decision by saying it would offer a better article to the readers. They said explaining the agreement would detract from the story and that it was not necessary to be so "up front" with the readers. In the end, we did not tell the readers about the agreement and we required the couple to set up a fund at a bank that readers could send donations to directly.

This brought up our second ethical decision. This story evolved over a three-week period. I met at length with the couple. I soon realized they had a six-week-old daughter who was healthy except for a large hole in her heart. They would not know for four months if their newborn daughter would require open-heart surgery. The daughter who was in the Critical Care Unit of Children's Hospital in Washington, DC, was born severely mentally retarded, deaf, blind, and having two holes in her heart. She had two open-heart operations in her first year of life. She never spoke a word, never learned to walk, and had been near death numerous other times. Each time she developed a rare form of pneumonia because she vomited into her lungs due to lack of control over her swallowing. The husband, John, was 26 and had been unemployed for over a year. The mother, Teresa, was 23 and had been unemployed since the second month of her second pregnancy. Both were unskilled laborers and they lived on unemployment checks.

So I became aware that this was a couple under great stress who, I felt, had many motivations for coming to my newspaper to publicize their story. They were unsophisticated in their knowledge of how harsh journalists can be, so they candidly answered all my questions about the state of their marriage, their finances, their debts, and their feelings about "pulling the plug" on their daughter. At least three times during the three weeks they each asked me how much money I thought readers would send once the story ran. So I discussed this with my editors, and again it was the editor-in-chief who insisted that the couple set up a fund in the daughter's name. He said this would have two advantages: (1) readers feel more comfortable sending money to a fund and (2) it would ensure to some extent that the donations would be in a separate account, at least initially.

I was facing a moral problem. I began to like this couple. I met their parents and siblings and the couple told me much more about themselves than I had expected. I learned of their parents' alcoholism and how one grandmother had completely rejected Tina because of her handicaps. I learned of the stress in their marriage. I found out, in a private interview without the wife present, that the husband was very undecided about stopping life support, but he felt his wife was really pushing it. She told me in private that she had a tubal ligation. (I decided on my own not to run this fact.) I felt compassion for the couple, but at the same time I was still a bit suspicious of their motives. My biggest concern, however, was that the couple was completely unaware that there might be some opposition from readers. Teresa and John were giving me quotes about the quality of their daughter's life and how it was an easy decision "because she's suffering and we don't want to see her suffer anymore."

It was at this point that I felt compelled to tell the couple that they might receive some hate mail, or worse, that someone might confront them in public after reading the article. Many journalists would not have done this, and I never told my editors about this conversation. Frankly, no story was worth it to me to have this young couple feel guilt the rest of their lives by some insensitive reader. Many journalists would have printed the information about the tubal ligation, because it was said on the record. However, I made a decision that it would be morally wrong for me to reveal information that I knew Teresa told me thinking I would keep it confidential.

After two weeks of meeting with doctors and watching the doctors try every effort to get the little girl off life support on her own, Tina died on a Friday night. It was very hard interviewing the parents just two hours after she died. The father seemed in shock, and for the first time I felt resentment toward me from him. I really felt like I was invading a painful, private moment. I knew that he had no way of knowing how hard it would be when he agreed to let a reporter follow him through the whole process. He began crying during the interview and ended it soon thereafter. I sensed this was an embarrassing moment for him and, again, I felt resentment from him. From that night and throughout the funeral and burial, I felt like there was something ethically wrong about a newspaper prying into the private lives of this young couple.

But, like all ethical problems, it was a decision between the better of two rights. I knew this story would touch hundreds of people who would identify with the couple's pain. I knew this was a rare glimpse of human life that people would learn something from, and that they would relate to their own lives. In many respects, I felt this story was journalism at its best. This was truly a touching human-interest story that was also educational and made the reader think about medical ethics.

We decided to do a sidebar with the story. The story was 85 inches, and the sidebar was about 30 inches. My editors gave this story great play. The sidebar was also compelling, featuring interviews with the doctors at Children's Hospital who deal with these types of situations daily. One doctor was the chief of genetics, the other doctor was the head of the Critical Care Unit. They gave me excellent quotes and they did not hold back in the discussions on the ethics of pulling the plug on terminally ill children. All the doctors interviewed said they supported such decisions completely. They criticized the hospital's policy on insisting that terminally ill children be kept alive long after they had lapsed into irreversible comas. The sidebar also looked at the personal side of the doctors. What was it like for them personally to deal with these types of situations daily? Again, they really opened up and they seemed to enjoy having a journalist ask them those types of questions. The sidebar turned out great and it was one strong argument that helped to justify the story in all the ethical debates.

One of the final ethical problems my editors and I faced with this story was what type of art to run. We wanted to get a picture of Tina in the hospital bed hooked up to the 18 monitors that she was on. The photographers and the editors thought it would be a powerful picture. We had several fights with the hospital administration, including a face-to-face meeting between the editor-in-chief and the director of hospital public relations. The hospital won out and we could not get a picture. The parents were furious and said it was their child and they wanted the picture to run in the paper. So we all came up with the same idea at roughly the same time. The parents took a picture with their own camera and gave it to us.

What became interesting was that once the little girl died and the story was written, the editors decided it was inappropriate to run the photo. The caption was to read that the picture was taken two hours before she died, which it was. But after the editors read my story, I think it changed their perspective on the situation and made it much more human to them. After all the battling with the hospital staff to get that photo, the editors in the end felt it would be an indignity to the child. I think this was a good ethical decision and it shows that editors have values and principles.

One interesting note here: The parents gave me a picture of Tina in her coffin and they wanted us to use it for the story. One editor liked the idea, but everyone else involved in the decision said it was inappropriate and readers would react violently. Ethically, the newspaper was not a sensationalist "rag" that ran those types of photos.

So this was an interesting case all around. It certainly tested the values, principles, and morals of each person involved. Many levels of responsibility, loyalties, philosophy, and even religion entered into these decisions. I think each person faced his or her own moral decisions along with the larger ethical decisions affecting the newspaper. It was not an easy situation for me, but I was glad I went through it because I learned a great deal about ethics from this story. In the end, the couple received enough money from readers to cover the cost of the funeral, and there was no hate mail—only very kind gestures from readers. One reader bought the newborn an entire wardrobe for her first year.

I think the size of the newspaper also made a difference in this case. Certainly if this story ran in a large metropolitan daily there would be hate mail and maybe some personal attacks on the couple. Knowing I was writing for a fairly limited, middle-class, suburban audience influenced my ethical decisions in this situation. Editors for a larger newspaper would certainly have insisted on a much harder line with the couple.

EDITOR'S NOTE: *As in the preceding essay by Virginia Mansfield Richardson, the following account—documenting the death of a man with AIDS—contains ethical considerations about privacy, conflict of interest, fairness, and power. But John Lenger's essay also deals with two other issues: bias against homosexuals and taste considerations—from an editor's perspective. It illustrates that a simple decision—scheduling a sensitive, powerful story about AIDS on Mother's Day—can anger certain segments of the audience. Nonetheless, Lenger endured that anger because he chose to do the right thing, according to his value system and sense of social responsibility. Ultimately, as you will learn, that courage was rewarded.*

AIDS on Mother's Day

John Lenger, Free-Lance Writer

The rewards of a newspaper career are not only many and varied, but they often come when you expect them least and need them most. I would put any paycheck or promotion I have earned against a single anonymous letter I received three years ago. Though it never appeared in print, that letter let me know that I had done the right thing by scheduling an AIDS story on Mother's Day.

It began simply enough. Carolyn Shapiro, who was then the education reporter at the *Post-Star* in Glens Falls, New York, had covered a meeting dealing with programs to combat AIDS. The *Post-Star* was placing a great deal of emphasis on good writing, and another editor suggested that Carrie should get more of a human angle on the story. Mark Mahoney, who later became city editor at the *Post-Star*, told Carrie that people want stories about people, not about programs. Mark suggested that Carrie do a Sunday feature on AIDS. I was the Sunday editor, and I readily agreed.

The Sunday features had largely been informative pieces on interesting points of public policy or local history. In my first few months as Sunday editor, we chronicled the reintroduction of the lynx into the Adirondack Mountains, for example, and began a series on historic area churches. Interesting stuff for sure, but not gripping human drama. We didn't get that until after Carrie had handed in her AIDS story.

Carrie approached all her assignments with a great deal of enthusiasm, but this story she really put her heart into. Through a social services agency, she located a man who was dying of AIDS, and did extensive interviews with him and his lover, who had also become his caregiver. Carrie walked and talked with these men, ate with them, swapped jokes and stories with them; they became a part of her life.

The tragedy that she was witnessing deeply affected Carrie. I know she cried as she wrote her story, and I had tears in my eyes as I read it. It was real life, and it was moving stuff. I can't begin to explain here how well she captured these men who were wrestling with their own mortality, so I won't even try. But I felt it was the best piece that had been produced for the paper in my few short months as Sunday editor.

There was one question about the story that I posed to my fellow editors at our regular planning meeting. The story was scheduled to run on Mother's Day. We also had a story for the front page about a new mother, but that story was less gripping than the AIDS story. Which should we put above the fold?

The consensus was that the AIDS story should lead the paper. So we played it up big, with sidebars and lots of photos.

I guess I was naive, for I saw the story as an anti-AIDS piece, not a pro-homosexuality piece. A few readers didn't take it that way. The office phones started ringing on Sunday. I was there, and took most of the calls from very irate men yelling about "faggots on the front page on Mother's Day."

We were trying to undermine the very fabric of civilization, some callers said. Others wanted to question me about my politics, my sexual persuasion, and my sanity. All who called saw the story as a deliberate attack on Mom, apple pie, and the American way.

The angry letters started coming in later that week. Mixed among them were pieces of unsigned hate mail for Carrie and for me. That made me angry, and I responded with an op-ed piece explaining just why the story had run. I admitted to a certain amount of ignorance about homosexuality myself, but said in the era of AIDS, none of us could afford the luxury of ignorance any longer. As for running the story on Mother's Day, I wrote that Mother's Day was as appropriate as any other day, since no mother would ever want to see a child die of AIDS.

That largely killed the phone calls but drew another round of letters, both pro and con. The letters began to run in favor of printing the story, but I was still getting hate mail.

In the midst of the controversy, Managing Editor Steve Bennett called me into his office and told me that he had received a letter he thought I should read. It was handwritten, and there was no return address on the envelope.

Dear Editor:

I am writing re: the "letters to the editor" that have been printed in response to your article on Mother's Day re: AIDS. I am a mother! My son has AIDS. . . .

I agree with John Lenger. No mother wants to see her son die with AIDS. This disease is taking my life as well as his—for when he passes on, more than a part of me will go with him. It's hard enough to see him suffer, but the social stigma is really tough to face. There's little to reach out to in our isolation. My son doesn't want anyone to know he's afflicted with this disease, so he is treated at a hospital out of the area. I am with him constantly, and will be to the end. . . .

I say "hurrah" to John Lenger. To dare to be bold and stand up for what he believes in! Perhaps people will now be more aware of the dangers involved. Another "hurrah" to the men the article was about. Thank you for being brave enough to bare your souls to help others. . . .

Thank you, John Lenger, for a great Mother's Day present. With your help, perhaps I won't have to go through this with another son—or watch a friend struggling to cope with AIDS.

Of course, I can't sign this letter—no one knows about my son, but thank you for reading it.

Of course, we couldn't run the letter, even though we badly wanted to, because the *Post-Star* has a very strict policy against anonymous letters. Steve Bennett went so far as to put a notice in the paper asking the letter writer to call him. He explained in the notice that the writer's name could be withheld, but no call ever came.

The letter had its intended effect, however. It reaffirmed my mission as an editor, and demonstrated for me once again just how dramatically a newspaper can touch the lives of its readers.

I made two copies of that letter. One I keep with my important papers. The other I sent to my mother.

EDITOR'S NOTE: *In the following essay, written for* Living Ethics, *Therese Frare, a Seattle-based photojournalist, discusses the personal and ethical aspects of her award-winning photo "Final Moments." The portrait documenting the death of an AIDS activist originally appeared in* Life *magazine and later was picked up by Benetton in an advertising campaign emphasizing social issues. Frare's photo was at the center of a debate about the appropriateness of such a private moment being used in an advertisement. In her piece, she explains how she decided to allow such use. She also discusses several aspects of power and addresses an important issue regarding taste. Ethicists often argue against staged photographs in the news. But Frare poses the question—"Is it okay to use* real *photos in advertising?"—a medium that typically uses "staged" or set-up illustrations in campaigns. That simple but powerful question expands the boundaries of ethical debate, not only with regard to Benetton but also to photojournalism in general.*

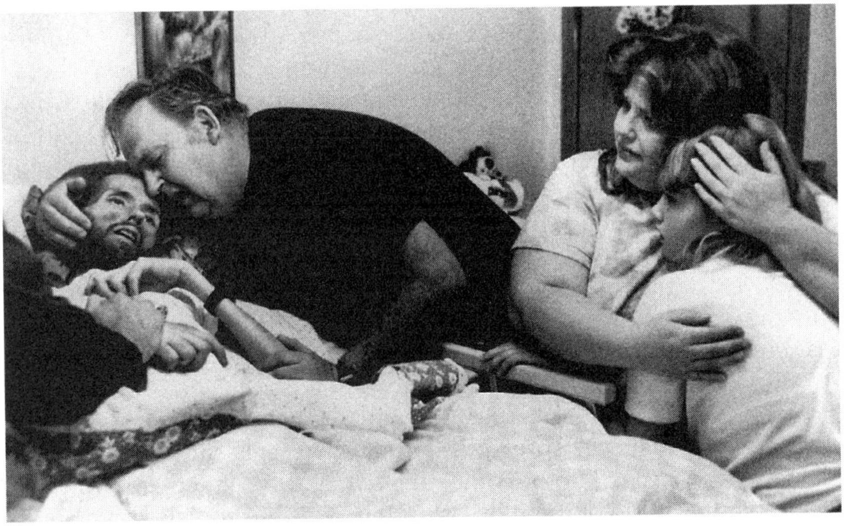

Final Moments. *This acclaimed photograph by Therese Frare documenting the final moments of a man dying of AIDS, surrounded by his family, received wide exposure when it was published in* Life *magazine and then reprinted in a Benetton advertising campaign on social issues.*

Lasting Moments

Therese Frare, Photojournalist

When I think of power in regard to the "Final Moments" photograph, I am reminded by the sheer power of death as the final experience of this life. I think of the power of family and the incredible love parents feel for their children. I think of the power of a moment—a real moment of intense emotion—a moment so personal and so raw that it overwhelms the senses.

It is impossible for me to discuss this photo without discussing the Kirby family to whom I am forever indebted for inviting me into their lives. David was an AIDS activist and had spent the last several years of his life trying to educate people about AIDS. When he met me, as a volunteer at the hospice-approach home in which he was living, I believe that he saw me as a vehicle for his message—that people with AIDS need care and love.

His father Bill is among the most loving people I have ever met and his mother Kate (not pictured; that's his sister and niece) is a strong, quiet woman who is dedicated and wise. Anyway, every week for a couple of months I visited David and his family and by luck or fate I happened to be visiting a caregiver friend of mine on the day that David died.

Knowing that it was a serious situation, I sat in the living room and my friend and David's family tended to David in the bedroom. I remember sitting there with my cameras by my feet and consulting a higher power, looking upward and thinking, "This one is your call. I need a sign if I am to take photographs here."

Within seconds, David's mother emerged and said, "Therese, we would like you to photograph people saying their final good-byes to David." I got up, quietly walked into the room, positioned myself in the corner and did not move. I made perhaps less than a dozen frames and then went back into the living room, cried with my friends, eventually drove home in a daze, slept for a day, and processed the film a couple of weeks later.

Power, in the case of this picture—*I cannot talk about my power*. There is only the power of death, the power of love and the power of fate—the force that brought me to David and his family in order for me to tell their story.

Several months after David's death, and with the permission of his family, I submitted the photo to the moments section of *Life* magazine, where it received a double truck spread. After that success, I sent a copy of the photo to the World Press Photo Competition, where it ended up winning two awards in the 1991 competition. With the award, it traveled to many countries and was picked up by various AIDS shows.

Eventually, Benetton saw the image in the World Press Yearbook and requested it for an issue-oriented campaign. Once again, I left the decision to a more knowledgeable source—in this case, David's family. They agreed to the photo being used. Even during the controversy that later ensued, the family maintained that Benetton did not take advantage of their son's death but had instead sponsored the photo to be seen by billions all over the world. Like I said, those Kirbys are amazing people.

I suppose this brings us to another power—power of the press and power of advertising. The same photo used in different ways brought about entirely different reactions. Is it okay to used staged photos in the news? Is it okay to use *real* photos in advertising?

In the end, the image has the power to move the audience—whether in a gallery, a magazine, or an advertisement—but the reaction to it is different depending on the context in which it is seen. If people are offended by its use, does that diminish its power or add to it? These are all questions to which I do not have the answer. I only know what happened and why.

Power. As a photojournalist, people lend you their power when they invite you in their lives. It is important to respect that. But the minute you take the photos out from the box under your bed and show them to the world, you lose your power to protect them. You cannot explain to a billion people what an image means. Like a child who grows, you can only put it out in the world and hope for the best.

V A L U E S   E X E R C I S E S

1. Without violating your own or another's privacy, recount in your journal a professional or academic dispute or situation in which you exerted power.

2. Without violating your own or another's privacy, recount in your journal a professional or academic dispute or situation in which you abused power.

3. Review the section of this chapter entitled Empowerment. Pay close attention to such concepts as ascertaining and evaluating your personal and professional power and taking prudent action and responsibility. Again in your journal, evaluate the disputes or situations in Exercises 1 and 2 according to these concepts. Do not hand in your notes but analyze them.

4. In a 250-word statement that does not violate your own or another's privacy, describe how, if at all, would you handle each dispute or situation in Exercises 1 and 2 differently today.

10

Values

Personal and Professional Standards

Newcomers to the workforce are often surprised about the emphasis many media corporations place on values. Why? Journalism programs often lack ethics courses and usually emphasize skills more than values. Want ads in the newspaper highlight duties and responsibilities, not morals, when soliciting for applicants. And recruiters want to know whether those applicants will be able to handle basic tasks on the job. Then new hires confront the biggest hurdle of their new careers, learning about ethics by trial and error or acknowledging that their values differ from that of their supervisers and/or employers. In either case, the unlucky novice understands the importance of values too late. He or she may have had the skills to get a job but not to keep or enjoy it.

During interviews, applicants emphasize words such as *ambition* and *objective.* An ambition is not a value but a desire. An objective is not a value but a goal. The words are often synonymous. In fact, you can plug *ambition, objective, goal, desire,* or *dream* into the following sentence and still mean the same thing: *My _____ is to replace Tom Brokaw as anchor for* NBC Nightly News. When you can substitute words like that with little or no change in meaning, the sentence lacks substance. It can mean the person works hard and achieves or takes shortcuts and deceives in pursuit of success. Unethical people can have ambitions and objectives, too. Recruiters know this. However the word *value* cannot be substituted for any of the terms in the sentence because a value has substance. If you told that recruiter for the local affiliate, *Tom Brokaw is my role model because he believes that truth may be elusive but integrity is not,* you just might get a callback for a second interview. Such a comment suggests that you have skills in addition to the maturity to use

291

them ethically on the job. (Brokaw shares his values in the Living Ethics section at the end of the chapter.)

Having a job objective on your resumé is not important. Having a values statement, however, is. David Peasback, president of Canny Bowen Inc., a New York City recruiting firm, says objectives on resumés "sometimes do more damage then good. Have you ever seen a job objective that said 'I want an unchallenging job with unlimited career potential'?"[1]

Values are becoming increasingly important in the business world where many public relations and advertising majors will work. Listen to how writers Russell Mitchell and Michael Oneal describe the corporate philosophy of Chairman Robert D. Hass, CEO of Levi Strauss, in a cover story titled "Managing by Values":

> Haas believes the corporation should be an ethical creature—an organism capable of both reaping profits and making the world a better place to live. . . . Haas is out to make each of his workers, from the factory floor on up, feel as if they are an integral part of the making and selling of blue jeans. He wants to ensure that all views on all issues—no matter how controversial—are heard and respected. The chairman won't tolerate harassment of any kind. He won't do business with suppliers who violate Levi's strict standards regarding work environment and ethics. A set of corporate "aspirations," written by top management, is to guide all major decisions.[2]

Authors of this article also note that Xerox, Johnson & Johnson, and MCI are known for values on diversity, and Nike, Microsoft, and Federal Express are known for values on fairness.

You can apply values to solve tricky, ethical situations on the job and thereby succeed, or you can learn by trial and error like most newcomers do. "I train so many people—I'm constantly training—and the hardest thing to train is not the ethics of good and bad," says Mike Ward, editorial director for several artist magazines published by F&W Publications in Cincinnati.

> Given a choice between a clearly right or clearly wrong decision, 99 percent of the people 99 percent of the time will make the right decision. But there are so many gray areas. It's when you have a choice between two flawed options, and you're trying to figure out which one is the best. That's the tough part, when you don't know what to do. Trainees have to know it's okay to make the wrong decision—that has to be an option—and there are times you just can't know all the ramifications of your actions without experience. I guess that's why people with more experience get paid more.

Because of their judgment and appropriateness, trainees with good value systems can solve gray-area problems and impress supervisors like Ward, a role model for several magazine graduates at Ohio University who have worked or interned for him.

Role models who pass their values to others have a significant impact on careers. Jimmie Baker, producer-director at KABC-TV in Hollywood and winner of five Emmy awards, says, "The one personal and professional value that has contributed to my success has been the influence of Dr. Harry Heath," former director of the School of Journalism and Broadcasting at Oklahoma State University. (In the Living Ethics section, Heath discusses the media's role in the erosion of cultural values.) "I learned from and admired Harry through Tulsa Central High School, when he was sports editor of the school newspaper and also worked for the *Tulsa Tribune* at the same time," Baker recalls. "At Tulsa University, he was my pledge father for Pi Kappa Alpha." Baker says that Heath passed along to him the values of truth and discipline to fulfill ambitions and goals. "This prepared me for my life after college," Baker adds. "I have never forgotten his advice. I have been with ABC for 45 years and still consult and treasure his advice to this day."

As we approach the end of this book, it is important to emphasize role models and values again. You might not be as fortunate as Jimmie Baker and have a significant mentor like Harry Heath. Moreover, when you enter the workforce, you will encounter supervisors like Baker who have strong values or corporations like Levi Strauss that enforce them. (Media companies emphasizing values are discussed later in the section entitled Student and Corporate Codes.) To prepare you, the author of this text asked successful journalists to share their most important values and serve as "textbook role models." As you read their replies, imagine working for each person and note in your ethics journal what compatibilities or conflicts may arise between their values and yours. If you have yet to work in your first media job, this will give you an indication of how your values and those of your manager must harmonize to achieve goals on the job.

Carolyn Kitch, senior editor for *Good Housekeeping,* says, "This is going to sound terribly Pollyannaish, but the value—personal and professional— that has served me best is hope, or optimism. While I make sure I am always prepared in case the worst happens, I go into any project or relationship with the attitude that the best will happen." Kitch's values motivate trainees in the editorial office at *GH,* a Hearst publication with a long-standing ethical reputation, extending limited warranties on products that carry its "seal of approval." According to Kitch, "Part of being successful is motivating the people who work for and with you to produce their best work. To do that, you have to believe they're capable of it, and you have to convey that belief to them." Hope has its consequences, Kitch observes.

Yes, there are "professionals" who ultimately don't merit your trust and respect, and yes, there are people who will try to walk all over you. You have to be prepared for those people and able to deal with them; you have to be ready to put out fires, and you have to know how to protect yourself. But I think it's worth it to take the risk of assuming the best about people at the start. For most people, confidence, appreciation and even basic courtesy are tremendous motivaters (and components of hope). Those people will work hard for you, and many of them will work well. That makes *you* work, and look, better. And over time, those people will give back to you—they will give you the emotional and professional support you need to continue, and grow, in your own work.

Jacques DeLier, retired vice-chairman of the board for KWTV, a CBS affiliate in Oklahoma City, says, "The one value that motivated me both personally and professionally would have to be the seeking of truth, not partial truth or embellished with personal bias, but the whole nine yards." DeLier, who started his career in the advertising department, says the station put his value into practice when the networks gave back to local affiliates the 6:30–7:00 P.M. central standard time slot, allowing KWTV to lengthen local news to a full hour. "Thus we were able to diminish the role of talking heads and inveigle the truth to our viewers by investigative and consumer reporting and by setting up an on-the-air ombudsman system to bring truth and fairness to our viewers."

Kay Dyer, first woman city editor at the *Oklahoman* and then at the *Oklahoma City Times,* worked at those publications for 21 years before returning to the family-owned *El Reno (Oklahoma) Daily Tribune.* Dyer, now publisher and editor, says, "Besides retaining a sense of humor—or developing one if you don't have it—I think the most important value a journalist should have is an interest in people"—a mix of curiosity and compassion. "Whether this has contributed to my success is a question," she observes. "I think this interest in people is what we (journalists) are all about and that we must consider them as humans, not just as the subjects of a news story." She adds, however, that "there may be very successful journalists who may not feel this way, but since we write for and about people, I find it hard to understand those who get into the profession without having this value."

Joseph C. Goulden, director of media analysis for Accuracy in Media, Inc., a journalism watchdog group, answered the question about values with the following anecdote:

In the spring of 1956, fresh from the University of Texas, I returned to my hometown of Marshall, Texas, to work on the local *News-Messenger* and await the draft. Marshall was perhaps the most rigorously segregated town in the state, more akin to, say, Mississippi or Alabama than the rest of Texas. I can't condemn the town and its people; both were simply caught in a time warp that ended about, say, 1865.

The *News-Messenger* did its duty in keeping racial segregation. Although perhaps half the 20,000 population was black, and there were two major black colleges (Wiley and Bishop). Negroes (the term used then) got their names in the paper most often in crime stories. Births, weddings, deaths, high school, and college activities—these sort of routine happenings were ignored.

In late spring, the city editor asked me to speak to a woman who was on the phone and to set up a time to take a photograph. She turned out to be an educator who was hosting a regional meeting of black school principals. We agreed that I would be at her office in early afternoon. I hung up, and the editor was at my side. "Wait until after you get back from lunch," he said, "and call her and tell her something has come up and you can't take a picture." Surprised, I protested, "But you just told me"—

"The hell with what I told you," the editor said. "We're not running a picture of a bunch of damned nigger teachers in my paper."

I left for lunch in a fury, and I drove the twenty miles to Longview, the nearest "wet" town, and had perhaps half a dozen bottles of Schlitz with my hamburger. I drove around East Texas the rest of the afternoon. In the evening I left my keys on my editor's desk with a note: "For $65 a week, you can tell your own damned lies."

"In later years, I quit two other newspaper jobs at the *Dallas Morning News* and the *Philadelphia Inquirer* over matters of principle," he adds, "and I learned the pleasures of working for a single boss with whom I agreed (myself)."

As you can see, Goulden embraces honesty—on a personal as well as professional level. "One sentence should suffice," he says. "If you ever ask yourself whether what you are contemplating is wrong, it probably is, so don't do it."

Joseph H. Carter has held positions in public relations, government, and print and broadcast media. Currently, he deals with the public as director of Will Rogers Memorial in Claremore, Oklahoma, and president of the Will Rogers Heritage Trust, Inc. He co-owned a public affairs firm in Washington DC for several years with veteran NBC-TV newsman Jim Hartz and was a staff writer and spokesperson on the White House staffs of Presidents Johnson and Carter, an aide to three members of Congress, and chief of staff to Governor David Hall of Oklahoma. He served as editor or reporter for several newspapers, including the *Honolulu (Hawaii) Advertiser.* More importantly, he was a United Press International correspondent who, among his other assignments, covered the November 1963 trip of President Kennedy to Dallas and heard the fatal shots of the assassination.

"The news value that has helped most in my career is the 'i'-factor," Carter says, "or the instinct, innovation, and initiative to pursue a story. The 'i'-factors were totally up to me. I tried to keep an ear open for the sidebar, angle, or event that was slipping past the herd and tried to pursue it." Sometimes, Carter admits, the formula didn't always work. "After covering the Kennedy assassination daylong, I attempted to intercept Richard Nixon at

Love Field as he departed Dallas, but was too late because of bureau duties. Yet, I contributed extensively, if not richly, to the report that day that largely carried Merriman Smith's UPI byline. That was appropriate since I was assigned as his 'back-up' reporter. I was on the bus behind Kennedy and heard the shots which gave me a great basis for many follow-up stories." Because of the confusion, Carter may have missed his interview with Nixon but, as he notes, "I believe it was my 'i'-factors that caused Jack Fallon, UPI division news editor, to assign me to the position that day."

"Incidentally," Carter adds, "I believe strongly today that the reports filed by UPI that day and during ensuring months—that Lee Harvey Oswald killed Kennedy and Jack Ruby killed Oswald without a lot of explanation, conspiracy, or motive—remains the truth. I personally spent days, months, and years with my 'i'-formula trying unsuccessfully to prove otherwise."

Jo Kemp, staff writer for Press Community Newspapers in Ohio, believes a value system is especially important at the local level. "I have stayed with the weeklies through many changes, including mergers, buyouts, office moves, computerization, centralization, decentralization, staff growth, beat changes, redesigns, and management restructurings. Through all the changes, however, my value system has served me well as long as I adhered to it," Kemp says. Like many respondents, Kemp notes her values have been shaped in part by religious beliefs. "There is no real contradiction, after all, in applying Christian principles on the job and being a good reporter. Both require a diligent search for and recounting of the truth. Both forbid slander and libel. Both call for a positive approach to people and situations, without prejudice or malice, being willing to acknowledge the good and not just the bad. Both require treating people with dignity and courtesy, honesty and trustworthiness. Both foster thoughtful consideration of the consequences of saying and doing certain things." There is a secular payoff for persons with religious-based values, Kemp observes. "A thought in time can save several inches of retraction, not to mention prevent law suits."

Harold Levine, founder of Levine, Huntley, Schmidt & Beaver, says responsibility is a personal and professional value.

> When I started the agency, I informed my partners that while I was in the office I would devote all my energy to the business, but at the end of the business day I would head home. I explained that I needed time in my life for business, for family, and for community service. I always felt that the person who devotes 100 percent of his or her time to business was less effective than one who made time for family life and all-important community involvement. I became aware that my involvement in various social issues encouraged employees to do the same. In addition, the agency became involved in a number of pro-bono ad campaigns.

James R. Blocki, a Chicago marketing consultant, spent more than 35 years as an executive at Kraft USA. Finding an employer with similar values was the most important element in his success, Blocki says. "The company was founded by James L. Kraft in 1903 with a horse, wagon, a few dollars, and strong religious beliefs, and henceforth was guided by a strong ethical corporate culture. Integrity, honesty, fairness, and professionalism were stressed in serving the grocery trade, distributors, suppliers, employees—all ultimately to serve the consumer." Blocki notes that long before consumer awareness was measured as part of a marketing strategy, Kraft had code dating ("best when purchased by . . . date") and a product guarantee ("satisfaction or your money back"). Kraft's and Blocki's stances toward the consumer harmonized and led to many promotions, culminating in his appointment as vice president and director of advertising and marketing services, a job he held for 20 years before becoming a consultant in 1987.

As Blocki's and others' responses indicate, successful careers are based on a balance of values—yours, your supervisor's, and your employer's. Those avenues must intersect. Job failure often has little to do with competence or competition. You may have strong values but work for a supervisor and/or company with weak ones. Or you may have weak values and work for a supervisor and/or company with strong ones. Or everyone's values may be strong (or weak) but essentially different on important issues or actions. Your goal upon graduation or reentry into the workforce may be, simply, to find a job. Salary levels and advancement opportunities are factors you will want to weigh, of course. But job dissatisfaction and termination are almost always based on value conflicts when they are not based on financial ones. A good way to determine your compatibility is to request ethics codes or statements about mission or corporate philosophy from potential employers. Another way is to prepare a values document to accompany your resumé, portfolio, or clipbook. Formats for such documents, based on ethical codes by major media outlets, are featured in the next section.

Student and Corporate Codes

Imagine this: You and another journalism graduate from a rival school have equal talent and experience and find yourselves as finalists for a public relations position at Ruder-Finn, a company with a well-known ethical reputation. The recruiter asks your rival about ethics and he hands her a copy of the Public Relations Society of America (PRSA) code, informing her, "I have memorized these." The recruiter asks you the same question and you hand her your *own* code of ethics, a professional-looking brochure showcasing your values. You inform the recruiter, "I created this document to accompany my portfolio because I feel so strongly about ethics. It's in line with the PRSA code, but more personal, discussing how I feel about truth, lies, and consequences, among other things."

Who makes the better impression?

You do. Does that mean you will get the job? Probably, at Ruder-Finn, because you share strong values about truth, lies, and consequences. Does that mean you will always beat out rivals in your job search? Not necessarily, because the company recruiting you may not take a strong ethical stance on issues, or the recruiter may believe your values might clash with its emphasis on profit. In such a case, you may be disappointed that your rival got the job. In the long term, however, your values were apt to clash with corporate ones anyway and impede promotions. Thus, having a values document helps you find an *appropriate* job where advancement will come naturally.

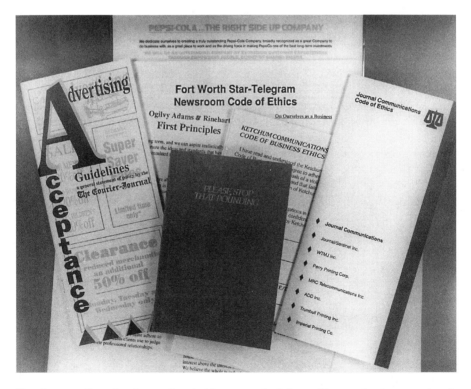

Here is a sampling of various codes of ethics or standards by media organizations mentioned in the text, including formats for resumé- and poster-like documents, brochures, files, booklets, and books.

At this point, it is important to note that codes of ethics by the various journalism associations are as important as your own. (Codes from the Society of Professional Journalists, the National Press Photographers Association, the Radio-Television News Directors Association, the American Advertising Federation, and the Public Relations Society of America are reprinted in the Appendix at the end of this book.) Such codes emphasize generally accepted standards in each industry. In the absence of a corporate code, a beginning employee usually will consult the association code to solve problems or resolve conflicts. Codes also provide grounds for more experienced employees or their supervisors to take action on an issue or a challenge. But the problem remains that codes can be memorized instead of practiced, whereas your own values document indicates a greater *personal* ethical commitment. (You will learn how to cast your values into codes in the Values Exercises at the end of the Living Ethics section.)

Following are some corporate codes that indicate the emphasis some outlets place on ethics. As you did in the previous section, read excerpts from each code and make notations in your ethics journal, commenting on compatibilities and conflicts between your values and the company's values. You can also analyze the format of the select codes and use them as models for your own documents.

Pepsi, for instance, uses a laminated 8½ × 11-inch poster-like document with an underscored red slogan in all caps centered on top: "Pepsi-Cola . . . The Right Side Up Company." The body text is in a blue upright display font (no serifs) with important concepts in red capitals or emboldened in blue. Type is set ragged right and left in a pleasing hourglass shape. The Pepsi mission statement reads: "WE WILL BE AN OUTSTANDING COMPANY BY EXCEEDING CUSTOMER EXPECTATIONS THROUGH EMPOWERED PEOPLE, GUIDED BY SHARED VALUES."

Pepsi's corporate contents are:

- A consistent CUSTOMER FOCUS for our company which all of our people understand and feel passionate about.
- An EMPOWERED ORGANIZATION, which is both motivated and supported to satisfy customers to the fullest extent of their capabilities.
- A set of SHARED VALUES, which guides all of our decisions and actions.

Those shared values are:

- **Diversity**—We respect the individual and will seek, value and promote differences of race, nationality, gender, age, background, experience and style.
- **Integrity**—We will do what we say.
- **Honesty**—We will speak openly and directly, with care and compassion, and work hard to understand and resolve issues.
- **Teamwork**—Working on real customer needs, we will combine functional excellence and cross-functional teamwork to produce exceptional results.

- **Accountability**—We all understand what is expected of us, and are fully committed to meeting those expectations.
- **Balance**—We will respect the decisions individuals make to achieve professional and personal balance in their life.

The back of the laminated document includes methods to execute Pepsi's mission and corporate and ethical philosophies.

Many media outlets use a resumé-like document to convey their ethical codes. One such document by the New York City communications agency Ogilvy Adams & Rinehart has a practical word-processor format on two pages of white bond paper. The company's name appears at the top in boldface; centered underneath is the title "First Principles." An upright serif font (ragged right) is used in the text. The corporate mission states: "We are in business for the long term, and we can aspire realistically to be the best in our business. To succeed, we must nurture the ideas and standards that have made possible our success to date. To that end, we are committed to these principles."

The principles are arranged in three categories bulleted in three-inch columns and include:

On Clients

- It is important to our effectiveness that we come to understand a client's business and learn what constitutes its business success. If we believe we cannot contribute to that success, we are obligated to inform the client and be prepared to terminate the relationship.

On Our People

- We know we can accomplish our objectives only if we have superior, highly productive people working at all levels of our firm. We consciously attempt, therefore, to hire only the best talent available to us—people of high intellect, integrity and potential—and we strive to provide an environment in which such individuals and attributes can flourish.

On Ourselves as a Business

- As a firm and as individuals, we know our good reputation is not only our most valuable asset, it is irreplaceable. We cannot safeguard it, let alone add to it, unless we conduct ourselves in accordance with the highest ethical standards. We will do no less.

Several advertising and public relations agencies also use the brochure to showcase their ethics. One of the most practical is by the New York City agency Ketchum Communications. The 5½ × 8½-inch card cover contains the company's name in a boldface and reversed upright font, positioned near the top in a box against a white and black field. "Code of Business Ethics" is centered on the cover. The date of the code appears toward the lower right corner, indicating updates and revisions. The inside cover contains a statement from the agency's president and CEO:

> Our mission at Ketchum is to be the best at what we do: to provide our clients with the most creative and effective solutions to their challenges. To do this, we constantly strive to think creatively, act decisively, manage through leadership and lead ourselves and our clients with vision and integrity.
>
> The idea of leading ourselves and our clients with integrity is written into our mission statement; it is a foundation of our company. Yet in a rapidly changing world, new technologies, new ideas and new forms of communications can create gray areas regarding integrity and ethical behavior.
>
> Therefore, it is good, from time to time, to review Ketchum's policies and to renew our understanding and acceptance of them. Please take a few minutes to read this revised Code of Business Ethics. It reflects our policies on client dealings, conflicts of interest and agency matters. We take these policies seriously and ask that all Ketchum employees acknowledge their acceptance by signing and returning the last page within one week's time.

Contents of the Ketchum brochure are listed in standard outline form with section headings in italic capital letters, topic headings in boldface, and text in an indented upright font. The outline numbers four pages covering three sections: "Client Dealings," "Conflicts of Interest," and "Agency Matters."

Here is the last:

III. AGENCY MATTERS

We will conduct ourselves and our business truthfully and honestly and in accordance with policy and law.

A. Accounting Control and Recordkeeping

We will not engage in false or misleading entries, estimates, timekeeping, or expense reporting. We will establish procedures to ensure that transactions are properly recorded and that the books and records of the agency properly reflect its business.

B. Human Resources

We will abide by the law and by the company's policies and practices regarding equal employment opportunity and safety in the workplace. We support Ketchum's policy of prohibiting "sexual harassment" and of providing for all employees a work environment free from discrimination, including race, religious creed, color, national origin, ancestry, physical disability, medical condition, marital status, sexual orientation, age or gender. We will read and periodically review these policies, and we will comply in spirit and in letter.

C. Political Contributions

We will not use company funds, services, property or facilities to support political parties or candidates or any volunteer efforts on their behalf. We will actively support whatever political candidates or causes we wish, but on our own time and independently of the agency.

D. Software/Copy Infringement

We will use all software in accordance with our licensing agreements. We will make no unauthorized copies of any software, nor will we misuse or give software to any outsiders. We will agree to ask questions when we are in doubt about our licensing agreements.

E. Unlawful Use of Computers

We will not alter, damage or destroy any computer, network, software or database, or without authorization access or give passwords to any outsiders.

F. Privacy

We recognize that all information and data on all computerized systems, including electronic mail and voice mail, are for business purposes and, when necessary, are accessible to the organization at all times.

G. Confidential Information

We will recognize and protect the confidentiality of all information concerning the agency, its business plans, new business efforts, clients, accounting and financial materials.

We will treat all data maintained by Ketchum, whether it belongs to the agency or one of its clients or some other outside user of Ketchum services, as proprietary and confidential. We agree not to disclose or use this data in any way, shape or form unless authorized by Ketchum management. We will seek the advice and counsel of management when we are in doubt regarding the proper use of such data.

We will understand the term "data" to refer to all information stored at or for the agency, in any fashion, either computerized or non-computerized, formally or informally.

Perhaps the most important aspect of this particular brochure is its inside cover and perforated inside flap cover. Both contain the same content with the back of the perforated inside flap listing the company's Human Resources officer and address so the page can be torn and mailed. The inside cover is for the employee's records. When the inside flap is torn and mailed, the brochure assumes a common format of cover and stapled inside page.

Here is the content:

KETCHUM COMMUNICATIONS
CODE OF BUSINESS ETHICS

I have read and understood the Ketchum Communications Code of Business Ethics. I agree to adhere to this Code, and I will advise the proper individuals of a violation by myself or another employee. I understand that failure to comply with this Code is a serious violation of Ketchum policy and may lead to immediate dismissal.

I understand that certain obligations in this Code, including but not limited to obligations of confidentiality, will continue after I am no longer employed by Ketchum Communications.

_____

PRINT NAME

_____

SIGNATURE

_____

TITLE   OFFICE/DIVISION

_____

DATE

One of the most popular formats for newspapers and broadcast outlets is the stapled file. Simply, the document is generated from a word-processing program and is printed, copied, collated, and fastened at the upper left corner. Ethical headings are usually boldface and some follow an outline, as in the preceding Ketchum example.

For instance, the *Fort Worth Star-Telegram* "Newsroom Code of Ethics" employs an outline format with category sections in a boldface headline display type centered over topics or items. Categories include "Outside Activities and Conflicts of Interest," "Reporting Standards," and "News Service Copy."

Text is justified in one long column across the page using an upright serif font. Here is how the topic of fairness is presented with items numbered in boldface and indented underneath:

Fairness:

1. Staffers are expected to be truthful and fair in all their dealings with readers, news sources and other *Star-Telegram* staff members. Deception can be a firing offense.

2. Staff members should never use their positions with the *Star-Telegram* for personal advantage. Company letterheads should not be used for purely personal activities outside company business. Nor should staffers use positions with the newspaper to obtain preferential treatment in personal matters associated with their roles as parents from business, industry or government organizations.

3. If a staffer concludes that he or she cannot be fair to all parties involved in a story, he or she should explain the situation to an editor and have the story reassigned. There should be no fear of penalty if such action is taken.

4. Because of the inherent conflict of interest, it is expected that no member of the News/Editorial staff will (a) seek election to public office; (b) accept appointment to a public board, commission or panel that makes or carries out policy or that advises elected or appointed officials; or (c) work for a politician or a political organization, either as a volunteer or for pay.

5. News sources should be disclosed unless there is clear reason not to do so. Every effort should be made to verify information from an anonymous source through at least one other source. The reporter may be expected to reveal the identity of an anonymous source to at least one supervising or senior editor. Editors informed of the identity of a source are bound equally by reporters' rules of confidentiality.

6. News stories should represent all sides of an issue. The *Star-Telegram* should not communicate charges or accusations affecting reputation or moral character without attempting to give the accused an opportunity to comment. If the accused chooses not to reply, or is not available for comment, the story should always state clearly why the comment was not included.

7. *Star-Telegram* newsroom personnel are urged to frequently ask themselves if our news stories are:
   • Complete and relevant, with care taken to include significant facts and omit irrelevant information.
   • On the level, with nothing that could consciously or unconsciously mislead or deceive the reader. Straight-forward, free of pejorative words that might mask a reporter's biases or emotions.

Another popular format is the booklet, used by several newspaper and broadcasting advertising departments and by communications conglomerates. The common 4 × 9-inch stapled document usually runs several pages. To illustrate, here is the contents section from the *Louisville Courier-Journal's* "Advertising Acceptance" booklet, one of the most comprehensive in the industry:

1. Abbreviations
2. Abortion Services
3. Adoption Services
3a. Surrogate Mother
4. Air Conditioners
5. Asterisks in Advertising
6. Auctions
7. Automobiles, Sale, Lease and Rental
8. Bait Advertising and Selling

9. Better Business Bureau, Use of Name in Ads
10. Blind Box
11. Blood Pressure Testing Devices
12. Business Opportunity Advertisements
13. Care for Elderly
14. Charities and Donations
15. Child Care
16. Church and Charity Rate
17. Comparative Pricing
18. Contests/Lotteries/Gambling Propositions
19. Cost (At, Under, Over, Etc.)
20. Credit Check
21. Credit Terms (Truth-in-Lending Act)
22. Currency Illustrations, Checks, Bonds,
23. Dating Services
24. Deaths and Funerals
25. Debt Responsibility
26. Derby (and Other Events) Tickets
27. Direct Sales
28. Disparagement
29. Employment
30. Errors, Mispricing, Etc.
31. Extra Charges
32. Factory to You, Etc.
33. False Advertising
34. Federal Excise Tax
35. Firearms, Fireworks, Tear Gas Guns, Etc.
36. Flag, United States
37. Food Freezer Plans
38. Former Employee Reference
39. Fortune Telling
40. Free, Use of the Word
41. Furs
42. Going Out of Business Sales
43. Government Buildings and Names
44. Hair and Scalp
45. Health Spas
46. Illustrations, Merchandise Pricing
47. Insurance
48. Jewelry
49. Loans, Stocks and Bonds
50. Mail Order
51. Massage Parlors
52. Meat, Meat Products and Bulk Beef
53. Medical and Health Promotions
54. Motion Picture/Amusement, General
55. Moving and Hauling
56. News Matter, Paid
57. News Matter Reproduction
58. News Style Advertisements
59. No Reasonable Offer Refused
60. Personals
61. Plumbing
62. Political and Issue
63. President's Name or Likeness, First Stamps, Coins, Family, Etc.
64. Price Predictions
65. Professional Advertising
66. Published Matter, Confidential Nature
67. Real Estate for Sale/Rent
68. Releases/Indemnification for use of Photographs, Names, Etc.
69. Sales and Use Tax
70. Schools, Instruction
71. Seconds, Irregulars, Imperfect
72. Sound Amplification Equipment
73. Sunday Opening
74. Teaser Advertisements
75. Testimonials
76. Ticket Sales
77. Transient Advertising
78. Underselling Claims
79. "Wholesale," Use of in Retail Ads
80. Wood Products

Another comprehensive booklet is the *Journal Communications Code of Ethics*, a touchstone in that its principles apply to a wide range of media outlets, including WTMJ-TV Milwaukee, the *Journal/Sentinel* newspapers, MRC

Telecommunications, and several other printing and publishing outlets. It also is in a 4 × 9-inch format using an upright display font on a white card cover and bond paper inside. Text is upright and unindented with white space separating paragraphs. Bulleted items are in blue with a dingbat symbol of scales to symbolize ethics at the top of the cover and each inside page. The inside cover is blank. A letter from the Chairman of the Board introduces the code as follows:

> Welcome to Journal Communications. You have joined a company that has prospered for more than 100 years by upholding the highest ethical standards.
>
> Our name is synonymous with integrity. We earn that reputation each day we do business by acting honorably and responsibly toward customers, competitors, the community and our fellow employees.
>
> Our reputation as a highly ethical company is measured one employee at a time. By conducting yourself according to the standards outlined in this booklet, you reaffirm the integrity of the company and help ensure its continued success.
>
> Ethical conduct is especially important for employees of Journal Communications because it is employee-owned and managed. Employee-owners not only have their jobs at risk but also their individual investments in the company.
>
> This booklet provides a clear, common set of guidelines for all of us to follow. By upholding the standards set forth in this booklet, you will contribute to the continued success of Journal Communications as it prepares to enter the 21st century.

The table of contents also is extensive, featuring these topics: "Overview; Ethical Standards; Reporting and Enforcement; Company's Respect for Employees; Employees' Respect for Each Other, Loyalty to Journal Communications; Conflicts of Interest; Competing, Relationships with Customers; Relationships with Suppliers; Relationships with News Sources; Favors, Gifts and Entertainment; Confidential Information; Use of Corporate Assets; Expense Reimbursement; Corporate Social Responsibility; and Political Involvement."

Here are representative entries:

Company's Respect for Employees

Journal Communications strives to create an environment in which we can pursue our careers unhindered by discrimination or harassment of any kind.

The company has and adheres to policies designed to ensure that it treats all employees equally. These policies ensure equal consideration to all employees and applicants for employment in connection with hiring, promotion, transfer, treatment during employment, compensation, participation in social and recreational functions and use of employee facilities.

Employees' Respect for Each Other

All employees must make a conscious effort to treat one another fairly and without discrimination or harassment of any kind. We should treat each other as we wish to be treated, respect one another's time and privacy and avoid gossip and rumors.

A rare but impressive ethics format is the book. Perhaps a potential employer should not be overwhelmed with an epic about your ethics. Suffice it to say, however, that at least one media outlet saw fit to employ such a design—Meldrum & Fewsmith, a Cleveland communications agency—in a work titled *Please, Stop That Pounding.* Chris Perry, president and CEO, cast the agency's ethical standards into "poem-ads," which are featured in the upcoming Living Ethics section. The unnumbered pages include 20 entries in a lightweight script font on heavy stock off-white paper with titles in capitals and the first letter of the first word in large point magenta (to match the matte cover and gold-ink title). The book is perfect-bound.

While you may not want to overwhelm an employer, you also should not limit yourself creatively when coming up with a format to enhance your values document. Some magazine students at Ohio University have created ethical calendars, memo pads with ethical inscriptions, and prototypes or magazine proposals. Some broadcasting students have produced radio or television demonstration tapes—accompanied by typewritten scripts—taping segments on political correctness, sexual harassment, and racism. Neither should you be content with formats presented here as models for your documents. Seek out ones from companies for which you aspire one day to work. Before graduation, many OU students solicit ethics codes or mission statements from potential employers, much the way freelance writers solicit editorial guidelines, and research corporations before applying for a position. They know that balancing their values with those of employers is the first step in their march toward career success after graduation.

Finally, after you secure a position, do not discard your ethics document but update it in the spirit of living ethics. Changes in values can be signs of growth or decline requiring amendments and/or revisions. The longer you work in mass media, the more apt your values are to metamorphose as you adapt to your working environment (with the exception of moral absolutes as covered in Chapter 2). The beauty of living ethics, or developing values, is in the amending so that your standards increase in proportion to your influence at work. Perhaps you now feel strongly about a political issue and would quit a job rather than handle a certain account or assignment. As you gain experience, however, you may still feel this way or you may lose interest in the issue or gain insight into handling such an account or assignment without compromising your values. Perhaps you now believe strongly in

Here is a sampling of the various formats for codes by students at Ohio University, including projects patterned after a poster-like document, brochure, booklet, and book.

free speech and candor, willing to speak your mind to anyone so that they know where you stand on important issues. As you advance in a company, however, you may still feel this way or you may have to keep your opinions to yourself because you may be a role model for others and do not want to overinfluence your trainees.

No one can predict the changes that will occur in your value system during your career. There is also good news, though. You may not have control over budgets, benefits, contracts, assignments, mergers, buy-outs, closures, office moves, promotions, demotions, reprimands, awards, hirings, firings, layoffs, and management restructures. You may not have control over deaths, births, marriages, divorces, illnesses, relocations, and other highs, lows, and turning points that may affect your performance at work. However, by exercising your values, you will *always* determine your response to those pressures and pleasures—and learn and grow in the process.

ENDNOTES

1. "Is a job objective essential on a resume?" no author, *New Woman,* June 1992, p. 38.
2. Russell Mitchell and Michael Oneal, "Managing by values," *Business Week,* 1 August 1994, p. 46.

L I V I N G   E T H I C S

Read the following interviews and articles and record your reactions in your ethics journal and/or discuss them with peers or mentors.

EDITOR'S NOTE: *Chris Perry's critical analysis of advertising titled "Nothing But Net" appears in the Living Ethics section in Chapter 2. Perry, Chairman and CEO of Meldrum & Fewsmith, shows his creative side here with "poem-ads" selected from his book,* Please, Stop That Pounding. *As for values, Perry says, these personal ones have served him throughout his professional career: "Perseverance. Resiliency. Treating people honestly and fairly. Developing a set of beliefs and principles and then having the courage to stand by them and stand up for them." Three of those beliefs appear here.*

Poetic Values

Chris Perry, Chairman and CEO,
Meldrum & Fewsmith Communications

PLEASE, STOP THAT POUNDING

Billions of dollars were spent
on advertising last year.

Here are the results:
About forty percent of consumers
    consider it degrading.
Nearly thirty percent found
    it insulting.
Before sending an advertising
    message to people, maybe it would
    be wise to listen to the message
    they're sending back.
Pounding a selling proposition
    into someone's head just isn't
    acceptable anymore.
People want more from ads
    and commercials than facts.
They want respect.

YOU WERE A KID ONCE

Do your recall your first job?
You probably sat there wide-eyed.
A little frightened. A little lost.
    Trying desperately to appear older.
    Wiser.
If you look around your office
    today, chances are you'll see someone
    who resembles you years ago.
Someone who could learn from
    your experience. Grow with your
    guidance.
Someone you can nestle comfortably
    under your wing.
Remember: Nothing is more
    important to someone who's a little
    wet behind the ears than a helping
    hand from one who's a little gray
    behind them.

THE ANSWER IS NO

When clients ask you to jump
    through hoops, say yes.

When they ask you to work
overtime, agree.
With a smile.
If they expect miracles, you'd
better damn well give them one.
And if they want you to shed a
little blood, sweat and tears on
their behalf, then bleed, perspire
and cry.
But what if you're asked to
compromise your beliefs, principles
and integrity?
Well, as Sam Goldwyn, the
movie mogul, once said, "I can
answer that in two words.
"Im. Possible."

EDITOR'S NOTE: *Harry E. Heath, Jr., was the director of the Oklahoma State University School of Journalism and Broadcasting from 1967 to 1982. Heath hired textbook author Michael J. Bugeja out of United Press International in Bugeja's first teaching job and later, like many other journalists, became one of Bugeja's role models. Heath says the value that shaped his personal and professional life has been honesty. "I have tried to ensure that my news and feature stories have been accurate, fair and balanced, insofar as I could achieve those goals." Heath had an extensive career in newspapers, television, and military public relations and has authored several texts, but perhaps his biggest contribution to journalism education is his extension work. Heath regularly lectures across Oklahoma at small panhandle and rural towns, training local journalists in concert with the Oklahoma Press Association (OPA). In the following essay, originally published in the OPA's newspaper, the* Oklahoma Publisher, *Heath expresses a concern for the erosion of cultural values.*

Eroding Values

Harry E. Heath, Jr., Professor Emeritus,
Oklahoma State University

Speaking of the United States, British-born journalist and broadcaster Alistair Cooke has offered a chilling perspective on his adopted country.

He prefaced his observation by describing America as a land of persistent idealism and bland cynicism, then said, "The race is on between [America's] decadence and its vitality."

The obvious inference is that if decadence wins, the nation's vitality will disappear—buried beneath the morass of a society that seemingly has lost its moral compass. The increasingly common coinage of popular culture is sex, violence, and vulgarity (i.e., a preoccupation with criminal behavior and what we once called bad taste).

Establishing values in an entertainment-driven society is admittedly difficult. With a faltering moral compass—one that seems to work only some of the time—commitment to integrity too often is overlooked.

The undisciplined and irresponsible use some mass communicators make of the First Amendment is as unprincipled as falsely shouting "Fire!" in a crowded theater. Freedom of expression has been carelessly used by filmmakers and broadcasters through so-called docudramas and news stories recreated by actors. Many of these mutations distort both historical perspective and current facts.

To all of this we have added the infomercial, disguising lengthy sales pitches as extended news reports.

Our high-tech tools make the electronic manipulation of reality increasingly tempting on Hollywood's big screen, television's small screen, and even on the printed page.

Are we forgetting integrity as we push free expression to the point of no return?

To many, the concept of taste as a component of human behavior has become virtually meaningless. Too long have we been surfeited in cheap sex, cheap language and an ever-increasing level of violence that has become a story-line crutch for both TV and the movies.

The result: a pervasive aura of malevolence in which some people act out their distorted imaginings with violent behavior. The sanctity of life itself has been cheapened.

Newspapers are not totally free of responsibility for the nation's weakened social contract. Community weeklies are largely guiltless, but the nation's daily newspapers in too many cases have energetically helped build the icons of popular culture.

Here are some questions to ponder:

- Have we lost sight of some of our basic ethical values in the rush to be first with the latest titillating details about celebrities and neo-celebrities?
- Have we let the supermarket tabloids erode our emphasis upon accuracy and objectivity?

- Is there something missing in the American character that was there in the first half of this century? If so, have newspapers contributed to the fact that it is hard to find a legitimate hero as a role model today?
- Has "image making" become so much a part of our sociopolitical environment that credibility is virtually nonexistent?

In short, it would seem that the only heroes today are to be found in the sports, theatrical, and music fields—and in the latter, the icons most revered are mainly those in the rock and country-western genres. Often these ersatz heroes are unworthy role models for their worshipping followers.

Popular culture has thrived upon the audiovisual media and their ability to build enormous followings for even tawdry heroes and sordid themes.

Daily newspapers have been too quick to jump on the pop-culture bandwagon, hoping to build readership among nonreaders. Their hoped-for converts are not likely to be lured from *Rolling Stone, GQ,* and *Playboy* for newspaper coverage of their heroes, most of whom are carefully "packaged" as anti-heroes.

Broadcasters, cablecasters, and motion picture producers talk out of both sides of their mouths when critics suggest that freedom of expression is a two-sided coin, with responsibility on one side balanced against freedom on the other. They insist that the plethora of violence people are immersed in today affects kids no more than the Grimm brothers' fairy tales of an earlier era. They also produce elaborate sales presentations to convince advertisers that they can sell anything from Preparation H to Cadillacs.

A growing number of behavioral scientists, some who earlier had sided with the audiovisual media, are taking a more serious look at the ability of the tube and screen to foster antisocial attitudes. If *Sesame Street* can teach preschoolers their ABCs, they ask, why can't violent programs teach violence? Are we to assume that violent programs have no affect whatsoever in the face of television's influence upon the buying habits of Americans? Tell that to Anheuser-Busch.

George Gerbner, a nationally respected communications research scholar, put it this way at a national colloquium a couple of years ago: "There's never before been the type of expertly choreographed brutality and violence that we have at the present time. It surrounds us from infancy. There's no question it influences the way in which we've been socialized into our roles. What we're dealing with is a kind of pollution that we have to understand and take care of."

Research analysts at the Center for Media and Public Affairs say that television violence is coming from more sources and in greater volume than ever before. In addition, four earlier government studies concluded that violence on TV leads to aggressive behavior.

Daily newspapers often publicize the worst sleaze merchants along with the finest entertainers as though they are all of the same cloth.

It's time to call a halt.

This is not a free-press issue. It is a choice between responsible and irresponsible editing or, in Alistair Cooke's terms, between decadence and vitality.

❖ EDITOR'S NOTE: *Tom Brokaw, South Dakota native, is one of the most experienced broadcasters in the business. His began his career in 1962 in Omaha and three years later took a job in Atlanta to cover the civil rights movement. In 1966, he moved to KNBC in Los Angeles to work as reporter and anchor. After covering the White House during the Watergate scandal, Brokaw was named anchor on* The Today Show *in 1976. Six years later, he was named co-anchor with Roger Mudd on* NBC Nightly News *and took over as sole anchor in July 1983. Brokaw has enjoyed a reputation for fairness since his college days at the University of South Dakota in Vermillion. Textbook author Michael J. Bugeja, a graduate of South Dakota State University, has followed his career since the early 1970s and asked Brokaw to share values with readers of* Living Ethics.

Fundamental Values

Tom Brokaw, Anchor, *NBC Nightly News*

After more than 30 years at this business of collecting, editing, and disseminating information under the broad definition of news, I am persuaded the most enduring personal rules of behavior are not so complicated. Yet they are profoundly important if the great freedoms we enjoy in American journalism are to flourish.

First, truth may be elusive but integrity is not. Viewers and readers are best served and most supportive when they have a daily appreciation of the vigorous and fair-minded effort their newspaper or news program has made in their behalf.

Next, just as the press in all of its forms—print, television, radio—has a societal obligation to examine change and decisions that affect the public welfare, so, too, does the press have an obligation to be a watchdog for excesses and failures *within* journalism.

Journalism, especially in this age of enormous competitive commercial pressure, does not have to be a nonprofit or money-losing proposition to be successful and respectable but neither should its owners measure its value solely by the bottom line.

Finally, to be a journalist in a society governed by a Constitution that has as its first amendment such an eloquent and robust statement of the place of a free press is an unparalleled privilege. It is a privilege that is best preserved and strengthened by an uncommon commitment to excellence by every journalist, whatever their station in the profession.

VALUES EXERCISES

It is now time to turn your values into codes for a document to present to a potential employer. Follow these guidelines:

1. Review the content in each chapter and note significant passages.

2. Review the Values Exercises from Chapters 1 through 9 and note significant passages.

3. Review your ethics journal entries.

4. Isolate one or two important items in passages and entries for each concept covered in the text: influence, responsibility, truth, lies, manipulation, temptation, bias, fairness and power.

5. Write a brief statement about how you feel about each item (about 50 to 100 words).

6. Turn to the codes of ethics in the Appendix, identify the one relating to your sequence (and/or media interest), and find a statement relating to each topic on your list.

7. Compare your statements with ones in the code and revise, if appropriate, clarifying terms or harmonizing content in keeping with industry standards.

8. Reevaluate each statement and circle key words and terms, listing them on a separate sheet.

9. Now condense each statement and keep or combine as many of those key terms as possible—about 10 to 50 words per item.

10. Assemble your codes in the same document and revise the wording of each so that all codes are similar in length and read in a consistent and parallel manner. (Common style errors include using the first person, *I*, in some codes and not in others and switching verb case or tense.)

11. Decide on the format. (News and photojournalism majors usually opt for a resumé-like or files document, although some broadcasting majors tape their codes with accompanying scripts; public relations majors usually decide on a resumé-like document or brochure; advertising majors often favor a brochure,

booklet, or poster; and magazine majors usually prefer a resumé-like document, brochure, booklet, or book.)

12. Show a draft of your code to a mentor or role model and/or share yours with peers in a group study or workshop. Ask for a critique and then revise your document so that it lacks embarrassing misspellings or grammatical mistakes.

APPENDIX

Codes of Ethics

Society of Professional Journalists

Code of Ethics

SOCIETY of Professional Journalists believes the duty of journalists is to serve the truth.

We BELIEVE the agencies of mass communication are carriers of public discussion and information, acting on their Constitutional mandate and freedom to learn and report the facts.

We BELIEVE in public enlightenment as the forerunner of justice, and in our Constitutional role to seek the truth as part of the public's right to know the truth.

We BELIEVE those responsibilities carry obligations that require journalists to perform with intelligence, objectivity, accuracy, and fairness.

To these ends, we declare acceptance of the standards of practice here set forth:

I. Responsibility: The public's right to know of events of public importance and interest is the overriding mission of the mass media. The purpose of distributing news and enlightened opinion is to serve the general welfare. Journalists who use their professional status as representatives of the public for selfish or other unworthy motives violate a high trust.

II. Freedom of the Press: Freedom of the press is to be guarded as an inalienable right of people in a free society. It carries with it the freedom and the responsibility to discuss, question, and challenge actions and utterances of our government and of our public and private institutions. Journalists uphold the right to speak unpopular opinions and the privilege to agree with the majority.

III. Ethics: Journalists must be free of obligation to any interest other than the public's right to know the truth.

1. Gifts, favors, free travel, special treatment or privileges can compromise the integrity of journalists and their employers. Nothing of value should be accepted.
2. Secondary employment, political involvement, holding public office, and service in community organizations should be avoided if it compromises the integrity of journalists and their employers. Journalists and their employers should conduct their personal lives in a manner that protects them from conflict of interest, real or apparent. Their responsibilities to the public are paramount. That is the nature of their profession.
3. So-called news communications from private sources should not be published or broadcast without substantiation of their claims to news values.
4. Journalists will seek news that serves the public interest, despite the obstacles. They will make constant efforts to assure that the public's business is conducted in public and that public records are open to public inspection.
5. Journalists acknowledge the newsman's ethic of protecting confidential sources of information.
6. Plagiarism is dishonest and unacceptable.

IV. Accuracy and Objectivity: Good faith with the public is the foundation of all worthy journalism.

1. Truth is our ultimate goal.
2. Objectivity in reporting the news is another goal that serves as the mark of an experienced professional. It is a standard of performance toward which we strive. We honor those who achieve it.
3. There is no excuse for inaccuracies or lack of thoroughness.
4. Newspaper headlines should be fully warranted by the contents of the articles they accompany. Photographs and telecasts should give an accurate picture of an event and not highlight an incident out of context.
5. Sound practice makes clear distinction between news reports and expressions of opinion. News reports should be free of opinion or bias and represent all sides of an issue.
6. Partisanship in editorial comment that knowingly departs from the truth violates the spirit of American journalism.
7. Journalists recognize their responsibility for offering informed analysis, comment, and editorial opinion on public events and

issues. They accept the obligation to present such material by individuals whose competence, experience, and judgment qualify them for it.

8. Special articles or presentations devoted to advocacy or the writer's own conclusions and interpretations should be labeled as such.

V. Fair Play: Journalists at all times will show respect for the dignity, privacy, rights, and well-being of people encountered in the course of gathering and presenting the news.

1. The news media should not communicate unofficial charges affecting reputation or moral character without giving the accused a chance to reply.
2. The news media must guard against invading a person's right to privacy.
3. The media should not pander to morbid curiosity about details of vice and crime.
4. It is the duty of news media to make prompt and complete correction of their errors.
5. Journalists should be accountable to the public for their reports and the public should be encouraged to voice its grievances against the media. Open dialogue with our readers, viewers, and listeners should be fostered.

VI. Mutual Trust: Adherence to this code is intended to preserve and strengthen the bond of mutual trust and respect between American journalists and the American people.

The Society shall—by programs of education and other means—encourage individual journalists to adhere to these tenets, and shall encourage journalistic publications and broadcasters to recognize their responsibility to frame codes of ethics in concert with their employees to serve as guidelines in furthering these goals.

National Press Photographers Association

Code of Ethics

The National Press Photographers Association, a professional society dedicated to the advancement of photojournalism, acknowledges concern and respect for the public's natural-law right to freedom in searching for the truth and the right to be informed truthfully and completely about public events and the world in which we live.

We believe that no report can be complete if it is not possible to enhance and clarify the meaning of words. We believe that pictures, whether used to depict news events as they actually happen, illustrate news that has happened or to help explain anything of public interest, are an indispensable means of keeping people accurately informed; that they help all people, young and old, to better understand any subject in the public domain.

Believing the foregoing, we recognize and acknowledge that photojournalists should at all times maintain the highest standards of ethical conduct in serving the public interest. To that end, the National Press Photographers Association sets forth the following Code of Ethics, which is subscribed to by all of its members:

1. The practice of photojournalism, both as a science and art, is worthy of the very best thought and effort of those who enter into it as a profession.
2. Photojournalism affords an opportunity to serve the public that is equaled by few other vocations, and all members of the profession should strive by example and influence to maintain high standards of ethical conduct free of mercenary considerations of any kind.
3. It is the individual responsibility of every photojournalist at all times to strive for pictures that report truthfully, honestly and objectively.
4. Business promotion in its many forms is essential, but untrue statements of any nature are not worthy of a professional photojournalist and we severely condemn any such practice.
5. It is our duty to encourage and assist all members of our profession, individually and collectively, so that the quality of photojournalism may constantly be raised to higher standards.
6. It is the duty of every photojournalist to work to preserve all freedom-of-the-press rights recognized by law and to work to protect and expand freedom of access to all sources of news and visual information.
7. Our standards of business dealings, ambitions and relations shall have in them a note of sympathy for our common humanity and shall always require us to take into consideration our highest duties as members of society. In every situation in our business life, in every responsibility that comes before us, our chief thought shall be to fulfill that responsibility and discharge that duty to that, when each of us is finished, we shall have endeavored to lift the level of human ideals and achievement higher than we found it.
8. No Code of Ethics can prejudge every situation; thus common sense and good judgment are required in applying ethical principles.

A Statement of Principle by the National Press Photographers Association

As journalists we believe the guiding principle of our profession is accuracy; therefore, we believe it is wrong to alter the content of a photograph in any way that deceives the public.

As photojournalists, we have the responsibility to document society and to preserve its images as a matter of historical record. It is clear that the emerging electronic technologies provide new challenges to the integrity of photographic images. This technology enables the manipulation of the content of an image in such a way that the change is virtually undetectable. In light of this, we, the National Press Photographers Association, reaffirm the basis of our ethics: Accurate representation is the benchmark of our profession.

We believe photojournalistic guidelines for fair and accurate reporting should be the criteria for judging what may be done electronically to a into photograph. Altering the editorial content of a photograph, in any degree, is a breach of the ethical standards recognized by the NPPA.

Radio-Television News Directors Association

Code of Ethics

The responsibility of radio and television journalists is to gather and report information of importance and interest to the public accurately, honestly and impartially.

The members of the Radio-Television News Directors Association accept these standards and will:

1. Strive to present the source or nature of broadcast news material in a way that is balanced, accurate and fair.
    A. They will evaluate information solely on its merits as news, rejecting sensationalism or misleading emphasis in any form.
    B. They will guard against using audio or video material in a way that deceives the audience.
    C. They will not mislead the public by presenting as spontaneous news any material which is staged or rehearsed.
    D. They will identify people by race, creed, nationality or prior status only when it is relevant.
    E. They will clearly label opinion and commentary.
    F. They will promptly acknowledge and correct errors.

2. Strive to conduct themselves in a manner that protects them from conflicts of interest, real or perceived. They will decline gifts or favors which would influence or appear to influence their judgments.
3. Respect the dignity, privacy and well-being of people with whom they deal.
4. Recognize the need to protect confidential sources. They will promise confidentiality only with the intention of keeping that promise.
5. Respect everyone's right to a fair trial.
6. Broadcast the private transmissions of other broadcasters only with permission.
7. Actively encourage observance of this Code by all journalists, whether members of the Radio-Television News Directors Association or not.

American Advertising Federation
Board of Directors

The Advertising Principles of
American Business

Truth: Advertising shall tell the truth, and shall reveal significant facts, the omission of which would mislead the public.

Substantiation: Advertising claims shall be substantiated by evidence in possession of the advertiser and advertising agency, prior to making such claims.

Comparisions: Advertising shall refrain from making false, misleading, or unsubstantiated statements or claims about a competitor or his products or services.

Bait Advertising: Advertising shall not offer products or services for sale unless such offer constitutes a bona fide effort to sell the advertised products or services and is not a device to switch consumers to other goods or services, usually higher priced.

Guarantees and Warranties: Advertising of guarantees and warranties shall be explicit, with sufficient information to apprise consumers of their principal terms and limitations or, when space or time restrictions preclude such disclosures, the advertisement should clearly reveal where the full text of the guarantee or warranty can be examined before purchase.

Price Claims: Advertising shall avoid price claims which are false or misleading, or savings claims which do not offer provable savings.

Testimonials: Advertising containing testimonials shall be limited to those of competent witnesses who are reflecting a real and honest opinion or experience.

Taste and Decency: Advertising shall be free of statements, illustrations or implications which are offensive to good taste or public decency.

Public Relations Society of America

Code of Professional Standards for the Practice of Public Relations

Declaration of Principles: Members of the Public Relations Society of America base their professional principles on the fundamental value and dignity of the Individual, holding that the free exercise of human rights, especially freedom of speech, freedom of assembly, and freedom of the press, is essential to the practice of public relations.

In serving the interests of clients and employers, we dedicate ourselves to the goals of better communication, understanding, and cooperation among the diverse individuals, groups, and institutions of society, and of equal opportunity of employment in the public relations profession.

We Pledge:

To conduct ourselves professionally, with truth, accuracy, fairness, and responsibility to the public;

To improve our individual competence and advance the knowledge and proficiency of the profession through continuing research and education;

And to adhere to the articles of the Code of Professional Standards for the Practice of Public Relations as adopted by the governing Assembly of the Society.

Code of Professional Standards for the Practice of Public Relations: These articles have been adopted by the Public Relations Society of America to promote and maintain high standards of public service and ethical conduct among its members.

1. A member shall conduct his or her professional life in accord with the **public interest.**
2. A member shall exemplify high standards of **honesty and integrity** while carrying out dual obligations to a client or employer and to the democratic process.
3. A member shall **deal fairly** with the public, with past or present clients or employers, and with fellow practitioners, giving due respect to the ideal of free inquiry and to the opinions of others.
4. A member shall adhere to the highest standards of **accuracy and truth,** avoiding extravagant claims or unfair comparisons and giving credit for ideas and words borrowed from others.
5. A member shall not knowingly disseminate **false or misleading information** and shall act promptly to correct erroneous communications for which he or she is responsible.
6. A member shall not engage in any practice which has the purpose of **corrupting** the integrity of channels of communications or the processes of government.
7. A member shall be prepared to **identify publicly** the name of the client or employer on whose behalf any public communication is made.
8. A member shall not use any individual or organization professing to serve or represent an announced cause, or professing to be independent or unbiased, but actually serving another or **undisclosed interest.**
9. A member shall **not guarantee the achievement** of specified results beyond the member's direct control.
10. A member shall **not represent conflicting** or competing interests without the express consent of those concerned, given after a full disclosure of the facts.
11. A member shall not place himself or herself in a position where the member's **personal interest is or may be in conflict** with an obligation to an employer or client, or others, without full disclosure of such interests to all involved.
12. A member shall not **accept fees, commissions, gifts or any other consideration** from anyone except clients or employers for whom services are performed without their express consent, given after full disclosure of the facts.
13. A member shall scrupulously safeguard the **confidences and privacy rights** of present, former, and prospective clients or employers.
14. A member shall not intentionally **damage the professional** reputation or practice of another practitioner.

15. If a member has evidence that another member has been guilty of unethical, illegal, or unfair practices, including those in violation of this Code, the member is obligated to present the information promptly to the proper authorities of the Society for action in accordance with the procedure set forth in Article XII of the Bylaws.
16. A member called as a witness in a proceeding for enforcement of this Code is obligated to appear, unless excused for sufficient reason by the judicial panel.
17. A member shall, as soon as possible, sever relations with any organization or individual if such relationship requires conduct contrary to the articles of this Code.

Official Interpretations of the Code

Interpretation of Code Paragraph 1, which reads, "A member shall conduct his or her professional life in accord with the public interest."

The public Interest is here defined primarily as comprising respect for and enforcement of the rights guaranteed by the Constitution of the United States of America.

Interpretation of Code Paragraph 6, which reads, "A member shall not engage in any practice which has the purpose of corrupting the integrity of channels of communication or the processes of government."

1. Among the practices prohibited by this paragraph are those that tend to place representatives of media or government under any obligation to the member, or the member's employer or client, which is in conflict with their obligations to media or government, such as:
   a. the giving of gifts of more than nominal value;
   b. any form of payment or compensation to a member of the media in order to obtain preferential or guaranteed news or editorial coverage in the medium;
   c. any retainer or fee to a media employee or use of such employee if retained by a client or employer, where the circumstances are not fully disclosed to and accepted by the media employer;
   d. providing trips, for media representatives, that are unrelated to legitimate news interest;
   e. the use by a member of an investment or loan or advertising commitment made by the member, or the member's client or employer, to obtain preferential or guaranteed coverage in the medium.
2. This Code paragraph does not prohibit hosting media or government representatives at meals, cocktails, or news functions and special events that are occasions for the exchange of news information

or views, or the furtherance of understanding, which is part of the public relations function. Nor does it prohibit the bona fide press event or tour when media or government representatives are given the opportunity for an on-the-spot viewing of a newsworthy product, process, or event in which the media or government representatives have a legitimate interest. What is customary or reasonable hospitality has to be a matter of particular judgment in specific situations. In all of these cases, however, it is, or should be, understood that no preferential treatment or guarantees are expected or implied and that complete independence always is left to the media or government representative.

3. This paragraph does not prohibit the reasonable giving or lending of sample products or services to media representatives who have a legitimate interest in the products or services.

4. It is permissible, under Article 6 of the Code, to offer complimentary or discount rates to the media (travel writers, for example) if the rate is for business use and is made available to all writers. Considerable question exists as to the propriety of extending such rates for personal use.

Interpretation of Code Paragraph 9, which reads, "A member shall not guarantee the achievement of specified results beyond the member's direct control."

This Code paragraph, in effect, prohibits misleading a client or employer as to what professional public relations can accomplish. It does not prohibit guarantees of quality of service. But it does prohibit guaranteeing specific results which, by their very nature, cannot be guaranteed because they are not subject to the member's control. As an example, a guarantee that a news release will appear specifically in a particular publication would be prohibited. This paragraph should not be interpreted as prohibiting contingent fees.

Interpretation of Code Paragraph 13, which reads, "A member shall scrupulously safeguard the confidences and privacy rights of present, former, and prospective clients or employers."

1. This article does not prohibit a member who has knowledge of client or employer activities that are illegal from making such disclosures to the proper authorities as he or she believes are legally required.

2. Communications between a practitioner and client/employer are deemed to be confidential under Article 13 of the Code of Professional Standards. However, although practitioner/client/employer communications are considered confidential between the parties,

such communications are not privileged against disclosure in a court of law.

3. Under the copyright laws of the United States, the copyright in a work is generally owned initially by the author or authors. In the case of a "work made for hire" by an employee acting within the scope of his or her employment, the employer is considered to be the author and owns the copyright in the absence of an express, signed written agreement to the contrary. A freelancer who is the author of the work and is not an employee may be the owner of the copyright. A member should consult legal counsel for detailed advice concerning the scope and application of the copyright laws.

Interpretation of Code Paragraph 14, which reads, "A member shall not intentionally damage the professional reputation or practice of another practitioner."

1. Blind solicitation, on its face, is not prohibited by the Code. However, if the customer lists were improperly obtained, or if the solicitation contained references reflecting adversely on the quality of current services, a complaint might be justified.
2. This article applies to statements, true or false, or acts, made or undertaken with malice and with the specific purpose of harming the reputation or practice of another member. This article does not prohibit honest employee evaluations or similar reviews, made without malice and as part of ordinary business practice, even though this activity may have a harmful effect.

Official Interpretation of the Code as It Applies to Political Public Relations

Preamble
In the practice of political public relations, a PRSA member must have professional capabilities to offer an employer or client quite apart from any political relationships of value, and members may serve their employer or client without necessarily having attributed to them the character, reputation, or beliefs of those they serve. It is understood that members may choose to serve only those interests with whose political philosophy they are personally comfortable.

Definition
"Political Public Relations" is defined as those areas of public relations that relate to:

a. the counseling of political organizations, committees, candidates, or potential candidates for public office; and groups constituted for the purpose of influencing the vote on any ballot issue;

b. the counseling of holders of public office;

c. the management, or direction, of a political campaign for or against a candidate for political office; or for or against a ballot issue to be determined by voter approval or rejection;

d. the practice of public relations on behalf of a client or an employer in connection with that client's or employer's relationships with any candidates or holders of public office, with the purpose of influencing legislation or government regulation or treatment of a client or employer, regardless of whether the PRSA member is a recognized lobbyist;

e. the counseling of government bodies, or segments thereof, either domestic or foreign.

Precepts

1. It is the responsibility of PRSA members practicing political public relations, as defined above, to be conversant with the various statutes, local, state, and federal, governing such activities and to adhere to them strictly. This includes, but is not limited to, the various local, state, and federal laws, court decisions, and official interpretations governing lobbying, political contributions, disclosure, elections, libel, slander, and the like. In carrying out this responsibility, members shall seek appropriate counseling whenever necessary.

2. It is also the responsibility of the members to abide by PRSA's Code of Professional Standards.

3. Members shall represent clients or employers in good faith, and while partisan advocacy on behalf of a candidate or public issue may be expected, members shall act in accord with the public interest and adhere to truth and accuracy and to generally accepted standards of good taste.

4. Members shall not issue descriptive material or any advertising or publicity information or participate in the preparation or use thereof that is not signed by responsible persons or is false, misleading, or unlabeled as to its source, and are obligated to use care to avoid dissemination of any such material.

5. Members have an obligation to clients to disclose what remuneration beyond their fees they expect to receive as a result of their relationship, such as commissions for media advertising, printing, and

the like, and should not accept such extra payment without their client's consent.

6. Members shall not improperly use their positions to encourage additional future employment or compensation. It is understood that successful campaign directors or managers, because of the performance of their duties and the working relationship that develops, may well continue to assist and counsel, for pay, the successful candidate.

7. Members shall voluntarily disclose to employers or clients the identity of other employers or clients with whom they are currently associated, and whose interests might be affected favorably or unfavorably by their political representation.

8. Members shall respect the confidentiality of information pertaining to employers or clients past, present, and potential, even after the relationships cease, avoiding future associations wherein insider information is sought that would give a desired advantage over a member's previous clients.

9. In avoiding practices that might tend to corrupt the processes of government, members shall not make undisclosed gifts of cash or other valuable considerations that are designed to influence specific decisions of voters, legislators, or public officials on public matters. A business lunch or dinner, or other comparable expenditure made in the course of communicating a point of view or public position, would not constitute such a violation. Nor, for example, would a plant visit designed and financed to provide useful background information to an interested legislator or candidate.

10. Nothing herein should be construed as prohibiting members from making legal, properly disclosed contributions to the candidates, party, or referenda issues of their choice.

11. Members shall not, through use of information known to be false or misleading, conveyed directly or through a third party, intentionally injure the public reputation of an opposing interest.

Official Interpretation of the Code as It Applies to
Financial Public Relations

"Financial public relations" is defined as "that area of public relations which relates to the dissemination of information that affects the understanding of stockholders and investors generally concerning the financial position and prospects of a company, and includes among its objectives the improvement of relations between corporations and their stockholders." The interpretation was prepared in 1963 by the Society's Financial Relations Committee, working with the Securities and Exchange Commission and with the advice of the Society's legal counsel. It is rooted directly in the Code with the full force of the Code behind it, and a violation of any of the following paragraphs is subject to the same procedures and penalties as violation of the Code.

1. It is the responsibility of PRSA members who practice financial public relations to be thoroughly familiar with and understand the rules and regulations of the SEC and the laws it administers, as well as other laws, rules, and regulations affecting financial public relations, and to act in accordance with their letter and spirit. In carrying out this responsibility, members shall also seek legal counsel, when appropriate, on matters concerning financial public relations.

2. Members shall adhere to the general policy of making full and timely disclosure of corporate information on behalf of clients or employers. The information disclosed shall be accurate, clear, and understandable. The purpose of such disclosure is to provide the investing public with all material information affecting security values or influencing investment decisions. In complying with the duty of full and timely disclosure, members shall present all material facts, including those adverse to the company. They shall exercise care to ascertain the facts and to disseminate only information they believe to be accurate. They shall not knowingly omit information, the omission of which might make a release false or misleading. Under no circumstances shall members participate in any activity designed to mislead or manipulate the price of a company's securities.

3. Members shall publicly disclose or release information promptly so as to avoid the possibility of any use of the information by any insider or third party. To that end, members shall make every effort to comply with the spirit and intent of the timely-disclosure policies of the stock exchanges, NASD, and the SEC. Material information shall be made available on an equal basis.

4. Members shall not disclose confidential information the disclosure of which might be adverse to a valid corporate purpose or interest and whose disclosure is not required by the timely-disclosure provisions of the law. During any such period of nondisclosure members shall not directly or indirectly (a) communicate the confidential information to any other person or b) buy or sell or in any other way deal in the company's securities where the confidential information may materially affect the market for the security when disclosed. Material information shall be disclosed publicly as soon as

its confidential status has terminated or the requirement of timely disclosure takes effect.

5. During the registration period, members shall not engage in practices designed to precondition the market for such securities. During registration, the issuance of forecasts, projections, predictions about sales and earnings, or opinions concerning security values or other aspects of the future performance of the company, shall be in accordance with current SEC regulations and statements of policy. In the case of companies whose securities are publicly held, the normal flow of factual information to shareholders and the investing public shall continue during the registration period.

6. Where members have any reason to doubt that projections have an adequate basis in fact, they shall satisfy themselves as to the adequacy of the projections prior to disseminating them.

7. Acting in concert with clients or employers, members shall act promptly to correct false or misleading information or rumors concerning clients' or employers' securities or business whenever they have reason to believe such information or rumors are materially affecting investor attitudes.

8. Members shall not issue descriptive materials designed or written in such a fashion as to appear to be, contrary to fact, an independent third-party endorsement or recommendation of a company or a security. Whenever members issue material for clients or employers, either in their own names or in the names of someone other than the clients or employers, they shall disclose in large type and in a prominent position on the face of the material the source of such material and the existence of the issuer's client or employer relationship.

9. Members shall not use inside information for personal gain. However, this is not intended to prohibit members from making bona fide investments in their company's or client's securities insofar as they can make such investments without the benefit of material inside information.

10. Members shall not accept compensation that would place them in a position of conflict with their duty to a client, employer, or the investing public. Members shall not accept stock options from clients or employers nor accept securities as compensation at a price below market price except as part of an overall plan for corporate employees.

11. Members shall act so as to maintain the integrity of channels of public communication. They shall not pay or permit to be paid to any publication or other communications medium any considera-

tion in exchange for publicizing a company, except through clearly recognizable paid advertising.

12. Members shall in general be guided by the PRSA Declaration of Principles and the Code of Professional Standards for the Practice of Public Relations of which this is an official interpretation.

Index